Grace A. Lewis   Iman Poernomo
Christine Hofmeister (Eds.)

Component-Based Software Engineering

12th International Symposium, CBSE 2009
East Stroudsburg, PA, USA, June 24-26, 2009
Proceedings

 Springer

Volume Editors

Grace A. Lewis
Carnegie Mellon® Software Engineering Institute
4500 Fifth Avenue, Pittsburgh, PA 15213, USA
E-mail: glewis@sei.cmu.edu
http://www.sei.cmu.edu/staff/glewis

Iman Poernomo
King's College London, Department of Computer Science
The Predictable Assembly Laboratory
Strand, London, WC2R 2LS, UK
E-mail: iman@dcs.kcl.ac.uk
http://palab.dcs.kcl.ac.uk

Christine Hofmeister
East Stroudsburg University, Computer Science Department
200 Prospect Street, East Stroudsburg, PA 18301-2999, USA
E-mail: chofmeister@po-box.esu.edu
http://www.esu.edu/~chrish

Library of Congress Control Number: Applied for

CR Subject Classification (1998): D.2, D.3, B.8, C.4, J.7, F.3, F.4.1

LNCS Sublibrary: SL 2 – Programming and Software Engineering

ISSN   0302-9743
ISBN-10   3-642-02413-0 Springer Berlin Heidelberg New York
ISBN-13   978-3-642-02413-9 Springer Berlin Heidelberg New York

springer.com

© Springer-Verlag Berlin Heidelberg 2009
Printed in Germany

Typesetting: Camera-ready by author, data conversion by Scientific Publishing Services, Chennai, India
Printed on acid-free paper   SPIN: 12696642   06/3180   5 4 3 2 1 0

Lecture Notes in Computer Science 5582

Commenced Publication in 1973
Founding and Former Series Editors:
Gerhard Goos, Juris Hartmanis, and Jan van Leeuwen

Preface

The 2009 Symposium on Component-Based Software Engineering (CBSE 2009) was the 12th in a series of successful events that have grown into the main forum for industrial and academic experts to discuss component technology.

Component-based software engineering (CBSE) has emerged as the underlying technology for the assembly of flexible software systems. In essence, CBSE is about composing computational building blocks to construct larger building blocks that fulfill client needs. Most software engineers are involved in some form of component-based development. Nonetheless, the implications of CBSE adoption are wide-reaching and its challenges grow in tandem with its uptake, continuing to inspire our scientific speculation.

Component-based development necessarily involves elements of software architecture, modular software design, software verification, testing, configuration and deployment. This year's submissions represent a cross-section of CBSE research that touches upon all these aspects. The theoretical foundations of component specification, composition, analysis, and verification continue to pose research challenges. What exactly constitutes an adequate semantics for communication and composition so that bigger things can be built from smaller things? How can formal approaches facilitate predictable assembly through better analysis? We have grouped the proceedings into two sub-themes that deal with these issues: *component models* and *communication and composition.* At the same time, the world is changing. While the engineering models and methods for component software development are slowly maturing, new trends in global services, distributed systems architectures, and large-scale software systems that cross organizational boundaries push the limits of established and tested component-based methods, tools, and platforms. These challenges are attacked within the remaining three sub-themes of the event: *component integration, extra-functional analysis,* and *components within the development life cycle.*

Our focus is ultimately about building better software. Consequently, effective communication and cooperation between universities and industry are essential if research challenges are to be appropriately identified and addressed. The CBSE symposium has a track record, maintained into 2009, of bringing together researchers and practitioners from a variety of disciplines to promote a better understanding of CBSE from a diversity of perspectives, and to engage in active discussion and debate. Due to the economic downturn of 2009, one might have expected a somewhat lower than usual attendance from industry representatives, but in spite of this trouble we maintained a good balance through continued industrial submissions, participation and solid industrial feedback within the reviewing process continuing to "keep the nerds honest."

CBSE 2009 had a special theme of components for large-scale systems of systems (SoS) and ultra-large-scale systems (ULS). Such systems involve the coordination of a vast array of decentralized, heterogeneous, and continually evolving subsystems, consequently meeting diverse and often conflicting requirements. The way that component technologies can move from assisting standard system architecture development to large-scale and ultra-large-scale system development is an important open question. Each of the topics listed above applies equally to the large-scale and ultra-large-scale case, but the context may demand radically novel solutions to deal with autonomous system components. We were lucky to have ULS expert Kevin Sullivan presenting a keynote on this topic.

While being the norm for the series, we nonetheless offer annual thanks for a superlative Program Committee of leading industry and academic experts in the field. We thank the committee and associated reviewers for their sterling efforts in facilitating a smooth and efficient process and ensuring a high-quality selection. We received 43 submissions, each of which was reviewed by three to four Program Committee members. In total, we accepted 16 papers.

Following a trend that we hope to continue in future years, CBSE was a part of COMPARCH, co-located with the 5th International Conference on the Quality of Software Architectures (QoSA 2009), a joint Industrial Day and the 14th International Workshop on Component-Oriented Programming (WCOP 2009). We thank Christine Hofmeister and her team at East Stroudsburg University for organizing the overall event. We also gratefully acknowledge the ACM Special Interest Group on Software Engineering (SIGSOFT) for their sponsorship and Springer for supporting the publication of the proceedings. Finally, as Program Chairs, we thank the Steering Committee for their invaluable expert mentoring.

As witnessed by these proceedings, the field of CBSE stands at an interesting point in its evolution: time will determine which of the themes addressed in this volume proves to be the most important as we move forward. Perhaps we will submit a reflection on this at the 24th CBSE event in 2021! Whatever the future holds, through scientific endeavor, may we learn to build bigger things out of smaller things better.

April 2009   Grace A. Lewis
                                                                   Iman Poernomo

Organization

Program Co-chairs

Grace A. Lewis   Software Engineering Institute, USA
Iman Poernomo   King's College London, UK

CompArch Organization Chair

Christine Hofmeister   East Stroudsburg University, USA

Steering Committee

Ivica Crnković   Mälardalen University, Sweden
Ian Gorton   Pacific Northwest National Lab, USA
George Heineman   Worcester Polytechnic Institute, USA
Heinz Schmidt   RMIT University, Australia
Judith Stafford   Tufts University, USA
Clemens Szyperski   Microsoft, USA

Program Committee

David Bentley   South Carolina Research Authority, USA
Judith Bishop   University of Pretoria, South Africa
Behzad Bordbar   University of Birmingham, UK
Michel Chaudron   Leiden University, The Netherlands
Kendra Cooper   University of Texas at Dallas, USA
Ivica Crnković   Mälardalen University, Sweden
Guglielmo De Angelis   National Research Council (CNR), Italy
Anthony Earl   Sun Microsystems Incorporated, USA
Xavier Franch   Universitat Politècnica de Catalunya, Spain
Rose Gamble   University of Tulsa, USA
Morven Gentleman   Dalhousie University, Canada
Sudipto Ghosh   Colorado State University, USA
Ian Gorton   Pacific Northwest National Lab, USA
Lars Grunske   Swinburne University of Technology, Australia
Richard Hall   Sun Microsystems, USA
George Heineman   Worcester Polytechnic Institute, USA
Dean Jin   University of Manitoba, Canada
Bengt Jonsson   Uppsala University, Sweden

Table of Contents

On Component Identification Approaches – Classification, State of the Art, and Comparison

Dominik Birkmeier and Sven Overhage

Component and Service Engineering Group,
Business Informatics and Systems Engineering Chair,
University of Augsburg,
Universitaetsstrasse 16, 86159 Augsburg, Germany
{dominik.birkmeier,sven.overhage}@wiwi.uni-augsburg.de

Abstract. Partitioning a design space to identify components with desired non-functional and behavioral characteristics is a crucial task in the component-based software development process. Accordingly, the issue of how to analyze design models in order to systematically derive a set of components constitutes a research question which has been investigated repeatedly. Component identification approaches that have been published in literature, however, make use of different component definitions and identification strategies. Furthermore, they vary from ad-hoc findings and general recommendations to more formalized methods and techniques which aim at an optimized partitioning. In this paper, we elaborate on the state of the art in component identification and provide a classification of approaches that highlights their respective strengths and weaknesses. To classify component identification approaches, we introduce a classification scheme that contains important distinguishing factors. It is used to compare existing approaches which have been compiled during a literature survey. In addition, it provides the basis to discuss significant differences between them and to identify remaining issues which give information about future research directions.

1 Motivation

Today's software systems have to satisfy a variety of demanding challenges: their complexity has to be *manageable* with a problem decomposition strategy, they need to be flexibly *adaptable* to changes in the field of application, and they must be *extensible* so that eventually required new functionality can be added efficiently [1,2,3]. With its underlying modular development paradigm, Component-Based Software Engineering promises to help solve these challenges. A prerequisite for its success in practice, though, is to better support this new modular development paradigm with adequate methods and tools [3,4].

Despite the questions of how components are to be specified, located in catalogs, and assembled to fulfill certain non-functional requirements, especially the issue of how to *systematically identify components* on the basis of design models constitutes an important research question which yet remains to be solved. The identification of components, which has to be accomplished at the beginning of the development process, provides the basis for the next design steps as well as the composition and usage

G.A. Lewis, I. Poernomo, and C. Hofmeister (Eds.): CBSE 2009, LNCS 5582, pp. 1–18, 2009.

of components later on. For this reason, it is of central importance for the component-based development process as a whole [2,5] and has been investigated in a variety of approaches that have been published in literature.

These approaches, however, show a significant heterogeneity. First of all, they range from *ad-hoc findings* (which have been gathered by creative thinking or charting an initial project) and *general recommendations* (which should be considered during the identification of components) to *structured methods* and *algorithmic procedures*. Moreover, their underlying component definition often differs and their respective strategy to identify components varies significantly. None of the approaches therefore was able to become broadly accepted so far, even more so as the systematic identification of components generally continues to be under research.

In this paper, we evaluate the state of the art in component identification and classify various approaches that have been published in literature. Therefore, we develop a *classification scheme* that takes distinguishing factors of component identification approaches from literature and combines them to form an overall picture. On the one hand, the classification scheme is used to *identify differences* which exist between individual approaches and to highlight their respective strengths as well as weaknesses. This comparison also reveals consequences for their applicability in different development scenarios and contexts. On the other hand, we use it to determine *complementary approaches*, which may be combined to obtain improved results, as well as *unresolved questions* that hint at issues interesting for further research. In so doing, we help structure the research agenda for the area of component identification and provide a means to better categorize future approaches.

The paper is organized as follows: to build the classification scheme, we start with determining and discussing characteristic criteria of component identification approaches in section 2. These criteria are being refined to form a set of distinguishing factors and then used to evaluate and classify component identification approaches. In section 3, we discuss various component identification approaches that have been published in literature and arrange them according to the specifications given in the classification scheme. In order to assemble the distinguishing factors as well as the component identification approaches, we conducted two literature surveys, which build the basic research method underlying this paper. Additionally, we brought in experiences gathered during the design and evaluation of the Business Component Identification (BCI) method [5]. To derive differences between the presented approaches and to highlight remaining issues, we use an argumentative-deductive approach. After giving an overview of related work in section 4, we finally conclude by discussing key findings and outlining future research directions in order to further improve existing component identification approaches.

2   Classification Scheme

When analyzing the component identification approaches published in literature more closely, they reveal significant differences, e.g. with respect to their conceptual design and the identification strategy. In order to compare and classify the individual approaches, we therefore firstly introduce a set of criteria which characterizes component identification methods and can be refined into distinguishing factors. For the derivation of characteristic criteria, we refer to the research focusing on the conception of systematic design methods in the software engineering as well as in other engineering disciplines [6,7]. From there, we take the following criteria as being characteristic for systematic methods in general:

- conceptual *foundations*, on which the approach is built;
- the *procedure* that is applied by the approach;
- the underlying *model* used by the approach;
- *supporting measures* which improve its application in practice.

These rather compact set of criteria allows a better understanding of whether an approach is able to contribute to the aspired *systematic identification of components* and where deficiencies exist. While they might not necessarily be complete, these abstract criteria have been proven to adequately describe systematic development approaches in theory [6,7]. For this reason, we used them as a starting point for building our classification scheme and refined them as documented below to describe component identification approaches in particular. In addition, we discussed augmenting the classification scheme with further aspects as, e.g., the scenario in which component identification approaches can be applied. Since we found that the aspects we discussed were already covered by the identified criteria, we decided on keeping this compact classification scheme. As we will see in section 3.3, the applicability of identification approaches in specific scenarios can, e.g., be assessed by looking at the underlying procedure and the models used.

2.1 Foundations

The conceptual design of a component identification approach is characterized by its *foundations*. They contain the understanding of central concepts, in particular the respective component definition which is underlying the approach. Furthermore, one has to distinguish approaches with respect to their degree of formalization and the integration into a comprehensive development process model. The first criterion gives information about how exact the component identification strategy is being described. The latter indicates whether the approach has been designed to work on data created during earlier development activities and provide specific results for later design steps.

Component definition. The approaches published in literature use different component definitions as a basis for the identification. These definitions range from domain-oriented component concepts, to architectural viewpoints, to more technical understandings (see fig. 1 for examples). Business-oriented component definitions, e.g., associate business components with domain-oriented concepts and require them to realize an autonomous business function or process [8,9]. More architecture-focused software component definitions usually do not contain a statement about the domain-specific functionality and instead concentrate on logical characteristics, e.g., a structuring in required and provided interfaces [3,10]. Technical component definitions, finally, concentrate on deployment and implementation aspects [11]. Since these definitions diverge in central aspects, they promote the emergence of different identification results.

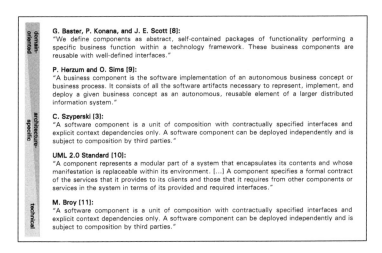

Fig. 1. Component definitions published in literature diverge

Degree of formalization. The degree of formalization ranges from a presentation of so-called ad-hoc findings, to general recommendations, to structured methods, to algorithmic procedures. Ad-hoc findings are based on creative thinking or experiences gathered by charting an initial project. Typically, they only allow for a fuzzy and opportunistic approach to identify components. General recommendations are proven practices that have been repeatedly applied to identify components with certain desirable characteristics. While they are based on more thoroughly researched findings, they usually concentrate on specific aspects or best practices that should be taken into consideration and do not combine these into a systematic procedure. Structured methods, in contrast, provide the designer with detailed work steps and arrange them to a component identification process. They also provide clearly specified identification criteria. Algorithmic procedures finally comprise a formal plan that combines individual work steps to a comprehensive work-flow.

Overall development process model. The identification of components usually is part of a software development project which is guided by a development process model. The process model defines the input and output of major development phases (such as design, implementation etc.) and coordinates the subsequent use of achieved results [2,12]. Component identification approaches should ideally be integrated into such an overall process model in order to define from which development phases the information taken as input should come from and how identified components are to be refined to serve as input for subsequent phases of the development process.

2.2 Procedure

The category *procedure* describes the technique that is applied by a component identification approach. While the overall development process model describes development phases in a rather coarse-grained manner (as process-in-the-large), the procedure describes concrete, fine-grained steps to identify components (as process-in-the-small).

It is characterized by the overall goal that is to be achieved with the identification, the direction in which the component identification is executed, the identification strategy, as well as the optimization of results that is eventually executed.

Goal. Component-based software is realized for a variety of reasons, above all because of its increased modularity (which allows for a more flexible adaptation [2]) and the fact that individual components can be generalized for reuse [3]. A component identification approach therefore can specifically opt for generating reusable components or look at a partitioning as a whole to achieve a well-modularized decomposition of a system. Additionally, there exist approaches that are able to strive for a balance between multiple goals, e.g. granularity and reuse (for a discussion of these contradicting goals see [3]).

Direction. The analysis to identify components can be carried out in two directions. Top-down approaches use domain-specific conceptual models (like business concept and process models) to identify components, which are then mapped onto a software landscape. Bottom-up approaches start by analyzing the existing software landscape and modularize this landscape. Identified modules of this landscape will be equipped with an according domain-specific semantics and provided as components. Meet-in-the-middle approaches try to combine both directions and strive for a compromise between a domain- and a technology-centric view.

Identification strategy. Components can basically be identified with different strategies. Some approaches use matrices to analyze relationships between design elements. E.g., they analyze create, read, update, and delete relationships between functions and data with the objective of finding clusters. Other approaches use graph-based or clustering algorithms to identify self-contained components.

Optimizing approach. An important characteristic of component identification approaches is whether they try to find an optimized choice, i.e. components with preferably optimal properties in terms of the designer's preferences. For example, optimizing approaches often try to identify a set of components with maximal cohesion and minimal dependencies following a principle already stated by Parnas [13]. Such requirements can be transferred to a mathematical optimization problem and then be approached with appropriate techniques (e.g. clustering methods). Thereby, one has to distinguish between approaches that use exact (finding the overall best solution – global optimum) or heuristic (identifying the best solution that can be found with reasonable effort – local optimum) methods.

2.3   Model

Generally, the identification of components is based on *models* which reflect reality. The examined approaches, however, diverge with respect to content and complexity of the utilized models. Differences become apparent regarding the analyzed model views, the consideration of legacy structures and system dependencies as well as the differentiation of component hierarchies or predefined component types.

Model views. Independent of the question whether a domain-oriented or technical perspective is being used, socio-technical systems in general and software systems in particular can always be described from three modeling views, which are widely used in software design methods such as Syntropy or Catalysis [12,14]: the *data view* describes processed information objects as well as their respective structure as system attributes. The *functions view* documents the system behavior and combines system attributes as inputs and outputs. A functional decomposition moreover describes the relationship between complex functions and their sub-functions. The *process view* finally describes the temporal relationships between functions and combines them to workflows. The identification of components basically can take all three model views into account, since only their synopsis provides a comprehensive view. Many approaches, however, only use a subset of these model views which leads to specific advantages and drawbacks.

Consideration of existing structures. The identification of components is often performed in an existent software environment with legacy systems or components in place. Many approaches, however, are unable to consider them appropriately and to weave existent structures into their procedure.

Consideration of system dependencies. Components are units of composition and normally provide their functionality in cooperation with other components only [3]. Some approaches, therefore, aim at identifying sets of collaborating components with thoroughly analyzed interdependencies. Others concentrate on identifying single components and disregard their potential dependencies to the environment.

Differentiation of component hierarchies. During the identification, one can generally distinguish between complex components, which themselves are composed of components, and elementary components. Identification approaches which explicitly support such a distinction implement a stepwise decomposition until no more complex components have been identified [15]. Others do not explicitly support a stepwise decomposition and leave the construction of a composition hierarchy to the designer.

Differentiation of predefined component types. Some of the component identification approaches generally distinguish components of predefined types [2,9]. Often, these approaches separate components whose primary purpose is the management of data (Entity Components) from those who coordinate and execute application-specific tasks (Process Components). Such an identification procedure inherently leads to a separation of data- and task-specific services. It is debatable, however, if such procedures deliver an optimal result, especially since many authors argue for a grouping of data and related tasks into a single part [13]. Other approaches, therefore, do not build upon a distinction of predefined component types.

2.4   Supporting Measures

Supporting measures enhance the applicability of component identification approaches in practice. They can be classified into tool support, quality assertions, and validation.

Tool support. The practical applicability of component identification approaches can be enhanced by providing software tools which guide the designer through the identification process and help managing the complexity.

Quality assertions. The quality of an identification result has a significant impact, since the implementation and roll-out of new software artifacts always is associated with considerable strategic and financial risks. Ideally, a component identification approach, therefore, is able to guarantee the correctness of a result, especially if it provides an algorithmic procedure. Optimizing approaches should additionally make sure that local optima are being prevented. If a formal guarantee is not feasible, approaches should support other forms of quality assertions. E.g., they could state the maximum deviation from an optimal result, allow for a sensitivity analysis, or at least provide an evaluation of the result.

Validation. Component identification approaches have to be validated to assess their correctness and applicability in practice. While a plausibility check demonstrates the principal correctness, only comprehensive use cases and best practices reveal terms of use as well as possible applications and limitations of an approach.

2.5 Classification Scheme

The previously mentioned distinguishing factors can be arranged to form a classification scheme as depicted in table 1. The values of the identified distinguishing factors have been summarized as a morphological box and serve as the basis to classify individual identification approaches. When looking at the classification scheme as a whole, one might suspect that distinguishing factors are not independent from each other.

Table 1. Classification Scheme

Classification Scheme for Component Identification Methods			
Component definition	Domain-oriented	Architectural	Technical	None
Degree of formalization	Algorithm	Structured	Recommendations	Ad hoc
Development process model	Yes		No	
Goal	Multi-criteria	Modularity	Reuse	Not defined
Direction	Top-down	Bottom-up		Meet-in-the-middle
Identification strategy	Matrix analysis	Graph-based	Clustering analysis	Other
Optimizing approach	Yes (exact)	Yes (heuristic)		None
Model views	Data	Functions		Processes
Consideration of existing structures	Yes		No	
Consideration of system dependencies	Yes		No	
Differentiation of component hierarchies	Yes		No	
Differentiation of predefined component types	Yes		No	
Tool support	Yes		No	
Quality assertions	Quality guarantee	Sensitivity analysis	Evaluation	None
Validation	Best practices	Use case	Plausibility check	None

A bottom-up approach to identify components might, e.g., probably use a technical component definition. Similarly, an approach that uses matrices to analyze relationships between design elements as part of its identification strategy might probably do this in a formalized (algorithmic) procedure.

However, when analyzing the distinguishing factors more closely, it becomes obvious that they are mostly orthogonal. It is, e.g., conceivable that a bottom-up approach might make use of a domain-oriented component definition. Such an approach will require moving from the underlying technical software system to its conceptual model which is used to identify meaningful components from a domain-oriented perspective. Identified components will then be mapped onto the existing software system. Accordingly, identification approaches might well use matrices to analyze relationships between design elements, but not conduct the analysis in an algorithmic procedure.

3   Component Identification Approaches

In this section, we provide an overview of the state of the art in component identification, and elaborate on various approaches published in literature. After briefly introducing these approaches in section 3.1, we compare and classify them in section 3.2. The introduced classification is built on the criteria defined in section 2, while the examined approaches were chosen from a broad and thorough literature survey in information systems, as well as computer science journals and proceedings.

3.1   Overview

Business Systems Planning (IBM). IBM describes an approach where *business information systems* can be decomposed systematically based on *business process* and *data models* [16]. Detailed steps are given to identify *system modules* through examining relations between process activities and data objects in a matrix analysis. The partitioning of corresponding activities is optimized using heuristics, in a way such that the number of shared data objects between the groups of activities is minimized.

FORM (Kang et al.). The *Feature-Oriented Reuse Method* (FORM) is an approach extending the FODA method, both introduced by Kang et al. in the *Domain Engineering* area [17]. The semi-formal method focuses on the identification and classification of *features*. By constructing and analyzing a *feature model*, a hierarchical organization of features in an *AND/OR graph* that captures logical structural relationships among features, the designer is able to develop domain architectures and candidate reusable components. However, detailed information on how to apply the technique is missing.

Units of... (Szyperski et al.). In his book about component-based software engineering Szyperski introduces *15 modularity criteria* which should ideally be satisfied by identified components [3]. According to these criteria, components should not only be *self-contained* with respect to their functionality, but also be *independently implementable*, *installable*, and *maintainable*. While the criteria are formulated in detail, they don't exceed the level of general recommendations. A structured procedure with concrete work steps to guide the designer is missing completely.

COMO (Lee, Yang et al.). Lee, Yang et al. propose the *object-oriented component development methodology* and *component modeling technique COMO*, which covers the phases domain analysis and component design [18]. In a first step UML use cases are clustered by considering *<<extends>>* relationships. Afterwards, a matrix-based use case and class clustering technique, built on an examination of *create*, *delete*, *write*, and *read* relationships, is applied. The component identification is only a fraction in the suggested process and therefore limited to rather basic steps and guidelines.

SADA (Sugumaran et al.). Sugumaran et al. suggest a methodology and software tool called *Systems Analysis and Design Assistant* (SADA), which combines system requirements with available software object repositories to obtain software components for a program design [19]. In four steps, higher level *object components* are extracted from a domain model and mapped to reusable *data attribute/method components* from a component repository, to achieve specific *software design components*. SADA was validated through an evaluation on four subjects.

UML Components (Cheesman et al.). In their book on *UML Components*, Cheesman et al. [2] describe a development process that includes a structured method to identify business components. They use a business type model to identify autonomous information objects, which are to be encapsulated and identified as entity components. Use cases and business process models are then used to identify additional components which execute application-specific tasks and process information objects. They are dependent on the entity components that have previously been identified.

O2BC (Ganesan et al.). The five step methodology *Objects to Business Components* (O2BC) from Ganesan et al. [20] is similar to the previously introduced *COMO* method [18], but has some significant differences in the clustering technique. *External Business Events* (EBE) with associated use cases and an object-oriented domain object model are used as input for the identification of candidate sets of logical components. *Entity components* (EC) are created in the first phase through an analysis of dependencies between EBEs and Entities. Taking the EBEs and the identified ECs as input, necessary *process components* (PC) are identified subsequently.

CompMaker (Jain et al.). Jain et al. are presenting an approach where they identify components from an *Analysis Level Object Model*, representing a business domain [21]. The domain model in UML notation contains at least object-oriented class diagrams, use cases and sequence or interaction diagrams. Structural and dynamic relationships between the different objects in the domain model are used to compute the *Class Relationship Strength*. Based on these, components are identified through grouping classes in a first step, using a *Hierarchical Agglomerative* clustering algorithm. Afterwards, automated *add-*, *move-* or *exchange-*, as well as *manual-heuristics* are applied for further improvement. Different measurements are used to identify a best possible solution, strongly depending on the designers' preferences. The identification process is supported in the *CompMaker* tool.

Component Identification Method (Lee, Jung et al.). A systematic component identification algorithm, that considers component coupling, cohesion, dependency, interface, granularity, and architecture, is suggested by Lee, Jung et al. [22]. Based on a domain model in UML-notation different aspects (amongst others: classes, class types, relations, use cases and required component interfaces) are examined by the designer in a stepwise procedure. Afterwards, the gained information is mapped onto a *Class Relation Graph* and a clustering algorithm is applied to identify candidate components. Based on a *Guideline for Well-Defined Components* the designer is able to choose appropriate components among the candidates.

Enterprise Component Identification (Levi et al.). An extension and refinement to the *Unified Process*, centered on enterprise component identification and specification, is introduced by Levi et al. [23]. The business-driven approach focuses on the two main business analysis activities *domain partitioning/decomposition* and the *creation of a goal model* to provide traceability of IT services to business goals. A software architect, together with a business analyst/modeler, identifies business processes and divides a domain into its functional areas (e.g. based on department boundaries and value chains). Each business process will be mapped onto an *Enterprise Component*. The subsystems are further decomposed into constituent business processes and business process steps. Moreover, *Services* are allocated to the components, using the goal model. A Service is hereby *'defined by interfaces: what a component exposes'*. The general procedure is outlined in six steps and recommendations are given based on a use case. Nevertheless, a thorough description of the process is lacking.

CUAT (Jang et al.). A component identification method, which leans on the previously introduced *Business Systems Planning* [16], is introduced by Jang et al. as the *class and use case affinity analysis technique* (CUAT) [24]. A business model, containing business need description, business type model and business use case model, as well as a software architecture, consisting of use case model, class model, interaction model and involvement matrix, are necessary for the two phases approach. Starting with a *class/class affinity analysis* and continuing with a *use case/class affinity analysis*, components are identified. However, detailed information on the proposed technique is missing. To show plausibility, the method is applied to the *Open Services Gateway Initiative* (OSGi) system.

Software Components (Kim et al.). Kim et al. propose a systematic UML-based method to identify components, which makes use of clustering algorithms, metrics and decision rules as well as a set of heuristics [25]. An object-oriented domain model is needed as input, including use case model, object model and sequence or collaboration diagrams. Components are identified in *four steps*, which fulfill three defined criteria for a good component identification process. After measuring the *functional dependencies* between the use cases, a matrix analysis is used to group coherent use cases. Afterwards, classes are allocated to use case groups depending on an analysis of the *dynamic* and *object models*. Finally a suggestion is given to select the group of components with the most promising qualities among all candidates.

BCI and BCI-3D (Albani et al.). In [5,26,27] the *Business Component Identification* (BCI) method, as well as the further development to *BCI-3D*, are described by Albani et al.. The basis for the component identification is a domain model, which can be available in any notation. Information about data objects, process steps and actors, plus their relationships is mapped onto vertices and edges of a graph. Weights are assigned to the edges depending on the relation type and the designers preferences. Using a combination of an *opening-* and an *improving-heuristic* from graph theory, the graph is partitioned and components are identified. The *BCI-3D* tool supports the designer in the identification process.

Components Grouping Technique (Blois et al.). A process, called *Component-Based Development - Architecture - Domain Engineering* (CBD-Arch-DE), which extends the *Odyssey-DE* process is proposed by Blois et al. [28]. From the three phases Domain *Planning*, *Analysis* and *Design*, only the last one, which contains the two parts *Component Generation* and *Architecture Generation*, is introduced in detail. For the creation of *business*, *utility* and *infra-structure components* in the first part, the authors rely on existing techniques. The focus lies on the *Component Grouping* through examining six defined criteria of an existing component structure and enabling the Domain Engineer to group components based on the four different aspects: *domain context*, *process component*, *component interfaces* and the *component itself*. A tool is provided as part of the *Odyssey Environment*.

Business Component Identification (Meng et al.). In their work on *Business Component Identification of Enterprise Information Systems*, Meng et al. are using a *hierarchical clustering technique* based on a graph [29]. Although differing between *business object components* and *business process components*, where the latter are composed of the former ones, they focus entirely on identifying object components. A domain model with function, process and information view is used as input. Mapping business objects onto the vertices of a graph and assigning weights to the edges after examining static and dynamic relationships, they are able to build *dendrograms* with a hierarchical clustering technique. Using different *linkage* methods, the designer is able to identify several candidate sets of reusable business components. Evaluating the candidate sets after the designers' preferences, helps to choose the most appropriate set of components.

3.2   Classification and Comparative Discussion

The majority of approaches were published between 1998 and 2001, but the ongoing research over the last years still shows the timeliness of the topic and the need for a well-engineered procedure model. Among the 15 different techniques, which face the task of identifying appropriate components from various angles, there is not a single one that convinces in all criteria, but rather all of them have their individual strengths and weaknesses. An overview on the classification results of the briefly introduced approaches is given in table 2. Below follows a differentiated examination of the methods, according to the criteria defined in section 2.

Foundations. The underlying *component definitions* vary heavily between the approaches. Whereupon technical [24] or domain-oriented [23,29] viewpoints are rather seldom, the majority of techniques are built upon an architectural definition of components. However, an interesting observation is that in six cases the authors identify components without any definition of what they try to find. Furthermore, even if a definition is given, it is oftentimes imprecise and therefore handicaps a comparison of the approaches. The *degree of formalization* is in seven cases structured, and general recommendations or algorithms are given in four cases each. The amount of information

Table 2. Classification of current component identification approaches

	IBM [16]	Kang et al. [17]	Szyperski et al. [3]	Lee, Yang et al. [18]	Sugumaran et al. [19]	Cheesman et al. [2]	Ganesan et al. [20]
Year of publication	1984	1998	1998, 2002	1999	1999	2001	2001
Component definition	n/a	None	Architectural	None	None	Architectural	Architectural
Degree of formalization	Structured	Recommendations	Recommendations	Structured	Recommendations	Structured	Structured
Development process model	✗	✓	✗	✓	✗	✓	✓
Goal	Modularity	Reuse	Multi-criteria	Not defined	Reuse	Modularity	Not defined
Direction	Top-down	Meet-in-the-middle	n/a	Top-down	Meet-in-the-middle	Top-down	Top-down
Identification strategy	Matrix analysis	Other	n/a	Matrix analysis	Other	Other	Other
Optimizing approach	✓ (heuristic)	✗	✗	✓ (heuristic)	✗	✗	✗
Model views	Processes and data	n/a [1]	n/a	Processes, data and functions	Processes	Processes and data	Processes and data
Existing structures	✗	✓	✓	✗	✗	✗	✗
System dependencies	✓	✗	✓	✗	✗	✓	✗
Component hierarchies	✗	✗	✗	✗	✓	✗	✗
Component types	✗	✓	✗	✗	✓	✓	✓
Tool support	✗	✗	✗	✗ [2]	✓	✗	✗
Quality assertions	None	None	None	Evaluation	None	None	None
Validation	Use case	None	None	Plausibility check	Plausibility check	Use case	Use case

[1] Features, [2] Not mentioned, but possible, [3] Not complete, [4] Mentioned, but not part of procedure,

and sub-steps explained alters noticeably in the evaluated literature. About half of the approaches are embedded in a *development process model*.

Procedure. In contrast to the newer approaches, where modularity is the dominating *goal*, two older ones focus solely on reuse [17,19]. Multi-criteria goals not only unite modularity and reuse, but for instance use combinations of managerial goals (i.e. cost effectiveness, ease of assembly, customization, etc.) and technical features (i.e. coupling, cohesion, complexity, etc.) [21]. Again, like the missing component definitions, some approaches work without defining goals for their results [18,20,23]. The *direction* of the analysis to identify components is top-down for most (nine) of the cases, only one uses a bottom-up strategy [28] and four follow a meet-in-the-middle course.

Table 2. *(Continued)*

Jain et al. [21]	Lee, Jung et al. [22]	Levi et al. [23]	Jang et al. [24]	Kim et al. [25]	Albani et al. [26,27,5]	Blois et al. [28]	Meng et al. [29]
2001	2001	2002	2003	2004	2005, 2006, 2008	2005	2005
Architectural	None	Domain-oriented	Technical	Architectural	None	None	Domain-oriented
Algorithm	Algorithm	Recommendations	Structured	Structured	Algorithm	Structured	Algorithm
✗	✗	✓	✗	✗	✓	✓	✗
Multi-criteria	Multi-criteria	Not defined	Modularity	Modularity	Modularity	Modularity	Multi-criteria
Top-down	Top-down	Top-down	Meet-in-the-middle	Meet-in-the-middle	Top-down	Bottom-up	Top-down
Clustering analysis	Graph-based	Other	Matrix analysis	Matrix analysis	Graph-based [5]	Other	Clustering analysis based on graph
✓ (heuristic)	✗	✗	✓ (heuristic) [3]	✓ (heuristic)	✓ (heuristic)	✗	✓ (exact) [7]
Processes and functions	Processes and functions	Processes	Processes and functions	Processes, data and functions	Processes and data	n/a	Processes, data and functions
✗	✗	✗	✗	✗	✓ [6]	✗	✗
✓	✗	✗	✗	✗	✓	✗	✗
✗	✗	✓	✗	✗	✗	✓	✓
✗	✗	✗	✗ [4]	✗	✗	✓	✓
✓	✗ [2]	✗	✗	✗	✓	✓	✗
Evaluation	None	None	None	Evaluation	Evaluation	None	Evaluation
Use case	Plausibility check	Use case	Plausibility check	None	Use case	Plausibility check	Plausibility check

[5] Older methods: matrix-based, [6] through integration in domain model, [7] Exact only for a subproblem

A matrix analysis was used in the first approach (Business Systems Planing [16]) and also many of the newer techniques utilize similar methods as stand-alone or as part of their *identification strategy* (categorized as 'other'). Furthermore, especially newer procedures propose a clustering analysis [21,29] or graph-based [5,22] technique. Less than half of the approaches try to *optimize* the identified component structure using a heuristic. The exact solution proposed by Meng et al. [29] only covers the smaller subproblem to choose the best component structure from a given candidate set.

Model. Almost all of the strategies are based on a process *view* on the model. Oftentimes this is completed by additionally considering information on functions and/or data. Whereas, *existing structures* are taken into account by three approaches only [3,5,17], and just five procedures analyze *system dependencies* [2,3,5,16,21]. Four authors care for *component hierarchies* and include according arrangements in their strategy [19,23,28,29]. The differentiation of predefined *component types* is covered in several papers, though only six of them integrate suitable support in their procedure.

Supporting Measures. A support of the proposed component identification approaches through corresponding *tools* is only mentioned in four cases [5,19,21,28]. Moreover, the integration into a tool-suite, covering the whole development process, might be helpful for the designer (cf. [28]). Especially for clearly structured methods and algorithms with high complexity a software tool is essential. Quality assertions are missing in most cases and the provided *evaluation* of components in five cases [5,18,21,25,29] does not go far enough to ensure and proof a high quality solution. A similar conclusion can be drawn for the *validation* of the proposed approaches, where use cases and plausibility checks are provided in six cases each, but none is validated through best practices. However, this would be crucial for the further development of the procedures.

3.3   Implications

Several implications can be derived from the identified state of the art for researchers in the field of component identification methods, as well as for software engineers of component-based software systems. The former ones can use the results from table 2 to identify areas requiring further research, improve their own approaches and fill out the blanks. To improve the usability of several methods, an analysis of the *supporting measures* shows that software tools are needed, especially in the case of optimizing approaches. Furthermore, the given quality assertions and validations are mostly quite rudimental. So far, none of the approaches considers existing structures as well as system dependencies and differentiates component hierarchies as well as predefined component types at the same time. Additionally, researchers might be able to use combinations of existing, complementary approaches for further improvements of the state of the art in component identification. For example we see a good chance that the *BCI* approach from Albani et al. [5,26,27] might be successfully combined with the *Components Grouping Technique* from Blois et al. [28], since the former one identifies components from a domain model and the latter one elaborates on existing component structures to form a hierarchy.

A software engineer can use the provided comparison of approaches to select one that is most appropriate for his/her particular development scenario. Above all, the utilized component definition, the direction of the approach as well as the required model views provide insights whether an approach is suited to support a development scenario or not. In a *greenfield software development project*, where components can be identified during the early design phases and without taking existing software systems into account, top-down approaches such as [2,16,21,22,26,29] which use a domain-oriented or architectural component definition should be chosen. The decision for a specific approach furthermore should be depending upon whether the overall goal during the identification is to identify reusable components [21,22,29] or to primarily create a modular system design [2,16,26].

In a scenario where existing software systems have to be modularized or at least to be integrated into the identification of components, bottom-up or meet-in-the-middle approaches are to be preferred. These approaches either start from existing software systems and aggregate implementation classes to form components [28] or at least take existing software structures into account during the identification of components [17,19,24,25]. As the classification shows, an integrated component identification approach, which combines the strengths of the mentioned approaches and is able to cover all depicted scenarios, is not available however. Therefore, it currently depends on the knowledge of the designer if a suitable approach is chosen and useful results can be achieved. Our paper thus provides useful insights by identifying and detailing on the state of the art.

4 Related Work

As the variety of analyzed approaches shows, the identification of components has been under research for several years and repeatedly addressed in various publications. While many of these publications contain a section discussing individual related approaches, systematic overviews and comparisons of component identification approaches are mostly missing. Especially, there is only little work specifically devoted to structure and present the state of the art. Such a survey of methods to identify components has been provided by Wang et al. [30]. While this survey had a similar goal of structuring the state of the art, the scope was limited and solely focused on approaches tailored to identifying business components. In addition, the authors did not provide a detailed scheme to classify identification approaches but heuristically distinguished between approaches with domain-engineering, CRUD (create, read, update, delete) matrix, or cohesion-coupling clustering strategies. This distinction, however, is neither necessarily disjoint nor the only distinguishing factor for component identification methods. This paper, therefore, specifically aims at introducing a comprehensive classification scheme that is more suitable to discuss existent (and future) component identification approaches. In addition, we did not limit the scope of our survey to identification approaches that have been tailored for a specific application domain.

5 Conclusions and Future Directions

In this paper we elaborated on the state of the art in component identification and discussed several approaches which have been published in literature. The discussion was centered around a classification scheme that contains various characteristics of component identification approaches and has specifically been developed to compare existent as well as future developments. The assembled characteristics, thereby, were initially based on results from research focusing on the conception of systematic design methods in general. These results have been refined with specific properties so that they describe component identification approaches. The classification scheme was mainly used to compare various component identification approaches and reveal differences in their conceptual design as discussed in section 3.2.

However, the classification also revealed some fundamental findings: as already mentioned, it is noteworthy that a significant number of component identification approaches has been presented without mentioning the underlying component definition at all. Since the underlying component definition, however, determines what has to be identified, this finding gives reasons for questioning the aspired systematic design of such approaches. When arranging the collected approaches in historical order, a certain shift regarding the identification strategy becomes obvious. While older approaches often build upon a matrix analysis, especially many younger approaches rely on graph-based and clustering analyses to identify components. Since nearly all of the approaches have not been validated in the aspired manner, it yet has to be examined which strategy will be able to prevail. This is also true for the question, whether approaches should use a setting of predefined component types (e.g. entity and process components) for the identification process. Many approaches use such a scheme of component types to form components, while others prefer to constitute components without a predefined type.

An important step forward would thus be to comparatively evaluate the collected approaches and gain a better understanding of the advantages and limitations of varying identification concepts. Efforts towards such a comparative study, however, are handicapped by the fact, that many approaches do not come with tools that might support their application. Because many approaches moreover are not described in a sufficiently operative manner, a comparative evaluation had to be left out as a research activity to be accomplished in the future. As discussed, another research direction should be to combine complementary approaches for the identification of components. To realize the aspired systematic component identification as part of an engineering process, existing approaches will finally have to be enhanced in various aspects. Above all, their identification technique often needs to be advanced in order to implement a structured or even algorithmic procedure. This also is the basis for the claimed provisioning of supporting tools. Finally, component identification approaches need to be advanced with respect to their maturity level. To reach this goal, they need to be applied in complex projects more extensively to generate best practices. With many component identification approaches already in place, these open questions gain in importance and should direct future research activities in this area.

References

1. Brown, A.W.: Large-Scale, Component-Based Development. Prentice Hall, Upper Saddle River (2000)
2. Cheesman, J., Daniels, J.: UML Components. A Simple Process for Specifying Component-Based Software. Addison-Wesley, Upper Saddle River (2001)
3. Szyperski, C., Gruntz, D., Murer, S.: Component Software. Beyond Object-Oriented Programming, 2nd edn. Addison-Wesley, Harlow (2002)
4. Speed, J., Councill, W.T., Heineman, G.T.: Component-Based Software Engineering as a Unique Engineering Discipline. In: Councill, W.T., Heineman, G.T. (eds.) Component-Based Software Engineering: Putting the Pieces Together, pp. 673–691. Addison-Wesley, Reading (2001)

5. Albani, A., Overhage, S., Birkmeier, D.: Towards a Systematic Method for Identifying Business Components. In: Chaudron, M.R.V., Szyperski, C., Reussner, R. (eds.) CBSE 2008. LNCS, vol. 5282, pp. 262–277. Springer, Heidelberg (2008)
6. Pahl, G., Beitz, W., Feldhusen, J., Grote, K.H.: Engineering Design: A Systematic Approach. Springer, Heidelberg (2007)
7. Sommerville, I.: Software Engineering. Addison-Wesley, Reading (2006)
8. Baster, G., Konana, P., Scott, J.: Business Components - A Case Study of Bankers Trust Australia Limited. Communications of the ACM 44, 92–98 (2001)
9. Herzum, P., Sims, O.: Business Component Factory: A Comprehensive Overview of Component-Based Development for the Enterprise. John Wiley & Sons, New York (2000)
10. Object Management Group (OMG): Unified Modeling Language Specification: Version 2, Revised Final Adopted Specification, ptc/05-07-04 (2005)
11. Broy, M.: Towards a Mathematical Concept of a Component and its Use. Software - Concepts and Tools 18, 137–159 (1997)
12. D'Souza, D.F., Wills, A.C.: Objects, Components, and Frameworks with UML. In: The Catalysis Approach. Addison-Wesley, Upper Saddle River (1999)
13. Parnas, D.L.: On the Criteria to be Used in Decomposing Systems into Modules. Communications of the ACM 15, 1053–1058 (1972)
14. Cook, S., Daniels, J.: Designing Object Systems. In: Object-Oriented Modelling with Syntropy. Prentice Hall, Englewood Cliffs (1994)
15. Atkinson, C., Bayer, J., Bunse, C., Kamsties, E., Laitenberger, O., Lagua, R., Muthig, D., Paech, B., Wust, J., Zettel, J.: Component-Based Product Line Engineering with UML. Addison-Wesley, Reading (2001)
16. IBM Corporation: Business Systems Planning: Information Systems Planning Guide. Technical report ge20-0527-4, International Business Machines Corporation (1984)
17. Kang, K.C., Kim, S., Lee, J., Kim, K., Shin, E., Huh, M.: FORM: A Feature-Oriented Reuse Method with Domain-Specific Reference Architectures. Annals of Software Engineering 5, 143–168 (1998)
18. Lee, S.D., Yang, Y.J., Cho, E.S., Kim, S.D., Rhew, S.Y.: COMO: A UML-Based Component Development Methodology. In: APSEC 1999: Proceedings of the Sixth Asia Pacific Software Engineering Conference, Washington, DC, USA, p. 54. IEEE Computer Society, Los Alamitos (1999)
19. Sugumaran, V., Tanniru, M., Storey, V.C.: Identifying Software Components from Process Requirements Using Domain Model and Object Libraries. In: ICIS '99: Proceedings of the 20th international conference on Information Systems, Atlanta, GA, USA, Association for Information Systems, pp. 65–81 (1999)
20. Ganesan, R., Sengupta, S.: O2BC: A Technique for the Design of Component-Based Applications. In: TOOLS 2001: Proceedings of the 39th International Conference and Exhibition on Technology of Object-Oriented Languages and Systems (TOOLS39), Washington, DC, USA, pp. 46–55. IEEE Computer Society Press, Los Alamitos (2001)
21. Jain, H., Chalimeda, N., Ivaturi, N., Reddy, B.: Business Component Identification - A Formal Approach. In: EDOC 2001: Proceedings of the 5th IEEE International Conference on Enterprise Distributed Object Computing, Washington, DC, USA, pp. 183–187. IEEE Computer Society Press, Los Alamitos (2001)
22. Lee, J.K., Jung, S.J., Kim, S.D., Jang, W.H., Ham, D.H.: Component Identification Method with Coupling and Cohesion. In: Proceedings of the 8th Asia-Pacific Software Engineering Conference (APSEC 2001), Macau, China, Washington, DC, USA, December 4-7, pp. 79–86. IEEE Computer Society Press, Los Alamitos (2001)
23. Levi, K., Arsanjani, A.: A Goal-Driven Approach to Enterprise Component Identification and Specification. Communications of the ACM 45, 45–52 (2002)

24. Jang, Y.J., Kim, E.Y., Lee, K.W.: Object-Oriented Component Identification Method Using the Affinity Analysis Technique. In: Konstantas, D., Léonard, M., Pigneur, Y., Patel, S. (eds.) OOIS 2003. LNCS, vol. 2817, pp. 317–321. Springer, Heidelberg (2003)
25. Kim, S.D., Chang, S.H.: A Systematic Method to Identify Software Components. In: APSEC 2004: Proceedings of the 11th Asia-Pacific Software Engineering Conference, Washington, DC, USA, pp. 538–545. IEEE Computer Society Press, Los Alamitos (2004)
26. Albani, A., Dietz, J.L., Zaha, J.M.: Identifying Business Components on the Basis of an Enterprise Ontology. In: Konstantas, D., Bourrieres, J.P., Leonard, M., Boudjlida, N. (eds.) Interoperability of Enterprise Software and Applications, Geneva, Switzerland, pp. 335–347. Springer, Heidelberg (2005)
27. Albani, A., Dietz, J.L.: The Benefit of Enterprise Ontology in Identifying Business Components. In: IFIP World Computing Conference, Santiago de Chile, Chile (2006)
28. Blois, A.P.T.B., Werner, C.M.L., Becker, K.: Towards a Components Grouping Technique within a Domain Engineering Process. In: EUROMICRO 2005: Proceedings of the 31st EUROMICRO Conference on Software Engineering and Advanced Applications, Washington, DC, USA, pp. 18–27. IEEE Computer Society Press, Los Alamitos (2005)
29. Meng, F.C., Zhan, D.C., Xu, X.F.: Business Component Identification of Enterprise Information System: A Hierarchical Clustering Method. In: Lau, F.C.M., Lei, H., Meng, X., Wang, M. (eds.) ICEBE, pp. 473–480. IEEE Computer Society, Los Alamitos (2005)
30. Wang, Z., Xu, X., Zhan, D.: A Survey of Business Component Identification Methods and Related Techniques. International Journal of Information Technology 2, 229–238 (2005)

Domain-Specific Software Component Models

Kung-Kiu Lau and Faris M. Taweel

School of Computer Science , The University of Manchester
Manchester M13 9PL, United Kingdom
{Kung-Kiu,Faris.Taweel}@cs.manchester.ac.uk

Abstract. We believe that for developing applications in a specific domain, the best kind of software component model to use is a domain-specific one. We also believe that current component models intended for specific domains are actually not domain-specific. In this paper we present an approach for deriving domain-specific component models from the domain model of a given domain, and show why such a component model is better than existing models that are not domain-specific.

1 Introduction

The usefulness of software components for constructing systems is recognised in increasingly diverse problem domains. General-purpose software component models [11,17] like EJB [7] and architecture description languages (ADLs) [19] are well-established for CBSE in generic problem domains. More recently, the principles of CBSE have been adopted by specialised problem domains like embedded systems [9], and even hardware design [24].

We believe that for a specialised domain, the best kind of component model is a domain-specific one. Moreover, we believe that such a model should be derived from the *domain model* [12]. By and large, this is not the case for current component models that are meant for special domains, e.g. Koala [22] for consumer electronics, PECOS [20] for field devices and SaveCCM [1] for vehicular systems. These models tend to be generic ADLs. They take account of the domain by incorporating its context into architectural units. Their connectors remain generic and simply link the ports of the architectural units. We do not therefore, regard these models as domain-specific because they are not derived directly from the underlying domain model. We believe that a domain-specific component model should have not only components that are domain specific, but also composition operators that are domain-specific, following the definition of component models in [11,17].

In this paper, we present an approach for deriving a component model from a domain model. In general, a domain model consists of many sub-models, such as the functional model [12,10] and the feature model [6]. The functional model describes data and control flow in the domain, starting from data and control I/O to the domain, via intermediate data processing operations, to the most basic data processing functions. The feature model specifies the functional units and their inter-relationships, in the domain, as well as which are mandatory or optional.

A component model consists of components and composition connectors. In this paper, we show how we can derive a domain-specific component model from a domain

G.A. Lewis, I. Poernomo, and C. Hofmeister (Eds.): CBSE 2009, LNCS 5582, pp. 19–35, 2009.

model. We derive domain-specific components from the most basic data processing functions, and we derive domain-specific composition operators from the control flow specification, in the functional model (of the domain model). A domain-specific component model not only makes it easier to build applications, by the use of pre-defined components and composition operators, but it can also take into account important domain knowledge such as variability, which generic ADLS cannot do.

2 Domain Models

There are various definitions of what a *domain* is. In this paper, we follow Czarnecki's definition [6]: "an area of knowledge scoped to maximise the satisfaction of the requirements of stakeholders, which includes concepts and terminology understood by practitioners in that area and the knowledge of how to build (parts of) systems in the area". We loosely interpret a domain as a problem domain.

A domain is described in a *domain model*, which is defined in a *context* described by a context model. A context model defines interactions between the candidate domain and external domains, together with any external constraints on these interactions [12]. In addition to the context model, the domain model consists of many other (sub)models (Fig. 1), each describing a different aspect (or view) of the domain. For example, the *feature model* (Fig. 1(b)) represents the common and variable features of a concept instance (an application in the domain), together with the dependencies among variable features. Other (sub)models include the *functional* model, *object* model, the *entity-relationship* model, etc. Domain modelling is a well-established research area, and has a more or less standard terminology. We will follow [8,10,12] for terminology.

In this work, we focus on the *functional* and *feature* models. The functional model describes the *data (or structural) model* and the *control model* (Fig. 1(a)). In Fig. 1(a), starting from the context (top), the functional model specifies functional structure and behaviour in terms of a *data model* (left) and a *control model* (right) respectively. The data model describes data flow in the domain, starting from data I/O to the domain (specified in the context), as a hierarchical decomposition of functionality in the domain where each node is a *data flow diagram* (DFD). Within a DFD (Fig. 2), functions are specified as *data transformations* (*dt*'s) interconnected by data flows (solid lines). The decomposition process of data ends with *primitive* data transformations (*pdt*'s). Each primitive data transformation is associated with a specification for data access or

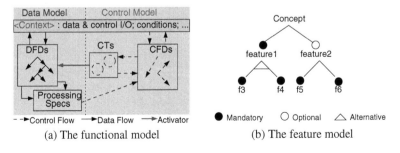

(a) The functional model   (b) The feature model

Fig. 1. Sub-models of a domain model

general data processing. The control model reuses the same hierarchy of DFDs of the data model, but without the data flows. It instead shows control flows (dashed arrows) for data transformations, and is captured in *control flow diagrams* (CFDs). Each CFD can be associated with a *control transformation* (ct),[1] which receives input control signals form its CFD, processes or transforms them, outputs them, and activates or deactivates data transformations in the corresponding DFD (activation/deactivation is represented by open arrows as in Fig. 1(a)). For example, in Fig. 2, *ct2* inputs control flows that are handled by the primitive data transformations *pdt2* and *pdt3*.

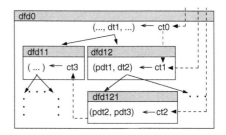

Fig. 2. Hierarchical decomposition of DFDs

A control transformation is a specification for a finite-state machine (FSM). A pair of corresponding DFD and CFD forms a *decomposition level* which may or may not have a control transformation. We introduce a visual simplification here embedding each *ct* in the relevant DFD and dropping CFDs, and control flows from the CFDs are represented as arrows arriving directly at *ct*'s.

As a result of tests on input data flows by their primitive data transformations, control flows are generated and propagates back to control transformations at the same or different decomposition levels. In particular, primitive data transformations can feed control signals back to an arbitrary control transformation, e.g. in Fig. 2, *pdt3* may feed control back to *ct2*.

Finally, for domain-specific development approaches such as generative programming [6] and product-lines engineering [4], a domain model provides the starting point. In these approaches, the domain model is used to build architectures and domain-specific languages. An architecture must capture variability so as to represent product families [23], and domain-specific languages are used to define such families and generate individual products. In generative programming, for example, an architecture is represented as templates based on GenVoca grammar [3], and code for different products can be generated from instances of such templates. In this paper we propose an alternative approach. From a domain model, we derive a domain-specific component model. This model encapsulates domain knowledge in its components and composition operators. These can be deposited in a repository for the domain, and reused for building any product (in the domain). Therefore our approach obviates the need for designing (and implementing) both architectures and domain-specific languages. Rather our domain-specific component model combines both.

3 Our Component Model

Our approach to deriving domain-specific component models is based on a component model that we have defined for a generic domain [16,14]. In this section, we briefly describe the component model which we refer to as the generic (component) model.

---

[1] In Fig. 1(a), CTs are put outside DFDs, but henceforth we put them inside for clarity.

The generic model has two kinds of basic entities: (i) *computation units*, and (ii) *connectors* (Fig. 3). A computation unit *CU* encapsulates *computation*. It provides a set of methods (or services). Encapsulation means that *CU*'s methods do not call methods in other computation units; rather, when invoked, all its computation occurs in *CU*. Thus *CU* could be thought of as a class that does not call methods in other classes.

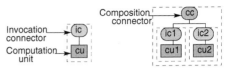

(a) Atomic component   (b) Composite component

Fig. 3. Our component model

There are two kinds of connectors: (i) *invocation*, and (ii) *composition* (Fig. 3). An invocation connector provides access to the methods (and data) of a computation unit. A composition connector encapsulates *control*. It defines and coordinates control flow between a set of components (atomic or composite). For example, a *sequencer* that composes components $C_1, \ldots, C_n$ can call methods in $C_1, \ldots, C_n$. This is illustrated in Fig. 4(a) for two atomic components. The

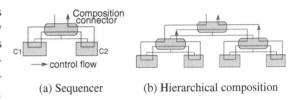

(a) Sequencer   (b) Hierarchical composition

Fig. 4. Composition in our model

control encapsulated by the composition connector determines the control flow between the two components.

Another example is a *selector* composition connector, which selects (according to some specified condition) one of the components it composes, and calls its methods.

Components are defined in terms of computation units and connectors. There are two kinds of components: (i) *atomic*, and (ii) *composite* (Fig. 3). An Atomic component consists of a computation unit with an invocation connector that provides an interface to the component. A composite component consists of a set of components (atomic or composite) composed by a composition connector. The composition connector provides an interface to the composite.

Invocation and composition connectors form a hierarchy [16]. This means that composition is done in a hierarchical manner. Furthermore, each composition preserves encapsulation. This kind of compositionality is the distinguishing feature of the generic component model. An atomic component encapsulates computation, namely the computation encapsulated by its computation unit. A composite component encapsulates computation and control. The computation it encapsulates is that encapsulated in its sub-components; the control it encapsulates is that encapsulated by its composition connector. In a composite, the encapsulation in the sub-components is preserved. Indeed, the hierarchical nature of the connectors means that composite components are self-similar to their sub-components, i.e. composites have the same structure as their sub-components; this property provides a basis for hierarchical composition.

Fig. 4(b) illustrates this: it shows that a generic composition connector receives control, passes it to its sub-connectors, and returns control. The control it receives comes from a composition connector at the next level of composition, i.e. the next level up, and the control it returns goes to a composition connector at the next level up too.

Finally, the generic model defines only *sequential* systems, i.e. systems that execute only one process, sequentially. It is also worth noting that components are *passive*, and executes only when invoked.

4   Deriving a Domain-Specific Component Model

To derive a domain-specific component model, we examine the domain model, and identify data transformations as candidates for atomic or composite components, and control transformations as candidates for composition connectors. Clearly to turn these into elements of the component model, we need to map or transform them into the latter. In this section, we discuss how this can be done.

4.1   Atomic Components

First we need to adapt atomic components in our model, in order to interpret control transformations according to our model. As we have seen in Fig. 2, a decomposition level in the functional model of a domain model comprises a DFD, a CFD and possibly a control transformation. A control transformation transforms a control flow from one type to another and activates or deactivates data transformations. In general, activation starts an *active* component executing, and deactivation stops it executing. Active components have their own thread of execution (unlike passive components, e.g. those in our component model), and are commonly elements of reactive or concurrent systems [2]. Since our component model does not have concurrency, we have to interpret activation and deactivation as method invocation in a (passive) atomic component. An invocation may succeed or fail, depending on whether the component has been activated or not. Therefore we need to add a *guard* to an atomic component; this is an adaptor connector that guards control flow to the computation unit by storing the state of a flag for the activated/deactivated status. The behaviour of a guard is shown in Fig. 5(b), where the two control flows show activation and deactivation as successful and failed invocation respectively. For simplicity, we will not show the guard in atomic components explicitly in any figures after Fig. 5(b).

With this adaptation, we can identify atomic components in a given functional model. Every primitive data transformation (*pdt*) is mapped to an atomic component, with its own invocation connector and a guard connector. A group of *pdts* associated with a control transformation (*ct*) is also mapped to an atomic component if the *ct* activates only one *pdt*, and all the other associated *pdts* return only

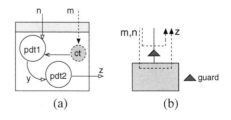

Fig. 5. Atomic components

data values, but no control signals at all. Fig. 5(a) shows an example of this. In this case, all the *pdts* (pdt_1, pdt_2) become one atomic component with a guard, as in Fig. 5(b).

In general, there can be many additional *pdt*s that are not part of the *ct* specification. These can be aggregated around *pdt*s that are specified in the *ct*, as in Fig. 5(a).

In the figures, we use variables to denote data values that accompany control flow; we use $m, n, p, \ldots$ to represent input values, and $x, y, z \ldots$ to represent output values for a connector. For example, in Fig. 5(b), m, n is the input to the guard (and the invocation connector which is not shown), and z the output from it.

4.2 Composition Connectors

In general, a *ct* is a control coordinator; a property that it shares with composition connectors of our component model (Section 3). However, unlike our composition connectors (Fig. 4), *ct*s do not encapsulate control. At any decomposition level of the functional model, a *pdt* may produce *feedback control flow*, i.e. it may output a control signal. In particular, such feedback control flow may ultimately arrive at a *ct* at another decomposition level, bypassing the *ct* at its own level.

Our strategy for deriving composition connectors from *ct*s is to identify groups of *ct*s which together do encapsulate control (as in Fig. 4). We call such a group a *control-encapsulation region* (*CER*). Of course, in general, for a given domain model, there are different ways to form *CER*s. However, for each *CER* we can derive a composition connector as defined in our component model. Such a connector is typically a composite connector [13] in the generic model. It is a domain-specific connector.

To determine *CER*s in a given functional model, we work up from the bottom decomposition level of the functional model. At each level, if there is a *ct*, say ct_1, then we check the control flow that starts from ct_1 and trace the control flow through the *pdt*s and to any other control transformation ct_2, and so on, until we reach the end of the control flow path. All the *ct*s in the control flow path then define a *CER*, and hence one composite composition connector in our model [13]. This composite connector encapsulates the control defined by all the control transformations $ct_1, ct_2, \ldots$ in this *CER*.

*CER*s can be broadly classified into two groups, depending on whether or not there is any feedback control flow therein. For each of these groups, we can also identify different cases, depending on the nature of the feedback control flow, if any, or depending simply on the interactions between the *pdt*s and the *ct*s. For each of these cases, we can define a corresponding composition connector in terms of connectors in the generic model. Here we briefly discuss the different categories of *CER*s we have identified so far and the corresponding composition connectors.

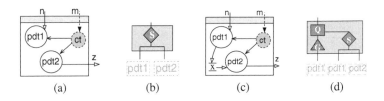

Fig. 6. No *pdt*s producing any feedback control

Category 1. A *CER* may contain no feedback control flows. A possible case is depicted in Fig. 6(a). Here the *ct* activates one *pdt*, but deactivates all other ones. The specification of the derived connector depends on whether these *pdt*s exchange data flows or not. A *ct* activating two *pdt*s that do not exchange data flows with one another maps to a *selector* composition connector, S in Fig. 6(b). However, a data flow from one to another requires a data store to allow passing the data values, and imposes a precedence on which *pdt* to perform first. The specification of the derived connector therefore must reflect these requirements for the connector to correctly achieve the desired functionality in the domain. Fig. 6(c) and (d) show the *CER* and the resulting composite connector in the case of interacting *pdt*s. The connector is a hierarchy comprising a selector (S), a sequencer (Q) and guard (G).

Category 2. A *CER* in this category contains a *ct* which receives feedback control flows from *pdt*s in the same decomposition level, as in Fig. 7(a). The only meaningful way to handle the feedback control flow is to activate other *pdt*s in the *CER* (and deactivating its source). Effectively, the feedback control flow is processed by the *ct* such that a sequence of one or more *pdt*s are performed next as a result of the feedback control flow. In the generic component model, this corresponds to sequencing the source *pdt* of the control flow with a guarded sequencer or pipe. Guarding is necessary to cater for scenarios where the control flow does not occur. Actually, the guard is equivalent to moving the source of the feedback control flow from the *pdt* to the control hierarchy, leaving the *pdt* with computation only. In general, to derive a connector for *CER*s in this category (e.g. Fig. 7(a)), we proceed in two phases: (i) a connector is derived by ignoring feedback control flows, but labelling their sources (Fig. 7(b)); and (ii) replacing the labelled branches by composites each consisting of a pipe/sequencer and guard connector (Fig. 7(c)).

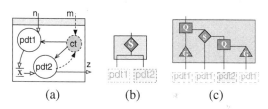

(a)   (b)   (c)

Fig. 7. Feedback control that stays within one level

Category 3. Feedback control flows can be returned by *pdt*s to *ct*s at levels different from their own, bypassing their level's *ct*s altogether. Such *CER*s form the third category. In Fig. 8(a), feedback control leaves one level and goes to another *ct* in the next level. A non-primitive *dt* A contains a *pdt* (pdt_1) and a non-primitive *dt* B, associated with a *ct* (ct_1). B is decomposed into two *pdt*s (pdt_2 and pdt_3) and is associated with its own *ct* (ct_2). A feedback control flow is initiated in pdt_2 and arrives (and terminates) at ct_1; one level higher in the model. The resulting *CER* therefore contains the two *ct*s, ct_1 and ct_2. Deriving a connector for this *CER* involves ct_1 and ct_2, in addition to piping/sequencing and possibly guarding. The derivation of a connector specification from Fig. 8(a) can be achieved by (i) abstracting the details of the *dt* that generates the feedback control flow, and (ii) applying steps used for deriving connectors from *CER*s in Category 2. Applying these steps to Fig. 8(a) reduces it to Fig. 8(b) which automatically contributes the composite connector in Fig. 8(c) (similar to that in Fig. 7). The

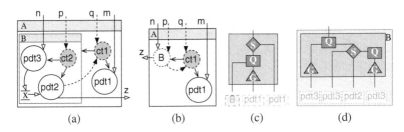

Fig. 8. Feedbacl control that goes to another level

final specification of the composite connector derived from A is achieved by replacing B in Fig. 8(c), by that in Fig. 8(d).

The composition connector derived for each *CER* is domain-specific because it encapsulates not only generic control structures that correspond to the composition connectors in our generic model, but it also encapsulates control behaviour defined in control transformations. Such control behaviour is defined in terms of state transitions between the states of the domain. Thus a derived composition connector contains domain-specific state-based behaviour.

Additionally, connectors also define place holders for control and data values, and specify how they are initialised and accessed. Data in the domain model is specified in terms of data stores defined in data transformations. Moreover, connectors are responsible for input and output data flows.

In summary, a derived composition connector is domain-specific because it specifies domain knowledge expressed in terms of control behaviour, data and data flows described in a given domain model. This will become clear in the next section when we discuss an example in some detail.

Finally, it is worth noting that in our approach, composition connectors provide an interesting means for modelling variability in domains. Based on the feature model, variants of connectors are specified to cater for optional features and their dependencies. Component models supporting domain variability specify it in terms of configuration interfaces and parametrised components, as exemplified by Koala [21]. In our approach, a set of *base* connectors are defined first, by ignoring all optional features (data transformations). A variant for a base connector is then defined, to coordinate control and data flows to an optional data transformation. In Fig. 8(a), if B is an optional data transformation, then following the same rules above, first a base connector is defined for A ignoring B (and its flows), and then a variant connector is defined from A and B. That is, we have one base connector and a variant connector.

5   Example: A Component Model for Vehicular Systems

In this section, we illustrate our strategy for deriving domain-specific component models by showing how to derive one for the vehicular systems domain (VSD). In particular, in VSD, we will identify *CER*s of categories 1, 2 and 3, as described in the previous section, and derive the corresponding composition connectors.

The domain model that we will use for VSD is a simplified (and adapted) version of an existing model for a vehicle management system presented in [10] (Chapter 26). A system in VSD is one of three possible variants. The *monitoring system* is a mandatory feature in all systems. It is used for monitoring fuel, average speed and the need for maintenance services. The *cruise control system* is a variant which allows the driver to set a value for a cruising speed that the system maintains, and enables the driver to resume to that speed at later times in the trip. The *adaptive cruise control system* is the third variant which involves an object detection functionality which allows the vehicle to automatically adapt its speed to safe levels with respect to the traffic in front of the vehicle, but when possible, allows it to return to the desired speed set by the driver during a given trip.

Fig. 9 depicts a feature model for VSD. It summarises the requirements for the three aforementioned variants. The monitoring feature, which is mandatory in all variants, will have the mandatory features *Measure Motion*, *Calibrate* and *Status*. A cruise control system will have the *Cruise* feature, whilst an adaptive cruise control system will have the *cruise* feature as well as the *Object Detection* feature, in addition. The *Object Detection* feature requires the *Cruise* feature, and Fig. 9 also shows this dependency.

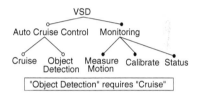

Fig. 9. Feature model for VSD

For lack of space, we only present part of the functional model. At the top level (level 0) of the functional model, we have a DFD (Fig. 10(a)), which contains one *ct* (ct_0) and five *dt*s: pdt_1 (1) for calculating vehicle speed and acceleration; pdt_2 (2) for calibrating the system; dt_3 ([3]) for calculating the throttle position necessary to accelerate, maintain speed at a desired speed, and optionally adapt speed to traffic in front of the vehicle; dt_4 (4) to monitor fuel levels, average speed and maintenance status; and dt_5 ([5]) for scanning obstacles, calculating safe speeds and triggering dt_3 to process the safe speed. The specification of ct_0 is a state transition diagram shown in Fig. 10(b). The diagram specifies a set of states and a number of valid transition between these states. Each transition is triggered by an input control flow to ct_0, and is then associated with a sequence of actions performed by *pdt*s in the same level. For example, when the Calibration Commands input the control signal START MEASURE to ct_0 in Fig. 10(a), this causes a

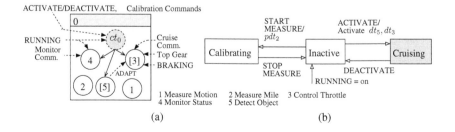

(a)   (b)

Fig. 10. Level 0 in the functional model for VSD

transition from the Inactive state to the Calibration state in Fig. 10(b). This transition activates pdt_2 as an action for handling the control signal START MEASURE.

We can identify several *CER*s in Fig. 10(a), depending on whether the optional *dts* (pdt_3 and pdt_5) are included or not. According to the feature model, each of pdt_3 and pdt_5 may or may not exist. If only pdt_3 exists, then we have the cruise control system; and if both pdt_3 and pdt_5 co-exist then we have the adaptive cruise control system.

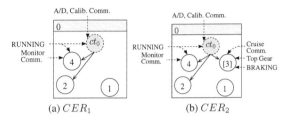

(a) CER_1 (b) CER_2

Fig. 11. Category 1 *CER*s of Level 0

Looking at Fig. 10(a), if both pdt_3 and pdt_5 are included then we can immediately define a Category 3 *CER* (let us call it CER_3) which is attributed to the control signal ADAPT returned by pdt_5 to pdt_3. If both pdt_3 and pdt_5 are dropped, then we can identify a Category 1 *CER* (CER_1 in Fig. 11(a)). If only pdt_3 is included then we have another Category 1 *CER* (CER_2 in Fig. 11(b)). We will revisit CER_3 to clarify it further below.

We can decompose the top decomposition level by decomposing the non-primitive *dts* (dt_3 and dt_5). dt_5 can decomposed into two primitives $pdt_{5.1}$ and $pdt_{5.2}$, together with a *ct* (ct_5), as shown in Fig. 12(a). $pdt_{5.1}$ analyses the Signal data flow input by a

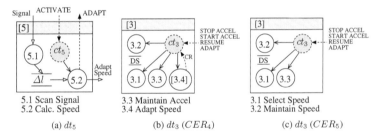

| 5.1 Scan Signal | 3.3 Maintain Accel | 3.1 Select Speed |
| 5.2 Calc. Speed | 3.4 Adapt Speed | 3.2 Maintain Speed |

(a) dt_5 (b) dt_3 (CER_4)   (c) dt_3 (CER_5)

Fig. 12. Level 2 for dt_3 and dt_5 in the functional model for VSD

sensor (e.g. a radar) and calculates the distance separating the vehicle from the traffic in front of the vehicle. $pdt_{5.2}$ calculates a safe speed and alerts dt_3 to reduce the vehicle speed to the safe speed. ct_5 is activated together with dt_3 as a result of receiving the ACTIVATE signal, as in Fig. 10(b). Clearly, the ADAPT control flow is returned by $pdt_{5.2}$ to dt_3, thus confirming that CER_3 identified above is a Category 3 *CER*. Indeed, by substituting dt_5 in Fig. 10(a) by its decomposition in Fig. 12(a) we get a match with that in Fig. 8(a).

dt_3 is decomposed into four *pdts*: $pdt_{3.1}$ for recording the driver's choice of the desired speed (DS) and keeping it in a data store throughout a trip; $pdt_{3.2}$ maintains speed at the desired level; $pdt_{3.3}$ to accelerate the vehicle to a speed that a driver may wish to cruise at; and $pdt_{3.4}$ (optional) to reduce the vehicle speed to a safe speed.

These *pdt*s are associated with *ct*₃, which processes a set of cruise commands (START/STOP ACCEL, RESUME, CRUISE and ADAPT). Fig. 12(b) shows the decomposition level for dt_3. The detailed behavioural specification of ct_3 is shown in Fig. 13, where the state Adapting is optional. The decomposition of dt_3 reveals two more *CER*s: a Category 2 *CER* defined by optional and mandatory *pdt*s (CER_4 in Fig. 12(b)); and a Category 1 *CER* defined by excluding the optional $dt_{3.4}$ (CER_5 in Fig. 12(c)).

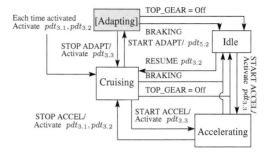

Fig. 13. Specification of ct_3

The decomposition of dt_4 is more detailed and is omitted here.[2] However, we include composition connectors derived from various decomposition levels of dt_4.

So far we have identified five *CER*s, covering all the categories presented in Section 4. Now we choose (the most interesting) three out of these *CER*s: CER_3, CER_4 and CER_5, and derive their corresponding composition connectors. In the derivation process, we start by ignoring optional *dt*s to derive base connectors. Then, we introduce gradually the optional *dt*s and any corresponding states in *ct*s, and derive variant connectors for the base connector. Additionally, while working on connectors, we identify atomic components from *pdt*s. Both, *pdt*s and connectors obtained from the derivation process are candidates for depositing in a repository for that domain. Because composition is bottom-up in component-based development, we also derive components and connectors bottom-up.

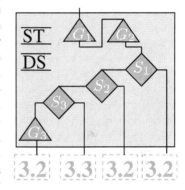

Fig. 14. CC_3

To derive a composition connector for a *CER*, we proceed as follows. We examine the state transition diagram for the *ct*, and map each transition to a guard or selector (in the generic model). Then we compose these connectors using our generic connectors, according to the transition conditions. The result of such a translation is a composite composition connector that is a domain-specific instance of a connector in our generic model. This is the case because of control encapsulation in a *CER*.

Consider CER_5 in Fig. 12(c) at the lowest level in the domain model. CER_5 is a member of Category 1 (Fig. 6(a)) whose *pdt*s exchange no direct data flows. This *CER* contributes a connector (designated CC_3) whose control behaviour is defined by the specification of ct_3 in Fig. 13, excluding the optional state. Table 1 lists the connectors in CC_3's specification, the condition each connector tests for enabling a sequence of actions on *pdt*s, and the intial states (S_f) and final states (S_i) for the transitions. (DS

---

[2] See the original case study in [10] (Chapter 26).

Table 1. Explanation of control processing performed by CC_3

Connector	S_i	Control Flow	DS Initialised	S_f
G_1	Accelerating OR Cruising	BRAKING	ANY	Idle
G_2	Accelerating OR Cruising	TOP_GEAR=Off	ANY	Idle
S_1	Idle	RESUME	Initialised	$pdt_{3.2}$
S_2	Cruising OR Idle	START ACCEL	ANY	$pdt_{3.3}$
S_3	Accelerating	STOP ACCEL	NOT BRAKING	$pdt_{3.1}; pdt_{3.2}$
G_3	Idle	Activate = CRUISE	ANY	$pdt_{3.1}; pdt_{3.2}$

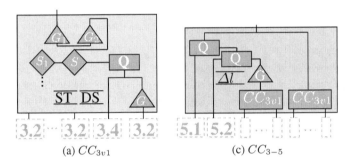

(a) CC_{3v1} (c) CC_{3-5}

Fig. 15. Connectors derived from CER_3

is a data store, see below.) CC_3 specifies no sequences because $pdt_{3.1}$ is a pure data access operation that is performed by connectors in our model [15]. Fig. 14 shows CC_3's specification. Obviously, CC_3 is specific to VSD because its control behaviour originates from the domain model (ct_3); encapsulates and accesses two data stores: DS and the state of the connector ST; and defines interfaces ($pdt_{3.2}$ & $pdt_{3.3}$) it accepts for composition. We identify $pdt_{3.2}$ & $pdt_{3.3}$ as atomic components.

Similarly we can derive composition connectors for CER_4 (Fig. 15(a)) and CER_3 (Fig. 10). Since CER_4 is defined from pdt_3, the resulting connector (CC_{3v1}) is a variant of the base connector CC_3. Finally, CER_3 defines a connector (CC_{3-5}) based on dt_3 and dt_5, including their optional pdts and the optional state in ct_3. The connector CC_{3-5} (15(b)) is also a variant of CC_3.

5.1 Comparison with SaveCCM

It is now possible to demonstrate the advantages of our approach over other component models intended for specific domains. We have selected SaveCCM [1], a component model for vehicular systems, as a representative model. In this section, we show the design of the cruise control system (CCS) using both our domain-specific component model (Fig. 16(a)) and SaveCCM (Fig. 16(b)).

With a repository at our disposal (Fig. 17), CCS can be designed and deployed from existing connectors and atomic components. These include four connectors (CC_3, CC_4, a pipe P and a selector S); and atomic components including "Measure Mile" and "Measure Motion" (Fig. 16(a)). Two of these components ("Maintain Speed" and

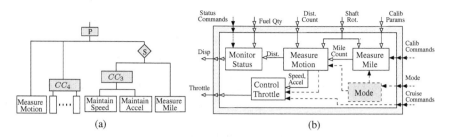

Fig. 16. Speed Controller designed using our model (a) and SaveCCM (b)

Connectors			Atomic Components	Origin
Connector	Description	Variant	Maintain Speed	$pdt_{3.2}$
CC_3	Speed controller	base	Maintain Accel	$pdt_{3.3}$
CC_{3v1}	Speed Controller	Variant of CC_3	Adapt Speed	$pdt_{5.2}$
CC_{3-5}	ACC controller	Variant of CC_3	Scan Signal	$pdt_{5.1}$
CC_4	Monitor Controller	base	Measure Mile	pdt_1
S	Selector	base	....	....
P	Pipe	base		

Fig. 17. Partial list of VSD repository

"Maintain Accel") are composed using CC_4 to construct a control cruising composite, and a number of other atomic components (not listed here) are composed by CC_4 to create the monitoring composite. CCS can either be in the calibrating mode or cruise mode, and hence "Measure Mile" and the cruising components are composed with S. The resulting composite is further composed with a pipe connector P to create CCS.

To build CCS in SaveCCM however, a set of components is selected to realise the "Cruise" and "Monitoring" features required in the domain (Fig.9). The corresponding dts to these features are pdt_1, pdt_2, dt_4 for "Monitoring" and dt_3 for "Cruise" in Fig. 10. Starting with an atomic component type in SaveCCM, we create two atomic components from pdt_1 and pdt_2, and two composite components for pdt_3 and pdt_4. For example, the composite component for pdt_3 is built from three atomic components created from $pdt_{3.1}$, $pdt_{3.2}$ and $pdt_{3.3}$. Creating a composite component in SaveCCM may also require switch components. That is, each time a system is designed, we have to start from the generic types of components and connections, embed into components only domain knowledge (possibly from a domain model) and compose these components to realise the system (connections are always generic). Types in SaveCCM are not domain specific, the gap between these types and components created from them is comparable to the gap between generic programming languages and domain-specific languages [26]. Our approach delivers a set of domain-specific connectors and atomic components that comprise a repository exclusive to that domain. It is very unlikely that CC_3 can be reused in systems outside VSD. Furthermore, we have not found any literature indicating that SaveCCM components can be stored into a repository and reused.

Moreover, data access $pdt_{3.1}$ are atomic components in SaveCCM, which makes the number of sub-components in a composite large.

Having built components from dt_3 and dt_4, they can be used with pdt_1 and $pdt_3 2$ together with a switch component to construct CCS. Fig. 16(b) depicts one design for CCS using SaveCCM. The "Mode" component is required to select between performing "Measure Mile" functionality for calibrating the system and "Cruise" functionality. The composite component is constructed in two steps: (i) sub-components are connected by linking their ports to create a composite which is (ii) encapsulated by a layer (shaded circumference) specifying which of its internal ports are to be imported or exported (e.g. Throttle and Mode ports). Accordingly, the designer decides which component ports to connect and which unconnected ports to export/import. However, these two steps may not result in a component, but in an assembly. In our model, connectors are compositional and using them with atomic components always creates components. For example, P is a pipe whose control behaviour is to invoke methods in components (from left to right) passing data output by a former component's method as argument for the next component's method, and so on. The same applies to domain-specific connectors such as CC_3 which is compositional, as defined by its specification in Fig. 14 and has a pre-defined control behaviour (specified in Table 1).

Executing CCS sequentially in SaveCCM requires a Clock component to trigger the system at a fixed time period. The order of executing the CCS is not clear from the design in Fig. 16(b). Actually, to execute CCS, the clock must trigger sub-components in an order that needs to be defined. In contrast, in our model, the execution behaviour is explicit and there is always one unique point through which the system can be started: the top-level connector of the component/system (e.g. P in our design).

In Fig. 16(a), it is possible to replace the CC_3 sub-tree with another whose top-level connector is CC_{3-5} leaving other parts of the architecture untouched. This swap generates the adaptive cruise control system. This shows that our domain-specific model supports variability in terms of (variant) connectors and parametrised atomic components, which is not an intrinsic property of SaveCCM, or similar ADLs intended for specific domains.

6   Discussion

We have endeavoured to show that given a generic component model and a domain model, a new component model conforming to the semantics of the generic model can be derived from the domain model. That is, atomic components in derived models are still defined according to the rules of the generic model, and components are composed according to the composition scheme of the generic model. The resulting model is a domain-specific component model, which is main contribution of this work.

We believe that domain-specific component models are the best kind of models to use for developing applications in a given domain. This view is echoed by [18] for ADLs, and by [5,9] for embedded systems. Of course the more established field of domain engineering, including product-lines engineering [4] and generative programming [6], has always emphasised the use of domain-specific knowledge in terms of product families, and our idea of domain-specific component model is in our view a logical extension of this field. Our contribution here is to add domain-specific component models to their armoury.

We go even further in the sense that we believe a domain-specific component model should be derived from the domain model. In this regard we are unique, as far as we know. As already mentioned, existing component models intended for specific domains are not domain-specific, according to our criteria. The main examples of these models are Koala [22], PECOS [20] and SaveCCM [1]. Although Koala is intended for the domain of consumer electronics, it does not explicitly define this domain; nor is it derived from a domain model. PECOS is intended for modelling applications in the domain of field devices. The model (component) types are generic and are derived from the control loops architectural style [25], but the domain model is not defined, and consequently any application having this architectural style could be regarded as a PECOS device. SaveCCM shares with Koala the architectural style of pipes-and-filters [25] and a Switch type. Like Koala, therefore SaveCCM is also not domain-specific.

More interesting, SaveCCM is intended for the same domain (vehicular systems) as the model we have derived in Section 5. Therefore, it provides us with a model to evaluate the feasibility of our approach. The core semantics of SaveCCM defines atomic and composite component types and conditional connections, which are all generic. Like PECOS and Koala, SaveCCM does not define the domain either. Comparing our model derived in Section 5 with SaveCCM, we see that connectors and component are specific to VSD. Whereas SaveCCM components are generic types to be used in creating domain-specific components in the design phase. Our model has more domain-specific composition connector types such as CC_3, CC_{3-5}, etc. All these connectors are unlikely to be reusable in other domains. Clearly, our approach delivers component models that reflect strong domain-specificity in terms of its types.

Unlike Koala, PECOS and SaveCCM, our approach also yields component models that support variability in the domain that is based on product families [23], a characteristic necessary for applying product-lines engineering. We claim that support of product-line engineering is an intrinsic property of domain-specific component models derived according to our approach.

7 Conclusion

Our contribution in this paper is an approach for deriving component models from the domain model. In particular, we have showed that a component model for a specialised domain can be derived from the functional model and the feature model. The resulting component model is domain-specific, not only by virtue of its types (connectors and components), but also by the fact that product families propagated into the model types via the domain. A property that these models shares with domain-specific software development approaches. We have observed that the derived models naturally support approaches such generative programming and product-line engineering.

By way of contrast, in generic ADLs for specific domains, architectural units may incorporate data transformations in general, but not specifically primary data transformations. They may also incorporate control transformations, in contrast to our approach where such transformations are in connectors, which are highly likely to be composite connectors.

References

1. Åkerholm, M., Carlson, J., Håkansson, J., Hansson, H., Nolin, M., Nolte, T., Pettersson, P.: The saveccm language reference manual. Technical Report ISSN 1404-3041 ISRN MDH-MRTC-207/2007-1-SE, Mälardalen University (January 2007)
2. Bacon, J.: Concurrent Systems: An integrated approach to Operating Systems, Distributed Systems and Databases (Open University Edition), 3rd edn. International Computer Science Series. Addison-Wesley, Reading (2003)
3. Batory, D., O'Malley, S.: The design and implementation of hierarchical software systems with reusable components. ACM Trans. Softw. Eng. Methodol. 1(4), 355–398 (1992)
4. Clements, P., Northrop, L.: Software product lines: practices and patterns. Addison-Wesley, Boston (2002)
5. Crnkovic, I.: Component-based approach for embedded systems. In: Proceedings of 9th International Workshop on Component-Oriented Programming, Oslo (2004)
6. Czarnecki, K., Eisenecker, U.W.: Generative programming: methods, tools, and applications. Addison Wesley, London (2000)
7. DeMichiel, L.G. (ed.): Enterprise JavaBeans Specification, Version 2.1. Sun Microsystems, Inc., 4150 Network Circle, Santa Clara, California 95054, U.S.A, November 12 (2003)
8. Gomaa, H.: Software Design Methods for Concurrent and Real-Time Systems. Addison-Wesley Longman Publishing Co., Inc., Boston (1993)
9. Hansson, H., Akerholm, M., Crnkovic, I., Torngren, M.: Saveccm - a component model for safety-critical real-time systems. In: EUROMICRO 2004: Proceedings of the 30th EUROMICRO Conference, USA, pp. 627–635. IEEE Computer Society, Los Alamitos (2004)
10. Hatley, D.J., Pirbhai, I.A.: Strategies for real-time system specification. Dorset House Publishing Co., Inc., New York (1987)
11. Heineman, G.T., Councill, W.T. (eds.): Component-based software engineering: putting the pieces together. Addison-Wesley, London (2001)
12. Kang, K., Cohen, S., Hess, J., Novak, W., Peterson: Feature-oriented domain analysis (FODA) feasibility study. Technical Report CMU/SEI-90-TR-021, Software Engineering Institute, Carnegie-Mellon University (November 1990)
13. Lau, K.-K., Ling, L., Velasco Elizondo, P., Ukis, V.: Composite connectors for composing software components. In: Lumpe, M., Vanderperren, W. (eds.) SC 2007. LNCS, vol. 4829, pp. 266–280. Springer, Heidelberg (2007)
14. Lau, K.-K., Ornaghi, M., Wang, Z.: A software component model and its preliminary formalisation. In: de Boer, F.S., Bonsangue, M.M., Graf, S., de Roever, W.-P. (eds.) FMCO 2005. LNCS, vol. 4111, pp. 1–21. Springer, Heidelberg (2006)
15. Lau, K.-K., Taweel, F.M.: Data encapsulation in software components. In: Schmidt, H.W., Crnković, I., Heineman, G.T., Stafford, J.A. (eds.) CBSE 2007. LNCS, vol. 4608, pp. 1–16. Springer, Heidelberg (2007)
16. Lau, K.-K., Velasco, P.I., Wang, Z.: Exogenous connectors for components. In: Heineman, G.T., Crnković, I., Schmidt, H.W., Stafford, J.A., Szyperski, C., Wallnau, K. (eds.) CBSE 2005. LNCS, vol. 3489, pp. 90–106. Springer, Heidelberg (2005)
17. Lau, K.-K., Wang, Z.: Software component models. IEEE Trans. on Software Engineering 33(10), 709–724 (2007)
18. Medvidovic, N., Dashofy, E.M., Taylor, R.N.: Moving architectural description from under the technology lamppost. Information and Software Technology 49(1), 12–31 (2007)
19. Mehta, N.R., Medvidovic, N., Phadke, S.: Towards a taxonomy of software connectors. In: ICSE 2000: Proceedings of the 22nd ICSE, pp. 178–187. ACM, New York (2000)
20. Nierstrasz, G.A.O., Ducasse, S., Wuyts, R., Black, P.M.A., Zeidler, C., Genssler, T., van den Born, R.: A component model for field devices. In: Bishop, J.M. (ed.) CD 2002. LNCS, vol. 2370, p. 200. Springer, Heidelberg (2002)

21. Ommering, R.C.: Building product populations with software components. Phd. thesis, Proefschrift Rijksuniversiteit Groningen, Met lit. opg. - Met samenvatting in het Nederlands (2004)
22. Ommering, R.C., Linden, F., Kramer, J., Magee, J.: The koala component model for consumer electronics software. IEEE Computer 33(3), 78–85 (2000)
23. Parnas, D.: On the design and development of program families. IEEE Transactions on Software Engineering SE-2(1), 1–9 (1976)
24. Preis, V., Henftling, R., Schutz, M., Marz-Rossel, S.: A reuse scenario for the vhdl-based hardware design flow. In: Proceedings EURO-DAC 1995, September 1995, pp. 464–469 (1995)
25. Shaw, M., Garlan, D.: Software Architecture: Perspectives on an Emerging Discipline. Prentice-Hall, Englewood Cliffs (1996)
26. van Deursen, A., Klint, P., Visser, J.: Domain-specific languages: An annotated bibliography. SIGPLAN Notices 35(6), 26–36 (2000)

A Model-Driven Engineering Framework for Component Models Interoperability*

Ivica Crnković[1], Ivano Malavolta[2], and Henry Muccini[2]

[1] Mälardalen University, Mälardalen Real-Time Research Center
[2] University of L'Aquila, Dipartimento di Informatica
ivica.crnkovic@mdh.se, ivano.malavolta@univaq.it,
muccini@univaq.it

Abstract. A multitude of component models exist today, characterized by slightly different conceptual architectural elements, focusing on a specific operational domain, covering different phases of component life-cycle, or supporting analysis of different quality attributes. When dealing with different variants of products and in evolution of systems, there is a need for transformation of system models from one component model to another one. However, it is not obvious that different component models can accurately exchange models, due to their differences in concepts and semantics. This paper demonstrate an approach to achieve that. The paper proposes a generic framework to interchange models among component models. The framework, named **DUALL**y allows for tool and notations interpretability easing the transformation among many different component models. It is automated inside the Eclipse framework, and fully-extensible. The **DUALL**y approach is applied to two different component models for real-time embedded systems and observations are reported.

1   Introduction

A multitude of component models exist today [1]. While they share the same objectives and some common foundational concepts, they all have some specific characteristics that make them different in many ways. For example, the Progress component model (ProCom) [2] supports the engineering process of embedded systems including quality aspects such as response and execution time, while the Palladio Component Model (PalladioCM) [3] contains annotations for predicting software performance. As a result, a proliferation of component models can be noticed today, each characterized by slightly different conceptual architectural elements, different syntax or semantics, focusing on a specific operational domain, or only suitable for specific analysis techniques.

While having domain- or analysis-specific component models allows component-based engineers to focus on specific needs, interchange [1] among component models becomes limited. Many factors, instead, demonstrate the need of interchange. European

---

* This work has been partly supported by the national FIRB Project ART DECO (Adaptive InfRasTructures for DECentralized Organizations), the Swedish Foundation for Strategic Research via the strategic research centre PROGRESS, and EU FP7 Q-ImPrESS project.
[1] Terminology: to be able to transform application models specified in a modelling language (i.e. a component model) to another modelling language (i.e. another component model) we need to enable interchange between these component models, i.e. interoperability between them.

projects like Q-Impress[2] or PROGRESS[3] aim to predict performance, reliability, and other quality attributes by integrating analysis features available in existing component models (Klaper, SOFA, PalladioCM, and ProCom in Q-Impress, SaveCCM and Pro-Com in PROGRESS). Artifacts interchange is required to propagate results and feed-backs from one notation/tool to another. Different component models cover different phases of component life-cycle. An example of such case is the use of SaveCCM and JavaBeans component models; SaveCCM supports modelling of time-related proper-ties, but has different implementations; one of them is achieved by transformation of an application model specified in SaveCCM to JavaBeans, which then are implemented in Java running on a Java platform [4]. Another example of need for interchange is a migration from one component model to another due to technology change. An exam-ple, later discussed, is a transformation from SaveCCM to a new generation, ProCom. Interoperability between SaveCCM and Procom models enables reuse of both design models (and their associated modeling tools) and of different quality attributes.

This work focusses on how to tackle interoperability from a model-driven engineer-ing (MDE) perspective. Specifically, considering component models as meta-models (thus without focusing on components' implementation) allows us to apply model trans-formation techniques to translate one model (conforming to a component model) to something equivalent conforming to a different component model.

Purpose of this work is to show how **DUALLY** [5], a framework for multipoint-to-multipoint transformations initially devised for allowing interoperability among ar-chitecture description languages, can be utilized in the context of component models. **DUALLY** transforms a source model into its target by passing through a pivot meta-model (named A_0 in Figure 1) enabling a star architecture of transformations. Order of n transformations (between the reference model and the pivot) are thus sufficient for transforming n notations, compared to the order of n^2 transformations required in traditional point-to-point ad hoc model transformations. While **DUALLY** scales better than traditional point-to-point approaches, the accuracy of transformations is in general lowered by passing through the pivot meta-model. In order to investigate the degree of accuracy we can achieve when transforming a component model into a different one, and to analyze cons' and pros' in using **DUALLY** compared to specialized point-to-point model transformations, we have applied the **DUALLY** approach to automatically build up transformations between two component models (namely, SaveCCM and Pro-Com, introduced in Section 2) and executed them on specific models.

In the following of this paper, after having provided an overview on **DUALLY**, we focus on the specific component models that exemplify evolution of component mod-els, and we show how **DUALLY** can facilitate their interchange. For this purpose, a demonstration of the approach is illustrated in Section 3: it will show how **DUALLY** semi-automatically provides the means to exchange models between SaveCCM and ProCom and how it may scale to other component models (thanks to its extensibil-ity mechanisms). Considerations are provided in Section 4, while Section 5 discusses related work. Section 6 concludes the paper with final remarks and suggestions for future work.

---

[2] http://www.q-impress.eu/Q-ImPrESS/CMS/index_html
[3] http://www.mrtc.mdh.se/progress/

2   Technologies Overview

This section introduces **DUALLY**, the generic framework for notations interoperability (Section 2.1), then focusses on two component models for Embedded Real-time systems: the SaveComp Component Model (Section 2.2) and ProCom (Section 2.3).

2.1   The DUALLY Framework

DUALLY provides a mechanism to automatically generate transformations allowing to pass from a notation to another and vice-versa. The configuration of the **DUALLY** framework is depicted in Figure 1.

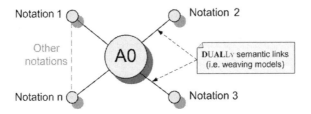

Fig. 1. Notations topology in **DUALLY**

Conceptually, **DUALLY** is a multipoint-to-multipoint transformation framework that permits transformation of elements of a model M1 into semantically equivalent elements in the model M2 (as shown in Figure 2). Each Mi conforms to its MMi that is a meta-model or a UML profile. The semantic mappings (and its corresponding generated transformation) relates MM1 to MM2 (as well as M1 to M2) passing through what we refer to as A_0.

The main purpose of A_0 is to provide a centralized set of semantic elements with respect to which relations must be defined. As clearly shown in Figure 1, for the realization of **DUALLY** we chose a "star" architecture: A_0 is placed in the center of the star, while the transformation engine is in charge of maintaining the transformation

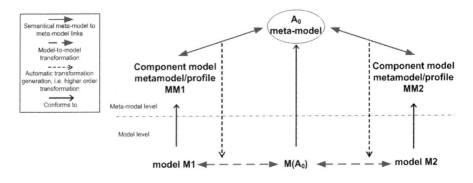

Fig. 2. **DUALLY** Conceptual overview

network. Whenever a model M1 has to be transformed into M2, a two-step process is realized that transforms M1 into $M(A_0)$, and successively $M(A_0)$ to M2. Thanks to the depicted star architecture a linear relationship between the selected language and A_0 is created, thus reducing the number of connections needed. While the star architecture clearly reduces the number of transformations needed, what may happen is that two notations, say M_i and M_j, share some domain specific concepts that are not contemplated in A_0. In general cases, this would strongly reduce the transformation accuracy, since those common concepts could not be transformed (since missing in A_0). However, since **DUALLY**'s A_0 can be extended, accuracy can be improved by including domain specific concepts (an extension to A_0 will be shown in Section 3). A_0 is implemented as a MOF compliant meta-model whose main elements are:

- **SoftwareArchitecture:** A collection of components and connectors instantiated in a configuration. It may contain also a set of architectural types, a Behavior and SAinterfaces representing points of interaction between the external environment and the architecture being modeled.
- **SAcomponent:** A (hierarchically structured) unit of computation with internal state and well-defined interface. It can contain a behavioral model and interacts with other architectural elements either directly or through SAinterfaces.
- **SAconnector:** Represents a software connector containing communication and coordination facilities. It may be considered as a special kind of SAcomponents.
- **SAinterface:** Specifies the interaction point between an SAcomponent or an SAconnector and its environment. It is semantically close to the concept of UML port and can have either input, output or input/output direction.
- **SArelationship:** Its purpose is that of delineating general relations between A_0 architectural elements; it can be either bidirectional or unidirectional.
- **SAchannel:** A specialization of an SArelationship representing a generic communication mean; it supports both unidirectional and bi-directional communication, and both information and control can be exchanged.
- **SAbinding:** Relates an SAinterface of a component to an SAinterface of one of its inner components; it is semantically close to the concept of UML Delegation Connector.
- **SAtype, SAstructuredType:** They define architectural types, so any architectural element can potentially be an instance of a particular SAtype. Each SAtype can contain a set of properties and the behavior of its instances, its internal structure is specified in case it is also a SAstructuredType.
- **Behavior:** Represents the behavior an architectural element. It is an abstract meta-class that plays the role of a "stub" for possible extensions of the meta-model representing dynamic aspects of the system.
- **Development:** Represents the direct relation between the architectural and the technological aspects, such as the process that will be used to develop the system, or the programming languages used to develop a certain component. Development is an abstract meta-class and its realization is left to future extensions of the A_0 meta-model.
- **Business:** An abstract meta-class to be specialized via future extensions of A_0 and represents the link to business contexts within which software systems and development organizations exist.

 - **Group:** A logical grouping of any element of A_0, it can contain architectural elements, properties, other groups and so on.

The A_0 meta-model contains other minor concepts like properties, abstract typed elements, generic components; we do not describe them in this work because of their basic nature and for the sake of brevity. For more details about A_0 we kindly refer the reader to [5].

Figure 2 shows that **DUALL**Y operates at two levels of abstraction: meta-modeling and modeling. At the meta-modeling level, MDE experts provide the concepts of each notation through either a meta-model or a UML profile. Then, a set of semantic links between $MM1$ (or $MM2$) and the corresponding elements in A_0 are defined. Such links are contained in a weaving model [6], a particular kind of model containing links between either meta-models or models.

Each weaving model (WM, in Figure 3) conforms to a specific weaving meta-model WMM provided by **DUALL**Y [5]. It's main elements are: correspondences (Left2Right, Right2Left and Equivalence) to relate two or more concepts, feature equivalences to relate attributes or references, bindings to a constant defined by the user, links to a woven element, and the various auxiliary elements referring the meta-classes to relate. **DUALL**Y provides a graphical editor for weaving models identification and a mechanism to automatically generate model-to-model transformations that reflect the logic of the semantic links.

Figure 3 highlights also that model-to-model transformations are generated through the execution of higher-order transformations (HOTs): *Left2Right* and *Right2Left*, depending on the direction of the transformation to be generated at the modeling level (i.e. *MM1_2_A0* or *A0_2_MM1*). The input of a HOT is composed of three models: (i) the weaving model WM, (ii) the left meta-model and (iii) the right meta-model (MM1 and A_0 in Figure 3, respectively). The output is a model transformation generated on

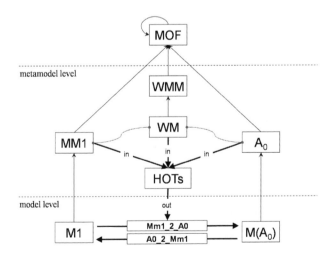

Fig. 3. Higher-order transformations in **DUALL**Y

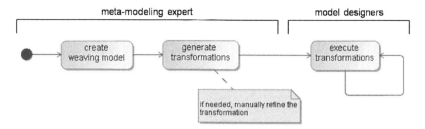

Fig. 4. DUALLY-zation process for each meta-model

the basis of the mappings defined into the weaving model. At a high level of abstraction, the current version of **DUALLY** translates each correspondence into an specific transformation rule and each feature equivalence into a binding between the involved attributes or references. The higher-order transformations are meta-model and A_0 independent; this gives the possibility to reuse **DUALLY** with different pivot meta-models, i.e. to reuse its approach in different domains.

At the modeling level, system designers create the model $M1$ and execute the previously generated transformations $t1$ and $t2$. This produces first the intermediate model $M(A_0)$ and then the final model $M2$ in the target notation.

Figure 4 shows the basic steps to **DUALLY**-ze a notation, i.e. to include it in the star topology implied by **DUALLY**. **DUALLY** provides a clear separation between its main users:

- meta-modeling experts play the role of technical stakeholders, they have to know the language to relate and semantically link it to A_0; they can also refine the generated transformations if there is the need for more advanced constructs within them;
- component-based systems designers play the role of final users, they deal with models only and apply the transformations automatically generated by **DUALLY**.

The preliminary steps of determining the pivot meta-model, or in case the extension of A_0, are not part of this process because they are not performed for each **DUALLY**-zation, but rather once for each specific domain the framework is being used in.

DUALLY is implemented as an Eclipse plugin in the context of the ATLAS Model Management Architecture (AMMA) [6]. Weaving models are expressed through the ATLAS model weaver (AMW) [7] and transformations in the Atlas Transformation Language (ATL [8]). Both models and meta-models are expressed via the XML Metadata Interchange (XMI), the interchange standard proposed by the OMG consortium.

2.2 SaveCCM

The SaveComp Component Model (SaveCCM) aims for design of software for embedded systems with constraints on the system resources such as memory and CPU, and requirements of time characteristics such as execution or response time. The graphical notation of the SaveCCM component model is presented in Figure 5.

SaveCCM contains three architectural elements: components, switches and assemblies. The interface of these elements consists of input- and output ports. The model is

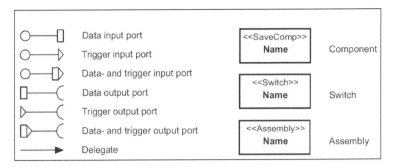

Fig. 5. The graphical notation of SaveCCM

based on the control flow (pipes-and-filters) paradigm, and on the distinction between data transfer and control flow. The former is captured by connections between *data ports* where data of a given type can be written and read, and the latter by *trigger ports* that control the activation of components. A port can also comprise both triggering and data functionality. The explicit notation of control flow makes the design analyzable with respect to temporal behaviour allowing analysis of schedulability, response time, etc., factors which are crucial to the correctness of real-time systems.

Components are the main architectural element in SaveCCM. In addition to an interface a component contains a series of quality attributes (e.g. worst case execution time, reliability estimates), each associated with a value and possibly a confidence measure. Quality attributes are used for analysis, model extraction and for synthesis. Components have a strict"read-execute-write" semantics that ensures once a component is triggered, the execution is functionally independent of any concurrent activity. This facilitates analysis since component execution can be abstracted by a single transfer function from input values and internal state to output values. The switch construct provides the means to change the components interconnection structure, either statically or dynamically. switches specify a number of guarded connection patterns, i.e., partial mappings from input to output ports. To enable increased reusability and design efficiency SaveCCM also defines assemblies. An assembly can be considered as a means for naming a collection of components and hiding its internal structure.

SaveCCM enables time and resource analysis using techniques are the basis in the context of real-time systems and the current version of the SaveCCM development Environment includes two analyzers: LTSA (Labelled Transition System Analyzer) [9] and Times Tool [10].

2.3 ProCom

ProCom [2] is the component model designed as a "new generation of SaveCCM" with extended functionality and somewhat different philosophy. While SaveCCM is designed for small embedded systems, ProCom is aimed for design and modelling of distributed embedded systems of larger complexity. ProCom enables distinguishing of two layers called ProSys and ProSave. The former deals with elements of coarse granularity, like subsystems and channels; the latter contains concepts to internally describe a

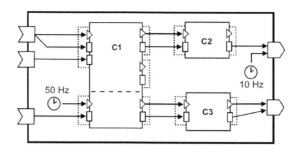

Fig. 6. A subsystem internally modelled by ProSave

ProSys system as a collection of concurrent components. A ProSys subsystem is specified by its input/output message ports, and its external view can optionally include attributes and auxiliary models. A subsystem is always active since it may perform activities periodically or in response to internal events. Subsystems are not directly connected, but rather they communicate through message-channels, which are specific elements for sharing information between senders and receivers of each message.

ProSave concerns the internal design of subsystems through its contained elements. Components in ProSave differ from ProSys subsystems since they are passive and the communication is based on the pipes-and-filters paradigm as in SaveCCM. Similar to SaveCCM, this component model explicitly separates data and control flow that are captured by data and trigger ports respectively. A new feature, compared to SaveCCM, is that ports can be grouped into services. They are part of the component and allow external entities to make use of the component functionality at an higher level of abstraction. Services are triggered independently and can run concurrently. ProSave does not have switches like SaveCCM, but a rich set of predefined connectors that provide more elaborate constructs, such as data/control fork, join, data muxer and demuxer.

ProSave elements are used to decompose ProSys subsystems (as exemplified in Fig. 6).This is is done in a similar way to how composite ProSave components are defined internally (i.e., as a collection of interconnected components and connectors) but with some additional connector types to allow for (i) mapping between message passing (used in ProSys) and trigger/data communication (used in ProSave), and (ii) specifying periodic activation of ProSave components. This is provided by the *clock* connector that repeatedly triggers ProSave elements at a given rate.

3   Demonstration of the Approach

This section shows how we apply the **DUALL**y approach to SaveCCM and ProCom modeling languages. Since both notations have common concepts and **DUALL**y's A_0 covers many of them, A_0 is still suitable as the pivot meta-model. However, there are also concepts that are contemplated in both SaveCCM and ProCom but not in A_0. This is not a desirable situation, because such concepts will not be preserved during transformation due to A_0's lack of them. The extensible structure of A_0 allows to overcome this issue: we extended A_0 in order to capture such elements an avoid their loss while

Table 1. Elements extending the A_0 pivot meta-model

Added element	A_0 base element	Description
System	SAcomponent	Coarse-grained independent component with complex functionality.
DataSAinterface	SAinterface	Specific interface for data transfer to which typed data may be read or written.
ControlSAinterface	SAinterface	Specific interface for control flow handling the activation of components.
Clock	SAcomponent	Component triggering other elements of the system when its given period expires.

passing from either SaveCCM and ProCom to A_0. We discuss this choice and its possible pros and cons in Section 4. Table 1 presents such an extension.

The line of reasoning we followed to create such extension is purely pragmatic: if (i) there are two elements x and y in SaveCCM and ProCom respectively that represent the same semantic concept z, and (ii) there is not a corresponding element in A_0, then extend A_0 with z. During the creation of weaving models, both x and y will be linked to z so that the execution of the generated transformations will preserve z while passing through A_0. An example of a common semantic concept is the data-transfer interface represented by DataSAinterface in A_0 (second row in table 1), it corresponds to the concepts of SaveCCM and ProCom DataPort.

The remaining of this section is organized so as to reflect the two roles of **DUALLY**'s users. In Subsection 3.1 we act as meta-modeling experts: for each language we follow the steps of the activity diagram in Figure 4 until the generation of model-to-model transformations. In Subsection 3.2 we act as software architects, i.e. we provide an example model conforming to SaveCCM and we apply the transformations generated from the previous steps. This allows us to get first a model conforming to the A_0 meta-model and then the final model conforming to the ProCom meta-model. We evaluate and compare the various models obtained within each phase of the process.

3.1 Semantic Links Definition

The first step is to import the SaveCCM and ProCom meta-models into the **DUALLY** framework; in our case it is straightforward since such meta-models have been developed in the context of Eclipse. Next step is the creation of the weaving models. Since a weaving model defines the links between a notation and A_0, we need two weaving models: $SaveCCM\_A_0$, which contains the semantic links between SaveCCM and A_0 and $ProCom\_A_0$ that relates ProCom concepts to A_0 elements. Due to space restrictions, in this paper we describe each weaving model in an informal way, abstracting from the technical details and presenting only its basic semantics.

In $SaveCCM\_A_0$ a SaveCCM System is mapped into an A_0 System. If the source System element is the root of the model, an A_0 SoftwareArchitecture element is also created (it will contain all the A_0 target elements). SaveCCM Component and Connection are mapped to SAComponent and SAchannel, respectively.

`Assembly` and `Composite` components are both mapped to `SAcomponent` annotating the type of its corresponding source element in the *description* field. By doing this we will not lose which kind of element the `SAcomponent` was generated from during the translation to an A_0 model. A SaveCCM `Clock` corresponds to the `Clock` entity specified in the extension of A_0, the `Delay` element is mapped into a generic `SAcomponent`, `Switch` is mapped into an `SAConnector`. `DataPort` and `TriggerPort` correspond to `DataSainterface` and `ControlSAinterface` respectively, their *direction* attribute is set accordingly to the type of the SaveCCM ports (i.e. whether they are input or output ports) and vice-versa. We applied a specific mechanism to manage combined SaveCCM ports: a combined port is splitted to a `DataSainterface` and a `ControlSAinterface` with the same name and direction; doing this, the generated $SaveCCM2A_0$ transformation splits combined SaveCCM ports to two A_0 interfaces, while the $A_02SaveCCM$ transformation merges two A_0 interfaces with the same name and direction to a single combined SaveCCM port. Both generic and SaveCCM-specific attributes (e.g. "delay" and "precision" attributes in `Delay`) correspond to A_0 properties.

$ProCom\_A_0$ contains links between concepts of A_0 ProCom at both system (i.e. ProSys) and component (i.e. ProSave) levels. At the system level, `Subsystems` correspond to `SAtypes` and `SubsystemInstances` are related to A_0 `Systems`. ProSys `Connections` are mapped to `SAChannels`, while `MessagePorts` correspond to generic `SAPorts`. The `MessageChannel` entity is linked to `SAconnector`. At the component level, `CompositeComponent` and `PrimitiveComponent` are mapped to `SAtype`. The concept of `SubcomponentInstance` is linked to the concept of `SAcomponent`; `Sensor`, `ActiveSensor` and `Actuator` also relate to `SAcomponent` along with the corresponding real-time attributes, in this cases the type of the source ProCom entity is annotated in the *description* attribute of the generated `SAcomponent`. A_0 `Clocks` are mapped to ProCom `Clocks`, and the corresponding period attribute is set. Each kind of ProCom port is mapped into $SAPort$, while the corresponding `Services` and port groupings are not matched because both A_0 and SaveCCM do not have entities semantically close to them; such elements are lost during the translation to A_0 and can be restored when "going back" to ProCom thanks to **DUALL**y's lost-in-translation mechanism [5].Furthermore, $ProSave$ `Connections` are mapped into `SAchannels` and every kind of `Connector` (e.g. `DataFork`, `ControlJoin`) corresponds to an `SAConnector`; the specific type of the $ProSave$ `Connector` can be inferred by analysing its own ports and connections pattern, e.g. a connector with one input data port and n output data ports can be considered a `DataFork` connector, a connector with n input control ports and a single output control port is a `ControlJoin` connector, etc. A number of low-level correspondences have been abstracted to make the description of the weaving models as readable as possible and complete at the same time. Most of them are contained into the $ProCom\_A_0$ weaving model; for example there is a system of correspondences and conditions to correctly arrange $ProSave$ Components and their internal realization or the mechanism to infer the type of $ProSave$ Connectors sketched above.

The next step is the execution of the **DUALL**y HOTs in order to get the model-to-model transformations. We generate two transformations from each weaving model:

(i) $Save2A_0$ and A_02Save from the weaving model between SaveCCM and A_0; (ii) $ProCom2A_0$ and $A_02ProCom$ from the $ProCom\_A_0$ weaving model. The logic of the generated transformations reflects that of the links in the weaving models. Since obtained transformations suit well with the models that we use, at the moment there is no need to refine them, i.e. the generated transformations are ready to be used by software architects.

3.2   Model Transformations Execution

After the generation of model transformations, designers can use them to translate models into other notations. Generated transformations can be executed in any order, in this work we focus only on how to produce ProCom models from SaveCCM specifications; this process is composed of three main phases:

1. development of a model conforming to SaveCCM;
2. execution of the $Save2A_0$ transformation that produces an intermediate A_0 model;
3. execution the $A_02ProCom$ transformation in order to translate the A_0 model into a ProCom specification.

The initial SaveCCM model is a specification of an Adaptive Cruise Controller (ACC), an enhanced version of the traditional vehicular Cruise Control. It has the basic function to actuate brake or throttle controls in order to keep the speed of the vehicle constant; it is geared also with a set of sensors (mainly radars and cameras) that allow the controller to (i) check if there is another vehicle in the lane, allowing the driver to maintain a safe distance with the preceding vehicle and (ii) check the presence of speed road signs and adapt the actual speed according to them. Figure 7 presents a simplified version of the ACC system developed using Save-IDE [11], the SaveCCM dedicated modeling toolkit.

The ACC system contains two main components, $Sensors$ and $ACC\_application$. The former represents a group of sensors that periodically provides data about the distance towards the preceding vehicle, actual speed, status of the whole controller and the degree of pressure on the brake pedal by the driver. Such sensors have been grouped into a single component in order to leave the model as simple as possible. The core of the system is the latter component, it performs three main tasks: (i) analyze information provided by sensors and return which actions forward to the actuators; (ii) log the status of the system; (iii) provide data to the Human Machine Interface (HMI).

For the sake of simplicity, we do not show the internal structure of $ACC\_application$ and the external context of the whole system. The system is also composed of two clock components that periodically trigger the corresponding components. More specifically, $clk50hz$ triggers $Sensors$ to gain the available current data and $ACC\_application$ to set its status according to the newly available informations. The Splitter switch periodically receives a trigger generated by the clock at 50Hz and splits it triggering simultaneously the $Sensors$ and $ACC\_application$ components. $clk10hz$ triggers $ACC\_application$ to log the status of the systems and to provide data to the HMI; $clk10hz$ operates at a lower rate since it is not related to safety-critical activities.

Once the ACC model has been created, we give it as input to $SaveCCM2A_0$ (the transformation automatically generated by **DUALLY**). The produced model is composed of a main SoftwareArchitecture containing all the elements of the ACC

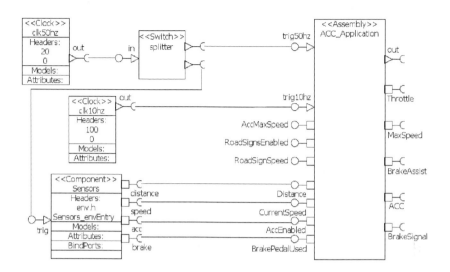

Fig. 7. ACC system designed using SaveCCM

system. Each SaveCCM component has been transformed into an SAcomponent, two clock entities have been created from the 10Hz and 50Hz SaveCCM clocks and their *period* attribute is represented as an A_0 Property. Data and Trigger ports have been translated into DataSAinterfaces and ControlSAinterface, respectively. All the $Save_CCM$ Connections have been translated into SAchannels, while the *Splitter* switch is transformed into an SAconnector with a single input ControlSAinterface and two output ControlSAinterfaces. Attributes specific to the SaveCCM language (e.g. the attribute specifying the implementation in C programming language of $ACC\_application$) are preserved in the A_0 model through generic properties; they will be looked up when passing to the ProCom specification.

At this point, we execute the $A_0 2 ProCom$ transformation on the A_0 model that we just obtained. The produced specification is a complete ProCom model containing both a *ProSys* and *ProSave* layer. The *ProSys* part of the model is made of only the ACC System containing its internal *ProSave* specification (depicted in Figure 8).

The obtained ProCom model, even though we passed through A_0, is similar to the initial SaveCCM specification, e.g. the topography of the two models remains the same. We mapped every A0channel to a *ProSave* Connection since the connected elements are only components (in case they were systems, *ProSys* Connections were generated); the two Clock components have been translated and their period attribute has been preserved. The thick dot shown in 8 represents a ControlFork connector that splits the control flow into two paths. The various data/control ports have been translated and their direction and type are also preserved; the only concern that we did not manage to map is grouping *ProSave* ports into services. Actually we expected it since there is no concept of service neither in SaveCCM nor in A_0. This is the typical case in which model designers have to manually arrange obtained models. A possible alternative solution to this issue is to generate services applying some heuristics, e.g.

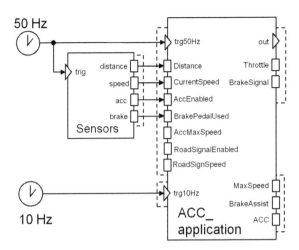

Fig. 8. The ACC specification obtained from the execution of $A_02ProCom$

analyze ports using a dictionary or an ontology so that ports whose names represent a common semantics may be grouped into a single service.

In conclusion, in this section we showed how **DUALL**y can be used to pass from a real-time notation (SaveCCM) to another (ProCom) applying a model-driven approach; designers need to specify only semantic links at the meta-modeling level and modellers execute automatically generated transformations to migrate models. The results of such executions strongly depend on the accuracy of the semantic links between meta-models; this and other issues are discussed and evaluated in the next section.

4   Evaluation and Considerations

Purpose of this paper has been to investigate the feasibility in utilizing **DUALL**y as a generic transformation framework in the context of component models and its advantages and limitations in comparison to manual and specialized model-to-model transformations. For this purpose and based on the experience reported in the previous section, we identified a set of generic dimensions to reason about which strategy best suites our needs: i) number of required transformations (NTrans) for achieving interchange among n notations, ii) number of additional transformations (AddTrans) required when a new notation is added, iii) accuracy (Acc) of the transformations results. Other (secondary) dimensions are also analyzed. Table 2 summarizes the main findings.

From the first row, we can see that the point-to-point strategy requires the development of order of n^2 transformations, while the pivot-based solution requires order of n transformations. Since many component models exist in real-time embedded systems, the traditional point-to-point strategy would require possibly too many transformations. Specifically, since our intent is to link several additional notations such as AADL, UML

Table 2. Comparison between point-to-point and DUALLY

	point-to-point transformations	DUALLY
NTrans	$n*(n-1)$	n
AddTrans	n	2
Acc	semantic loss	semantic loss + pivot inaccuracy
automation	manually coded transformation	automatically generated transformations
steps	one-step transformation	two-step transformation

models using the MARTE profile or Timed Automata, the pivot meta-model proposed in **DUALLY** seems to be more appropriate.

Moreover, the second row points out that adding a further notation to the interoperating network of notations requires n new transformations implemented from scratch in the point-to-point strategy. The pivot meta-model strategy in **DUALLY**, instead, requires only one new transformation between the added notation and A_0. More importantly, the full-mesh strategy requires a deep knowledge of the n existing notations, while the pivot-based solution requires knowledge on A_0 only.

As outlined in the third row, loss of information may happen in both the point-to-point and pivot-based strategies, since the expressiveness of the notations to relate can vary (i.e., if a notation is more expressive than the other, the extra expressiveness cannot be typically mapped). Apart from this, the pivot-based strategy is in principle less accurate than the point-to-point solution, since the (domain-specific but generic) intermediate model can increase the probability to loose concepts during the translation. Even a well designed pivot meta-model might be less accurate than a point-to-point transformation. Heterogeneity between notations to relate exacerbates this issue. In order to limit such an issue, **DUALLY** provides extensibility mechanisms as a way to minimize the loss of information. As shown in Section 3 we created an ad hoc extension including all those elements in SaveCCM and ProCom not contemplated in A_0. Specifically, we added the concepts of *system* (meant as coarse-grained component), *data/control interfaces* and *clock* components. This allowed us to not lose such elements while passing through A_0; this was an undesirable issue because elements would have been lost only because of the pivot meta-model and not for a real mismatch between SaveCCM and ProCom. For example, SaveCCM *data port* would have been mapped to A_0 *SAinterface*, but when passing to ProCom we did not know to which kind of ProCom port we had to translate it; so, extending A_0 allowed us to map SaveCCM *data ports* to ProCom *data ports* passing through A_0's `DataSAinterfaces` without losing their semantics. As illustrated in Section 3, this activity has not required a big effort, due to the similar expressive power and conceptual elements exposed by the two notations and the similarity between the concepts already in A_0 and those in component models. Indeed, when deciding to **DUALLY**ze notations in a completely different domain, extending A_0 might not be enough. We are currently evaluating how to deal with such a situation.

The fourth row points out that while traditional point-to-point transformations require ad hoc and manually coded transformations in some transformation language

Table 3. Efforts to relate SaveCCM and ProCom

	SaveCCM	ProCom
import meta-model	0	0
learn meta-model	4 (7,2%)	10 (18,1%)
create weaving model	9 (16,2%)	20 (36,2%)
refine transformation	0	0
develop models	2 (3,6%)	0
	15 (29,8%)	30 (56,1%)

(e.g., ATL [8] or QVT [12]), **DUALL**Y automatically generates the transformation code out of the weaving models.

In the fifth row, we put in evidence that **DUALL**Y uses a two-steps transformation, while a single-step is required in point-to-point strategies. The main issue about the two strategies is that of accuracy, i.e. passing through a pivot meta-model could lower down the quality of the models produced by the transformations; we managed to overcome this problem extending A_0 so that no common element is lost because of A_0's expressivity. So, in this specific case, extending A_0 and applying the **DUALL**Y approach leads to the same degree of accuracy as if a point-to-point strategy is applied. In addition, applying the pivot-based strategy gives us also other benefits in the context of future work; for example it is possible to reuse the **DUALL**Y-zations of both SaveCCM and ProCom while relating other notations to A_0, or quantifying how many elements SaveCCM and ProCom have in common with respect to other **DUALL**Y-zed notations.

Table 3 quantify the efforts needed to **DUALL**Y-ze SaveCCM and ProCom. Each notation has a dedicated column, while the rows describe specific activities performed during our experience. The value of a cell is both represented in terms of person-hour, (i.e. the amount of work carried on by an average worker) and in percentage with respect to the whole process. All the percentage values do not sum to one hundred since we leaved out around eight person-hours to define which topology adopt to relate the notations and to specify which elements form the extension of the A_0 meta-model.

Since each meta-model is already in the XMI format, the effort related to the import phase can be considered equal to zero. The second row represents the time to "learn" each notation, that is how much it took to understand its constructs and manage its models. Table 3 highlights that creating weaving models is the activity that requires much effort, since the resulting weaving model must be very accurate and the generation of well-formed transformations directly depends on it. This specific experiment did not require to manually refine the generated transformations.

The *develop models* row specifies how much time it took to create a model in each notation. The *ProCom* column value is equal to zero because the ProCom model has been automatically derived by executing the $A_02ProCom$ transformation. The efforts associated to the meta-modeling expert represent almost the 80% of the whole process but are performed only once for each notation. Further, **DUALL**Y hides most of the complexity to the final users, since they deal with models development and transformations execution only.

5   Related Work

Related work mainly regards model-based tool integration, automatic derivation of model transformations and semantic integration. The authors of [13] present Model-CVS, a framework similar to **DUALL**Y in which meta-models are lifted to ontologies and semantic links are defined between such ontologies, they will serve as a basis for the generation of model transformations; this approach manages also concurrent modeling through a CVS versioning tool. **DUALL**Y is somewhat different because it implies the A_0-centered star topology (it scales more when dealing with multiple notations) and the preliminary step of meta-model lifting is not performed.

The role of **DUALL**Y's A_0 is similar to the Klaper language in the field of performability. Grassi et al. in [14] propose the Klaper modeling language as a pivot meta-model within a star topology; however the Klaper-based methodology is different from **DUALL**Y's approach since model transformations are not "horizontal" (Klaper is designed as a mean between design-level and analysis-oriented notations). Moreover model transformations are not derived from semantic bindings, they must be manually developed.

In the field of software architectures, the ACME initiative [15] is famed for being one of the very first technologies to tackle the interoperability problem. It benefits from both a good tooling set and a good level of expressivity, but it is neither MOF compliant nor automatized; further on, a programming effort (rather than graphically designed semantic links) is needed every time a notation must be related to the ACME language.

Finally, the Eclipse project named Model Driven Development integration (MDDi[4]) presents an interesting approach based on the concepts of model bus and semantic bindings, but it is still in a draft proposal state.

6   Conclusion and Future Work

In model-driven engineering transformations of models are crucial activities in the development process. In component-based development, along with increasing support for specification, analysis and verification of quality attributes, and evolution of the component-based systems, transformation models between different component models becomes increasingly important. We have analyzed possibilities of increasing interchange between component models by applying a principle multipoint-to-multipoint transformation engine and using a pivot-metamodel, both implemented in **DUALL**Y. Although **DUALL**Y was originally designed for transformation of different architecture description languages, we have demonstrated feasibility of this approach. The component models SaveCCM and ProCom, used in our investigations, are examples of evolution of component models; for this reason they have many similar elements, but also elements that are quite different. We have shown that it is possible to find a common core, in spite of these differences. Actually we have demonstrated that the pivot-metamodel expressed in A_0 is sufficient. The interoperability between component models and A_0, depends of course on similarities of the component models. We have addressed the structural part of the architectural interoperability, which does not cover the

---

[4] http://www.eclipse.org/proposals/eclipse-mddi/

complete interoperability; for example we have not addressed behavioral models, and models of quality attributes. Our future work is focused on (i) adding new component models , and (ii) adding behavioral models. Architectural interoperability is however the most important since it is used as a common reference point for other models both functional and non-functional. Further it is the only part that is included in most of the component models.

So far in the Component-Based Development approach, interoperability between component-based applications have been addressed in research in order to increase reusability of existing components or component-based systems. We have investigated interoperability between models which increases reusability of models, this is crucial for analysis and verification of components and component-based systems.

References

1. Crnkovic, I., Larsson, M. (eds.): Building Reliable Component-based Software Systems. Artech House (2002)
2. Sentilles, S., Vulgarakis, A., Bures, T., Carlson, J., Crnkovic, I.: A component model for control-intensive distributed embedded systems. In: Chaudron, M.R.V., Szyperski, C., Reussner, R. (eds.) CBSE 2008. LNCS, vol. 5282, pp. 310–317. Springer, Heidelberg (2008)
3. Becker, S., Koziolek, H., Reussner, R.: The Palladio component model for model-driven performance prediction. Journal of Systems and Software 82, 3–22 (2009)
4. Feljan, J., Carlson, J., Zagar, M.: Realizing a domain specific component model with javabeans. In: 8th Conference on Software Engineering Research and Practice in Sweden (SERPS 2008) (2008)
5. Malavolta, I., Muccini, H., Pelliccione, P., Tamburri, D.A.: Providing architectural languages and tools interoperability through model transformation technologies. IEEE Transactions on Software Engineering (to appear, 2009)
6. Bézivin, J., Jouault, F., Rosenthal, P., Valduriez, P.: Modeling in the large and modeling in the small. In: Aßmann, U., Aksit, M., Rensink, A. (eds.) MDAFA 2003. LNCS, vol. 3599, pp. 33–46. Springer, Heidelberg (2005)
7. Didonet Del Fabro, M., Bézivin, J., Jouault, F., Breton, E., Gueltas, G.: AMW: a generic model weaver. In: Proc. of 1ére Journée sur l'Ing. Dírigée par les Modéles, Paris, France, pp. 105–114 (2005)
8. Jouault, F., Kurtev, I.: Transforming Models with ATL. In: Bruel, J.-M. (ed.) MoDELS 2005. LNCS, vol. 3844, pp. 128–138. Springer, Heidelberg (2006)
9. Magee, J., Kramer, J., Giannakopoulou, D.: Behaviour Analysis of Software Architectures. In: First Working IFIP Conference on Software Architecture, WICSA1 (1999)
10. Amnell, T., Fersman, E., Mokrushin, L., Pettersson, P., Yi, W.: Times: a tool for schedulability analysis and code generation of real-time systems. In: Larsen, K.G., Niebert, P. (eds.) FORMATS 2003. LNCS, vol. 2791, pp. 60–72. Springer, Heidelberg (2004)
11. Sentilles, S., Håkansson, J., Pettersson, P., Crnkovic, I.: Save-ide an integrated development environment for building predictable component-based embedded systems. In: Proc. of the 23rd IEEE/ACM Int. Conf. on Automated Software Engineering (2008)
12. OMG: MOF QVT Final Adopted Specification. Object Modeling Group (2005)
13. Kappel, G., Kapsammer, E., Kargl, H., Kramler, G., Reiter, T., Retschitzegger, W., Schwinger, W., Wimmer, M.: Lifting metamodels to ontologies - a step to the semantic integration of modeling languages. In: Nierstrasz, O., Whittle, J., Harel, D., Reggio, G. (eds.) MoDELS 2006. LNCS, vol. 4199, pp. 528–542. Springer, Heidelberg (2006)

14. Grassi, V., Mirandola, R., Randazzo, E., Sabetta, A.: KLAPER: An Intermediate Language for Model-Driven Predictive Analysis of Performance and Reliability. In: Rausch, A., Reussner, R., Mirandola, R., Plášil, F. (eds.) The Common Component Modeling Example. LNCS, vol. 5153, pp. 327–356. Springer, Heidelberg (2008)
15. Garlan, D., Monroe, R.T., Wile, D.: Acme: Architectural description of component-based systems. In: Leavens, G.T., Sitaraman, M. (eds.) Foundations of Component-Based Systems, pp. 47–68. Cambridge University Press, Cambridge (2000)

Process Patterns for Component-Based Software Development

Ehsan Kouroshfar, Hamed Yaghoubi Shahir, and Raman Ramsin

Department of Computer Engineering
Sharif University of Technology
kouroshfar@ce.sharif.edu, yaghoubi@ieee.org, ramsin@sharif.edu

Abstract. Component-Based Development (CBD) has been broadly used in software development, as it enhances reusability and flexibility, and reduces the costs and risks involved in systems development. It has therefore spawned many widely-used approaches, such as Commercial Off-The-Shelf (COTS) and software product lines. On the other hand, in order to gain a competitive edge, organizations need to define custom processes tailored to fit their specific development requirements. This has led to the emergence of process patterns and Method Engineering approaches.

We propose a set of process patterns commonly encountered in component-based development methodologies. Seven prominent component-based methodologies have been selected and reviewed, and a set of high-level process patterns recurring in these methodologies have been identified. A generic process framework for component-based development has been proposed based on these process patterns. The process patterns and the generic framework can be used for developing or tailoring a process for producing component-based systems.

Keywords: Component-Based Development, Software Development Methodologies, Situational Method Engineering, Process Patterns.

1 Introduction

Although *Component-Based Development* (CBD) is not a novel approach, it is still extensively used for building various types of software systems, and is expected to remain popular for the foreseeable future. There exist several software development methodologies that support the construction of component-based systems, and the domain has matured over the years. When viewed collectively, CBD methodologies have indeed addressed all the relevant issues; however, none of the methodologies covers all the aspects of component-based software development. A general methodology can resolve this through addressing the deficiencies while being customizable according to the specifics of the project situation at hand. An alternative approach to tackling this problem is *Assembly-Based Situational Method Engineering* (SME), in which a bespoke methodology is constructed according to the characteristics of the project situation at hand. The construction process involves selecting and assembling reusable process *fragments* from a repository [1, 2].

G.A. Lewis, I. Poernomo, and C. Hofmeister (Eds.): CBSE 2009, LNCS 5582, pp. 54–68, 2009.
© Springer-Verlag Berlin Heidelberg 2009

Process patterns were first defined as "the patterns of activity within an organization (and hence within its project)" [3]. Later definitions focused on defining patterns as practical process chunks recurring in relevant development methodologies. One such definition, focusing on the object-oriented paradigm, defines a process pattern as "a collection of general techniques, actions, and/or tasks (activities) for developing object-oriented software" [4]. Process patterns are typically defined at three levels of granularity: *Tasks*, *Stages* and *Phases* [4]. A *Task* process pattern depicts the detailed steps to perform a specific task. A *Stage* process pattern includes a number of *Task* process patterns and depicts the steps of a single project stage. These steps are often performed iteratively. Finally, a *Phase* process pattern represents the interactions between its constituent *Stage* process patterns in a single project phase. *Phase* process patterns are typically performed in a serial manner.

Since process patterns describe a process fragment commonly encountered in software development methodologies, they are suitable for being used as *process components*. They can thus be applied as reusable building blocks in an assembly-based SME context, providing a repository of process fragments for assembling processes that are tailored to fit specific projects or organizational needs. The OPEN Process Framework (OPF) is an example of using process patterns for general method engineering purposes [5]. Sets of process patterns can also be defined for specific development approaches; the *object-oriented* process patterns of [4], and the *agile* process patterns proposed in [6] are examples of domain-specific patterns, and have indeed inspired this research.

Although a number of process patterns have been introduced in the context of component-based development [7], a comprehensive set of patterns providing full coverage of all aspects of component-based development has not been previously proposed. We propose a set of process patterns commonly encountered in component-based development. The patterns have been identified through studying seven prominent component-based methodologies. A generic process framework, the *Component-Based Software Development Process* (CBSDP), has been constructed based on these process patterns. The generic framework and its constituent process patterns can be used for developing or tailoring a methodology for producing component-based systems. It should be noted that the proposed framework is not a new methodology for component-based development, but rather a generic pattern-based SME model for CBD: method engineers can instantiate the generic framework and populate it with instances of the constituent process patterns according to the particulars of their CBD projects. This approach is already prevalent in methodology engineering frameworks such as OPEN/OPF [8], SPEM-2 [9], and the Eclipse Process Framework (EPF) [10]; indeed, the proposed framework and process patterns can be defined and used as method plug-ins in the *Eclipse Process Framework Composer* (EPFC) tool.

The rest of the paper is structured as follows: Section 2 provides brief descriptions of the seven CBD methodologies used as pattern sources; Section 3 contains the proposed generic framework for component-based software development (CBSDP); in Section 4, the proposed phase-, stage-, and task process patterns are explained; Section 5 validates the patterns through demonstrating how the proposed patterns correspond to the methodologies studied; Section 6 contains the conclusions and suggestions for furthering this research.

2   Pattern Sources: Component-Based Software Development Methodologies

The seven methodologies that have been studied for extracting process patterns are: *UML Components*, *Select Perspective*, *FORM*, *KobrA*, *Catalysis*, *ASD*, and *RUP*. These methodologies were selected because they are well-established and mature, and also because adequate resources and documentation are available on their processes. We briefly introduce each of these methodologies in this section.

UML Components is a UML-based methodology aiming to help developers use technologies such as COM+ and JavaBeans for defining and specifying components [11]. The process shows how UML can be used in a CBD context; that is, to define components, their relations, and their use in the target software system.

Select Perspective was the result of combining the object modeling language introduced in [12] with the Objectory use-case-driven process (later integrated into RUP). In its original form, it incorporated business modeling, use case modeling and class modeling activities. A CBD extension was later added, addressing business-oriented component modeling, component modeling of legacy systems, and deployment modeling. *Select* is based on a service-oriented architecture adapted from the Microsoft Solution Framework application model. It constitutes of three types of services: user services, business service, and data services.

Feature-Oriented Domain Analysis (FODA) was introduced in 1990, and presented the idea of using features in requirement engineering [13]. It was later extensively used in several product-line engineering methods. One such method is the *Feature-Oriented Reuse Method* (FORM) [14, 15], which has added the features of architectural design and construction of object-oriented components to *FODA*, thus providing a CBD methodology.

The *KobrA* methodology is based on a number of advanced software engineering technologies, including product-line engineering, frameworks, architecture-centric development, quality modeling, and process modeling [16, 17]. These methods have been integrated into *KobrA* with the specific aim of systematic development of high quality, component-based software systems.

The *Catalysis* methodology is a component-based approach based on object-oriented analysis and design [18]. It has been influenced by other object-oriented methodologies such as Syntropy and Fusion. *Catalysis* provides a framework for constructing component-based software.

The *Adaptive Software Development* (ASD) methodology was introduced in 1997 [18], and is the only Agile method that specifically targets component-based development.

The *Rational Unified Process* (RUP) is the most well known of the selected methodologies [18]. As a third-generation object-oriented methodology, RUP is use-case-driven and architecture-centric, and incorporates specific guidelines for component-based development. It should be noted, however, that RUP has evolved into a method engineering framework (*Rational Method Composer* – RMC); a further testimony to the changing nature of software engineering, stressing the importance of process patterns in this new trend.

3 Proposed Component-Based Software Development Process (CBSDP)

A thorough examination was conducted on the selected methodologies, as a result of which, 4 *phase* process patterns, 13 *stage* process patterns, and 59 *task* process patterns were identified.

The process patterns have been organized into a generic process framework for CBD methodologies. This framework, which we have chosen to call the Component-Based Software Development Process (CBSDP), is shown in Figure 1. CBSDP consists of four phases (each considered a phase process pattern): *Analysis*, *Design*, *Provision*, and *Release*.

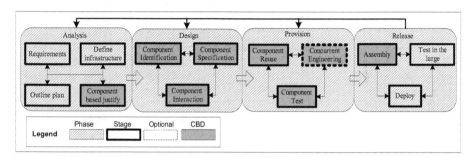

Fig. 1. The proposed Component-Based Software Development Process (CBSDP)

The process begins with the *Analysis* phase, in which the requirements of the system are elicited first. The applicability of the component-based approach to the project at hand is then investigated; after all, the component-based approach may not be suitable for the project. The infrastructure of the project is then defined, and a preliminary project plan and schedule is outlined. In the *Design* phase, the components of the system are identified; based on the interactions among these components, complete specifications are defined for each component. In the *Provision* phase, components are classified into two categories: Those which are retrieved from a repository of reusable components, and those which are constructed from scratch. Components are then developed and tested individually. In the *Release* phase, components are assembled together to form the system proper. After system testing is conducted, the end-product will be deployed into the user environment.

It is worth noting that CBSDP is a framework that guides the method engineer when assembling instances of process patterns. Not all stage process patterns in CBSDP are mandatory; pattern selection is based on the needs of the project situation at hand. For example, suppose that a method engineer needs to construct a methodology for a product line project that is similar to a previous project. Hence, the *Component-based Justify* stage will not be required in the *Analysis* phase. In addition, the *Concurrent Engineering* stage in the *Provision* phase could be omitted, since it may be possible to use existing components instead of constructing new ones.

4 Proposed *Stage* and *Task* Process Patterns

In this section, details of the *Stage* process patterns constituting each of the four aforementioned phases are discussed. Furthermore, some of the constituent *Task* process patterns are briefly reviewed in the descriptions. As previously mentioned, these process patterns can be used independently by method engineers to extend/enhance an existing process, or to construct a new component-based software development methodology.

It is important to note that the arrows connecting the task process patterns do not imply any sequencing. Although it is logical to assume that some of the tasks will precede others, we do not intend to impose any such ordering. The main purpose of this approach is to enable the method engineer to decide the order of the tasks based on the specifics of the project situation at hand.

4.1 Requirements

Requirements Engineering is where the high level *Requirements* of the target system are defined (Figure 2). The inputs to this stage include the *Project Vision* and the *Customer's Viewpoints* on the different aspects of the project. The key factor in component-based development projects – as emphasized in many component-based methodologies such as Select Perspective, UML Components, and KobrA – is how to use previous experience and existing components in future projects. In order to support this purpose, *Existing Components* and *Previous Projects' Assets* are two important inputs to this stage.

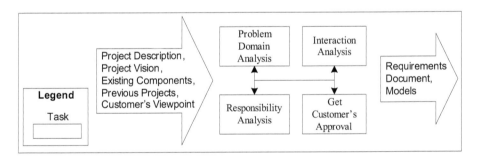

Fig. 2. Constituents of the Requirements stage process pattern

Requirements are defined during the *Problem Domain Analysis* task. During *Interaction Analysis*, the interactions of the system with its environment are examined. The system boundary and the external actors interacting with the system are thus determined. In the *Responsibility Analysis* task, the main functionalities of the system are investigated, and functional and non-functional requirements are identified through active collaboration with the customer. The customer's approval is obtained through the *Get Customer's Approval* task.

4.2 Define Infrastructure

The *Project Infrastructure* should be defined at the beginning of the project. As shown in Figure 3, it includes *Standards, Teams Definition, Tools* used during the project, and the *Development Platform*. The tailored version of the development process to be used in the project is also determined, with *Method Constraints* (covering modeling, testing, build, and release activities) duly defined. In product-line engineering and component-based projects, the *Project Infrastructure* is a key product because it can be used in various projects. Similarly, the infrastructure of previous projects can be tailored for use in future projects.

The inputs to this stage are the requirements extracted in the *Requirements* stage, along with previous experiences compiled in the *Previous Projects* document, *Existing Infrastructure,* and the *Project Plan.* As a result, the *Project Infrastructure Document* and *Team Definition* are produced. The requirements document may be refined during this stage.

In cases where the organization imposes predefined standards and development platforms, the *Select Standards* and *Specify Development Platforms* tasks are not applicable. These tasks have therefore been defined as optional.

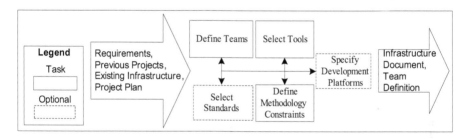

Fig. 3. Constituents of the Define-Infrastructure stage process pattern

4.3 Outline Plan

In this stage of the CBSDP (Figure 4), the initial project management documents (such as project scope, time schedule, etc.) are produced. The management documents are used and updated during the development lifecycle.

The inputs to this stage are the *Requirements Document, Infrastructure Document, Existing Components*, and *Project Objectives*. Preliminary estimation of time and resources and the definition of the project scope are also performed during this stage. An initial viable schedule is then outlined for the project. Based on the team definition provided in the infrastructure document, the work units are assigned to team members. Initial risk assessment activities are also conducted in this stage.

In component-based projects, there is a need to study the market in order to obtain information about existing systems, similar solutions, and reusable components. This information can be used in time and resource estimation, and also when preparing an initial schedule for the project.

The *Project Plan*, *Management Document* and *Risk Assessment* are the deliverables of this stage. The management document contains all the information needed for managing the project. It includes the project plan and schedule (among other things), and may be refined during later stages of the project.

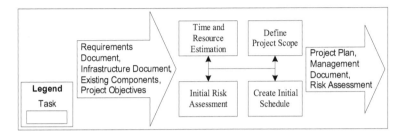

Fig. 4. Constituents of the Outline-Plan stage process pattern

4.4 Component-Based Justify

This stage determines whether the component-based approach can be used on the project at hand (Figure 5). It is a critical stage of the analysis phase since it checks if the project makes sense in a component-based context. It makes use of the *Requirements Document*, *Risk Assessment Document*, *Existing Components* and *Previous Projects* experience to produce the *Feasibility Study* and the *Business Case*, which justifies the project financially.

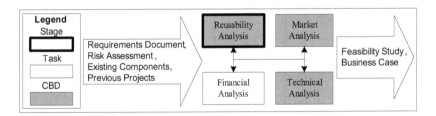

Fig. 5. Constituents of the Component-based-Justify stage process pattern

During the *Technical Analysis* task, we investigate whether it is possible to build the system and realize all of its functional features on the basis of components. Since *Reusability Analysis* contains various tasks, it is defined as a stage process pattern. In this stage, the component repository is first checked in order to assess the applicability of existing components; furthermore, the system components which are to be produced during the current project are explored as to their potential reusability. During the *Market Analysis* task, we search for similar components and systems available on the market. We also investigate the marketability of the components developed for the new system. Based on this information, *Financial Analysis* is performed to assess the economic feasibility of the project.

4.5   Component Identification

The second phase, *Design*, starts with the *Component Identification* stage (Figure 6). It accepts the *Requirements Document*, *Existing Interfaces*, *Existing Components*, *Previous Projects*, and the *Business Case* as input. The main goal of this stage is to create an initial set of interfaces and component specifications. It determines the *System Interfaces* from the interactions between the system and its environment. *Business Interfaces* and *Technical Interfaces* are also identified in this stage. *Business Interfaces* are abstractions of all the information that should be managed by the system, while *Technical Interfaces* manage the technical components (such as database components). The *Business Type Model* contains the specific business information that must be maintained by the system, and will be used in the *Component Specification* stage. Furthermore, an *Initial Architecture* and *Components Specification* are defined in this stage. At the end of this stage, the *Business Type Model*, *System Interfaces*, *Business Interfaces*, and *Component Specs and Architecture* will be produced.

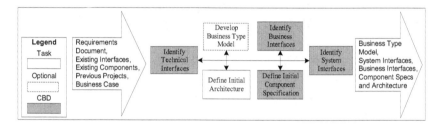

Fig. 6. Constituents of the Component-Identification stage process pattern

4.6   Component Interaction

After defining an initial set of components and their interfaces, we should decide how these components should work together. This task is performed in the *Component Interaction* stage (Figure 7), which uses and refines the *Business Interfaces*, *System Interfaces*, *Technical Interfaces*, and *Component Specifications and Architecture*.

Business operations needed by system to fulfill all of its expected functionality are defined. Existing design patterns are used for refining the *Interfaces* and *Component Specs*. Certain optimization criteria, such as minimization of calls, removal of cyclic dependencies, and normalization of operations and interfaces should be considered during this refinement.

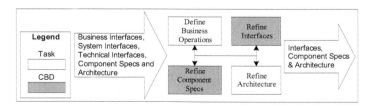

Fig. 7. Constituents of the Component-Interaction stage process pattern

4.7 Component Specification

This is the last stage of the *Design* phase; this means that all the information needed for building the components should be provided to the development teams. In this stage (Figure 8), *Design by Contract* is applied through specifying preconditions and postconditions for class operations. A precondition is a condition under which the operation guarantees that the postcondition will be satisfied. Furthermore, constraints are added to components and interfaces to define how elements in one interface relate to elements in others. Furthermore, *Business Rules and Invariants* are added to the component specifications. Finally, interfaces will be merged or broken in order to provide simpler interfaces.

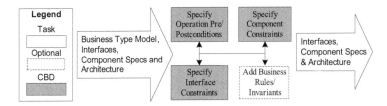

Fig. 8. Constituents of the Component-Specification stage process pattern

4.8 Component Reuse

The *Component Reuse* stage (Figure 9) determines a specific strategy for providing the components which can be constructed or purchased. All components should be classified according to this strategy. For example, one strategy is to build *Business Components*, and purchase all the others. Based on the acquisition strategy, component specifications can be issued to the organization's development teams, commissioned to trusted partners, or sought from commercial sources.

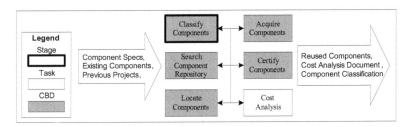

Fig. 9. Constituents of the Component-Reuse stage process pattern

When a candidate component arrives, it undergoes formal certification, which results in acceptance or rejection. If the component is certified, it will be stored in the component repository, and then published for access by developers in different projects. Component developers first search the component repository for components they require. Whenever components are discovered, they will be retrieved and examined, perhaps even tested, before they are reused. *Cost Analysis* is performed to determine which alternative is economically preferable: to build a new component or to reuse an existing one. At the end of this stage it would be clear which component should be constructed from scratch and which one should be reused.

4.9   Concurrent Engineering

As depicted in Figure 1, the *Concurrent Engineering* stage is an optional stage, since we may be able to reuse existing components instead of constructing new ones. Components to be built are assigned to development teams and are concurrently constructed in this stage (Figure 10). Since teams work in a parallel fashion, the development pace is sped up considerably. Each team first *Defines Cycles* for implementing the components assigned to it. Implementation is performed iteratively according to component specifications in fixed time-boxes. Test code and documentation can be written in tandem with coding the components. Code inspection, with the aim of code refactoring and optimization, may also be done during the *Components Implementation* task.

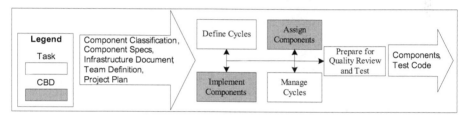

Fig. 10. Constituents of the Concurrent-Engineering stage process pattern

It is important to note that each team manages the project pace through continuous monitoring and control during the *Concurrent Engineering* stage. Keeping the cycles on track is the main concern of the *Manage Cycles* task. At the end of the stage, components should be prepared for quality review and testing. The *Concurrent Engineering* stage uses *Component Classification*, *Component Specs*, *Infrastructure Document*, *Team Definition* and the *Project Plan* to produce the new components.

4.10   Component Test

The *Component Test* stage (Figure 11) focuses on the verification and validation of the components. Documents, code and models should be tested and verified. The goal of *Component Testing* is to ensure that the components are ready to be delivered. *Component Test* is not a system-level test, and mainly consists of black box testing, unit testing and regression testing.

The *Requirements Document* and *Component Specs* are the inputs to this stage. After defining the *Test Plan*, *Test Cases* are either selected from the test base or generated according to *Component Specs*. The next step is to run the test cases on different components and record the results. Code inspection and review can also be conducted with the purpose of code refactoring, but this is not mandatory in all projects. During *Fix Bugs* tasks, minor defects would be resolved, but major errors should be addressed in the Concurrent Engineering stage.

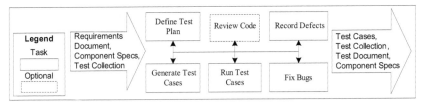

Fig. 11. Constituents of the Component-Test stage process pattern

4.11   Components Assembly

Assembly is the process of putting components and existing software assets together in order to build a working system. User interfaces of the system, which satisfy the user requirements, should then be designed (Figure 12). This stage shares many characteristics with standard configuration practices. Each individual component can be viewed as a separate configuration item, and the *Components Architecture* represents the system configuration definition.

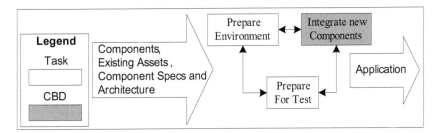

Fig. 12. Constituents of the Components-Assembly stage process pattern

The environment should first be prepared for installing the new component. Then the current system, which is integrated with the new component, will be prepared for testing. Components can be assembled simultaneously or incrementally based on the project strategy.

4.12   Test in the Large

System-level testing is conducted in this stage. The goal of *Test in the Large* (Figure 13) is to prove that the application is ready to be deployed. Defects found in this stage are either resolved by the *Fix Bugs* task, or referred to the *Provision* phase. The tasks of this stage are very similar to the *Component Test* stage, with one difference: the planning and generation of test cases is based on system-level testing strategies. *User Test* is an important stage during which the whole system is validated by users. Important tasks such as *Acceptance Testing* and *Quality Assurance* are conducted during this stage. The system will be ready to be deployed in the working environment after the completion of *Test in the Large* stage.

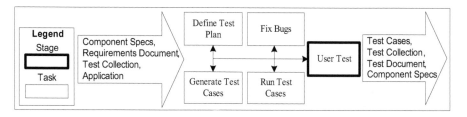

Fig. 13. Constituents of the Test-in-the-Large stage process pattern

4.13 Deploy

The aim of this stage (Figure 14) is to deploy the developed system into the user environment. The environment should first be set up for the deployment of the new system. Providing the necessary software and hardware is a prerequisite to the installation of the developed system. System users should then be prepared for working with the new system. To this aim, user manuals and appropriate application documents are provided, and users at different organizational levels are trained. The new system is then deployed. Deployment tasks should be performed with due attention to the project *Infrastructure Document*. In addition, components which have been tested and validated so far are added to the components repository for future reuse.

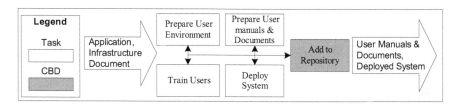

Fig. 14. Constituents of the Deploy stage process pattern

5 Realization of Proposed Process Patterns in Component-Based Methodologies

In this section, we demonstrate how different phases of the component-based methodologies studied can be realized by the proposed process patterns. Table 1 shows how the phases of the seven methodologies used as pattern sources correspond to the proposed stage process patterns. The results seem to indicate that the process patterns are indeed valid as to the coverage of activities that are typically performed in component-based development. In other words, all of these methodologies can be engineered by using the proposed framework and process patterns. It can therefore be concluded that the stated framework and process patterns are valid, although it is possible to enrich the repository by adding new process patterns.

Table 1. Realization of proposed process patterns in the source CBD methodologies

Methodologies	Phases	Corresponding Stage Process Patterns
UML Components	Requirements	Requirements, Define Infrastructure, Outline Plan, Component-based Justify
	Specification	Component Identification, Component Interaction, Component Specification
	Provisioning	Component Reuse, Concurrent Engineering, Component Test
	Assembly	Assembly
	Test	Test in the Large
	Deployment	Deploy
Select Perspective	Supply	Component Specification, Component Reuse, Concurrent Engineering, Component Test, Assembly, Test in the Large
	Manage	Component Reuse, Component Test
	Consume	Requirements, Outline Plan, Component Identification, Component Interaction, Deploy
FORM	Feature Modeling	Requirements
	Architecture Design	Component Interaction
	Architecture Refinement	Component Interaction
	Candidate Object Identification	Component Identification
	Design Object Modeling	Component Identification, Component Interaction
	Component Design	Component Specification
KobrA	Context Realization	Requirements
	Specification	Requirements, Component Identification
	Realization	Component Identification, Component Interaction, Component Specification
	Implementation & Building	Concurrent Engineering
	Component Reuse	Component Reuse
	Quality Assurance	Component Test, Assembly, Test in the Large
	Incremental Development	Concurrent Engineering, Assembly
ASD	Project Initiation	Requirements, Define Infrastructure, Outline Plan
	Adaptive Cycle Planning	Outline Plan, Component Identification, Component Interaction, Component Specification
	Concurrent Component Engineering	Component Reuse, Concurrent Engineering, Component Test, Assembly
	Quality Review	Test in the Large
	Final Q/A and Release	Test in the Large, Deploy
Catalysis	Requirements	Requirements, Define Infrastructure, Outline Plan, Component-based Justify
	System Specification	Requirements, Component Identification
	Architectural Design	Component Identification, Component Interaction
	Component Internal Design	Component Specification, Component Reuse, Concurrent Engineering, Component Test, Assembly, Test in the Large
RUP	Inception	Requirements, Define Infrastructure, Outline Plan
	Elaboration	Requirements, Component Identification
	Construction	Component Interaction, Component Specification, Component Reuse, Concurrent Engineering, Component Test
	Transition	Assembly, Test in the Large, Deploy

6   Conclusions

We have proposed a generic process framework for component-based software development. Within this general process, we have proposed a number of process patterns that are commonly used in component-based development. Extraction of these process patterns was based on a detailed review of seven prominent component-based development methodologies.

After the identification of the process patterns, they were checked against the source methodologies to demonstrate that they do indeed realize the phases of the methodologies. The results, as depicted in Table 1, seem to verify that the patterns do indeed cover the activities performed in the source methodologies.

The proposed process patterns can be used in component-based development projects for engineering a custom process tailored to fit the requirements of the project at hand.

The process patterns proposed in this paper were detailed at the phase and stage levels. Further work can be focused on detailing the task process patterns introduced. Through completing the specifications of the task process patterns, it will be possible to set up a repository of component-based development process patterns to enable assembly-based situational method engineering. The general process presented in this paper can be used as a template for defining component-based processes. A method engineer can use this general template and populate it with specialized instances of the proposed process patterns, thus instantiating a new component-based software development methodology. To this end, work is now in progress on defining our proposed framework and process patterns as method plug-ins in the *Eclipse Process Framework Composer* tool.

Acknowledgement. We wish to thank the ITRC Research Center for sponsoring this research.

References

1. Mirbel, I., Ralyté, J.: Situational Method Engineering: Combining Assembly-based and Roadmap-driven Approaches. Requirements Engineering 11(1), 58–78 (2006)
2. Ralyté, J., Brinkkamper, S., Henderson-Sellers, B. (eds.): Situational Method Engineering: Fundamentals and Experiences. In: Proceedings of the IFIP WG 8.1 Working Conference, Geneva, Switzerland, September 12-14. IFIP International Federation for Information Processing, vol. 244. Springer, Boston (2007)
3. Coplien, J.O.: A Generative Development Process Pattern Language. In: Pattern Languages of Program Design, pp. 187–196. ACM Press/ Addison-Wesley, New York (1995)
4. Ambler, S.W.: Process Patterns: Building Large-Scale Systems Using Object Technology. Cambridge University Press, Cambridge (1998)
5. Henderson-Sellers, B.: Method Engineering for OO Systems Development. Communications of the ACM 46(10), 73–78 (2003)
6. Tasharofi, S., Ramsin, R.: Process Patterns for Agile Methodologies. In: Ralyté, J., Brinkkemper, S., Henderson-Sellers, B. (eds.) Situational Method Engineering: Fundamentals and Experiences, pp. 222–237. Springer, Heidelberg (2007)
7. Bergner, K., Rausch, A., Sihling, M., Vilbig, A.: A Componentware Development Methodology based on Process Patterns. In: 5th Annual Conference on the Pattern Languages of Programs, Monticello, Illinois (1998)
8. Firesmith, D.G., Henderson-Sellers, B.: The OPEN Process Framework: An Introduction. Addison-Wesley, Reading (2001)
9. Object Management Group: Software and Systems Process Engineering Metamodel Specification v2.0 (SPEM), OMG (2007)
10. Haumer, P.: Eclipse Process Framework Composer, Eclipse Foundation (2007)
11. Cheesman, J., Daniels, J.: UML Components: A Simple Process for Specifying Component-Based Software. Addison-Wesley, Reading (2003)

12. Rumbaugh, J., Blaha, M., Premerlani, W., Eddy, F., Lorensen, W.: Object-Oriented Modeling and Design. Prentice-Hall, Englewood Cliffs (1991)
13. Kang, K.C., Cohen, S.G., Hess, J.A., Novak, W.E., Peterson, A.S.: Feature-Oriented Domain Analysis (FODA) Feasibility Study. Technical Report CMU/SEI-90-TR-21, Software Engineering Institute, Carnegie Mellon University, Pittsburgh, PA (1990)
14. Kang, K.C., Lee, J., Donohoe, P.: Feature-Oriented Product Line Engineering. IEEE Software 9(4), 58–65 (2002)
15. Sochos, P., Philippow, I., Riebisch, M.: Feature-Oriented Development of Software Product Lines: Mapping Feature Models to the Architecture. In: Weske, M., Liggesmeyer, P. (eds.) NODe 2004. LNCS, vol. 3263, pp. 138–152. Springer, Heidelberg (2004)
16. Atkinson, C., Bayer, J., Bunse, C., Kamsties, E., Laitenberger, O., Laqua, R., Muthig, D., Paech, B., Wüst, J., Zettel, J.: Component-Based Product-Line Engineering with UML. Addison-Wesley, Reading (2001)
17. Atkinson, C., Bayer, J., Laitenberger, O., Zettel, J.: Component-based Software Engineering: The KobrA Approach. In: 22nd International Conference on Software Engineering (ICSE 2000), 3rd International Workshop on Component-based Software Engineering, Limerick, Ireland (2000)
18. Ramsin, R., Paige, R.F.: Process-Centered Review of Object-Oriented Software Development Methodologies. ACM Computing Surveys 40(1), 1–89 (2008)

Selecting Fault Tolerant Styles for Third-Party Components with Model Checking Support

Junguo Li, Xiangping Chen, Gang Huang[*], Hong Mei, and Franck Chauvel

Key Laboratory of High Confidence Software Technologies, Ministry of Education,
School of Electronics Engineering and Computer Science, Peking University,
Beijing, 100871, China
{lijg05,chenxp04,huanggang,franck.chauvel}@sei.pku.edu.cn,
meih@pku.edu.cn

Abstract. To build highly available or reliable applications out of unreliable third-party components, some software-implemented fault-tolerant mechanisms are introduced to gracefully deal with failures in the components. In this paper, we address an important issue in the approach: how to select the most suitable fault-tolerant mechanisms for a given application in a specific context. To alleviate the difficulty in the selection, these mechanisms are abstracted as Fault-tolerant styles (FTSs) at first, which helps to achieve required high availability or reliability correctly because the complex interactions among functional parts of software and fault-tolerant mechanism are explicitly modeled. Then the required fault-tolerant capabilities are specified as fault-tolerant properties, and the satisfactions of the required properties for candidate FTSs are verified by model checking. Specifically, we take application-specific constraints into consideration during verification. The satisfied properties and constraints are evidences for the selection. A case study shows the effectiveness of the approach.

Keywords: Fault tolerance, model checking, fault-tolerant style, software architecture.

1 Introduction

Third-party components, such as COTS (Commercial Off-The-Shelf) components and service components, are commonly used to implement large-scale (often business related) applications, which contributes to their ability to reduce costs and time. These components share some common characters: a) they are produced and consumed by different people. Application developers work as consumers to integrate third-party components into applications, according to interfaces provided by components providers. b) They are reused as black boxes or "gray" boxes. Consumers are unaware of technical details about how such a component is implemented as well as what's the difference between its updated version and its previous version.

---

[*] Corresponding author.

G.A. Lewis, I. Poernomo, and C. Hofmeister (Eds.): CBSE 2009, LNCS 5582, pp. 69–86, 2009.

These characters raise a challenge to build highly available or reliable applications out of unreliable components that lack special Fault Tolerance (FT) design[1]. Most of the existing studies on the topic try to attach fault-tolerant mechanisms (for example, reboot, retry, or replication) to the external of COTS components [11] or services [24] as "wrappers" or "proxies". They specify such applications at Software Architecture (SA) level because SA is good at modeling interactions among multiple components. The approach works well except that a question is not well answered yet: which fault-tolerant mechanism is the most suitable one for a given third-party component in a specific application? The question stems from two facts. On the one hand, the effectiveness of a fault-tolerant mechanism depends on its fitness for an application context, including fault assumption, application domain, system characteristics, etc. [23]. None of the existing mechanisms, such as reboot, recovery blocks and N-Version Programming, are capable of tolerating all faults in all contexts. On the other hand, an anticipated fault characters in a third-party component may change due to its upgrade. So we need to select a suitable mechanism for third-party components during application development or maintenance, taking into consideration the components' fault assumption, the application's specific constraints, etc.

In the paper, we present a specification and verification-based solution to the problem. The contributions of the paper are two-fold. First, we offer solid evidences to selecting the most suitable fault-tolerant mechanism for a component running in a specific application. The evidences are obtained by model checking and they are necessary to resolve conflicts between continually evolving components and the specificity required by fault-tolerant mechanisms. Once a mechanism cannot successfully recover a fault in an upgraded component, the approach applies to the component again to select another. Second, we take application-specific dependency relationship into consideration in formal specification of an FTSA. This relationship affects the selection and usage of fault-tolerant mechanisms.

In the solution, we specify fault-tolerant mechanisms at first, which improve third-party components' availability or reliability, as a special software architectural style, i.e. fault-tolerant styles (FTSs). Then we define semantics of Fault-Tolerant Software

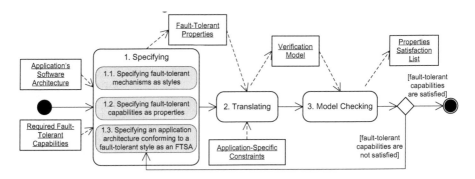

Fig. 1. A process for selecting suitable fault tolerance mechanisms for an component in an application

---

[1] We only discuss software-implemented fault tolerance (SIFT) design in the paper.

Architectures (FTSAs) conforming to an FTS. The definition supports an application-specific constraint (dependency relationships among components), which is seldom considered before. Based on formally specified fault-tolerant properties like fault assumptions, fault-tolerant capability, and application-specific constraints, we verify whether an FTS preserves required properties by model checking. The result determines the suitableness of a mechanism for a specific component in an application. An automatic translation from FTSAs' behavioral models into model checker's input (verification model) is also given. Fig. 1 presents an overview of the proposed approach.

The remainder of the paper is organized as follows: Section 2 gives an overview of FT and a motivating example of selecting an FTS for an EJB component. Section 3 describes the concept of FTS and FTSA, and how to model FTSs before Section 4 describes how to formalize FTSA, fault-tolerant properties and application-specific constraints. Section 5 focuses on translating the above formalized model into Spin model checker's input. Section 6 shows how to use the approach to solve the problem in the motivating example. Section 7 clarify some notable points in the approach and discuss the limits of the approach. At last, we give an insight into conclusions and future work in Section 8.

2 Background and a Motivating Example

In this section, we give an overview of software-implemented fault tolerance mechanism and a motivating example to clarify the problem solved in the paper.

2.1 Software-Implemented Fault Tolerance

Software-implemented fault tolerance is an effective way to achieve high availability and reliability. An activated fault in a component causes errors (i.e. abnormal states that may lead to failures), which is manifested as a failure to its clients. Failures prevent software from providing services or providing correct services for clients [3]. A fault-tolerant mechanism uses a set of software facilities to take two successive steps to tolerate faults: the error detection step aims to identify the presence of an error, while the recovery step aims to transit abnormal states into normal ones (some masking-based fault-tolerant mechanisms do not take the recovery step). The difference among various mechanisms is the way to detect errors and to recover states. Existing fault-tolerant mechanisms are classified as design diversity-based, data diversity-based or environment (temporal) diversity-based mechanisms. Design diversity-based mechanisms require different designs and implementations for one requirement. As a result, even if a failure happened in one version, correct results from other versions can mask it. Data diversity-based mechanisms use data re-expression algorithms to generate a set of similar input data, execute the same operation on those inputs, and use a decision algorithm to determine the resulting output. Environment (temporal) diversity-based mechanisms try to obtain correct results by re-executing failed operations, with different environment configurations. This kind of mechanism is efficient to deal with environment-dependent failure that only happened in a specific execution environment.

Fault-Tolerant Style (FTS) specifies the structural and behavioral characters of an fault-tolerant mechanism very well. Usually FTSs can be modeled in: a) Box-and-line diagrams and formal (or informal) behavioral descriptions [27]; b) Architectural Description Languages (ADLs) [10, 13, 25]; or c) UML or an UML profile [26, 14]. The latter two are widely used in current practices. We take an UML profile for both SA and FT as the modeling language in the study, but pure ADLs can also be used.

2.2 A Motivating Example

ECperf [9] is an EJB benchmark application, which simulates the process of manufacturing, supply chain management, and order/inventory in business problems. *Create-a-New-Order* is a typical scenario in ECperf, i.e. a customer lists all products, adds some to a shopping cart, and creates a new order. We use Software Architecture (SA) model to depict the interactions among EJBs in the scenario in Fig. 2. We assume these EJBs are black boxes and we have nothing known about their implementation details. The structural model of ECperf comes from runtime information analysis, with the monitoring support provided by a reflective JEE Application Server (AS) [16].

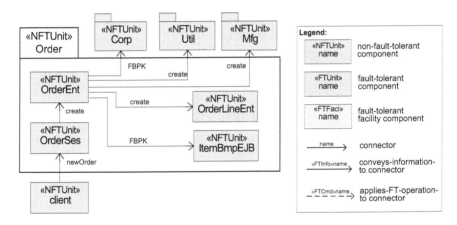

Fig. 2. The part of software architecture of ECperf in the Create-a-New-Order scenario

ECperf cannot tolerate any faults originally, but it needs to be fault tolerable, especially for *ItemBmpEJB*, which is a frequently used bean-managed persistent EJB in the Create-a-New-Order scenario. There are on average more than 400 invocations for ItemBmpEJB, compared with only one invocation for *OrderEnt* in the scenario. The availability of ItemBmpEJB may be imperiled by database faults or unreliable connections to databases. These faults are permanent – they do not disappear unless the database or the connections are recovered, unlike transient faults which may disappear in a nondeterministic manner even when no recovery operation is performed. In addition, these faults are activated only under certain circumstances like heavy-load or heavy communication traffic. So the first fault-tolerant requirement is to make ItemBmpEJB capable of tolerating environment-dependent and non-transient (EDNT) faults.

A common constraint in applications is dependency among components. A component in an application may use other components to fulfill desired functionalities. We call the former a *depending* component, and the latter a *depended-on* component and there is a dependency between them [17]. We classify dependencies as *weak* ones or *strong* ones: If every time a depending component C_1 uses a depended-on component C_2, and C_1 has to look up or acquire C_2 as the first step, there is a weak dependency. On the other hand, if C_1 can invoke C_2 directly by a reference R that is created during C_1's first initialization, it is a strong dependency. Strong dependency is common because the design improves application's performance if the invocation happens frequently. With the proliferation of Dependency Injection design in component-based development, the heavy dependency is more popular. Strong dependencies require a coordinated recovery capability. If C_2 failed at some time, the R in C_1 is invalid either. Any new invocation for C_2 by the R would definitely cause a failure. From the point of view of fault, it is a global error that needs to be recovered coordinately, which is stated in our previous work [17]. Either the R is updated or C_1 is recovered when recovering C_2. By analyzing runtime information, we find OrderEnt strongly depends on ItemBmpEJB because there is a *lookup* invocation in OrderEnt when it calls ItemBmpEJB at the first time, and there is not any lookup invocation later when calling ItemBmpEJB again. As a result, both of them should be configured with a fault-tolerant mechanism as a whole. Another application-specific constraint is that ItemBmpEJB's response time must be within 10 seconds because 10 seconds is long enough for a client waiting for a response.

When all fault-tolerant requirements and application-specific constraints are given, the problem is: which fault-tolerant mechanism is the most suitable one for ItemBmpEJB and OrderEnt, without any modifications on their source code? To solve the problem, we describe our approach step by step in the following sections.

3 Modeling Fault-Tolerant Mechanisms as Styles

In this section, we specify the structural and behavioral characters in fault-tolerant mechanisms as Fault-Tolerant Styles (FTSs) (Step 1.1 and 1.3 in Fig. 1). By surveying the literature on FT [2, 3], we derive some reusable parts that can be combined to form different FTSs. The well organized FTSs form the foundation of selecting a suitable mechanism for an application.

3.1 The Concept of Fault-Tolerant Styles

Although different fault-tolerant mechanisms are distinguished by their structure and interactions with functional components, their primary activities are similar. They control the messages passed in or received from a component, and monitor or control a component's states. An architectural style is a set of constraints on coordinated architectural elements and relationships among them. The constraints restrict the role and the feature of architectural elements and the allowed relationships among those elements in a SA that conforms to that style [21]. From the point of view of architectural style, entities in a fault-tolerant mechanism are modeled as components, interactions among the entities are be modeled as connectors, and constraints in a mechanisms are modeled as

Table 1. The stereotype definition for both fault-tolerant components and connectors in FTSA

UML Stereo-type	Type	Meaning
«FTUnit»	Component	Components that have fault-tolerant capabilities
«NFTUnit»	Component	Components that have not fault-tolerant capabilities
«FTFaci»	Component	Facility components that enable fault tolerance. By obeying specific structural constraints and coordination, «FTFaci» elements interact with «NFTUnit» elements, to make the latter fault-tolerable.
«FTCmd»	Connector	Changing states
«FTInfo»	Connector	Conveying information

an FTS [18, 26], which is a kind of architectural style. The architecture of a fault-tolerant application is a Fault-Tolerant Software Architecture (FTSA), which conforms to an FTS and tolerates a kind(s) of faults.

We use a UML profile for both SA and FT [20, 26] and made necessary extensions to specify FTSs and FTSAs (see Table 1), because UML is widely used and easy for communication. There are three kinds of components in the profile: *«NFTUnit»* components are business components without fault-tolerant capability; *«FTUnit»* components are business components with fault-tolerant capability either by its internal design or by applying a set of *«FTFaci»* components to an «NFTUnit» component. We define a stereotype «FTFaci» for well-designed and reliable components, which provide FT services for «NFTUnit»components. There are two kinds of connectors: «FTInfo» connectors are responsible for conveying a component's states to another; «FTCmd» connectors are responsible for changing an «NFTUnit» component's states. An «NFTUnit» component and its attached «FTFaci» components, which interact with each other in a specific manner, form a composite «FTUnit» component.

Based on the profile, we model fault-tolerant mechanisms as FTSs. Each mechanism's structure is modeled in UML2.0 component diagram (see Fig. 3 (a)). In order to model the mechanism's behavior in a similar manner, we use UML2.0 sequence diagram. UML2.0 sequence diagram provides a visual presentation for temporal relations among concerned entities, but its capability to explicitly specify internal states and states transition are limited. So we introduce a special *calculation occurrence* from the general *execution-occurrence* definition in UML2.0 sequence diagram. Execution-occurrences are rectangles drawn over lifelines in a sequence diagram, and represent the involvement of components in an interaction or scenario (see Fig. 3 (b)). A calculation occurrence is a special execution-occurrence to define, initialize or change variables in an interaction. The order of different calculation occurrences in a scenario stands for the temporal relations among interactions.

Micro-reboot mechanism [7] is an illustrative mechanism to be modeled as FTS. A Micro-reboot style consists of some «FTFaci» components (ExceptionCatcher, Reissuer, and BufferRedirector) and an «FTCmd» Reboot connector for an «NFTUnit» component (Fig. 3). The ExceptionCatcher catches all unexpected exceptions in the «NFTUnit» component. After the caught exceptions are analyzed and the failed component is identified, the failed component is rebooted. Meanwhile, the BufferRedirector blocks incoming requests for the component during recovery. When the failed component is successfully recovered, the BufferRedirector re-issues the blocked requests and the normal process is resumed.

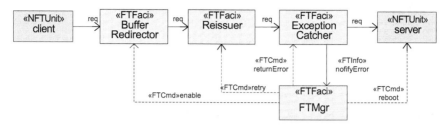

(a) The structure of *Micro-reboot* style

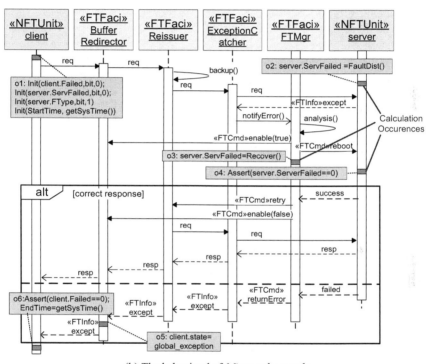

(b) The behavioral of *Micro-reboot* style

Fig. 3. The structural (a) and behavior (b) specifications of Micro-reboot style

We also model other FTSs such as Simple Retry style and Retry Blocks style. Simple Retry style is similar to Micro-reboot style except it only re-invokes a failed component again, without rebooting it. Retry Blocks style is similar to Simple Retry style except it uses data re-expression component to mutate inputs before retrying. These FTSs are not shown in the paper due to the space limitations.

3.2 The Classification of Fault-Tolerant Styles

We identify some common and key «FTFaci» components and «FTCmd» connectors in Table 2, which can be used for third-party components. They are classified by their functionalities: detecting errors, recovering error states, or smoothing the recovery procedures. A complete FTS consists of an error-detection part, a recovery part, and an auxiliary part (Some FTSs only have two parts or even one part, depending on different FT design principles). Combinations based on the above FT components or connectors form different FTSs. In Fig. 4, seven major FTSs are given by the combination of these entities. These FTSs stands for typical fault-tolerant mechanisms for third-party components. Recovery Blocks and N-Version Programming are design diversity-based mechanisms; N-Copy Programming and Retry Blocks are data diversity-based mechanisms; and Micro-reboot, Simple Retry, and Checkpoint-restart are environment (temporal) diversity-based mechanisms.

The identification of common «FTFaci» components and «FTCmd» connectors makes FTSs flexible. A FTS's error detection part or recovery part can be replaced by another if necessary. For example, Recovery Block style, which works on a primary component and a secondary component implementing same functions, requires an AcceptanceTest to determine whether the primary works correctly or not. But if the primary mainly thrown exceptions when a failure happened, AcceptanceTest is not good at dealing with such abnormal. It can be replaced by ExceptionCatcher, which

Table 2. Key modules in fault-tolerant mechanisms

Type	Component/ Connectors in FTSA	Explanation	Mechanism examples
Error Detection	«FTFaci» ExceptionCatcher	Catches thrown exceptions by a component	Micro-reboot.
	«FTCmd» Watchdog	Periodically sends a request to a component to testify its liveness.	Watchdog.
	«FTFaci» AcceptanceTest	Decides the correctness of a returned value	Recovery Blocks, Retry Blocks.
Recovery	«FTCmd» Reboot	Resets a failed component's states by reboot	Micro-reboot.
	«FTFaci» StateSetter	Set a component's states, according to given parameters.	Checkpoint-restart.
	«FTFaci» Switcher	Sends a request to a version/instance of a component.	Recovery Blocks.
	«FTFaci» DistributerCollector	Sends identical requests to multiple versions/instances of a component, and determines a result by comparing all the returned values.	N-Version Programming (NVP), N-Copy Programming (NCP)
Auxiliary	«FTFaci» DataReexpression	Slightly modifies an input	Recovery Blocks, NCP.
	«FTFaci» BufferRedirector	Buffers all requests to a failed component and redirects them when it is recovered	Micro-reboot.
	«FTCmd» Reissuer	Re-sends a request to the target component, after a varied waiting time	Checkpoint-restart.
	«FTFaci» FTMgr	Coordinates operations between error detector and recovery, or between several recovery operations	Used in All most all mechanisms.

is good at dealing with failures manifested as exceptions. The occasion of a replacement is usually decided by the time when a fault assumption is changed, and the verification of the correctness of the replacement is supported by our model checking approach described in Section 5 if only the correctness is also specified as a property.

The combined FTSs would be more plentiful if more «FTFaci» components or «FTCmd» connectors are included. But keep in mind that not all existing fault-tolerant mechanisms are meaningful for third-party components. Because implementation details of these components are hidden from application developers, and components' internal states are invisible except those accessed through a predefined interface. Most of the mechanisms in the classification can be externally attached to components. A notable example is checkpoint-restart mechanism. Almost all checkpoint-restart protocols require accessing a component's internal states. Considering an impractical assumption that all components provide an interface to get/set their internal states, checkpoint-restart can only apply to a considerably small number of third-party components that provide state manipulation operations. The similar situation exists in replication mechanism too.

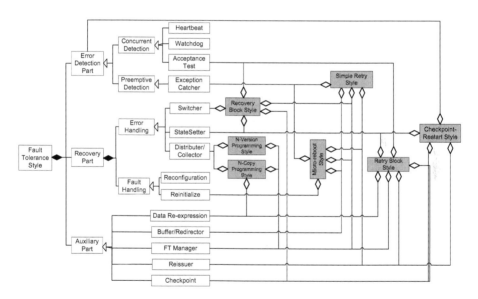

Fig. 4. The classification of FTSs according to their design principles. We assign the common «FTFaci» components and «FTCmd» connectors to a classification framework give by [3], and we show how to form a FTS by combining some of them.

4   Modeling Fault-Tolerant Properties and Application-Specific Constraints

4.1   Fault-Tolerant Properties and Application-Specific Constraints

Given a specific application, a set of requirements on fault-tolerant capabilities, and a set of candidate FTSs, it is critical to select the most suitable one for concerned components in the application to meet the requirements. In this section, we abstract both fault-tolerant capability requirements and fault assumptions on components as fault-tolerant properties, and specify application-specific constraints (Step 1.2 in Fig. 1). In the next section, we translate an FTS's behavioral models in UML sequence diagram, the properties, and the constraints into verification models, and use model checking to verify the FTS's satisfaction of the properties and the constraints.

Table 3. Fault-tolerant properties and application-specific constraints

Type	Property Name & Description
Fault Assumptions	**Transient fault assumption (P_1):** When a component is providing services and a transient fault is activated in it then, its states will be resumed if a fault-tolerant mechanism was applied. Transient faults are nondeterministic and are also called "Heisenbugs".
	Environment-dependent and non-transient (EDNT) fault assumption (P_2): When a component is providing services and an EDNT fault is activated in it then, its states will be resumed if a fault-tolerant mechanism was applied. EDNT faults are deterministic and activated only on a specific environment.
	Environment-independent and non-transient fault assumption (EINT) (P_3): When a component is providing services and an EINT fault is activated in it then, its states will be resumed if a fault-tolerant mechanism was applied. EINT faults are deterministic and are independent of specific environment.
Generic Fault-Tolerant Capabilities	**Fault containment (P_4):** If an error is detected in a component, other components would not be aware the situation.
	Fault isolation (P_5): When a failed component is being recovered, no new incoming requests can invoke the component.
	Fault propagation (P_6): If an un-maskable fault is activated in a component and it cannot be recovered successfully, the client, who issues the request and activates the fault, would receive an error response.
	Coordinated error recovery (P_7): If a global error, which affects more than one component, happened, the error can be recovered.
App.-Specific Constraints	**Weak dependency (P_8):** Component C_1 weakly depends on component C_2.
	Strong dependency (P_9): Component C_3 strongly depends on component C_2.
	Timely constraint (P_{10}): A component always delivers correct response within 10 seconds.

Fault assumption is a kind of important properties. It assumes the characters of faults in a component or an application. Only when an FTS can deal with a certain kind of fault, it is meaningful to discuss the FTS's other capabilities. Properties P_1, P_2, and P_3 shown in Table 3 denote three fault assumptions. These three properties form a dimension of selecting FTSs. Then fault containment, fault isolation, fault propagation, and recovery coordination are four generic fault-tolerant capabilities. They are shown in Table 3 as P_4 to P_7 and form another dimension of the selection. P_4 stipulates that the source of a failure should be masked, for fear of error propagation. Because not all errors can be masked, property P_6 states that if a failed component cannot be recovered, the error should be allowed to propagate to others to trigger a global recovery processes. This is important for some faults that can be tolerated by coordinated recovery among several dependent components. P_5 stipulates that new incoming requests cannot arrive at a failed component. P_7 is related to application-specific constraints P_8 and P_9, so it will be explained later. At last, application-specific constraints can also affect the selection of suitable FTSs. Properties P_8 to P_{10} describe some application-specific constraints. P_8 and P_9 stipulate weak and strong dependencies among components, respectively. Property P_{10} states a performance-related constraint: a component's response time must not be more than a certain time in all circumstances.

It should be noted that the above fault-tolerant properties only covers some important and typical ones, and they are distilled from a study of FT [3, 2]. Other properties, such as those presented in Yuan et al.'s study [13], can also be appended to the table.

4.2 Specifying Properties

Before formally specifying fault-tolerant properties, we define a base for FTSA. In an FTSA model, components $C=\{c_1, c_2, ..., c_n\}$, where each c_i $(1 \leq i \leq n)$ is a «NFTUnit» component. States of an component belong to a states set $S=\{normal, local\_error, global\_error\}$ and $\forall c \in C, c.state \in S$. Local errors are abnormal states that affect only one component and can be resumed by recovering this component individually, whereas global errors may affect more than one component and need to be recovered by coordination of all affected components. Each «NFTUnit» component has a variable *Failed* to indicate whether the component is failed or not, and *ErrorName* to indicate the name of an error.

$$\forall c \in C, c.Failed = \begin{cases} false, if\ c.state = normal \\ true, otherwise \end{cases}$$

The variable *ServFailed* is an alias of *Failed* in a component that provides services for others. Each «NFTUnit» component has an *Ftype* to indicate its fault assumption in a scenario. $\forall c \in C, c.Ftype \in \{transient, EDNT, EINT\}$. For each «NFTUnit» component, it is attached by a fault activation function *FaultDist*, which specifies faults' activation occasions and duration in the component decided by *Ftype* and the given failure-interval distribution. The function may transit a component's state from *normal* to *local_error* or *global_error*.

The above definition only covers FT-related issues. To represent application-specific constraints, we classify them as two types because application-specific constraints are various. Generally, if a constraint manifested as "*p implies q*", it is treated as fault-tolerant properties, like P_{10} in Table 3. If a constraint cannot be manifested as "*p implies q*", it would be treated as an extra modification of the state transition of FTSA. In our study, we take dependencies as an example of such constraints. It is one of important application-specific constraints in FT. For each c_1 and c_2 in C, we denote $c_1 \prec_w c_2$ if c_1 weak dependent on c_2, and $c_1 \prec_s c_2$ if c_1 strong dependent on c_2, otherwise, c_1 is independent from c_2 (i.e. there is no dependent relationships between them).

The lifecycle of a component is modeled as a process. The initial trigger of a components' state transition is a request for its service. A component's state transition function δ under the constraint of dependent relationship are: if $c_1 \prec_s c_2$,

$$\delta(c_1.state) = \begin{cases} FaultDist(c_1.Ftype), & \text{if } c_1.state = normal \text{ and } c_2.state = normal \\ c_1.state, & \text{if } c_1.state \,!= normal \text{ and } c_2.state = normal \\ local\_error, & \text{if } c_2.state \,!= normal \end{cases}$$

Otherwise (i.e. $c_1 \prec_w c_2$ or c_1 is independent from c_2),

$$\delta(c_1.state) = \begin{cases} FaultDist(c_1.Ftype), & \text{if } c_1.state = normal \\ c_1.state, & otherwise \end{cases}$$

An FTS's recovery part has a *Recover* function to transit a component's error state to a normal one. «FTFaci» FTMgr holds a list *comp* containing components which is configured to be fault tolerant. The components in *comp* have an extra *recovering* state, which is visible only by the FTMgr, and a variable to indicate the name of an error.

Based on the above definitions, informally expressed fault-tolerant properties and application-specific constraints in Table 3 are formalized as:

P_1: *client.o_1.Failed = false ∧ server.o_2.ServFailed = true ∧ server.o_2.Ftype = transient ⇒ server.o_4.Failed = false*

P_2: *client.o_1.Failed = false ∧ server.o_2.ServFailed = true ∧ server.o_2.Ftype = EDNT ⇒ server.o_4.Failed = false*

P_3: *client.o_1.Failed = false ∧ server.o_2.ServFailed = true ∧ server.o_2.Ftype = EINT ⇒ server.o_4.Failed = false*

P_4: *client.o_1.Failed = false ∧ server.o_2.ServFailed = true ⇒ client.o_6.Failed = false*

P_5: *client.o_1.Failed = false ∧ server.o_2.ServFailed = true ∧ FTmgr.o_3.comp[server]. state = recovering ⇒ ∀c ∈ C , c != server, c.ErrorName != FTmgr.o_3.comp [server].ErrorName*

P_6: *client.o_1.Failed = false ∧ server.o_2.ServFailed = true ∧ server.o_4.ServFailed = true ⇒ client.o_6.Failed = true*

P_7: *client.o_1.Failed = false ∧ server.o_2.ServFailed = true ∧ server.o_2.state = global_error) ⇒ client.o_6.Failed = false ∧ server.o_6.Failed = false.*

P_8: *$c_1 \prec_w c_2$*

P_9: *$c_3 \prec_s c_2$*

P_{10}: *client.o_1.Failed = false ∧ (server.o_2.ServFailed = false ∨ server.o_2.ServFailed = true) ⇒ client.o_6.EndTime - client.o_1.StartTime <= 10.*

The o_1, o_2, o_3, o_4 and o_6 in the above formal specification are calculation occurrences in the extended sequence diagram (based on Fig. 3 (b)). The *StartTime* and *EndTime* variables in P_7 are user defined variables which record the time of starting a request and receiving a response.

5   Translating Behavioral Models and Properties into Verification Models

We verify FTSs' satisfaction of fault-tolerant properties and application-specific constraints by Spin model checker [12], because it is proven effective in many industrial applications [12]. However a system to be verified in Spin must be modeled in Promela (Process Meta-Language). Programs in Promela cannot be visualized as UML diagrams, and are often called verification model.

We predefine a set of templates to automatically translate the extended UML2.0 sequence diagrams into Spin's verification model (Step 2 in Fig. 1). The automatic translation of standard elements in UML2.0 sequence diagram has been addressed in related literature [5]. Interaction elements in UML2.0 sequence diagram, such as timeline and message dispatch, are mapped to basic block or elements in Promela, such as process (*proctype*) and channel (*chan* element). Structured control operators in UML2.0 sequence diagrams, such as conditional execution and loop execution, are mapped to control-flow constructs in Promela, such as the selection statement (*if...fi*) and loop statement (*do...od*).

Calculation occurrences defined in our extension are mapped to code blocks in Promela processes, based on the position where the calculation occurrence is placed on. Variables defined in calculation occurrences are mapped to variables in Promela, and all of them are initialized in the Promela-defined init process. The variables may be re-assigned by *FaultDist* function that we defined to simulate faults, by *Recover* function that simulate a fault-tolerant mechanism, or by build-in functions such as obtaining system clock. The fault simulation function is mapped to a separate parameterized process that interacts with other processes.

Finally, conclusions in properties predicate are mapped to assertion statements in Promela. The positions of the assertions are decided by the quantifiers (universal or existential) of predicate and execution occurrences in which the conclusions covered. For example, a universal quantifier is prefixed to a component in the conclusion of property P_5 in Section 4.2, so the corresponding assertion should be placed in all processes corresponding to timelines of components, and its position in the processes must be after the position of the last execution occurrence (o_2) in P_5. For some application-specific properties that cannot be specified as predicates, such as P_8 and P_9, they are represented by affecting components' state transitions.

In model checking process (Step 3 in Fig. 1), Spin simulates an FTS's behavior and traverses all its states combinations. As we explained before, a component's states are defined and stored in variables defined in the calculation occurrences. These states are initialized at the beginning, and re-assigned by fault simulation function and state transit rules. When Spin control flow arrives at an assertion, it checks the truth or not of the assertion. It either confirms that the properties hold or reports that they are violated. A false assertion means the style does not preserve the property represented by the assertion and a counter-example is provided. Otherwise, the above verification process continues. When all assertions are true, it means the FTS satisfies all the concerned properties.

6   Utilization of the Approach for ECperf

In the previous sections, we explain how to specify fault-tolerant mechanisms that can be used for third-party components, how to specify fault-tolerant properties and application-specific constraints, and how to translate these specifications to verification model of Spin. In this section, we use the approach to selecting a suitable mechanism for ECperf.

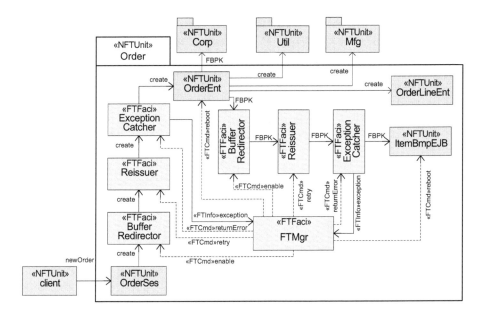

Fig. 5. The fault-tolerant architecture of ECperf that conforms to Micro-reboot style

Application-specific constraints can narrow the scope of candidate FTSs. ECperf runs on a sequential execution environment (JEE AS), so N-Version Programming style and N-Copy Programming style cannot be used because they require concurrent execution support. There exist no other variants of ECperf, so Recovery Blocks style cannot be used because it requires multiple alternatives for a same design. ItemBmpEJB does not provide interfaces to access its internal states, so Checkpoint and Restart style is excluded. Then the remaining candidates include Retry Blocks style, Simple Retry style, and Micro-reboot style. There are no more ECperf-specific characters help to select or exclude one of the above candidates. To select a suitable FTS from existing ones, we carry out a model checking process to verify if they satisfy fault-tolerant properties stated in Section 4.1 and ECperf-specific constraints.

We create three different versions of fault-tolerant ECperf by modifying its original SA. Each version conforms to one of the above three FTS (Fig. 5 shows the version conforming to Micro-reboot style). The behavioral models of the enhanced versions are translated into Promela programs, and we use Spin to verify their satisfactions on properties P_1 to P_7, and P_{10} listed in Table 3 in Create-a-New-Order scenario. To verify property P_{10}, we calculate the average response time of ItemBmpEJB with the help of runtime information, and estimate average response time of «FTFaci» components in Micro-reboot style. The result is shown in Table 4 and Micro-reboot style is the winner because it fits the EDNT fault assumption and supports coordinated recovery, but Retry Blocks style and Simple Retry style cannot.

We also perform a set of comparative experiments to validate the practical correctness of the selection. In the experiments, micro-reboot mechanisms and simple retry mechanism are attached to the components at the external, with the supports of the reflective JEE AS. We periodically inject Java exceptions into ItemBmpEJB to simulate EDNT faults. As a result, the rates of successful submitted orders using Micro-reboot and Simple Retry are 87.3% and 50.7%, respectively, compare to 45.4% with no FT. It is clear that Micro-reboot style works better than Simple Retry style. The experimental result is coincident with the model checking result.

Table 4. The satisfaction of properties for Retry Blocks style, Simple Retry style, and Micro-reboot style. (•: preserve; ○: do not preserve). Fault assumptions form a dimension, other fault-tolerant properties and some application-specific constraints form another dimension. The results in the dash-line rectangle shows that Micro-reboot style satisfied all concerned properties and constraints under EDNT fault assumption, while Retry Blocks style and Simple Retry style cannot.

(a) Retry Blocks style					(b) Simple Retry style					(c) Micro-reboot style				
P_4	P_5	P_6	P_7	P_{10}	P_4	P_5	P_6	P_7	P_{10}	P_4	P_5	P_6	P_7	P_{10}
P_1 •	•	•	•	•	P_1 •	•	•	•	•	P_1 •	•	•	•	•
P_2 ○	○	○	○	○	P_2 ○	○	○	○	○	P_2 •	•	•	•	•
P_3 ○	○	○	○	○	P_3 ○	○	○	○	○	P_3 ○	○	○	○	○

7 Discussion and Related Work

In the area of **Architecting Fault-Tolerant Systems** [1], components (computing entities), connectors (communication entities), and configuration (topology of components and connectors) have been used to model fault-tolerant software as FTSA. Previous work in the area mainly focus on how to model a specific fault-tolerant mechanism [10, 13, 14, 26, 27], for example, exception handling-based mechanism [14, 27]. A few studies consider the reasoning or analysis on an FTS. Yuan et al. [27] specify a Generic Fault-Tolerant Software Architecture (GFTSA), which obeys idealized Fault-Tolerant Component style, in formal language Object-Z, and perform manual formal proofs to demonstrate fault-tolerant properties the GFTSA preserves. The authors also present a template to automate the customization process when using the style. Sözer et al. [26] specify the structure of a local recovery style in an UML profile, and perform performance overhead and availability analysis. In contrast, we uniformly model and analysis various mechanisms that can be used for third-party components as fault-tolerant styles.

Verifying fault-tolerant software via model checking has been studied in previous work to prove the correctness of fault-tolerant design. Bernardeschi et al. [4] applies model checking to fault-tolerant software specified in Calculus of Communicating Systems (CCS)/Meije process algebra. Fault-tolerant properties are expressed in Action-based Computation Tree Logic (ACTL). Because a common prerequisite of model checking is that software model should be a formal one, this would be a barrier to its acceptance in practices. Some studies adopt another approach – after modeling software using popular modeling languages, translating the models into a formal one [8, 6]. Ebnenasir and Cheng [7] define a computation model and use UML state diagrams to specify fault, generic fault tolerant patterns, and fault-tolerant systems. The UML state diagram models are translated into Promela programs automatically. Thus the model is checked to verify its safety and liveness. The major difference between their work and ours is that we concentrate on the specificity of fault-tolerant mechanisms but they focus on the generality of them. They define detector pattern and corrector pattern to covers all error detection mechanism and all recovery mechanisms. But a specific mechanism (Micro-reboot, checkpoint and restart, etc.) cannot be distinguished from others in such a generic definition.

We use UML2.0 diagram to model FTSs, and use Spin to verify both fault-tolerant properties and application-specific constraints because both are widely used and well studied. Other specification languages and model checkers can also be chosen to implement our approach, but it should be noted that the translation between FTS models and verification models is specific to the choice. For example, if we use a traditional ADL to specify FTSs' behaviors and a model checker's formal language to specify properties, the translation is not necessary. This alternative is not preferred because it not only requires application developers to learn a formal language, but also requires a manual modification of the verification model if the FTS is changed.

The scalability of model checkers is a major limit of the technique, because the explored states are restricted by the computational resources. But it is not a serious problem in our study. The verifications of fault-tolerant properties and application-specific constraints are carried out at SA level, and the number of states in FTSs is considerably small (*state*, *Failed*, *Ftype*, *comp*, etc.). Moreover, although the state may be large when taking application into consideration, the verification process is oriented to a scenario (for example, Create-a-New-Order scenario in the case study), in which the number of components is restricted.

We talk little about other general requirements (such as safeness and correctness of an FTSA). The reason is not in that these requirements are minor, but in that we focus on the selection of FTSs in the paper and these requirements do nothing helpful to the selection. In fact, we take them as prerequisites for all valid FTSs. This means these requirements must be met at first. Moreover, we touch the fringe of the interaction among FT and other software qualities like performance. Performance works as an application-specific constraint for the selection of FT styles. We believe similar solution is also helpful to make a trade-off between fault-tolerant styles and performance optimization patterns [14].

It is also abstractive to use more than one FTSs for a component in an application, thus the component is capable of tolerate many kinds of faults. But FT is an expensive measure that will impact other system qualities, such as performance. Multiple fault-tolerant mechanisms for a component will definitely impose heavy penalty to the application. Moreover, intervenes among multiple FTSs will also make the configuration of FTSA much more complex and error-prone.

8   Conclusion and Future Work

The proliferation of the development using third-party components brings new challenges to high availability or reliability because these components are often treated as black boxes. We present two levels of abstraction for the problem: fault-tolerant mechanisms that can improve third-party components' availability or reliability are abstracted as a Fault-Tolerant Styles; and fault assumptions, fault-tolerant capabilities, and application-specific constraints are abstracted as properties. The virtual of the model checking based approach proposed in the paper is making the selection of FTS for a specific application more confidently. The approach is more meaningful when components' failure characteristics and execution environment change continually.

The work presented in the paper does not cover the problem of how to merge «FTFaci» components into an applications' architecture, which also affects the correctness of an FTSA. We assume the merge is performed by FT experts in the paper but we are working on an automatic model merging to do the task, similar to existing work [19, 22]. We are also going to finish the development of a GUI tool to integrate FTS modeling tool, translating tool, and Spin model checker.

Acknowledgments. This work is sponsored by the National Key Basic Research and Development Program of China (973) under Grant No. 2009CB320703; the Science Fund for Creative Research Groups of China under Grant No. 60821003; the National Natural Science Foundation of China under Grant No. 60873060; the High-Tech Research and Development Program of China under Grant No. 2009AA01Z16; and the EU Seventh Framework Programme under Grant No. 231167..

References

1. Workshop on Architecting Dependable Systems,
   http://www.cs.kent.ac.uk/ wads/
2. Anderson, T., Lee, P.A.: Fault Tolerance: Principles and Practice. Prentice-Hall, Englewood Cliffs (1981)
3. Avizienis, A., Laprie, J.-C., Randell, B., Landwehr, C.: Basic concepts and taxonomy of dependable and secure computing. IEEE Trans. on Dependable and Secure Computing 1(1), 11–33 (2004)
4. Bernardeschi, C., Fantechi, A., Gnesi, S.: Model checking fault tolerant systems. Software Testing Verification and Reliability 12, 251–275 (2002)
5. Bose, P.: Automated Translation of UML Models of Architectures for Verification and Simulation Using SPIN. In: Proceedings of the 14th IEEE Int'l Conference on Automated Software Engineering, pp. 102–109. IEEE Computer Society Press, Los Alamitos (1999)
6. Brito, P.H.S., Lemos, R., Rubira, C.M.F.: Verification of Exception Control Flows and Handlers Based on Architectural Scenarios. In: Proceeding of the 11th IEEE High Assurance Systems Engineering Symposium (HASE), pp.177–186 (2008)
7. Candea, G., et al.: JAGR: an autonomous self-recovering application server. In: Proc. of the 5th Int'l Workshop on Active Middleware Services, Seattle, USA, pp. 168–177 (2003)
8. Ebnenasir, A., Cheng, B.H.C.: Pattern-Based Modeling and Analysis of Failsafe Fault-Tolerance. In: 10th IEEE International Symposium on High Assurance System Engineering (HASE), Dallas, Texas, USA, November 14–16 (2007)
9. ECperf webpage, http://java.sun.com/developer/earlyAccess/j2ee/ecperf/download.html
10. Garlan, D., Chung, S., Schmerl, B.: Increasing system dependability through architecture based self-repair. In: de Lemos, R., Gacek, C., Romanovsky, A. (eds.) Architecting Dependable Systems. LNCS, vol. 2677. Springer, Heidelberg (2003)
11. de Guerra, P.A.C., Rubira, C.F., Romanovsky, A., de Lemos, R.: A fault-tolerant software architecture for COTS-based software systems. In: Proc. of ESEC/FSE-11, Helsinki, Finland, pp. 375–378 (2003)

12. Holzmann, G.J.: The Model Checker SPIN. IEEE Trans. on Software Engineering 23(5) (1997)
13. Issarny, V., Banatre, J.: Architecture-Based Exception Handling. In: Proc. of the 34th Annual Hawaii International Conference on System Sciences, vol. 9, p. 9058 (2001)
14. Lan, L., Huang, G., Wang, W., Mei, H.: A Middleware-based Approach to Model Refactoring at Runtime. In: Proceedings of the 14th Asia-Pacific Software Engineering Conference (APSEC 2007) (2007)
15. de Lemos, R., Guerra, P., Rubira, C.: A fault-tolerant architectural approach for dependable systems. IEEE Software 23(2), 80–87 (2006)
16. Mei, H., Huang, G.: PKUAS: An Architecture-based Reflective Component Operating Platform. In: IEEE Int'l Workshop on Future Trends of Distributed Computing Sys. (2004)
17. Mei, H., Huang, G., Liu, T., Li, J.: Coordinated Recovery of Middleware Services: A Framework and Experiments. Int. J. Software Informatics 1(1), 101–128 (2007)
18. Muccini, H., Romanovsky, A.: Architecting Fault Tolerant Systems. Technical report, University of Newcastle upon Tyne, CS-TR-1051 (2007)
19. Nejati, S., Sabetzadeh, M., Chechik, M., Easterbrook, S., Zave, P.: Matching and Merging of Statecharts Specifications. In: Proc. 29th Int'l Conference on Software Engineering, pp. 54–64 (2007)
20. Object Management Group, UML(TM) Profile for Modeling Quality of Service and Fault Tolerance Characteristics and Mechanisms,
    http://www.omg.org/docs/ptc/04-09-01.pdf
21. Perry, D.E., Wolf, A.L.: Foundations for the study of software architecture. SIGSOFT Software Engineering Notes 17(4), 40–52 (1992)
22. Pottinger, R.A., Bernstein, P.A.: Merging models based on given correspondences. In: Proc. 29th int'l Conference on Very Large Data Bases, pp. 862–873 (2003)
23. Romanovsky, A.: A Looming Fault Tolerance Software Crisis? ACM SIGSOFT Software Engineering Notes 32(2) (2007)
24. Salatge, N., Fabre, J.C.: Fault Tolerance Connectors for Unreliable Web Services. In: Proc. of 37th Annual IEEE/IFIP International Conference on Dependable Systems and Networks (DSN 2007), Edinburgh, UK, pp. 51–60 (2007)
25. Seo, C., et al.: Exploring the Role of Software Architecture in Dynamic and Fault Tolerant Pervasive Systems. In: Proc. of SEPCASE 2007, Minneapolis, MN, USA (2007)
26. Sözer, H., Tekinerdogan, B.: Introducing Recovery Style for Modeling and Analyzing System Recovery. In: Proc. of 7th IEEE/IFIP Working Conference on Software Architecture, Vancouver, Canada, pp. 167–176 (2008)
27. Yuan, L., Dong, J.S., Sun, J., Basit, H.A.: Generic Fault Tolerant Software Architecture Reasoning and Customization. IEEE Trans. on Reliability. 55(3), 421–435 (2006)

Extracting Behavior Specification of Components in Legacy Applications[*]

Tomáš Poch[1] and František Plášil[1,2]

[1] Charles University in Prague, Faculty of Mathematics and Physics
Department of Software Engineering
Malostranske namesti 25, 118 00 Prague 1, Czech Republic
{poch,plasil}@dsrg.mff.cuni.cz
http://dsrg.mff.cuni.cz
[2] Academy of Sciences of the Czech Republic
Institute of Computer Science
plasil@cs.cas.cz

Abstract. A challenge of componentizing legacy applications is to extract behavior specification of suggested components. It is desirable to preserve a relation between the original structure of the source code of a component and the extracted specification; in particular, this is important for both user comprehension and for interpretation of results of any further formal verification. Even though the reverse engineering techniques providing behavior specification have already been applied on object oriented software and components, none of them targets the interplay of both the externally and internally triggered activities on the component's provided and required interfaces from a single perspective. This paper targets the problem in the scope of Behavior Protocols and components given as a set of Java classes accompanied with information on component boundaries. To demonstrate viability of the proposed approach, this technique has been partially applied in the JAbstractor tool for the SOFA component model.

Keywords: Reverse engineering, Component behavior specification.

1 Introduction

1.1 Why Behavior Modeling of Legacy Components

Component-based software development eases production of complex systems by composition of precisely defined separated blocks of software – components. Since every component clearly states its purpose and assumptions on the environment in terms of provided and required interfaces, it can be developed independently of the other components. The isolation of components prevents from unexpected dependencies between unrelated parts of the system.

---

[*] This work was partially supported by the Grant Agency of the Czech Republic project 201/08/0266.

G.A. Lewis, I. Poernomo, and C. Hofmeister (Eds.): CBSE 2009, LNCS 5582, pp. 87–103, 2009.
© Springer-Verlag Berlin Heidelberg 2009

Component-based development allows reusing a component in different systems and contexts. Moreover, when a component is equipped with additional information like an abstraction of behavior it exhibits and performance characteristics, various kinds of analysis and verification (compliance of components' behavior, performance) can be applied already at design stage to shorten development cycle and lower the costs. The additional information also serves for documentation purposes and test case generation.

Even though the component technology has become used in practice during last decade, there is still a wide range of legacy applications run and maintained, design of which is far from being component-based. Thus, when such application is being modified, developers can not take an advantage of the component paradigm. Reimplementation from scratch using modern component-based methods would be extremely costly. Instead, it pays off to apply reverse engineering techniques to re-design the application in a component-based way.

In this context, to take advantage of formal verification of component behavior, two reverse engineering tasks have to be accomplished: (i) Extracting static structure (architecture) of the application. This means to identify individual components, their provided and required interfaces, and relations among them in the form of binding between interfaces. (ii) Providing the behavior specification for each component identified in the task (i).

This paper aims at the task (ii), assuming the source code of the application is available. Naturally, an automatized way to extract component behavior specification is very desirable. Even though the reverse engineering techniques providing higher level behavior specification were already applied on object oriented software [3][4][6], and components [17], none of them targets the interplay of both the externally and internally triggered activities on provided and required interfaces from a single perspective.

1.2   Goals and Structure of the Paper

In this paper, we assume a behavior specification/formalism (BF) of the power of finite state machine and a component C implemented in an object oriented language (oo language). The component C conforms to an underlying component model which introduces at least the abstractions of provided and required interfaces, each grouping methods, and the execution model of which is based on method calls triggered by both external and internal activities (threads) of components.

Problem statement. The challenge is to find a mapping among the underlying component model abstractions (and their relations) used in C which can be captured both by BF and the oo language representation of C. Based on the mapping, an automatized transformation from the oo language representation of C into behavior specification of C in BF is to be defined. Here, the challenge is to keep a "reasonable" relation between the structure of implementation and the structure of specification (while preserving important aspects of behavior), although the expressive power of BF and oo language significantly differs. Keeping the relation is very important both for human comprehension and for interpretation of results of a further formal verification. To achieve this important property, certain degree of over-approximation is necessary despite loosing some details. Since the components encapsulate implementation details and thus exhibit externally observable behavior of less complexity, there is a good chance that a "reasonable" specification (in terms of size, accuracy) exists. Nevertheless, this assumes a good architecture structuring which really hides the implementation details. If this is not the case, result of the transformation should serve as a feedback to reverse engineering (task (i)) to structure the application in a better way.

Goal. The goal of this paper is to present a technique for extracting the behavior of a component given as a set of Java classes. The extraction is done in an automatized way and the target formalism is Behavior Protocols [1]. This technique has been partially applied in the JAbstractor tool for the SOFA component model [19].

This goal is reflected in the structure of the paper as follows. The formalism of Behavior Protocols and running example is presented in Sect. 2, while Sect. 3 introduces the technique of behavior extraction. The remaining sections are devoted to evaluation and discussion, related work, and a conclusion.

2 Background

2.1 Running Example

The following example will be used in the paper for illustration of the presented ideas. Fig. 1 depicts a fragment of an information system. The `SessionManager` component is intercepting all communication between user interface and application business logic and manages user sessions. When a user wants to log into the system, `UserInterface` asks `SessionManager` to create a new session by invoking the `createSession` method on the `session` interface. Once the new session id is returned, it is used in subsequent requests (`invokeCommand` method on the `session` interface) to indentify the session and user. Within the `invokeComand` method, the session id is checked and if valid, the command is passed together with user information to the business logic. If an inactive session is terminated by `SessionManager`, the user interface is notified via the `uiNotify` required interface. The Java implementation of the `SessionManager` and `RndGenerator` components is in Appendix A.

2.2 Behavior Protocols Basic

The formalism of Behavior Protocols (BP) is a high level specification capturing the finite sequences of method calls allowed on the component provided and required interfaces. Having a BP specification ("frame protocol") available for each component in a system, a composition operator serves to detect communication errors.

A primitive term in BP represents: accepting a method call `?interface.method{reaction}`, issuing a method call `!interface.method`, and empty action (`NULL`). Expressions use the following operators: '+' alternative, ';' sequence, '*' repetition, '|' parallel operator. More details are in [1][2].

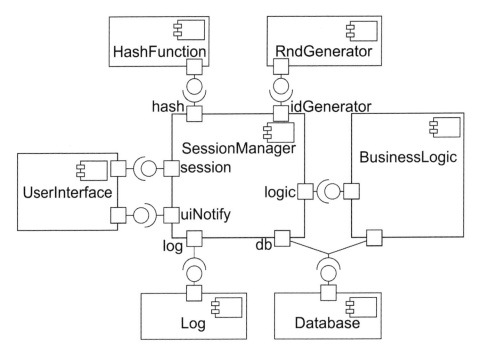

Fig. 1. Fragment of architecture of an information system involving the `SessionManager` component

The BP specification in Fig. 2 captures frame protocol of `SessionManager`. At the beginning, `SessionManager` opens the database connection (`!db.open`). Then, in parallel and repetitively, `SessionManager` can accept calls of `create-Session` and `invokeStatement`. Besides, there is an autonomous thread running in parallel, which notifies about session timeout. The reaction on `create-Session` first invokes `getHash` on the `hash` required interface to handle the password passed as a parameter. (Since parameters are not considered, just the

```
!db.open;(
(?session.createSession{
  !hash.getHash; (!db.query+NULL) ;
  ((!idGenerator.generate;!log.log) + (!log.log))
})*
|
(?session.invokeStatement{
  !log.log;!logic.invokeStatement+NULL
})*
|
(!uiNotify.sessionTerminated;!log.log)*
)
```

Fig. 2. Frame protocol of the SessinManager component in BP

method call is captured and no relation between parameters is apparent from the specification.) When the hash is returned, it is approved either by querying the database (!db.query) or (+ operator) the internal cache of SessionManager which does not have any externally observable effect (NULL). Depending on the result, new session id is generated (logged in any case).

At semantic level, a method call i.m is represented by pair of events (i.m↑, i.m↓) corresponding to issuing of method call and return from the method call. A component reaction may occur between them. BP expression semantics is given by an LTS labeled with those events. Composition of BP is then defined as synchronous product of the corresponding LTSs.

3 Strategy of Extraction

In principle, extracting a frame protocol from Java code of a component C boils down to finding a mapping among the underlying component model abstractions (and their relations) used in C which can be captured both by the frame protocol and the Java representation of C. Basically, the frame protocol determines what the reaction on a method call on a provides interface should be in terms of activities on the requires interfaces of C (reaction of an external thread activity), and, moreover, can determine autonomous activities on the required interfaces driven by an internal thread of C. Finally, the frame protocol determines what the corresponding interplay of both the externally and internally triggered activities should be (potential sequencing/interleaving, alternative execution, and repetition). Thus all these features have to be identified in the Java representation of C and mapped to the BP representation of the frame protocol of C. The following subsections describe how this can be done in three steps: (i) Extraction of reactions on method calls, (ii) Identification of autonomous activities (threads active on required interfaces, initialization), (iii) integration step defining the desired interplay of all activities (both external and internal).

In description of these steps, the Java representation of C is assumed to be provided in the form of a set of Java classes and architectural information mapping the Java concepts to the abstractions of the target component model. The architectural information consists of five Java declaration sets: $C^{Classes}$, $C^{Required}$, $C^{Provided}$ and C^{Init}. Here, $C^{Classes}$ contains the Java classes instantiated by the component model runtime infrastructure when a C's instance is being created. Then, $C^{Classes\bullet}$ contains all classes instantiated (transitively) from an element of $C^{Classes}$. $C^{Required}$ contains the member variables referencing the C's required interfaces, while $C^{Provided}$ contains the Java interfaces implemented by classes from $C^{Classes\bullet}$ (these Java interfaces correspond to C's provided interfaces). Finally, C^{Init} contains the initialization methods called by the component model runtime infrastructure when C is instantiated. The following properties hold for these sets (the relations here are defined intuitively): $A \in C^{Classes} \Rightarrow A \in C^{Classes\bullet}$; $A \in C^{Classes\bullet} \land A$ instantiates $B \Rightarrow B \in C^{Classes\bullet}$; $A \in C^{Required} \Rightarrow A\text{'parent} \in C^{Classes}$; $A \in C^{Provided} \Rightarrow \exists B \in C^{Classes}$ implementing A; $A \in C^{Init} \Rightarrow A\text{'parent} \in C^{Classes}$.

3.1   Extraction of a Reaction on a Method Call

The first step aims at capturing the BP specification of the effect of each method m from a C's provided interface. Precisely, m is a method of a class from $C^{Classes\bullet}$ and implements an interface from $C^{Provided}$. The effect of the method m is captured in terms of the corresponding events on the required interfaces of C – the specification captures the (externally) observable behavior performed by the component in reaction on any call of m. The basic idea is to "inline" all the internal objects' methods which appear in the calling chains defined by the Java body of m. The result of inlining is a method m^{inl} which contains only method calls on interfaces determined by $C^{Required}$.

For illustration, consider the implementation of the createSession method provided by SessionManager (Appendix A, line 37). Obviously createSession first invokes getHash on the hash interface. Then, the login name and password are checked and if valid, new session identifier is generated and returned as result. The validation is implemented by the internal object DBCache, which is accessing the required interface db.

In principle, the extraction omits all the behavior of m inexpressible in BP. The method m^{inl} is created from m in the following steps. First, all variables, parameters, and their usages are omitted, as well as the method calls that do not lead to a call on a required interface from $C^{Required}$. Then, method inlining is recursively applied, so that in m^{inl} remain only the method calls on members of $C^{Required}$ linked by control flow statements. Finally, empty control flow statements are removed. To convert the resulting m^{inl} into BP notation, the effect of Java control statements is transformed as defined in Table 1. As apparent from the table, all conditions are replaced by nondeterminism (an over-approximation).

For example, the resulting BP specification of the createSession method takes the form

```
createSession {!
    hash.getHash; (!db.query+NULL) ;
    ((!idGenerator.generate;!log.log) + (!log.log))
}
```

Table 1. Java statement to BP transformation

Java statement S	Corresponding protocol P(S)
requiredIf.method(p1,.. ,pn)	!requiredIf.method
S1;S2	$P(S_1);P(S_2)$
for(i;c;it) S1	$P(S_1)^*$
while(c) S1	$P(S_1)^*$
if (c) S1 else S2	$P(S_1) + P(S_2)$

switch   (e)   {
   case   a: Sa
   case   b: Sb
   ...
   default   Sd
 }
	$P(S_a)+P(S_b)+...+P(S_d)$

empty statement	NULL

There are more challenging issues in forming the reaction on a method call: (i) Any method m_i in Java is a virtual method, so that the actual implementation of m_i is selected at runtime. Thus, when a method m_i is being inlined into m, the call of m_i has to be replaced instead of single method body by a non-deterministic choice (the +operator) from all of the available implementations of m_i. In principle, points-to analysis [10] can be used to narrow the set of m_i implementations to those that can be actually called. (ii) All the method calls on the required interfaces of C have to be identified in the Java implementation. Although the fields referencing a required interface are statically captured in $C^{Requires}$, the reference can be copied to another variable (duplicated).

For illustration, the DBCache class (Appendix A, line 16) keeps the reference on required interface in variable db. This variable is initialized in the constructor, however it is not annotated. In this respect, a naïve solution is to consider all the variables sharing their type with a variable from $C^{Requires}$ also as referencing a required interface. However, this would not allow distinguishing two interface instances of the same type. A better solution is to use points-to analysis to distinguish different reference targets. (iii) During inlining, a recursive method may occur. Such recursive method definitely involves also a method call on an interface from $C^{Required}$ (otherwise it would be omitted in the previous step). Since exact number of iterations is not captured in BP anyway, such recursion can be replaced by non-deterministic loop.

Finally, the resulting BP specifications of m^{inl} have to be combined together – how this is done is described in Sect. 3.3

3.2 Extraction of Autonomous Activities

The goal of the second step is to create specification of the behavior performed by C on its own (as an active entity). In terms of Java, this means to analyze the behavior performed by the C's internal threads and initialization methods (an initialization method appears as an activity of C, since it is called by the underlying run time infrastructure of the component model, not by another component). Since this behavior is also explicitly expressed in Java, similar technique as the one described in Sect. 3.1 can be used for its extraction (transformation into BP). Initialization methods are given by the architectural information in C^{Init}.

A thread is considered to belong to C if its class is in $C^{Classes\bullet}$ and it is started by a method of a class in $C^{Classes\bullet}$, and it is accessing only $C^{Classes\bullet}$. However, a thread belonging to C that does not access any required interface does not contribute to the observable behavior of C and thus it is not interesting for the extraction.

For illustration, cleanupThread (Appendix A, line 79) is created and started during the initialization of SessionManager; it invokes cleanupOldSessions which modifies the data structure keeping the set of current sessions. Thus, the thread belongs to the SessionManager component. The result of this step is the BP specification of init and cleanupThread. Since init does not feature any (externally) observable behavior, its BP specification is db.open. The BP specification of cleanupThread can take the form (!uiNotify. sessionTerminated ; !log.log)*.

The thread concept in Java is quite powerful. There is no restriction posed on the number of thread instances, on the moment of start and termination, etc. On the other hand, due to the static nature of BP specification, extraction of thread behavior is possible only in specific cases though, e.g. for threads started within the initialization of C. This issue is more discussed in Sect. 5.

How the BP specifications produced in this step are combined together and how they are integrated with the results of the method reaction step is described in Sect. 3.3.

3.3 Integration Step

Finally, the third step puts the results of the previous steps together to state how the component C should be called in its provided interfaces and what the corresponding interplay of calls on its required interfaces is. As mentioned in Sect. 2.2 such specification of C's behavior expressed in BP is the frame protocol of C. The frame protocol states restrictions on the C's environment in terms of the allowed sequences/interleaving of method calls and internal thread actions. In contrast to the previous steps, information about the important mutual dependencies between individual code fragments is present in the primitive component code only in a "scattered way", since each method can contribute to the C's state modification differently and each state history implies specific desired call ordering. Moreover, the resulting frame protocol may also depend upon the actual usage of the component. However, the integration of the results of the previous two steps into a frame protocol is not a trivial task, having a straightforward generic solution. The following three approaches to frame protocol integration we found after many experiments most viable:

(a) *Maximal parallelism preventing race conditions.* If the C's implementation is protected from race conditions by an appropriate Java synchronization both in the provided methods and internal threads (the synchronization can be statically checked in both cases), the methods can be called in any order, even in parallel, and also in parallel with all the internal threads. Assuming C is initialized before any other action, the frame protocol takes the form

$$\text{init}; \, ?m_1\{r_1\}^* | \, ?m_2\{r_2\}^* | \ldots | ?m_n\{r_n\}^* | t_1 | \ldots | t_m \qquad \text{(I)}$$

where init is BP capturing the initialization phase, m_i is a name of a method, r_i is the reaction of m_i, and t_i is BP is specification of a thread. An example of (I) is the protocol in Fig. 2. When C is designed as single threaded (parallel execution of methods as well as existence of individual threads is not considered) the frame protocol may take a simpler form

$$\text{init}; \, (?m_1\{r_1\}+? \, m_2\{r_2\}+\ldots+? \, m_n\{r_n\})^* \qquad \text{(II)}$$

The frame protocols (I) and (II) are special cases considering all methods to be executed in parallel resp. sequentially. In general, however, C may feature groups of methods not allowed to be executed in parallel. Those groups may be identified by static analysis. In particular, static analysis can identify the pairs of methods that alternatively (i) may cause a race condition (may access the same variable without locking), (ii) are mutually excluded when accessing a shared variable, (iii) do not share a variable. To precisely characterize the pairs, we define a symmetric relation $RC(m,n)$ to hold for methods m and n if parallel execution of those methods may lead to race condition. Then, $RC^{\bullet}$ is a reflexive transitive closure of RC. $RC^{\bullet}$ is an equivalence relation and divides the set of methods into equivalence classes. Then, for each equivalence class E_i we create a protocol P_{Ei} by connecting methods call acceptance by + operator. Using these equivalence classes, the integrated frame protocol takes the form:

$$\text{init; } P_{Ei}* \mid \ldots \mid P_{Ek}* \mid t_1 \mid \ldots \mid t_m \qquad\qquad (III)$$

Such protocol, however, does not allow executing a method m many times in parallel even though the parallel execution can not cause a race condition ($\neg RC(m,m)$). To reflect this fact in the frame protocol and to allow g parallel executions of m, all occurrences of ?m in (III) can be safely replaced with ?m|...|?m, where m is repeated g times. The constant g can be determined from the component's environment [16].

As an example, consider again the `SessionManager` component. It provides two methods – `createSession` and `invokeCommand`. Although these methods share the field `activeSessions`, access to it is guarded by Java synchronization. Thus, these methods belong to different equivalence classes and the frame protocol takes form presented in Fig. 2 in Section 3.2. On the other hand, when the `RndGenerator` implementation from Appendix A is considered, there are also two methods – `generate` and `seed`, however in this case both of them access the same variable and the access is not mutually excluded. Thus, RC(`generate`, `seed`) holds and consequentially the frame protocol takes the form (`?randomGenerator.seed+?randomGenerator.generate)*`.

Note, that any pair of synchronized methods m_i and m_j (satisfying (ii)) is handled as if they were totally independent and satisfying (iii), falling thus into different equivalence classes. This is an over-approximation, since synchronized m_i and m_j bodies are never executed in parallel, even though the calls of m_i and m_j can be accepted in parallel.

(b) *Preventing the component from reaching an invalid state.* Although the frame protocols (I) – (III) indicate how an environment's usage should avoid race conditions within the component implementation, they still do not capture design dependencies of individual methods in terms of the desired sequences of their usage. As an example, consider the `RndGenerator` component which assumes the `seed` method is called before using the `generate` method (assume also, that this is checked in the code via an assertion – Appendix A, line 93). Thus, the resulting frame protocol of `RndGenerator` should take the form (`?idGenerator.seed; (?idGenerator.generate)*)*` to express this restriction and, as an aside, also the fact that `RandomGenereator` does not have to be used at all.

In general, if such a restriction is violated, the component is to reach an error state. To avoid the violation in the extracted frame protocol, such error states have to be explicitly determined. This can be done either directly by the user (e.g. by checking a predicate over member variables), or even implicitly (e.g., no low level exception is thrown). When error states are determined, elaborated approaches using model-checking can be used [4][6] to obtain the desired call sequencing. Here, the result of these methods is typically an LTS capturing the allowed sequences of method calls (parallelism is not considered). To form a frame protocol containing just method acceptation in BP, the LTS can be easily transformed to Behavior Protocol P using the algorithm from [12] since BP is based on regular expression. Then, the frame protocol is finalized by enhancing R by the reactions (such as r_i in (I)) provided by the Step 1 (Sect. 3.1).

(c) *Analysis of a complete application.* So far, approaches considering an isolated component C were discussed. However, having available an application using C correctly (in another words, an environment E_C of C is available), a valid usage specification can be obtained by analyzing E_C. Obviously, E_C must be correct in terms of C's usage and the result of the analysis does not yield the most general frame protocol of C, but captures only the behavior exhibited and employed by E_C. This can be improved by analyzing more applications using C (environments of C) and integrating the results. There are basically three approaches for analyzing E_C – runtime monitoring [3], static analysis [5] and state space traversal [13]. None of them, however, considers parallelism.

Overall, in order to provide a frame protocol featuring maximal parallelism, while still keeping the necessary sequencing of methods and preventing race conditions, the result provided by the approaches (b) and/or (c) can be improved by adding information from (a). Assuming the result of (b) or (c) in the form of BP, parallelism can be introduced in certain subexpressions of the repetition operator. Let us suppose a Behavior Protocol P in form $(P_1 + P_2 + \dots + P_n)^*$. As an aside, in a special case, P may thus take the form P_1^*. Then, we define a relation RC_P over the set of alternatives $\{P_1, \dots, P_n\}$. The relation RC_P holds for alternatives P_i and P_j if their parallel execution may lead to a race condition. RC_P is defined using the relation RC since their motivation is similar. In particular, $RC_P(P_a, P_b)$ holds if there is no method p invoked in P_a and no method q invoked in P_b such that $RC(p,q)$. Similar to the relation RC, the relation RC_P is symmetric and its reflexive transitive closure is denoted as $RC_P^\bullet$. Then, for each equivalence class E_i of $RC_P^\bullet$ we define a protocol P_{Ei} by connecting the alternatives from the equivalence class by the + operator. Then, the original protocol P can be replaced by protocol

$$P_{E1}^* \mid P_{E2}^* \mid \dots \mid P_{Ek}^* \qquad \text{(IV)}$$

Moreover, certain alternatives can run many times in parallel without risking a race condition which should be reflected in the frame protocol (alternatives P_i such that $\neg RC_P(P_i,P_j)$). Then, all occurrences of P_i in (IV) can be replaced by g copies of P_i connected by the parallel operator to allow g executions of P_i in parallel.

For illustration, consider the result obtained by method (b) for the implementation of the `RndGenerator` which takes form (`?idGenerator.seed;` (`?idGenerator.generate`)`*`)`*`. There are two repetition operators. There are no alternatives in the top level repetition operator (P_1^* form), so there is just one equivalence class E containing single protocol P taking the form `?idGenerator.seed;` (`?idGenerator.generate`)`*` and the associated protocol P_E is the same. Since `RC(seed,generate)` holds, the relation $RC_P(P_E,P_E)$ holds too. Thus, we can not put more protocols P_E in parallel in the result. In contrary, when the second repetition operator is taken in account, there are also no alternatives, thus there is single equivalence class and the associated protocol P_E takes the form `?idGenerator.generate`. However, here $RC_P(P_E,P_E)$ does not hold, as `¬RC(generate, generate)` and there is no other method in P_E. Thus, the overall result allowing two parallel invocations of the generate method takes the form (`?idGenerator.seed;` (`?idGenerator.generate`)`* | ?idGenerator.generate`)`*`)`*`.

4   Prototype Tool: JAbstractor

To evaluate and verify viability of the ideas presented in the previous sections, a proof-of-the-concept prototype tool (JAbstractor) has been developed. As input, JAbstractor takes Java source code of a primitive component. The code has to be compilable, which implies that also declarations of all the employed types are to be available. Since the static architecture reconstruction is separate task the architectural information (sets from Sect. 3) is defined via Java annotations directly in the code (those annotations can be obtained by an third party tool [7] or specified manually).

The current JAbstractor version extracts reactions on method calls (Sect. 3.1) using a sequence of AST transformations. It also detects autonomous threads created and started within initialization methods and extracts their behavior. Regarding the integration step of behavior extraction, just the simple solution using the frame protocol in the form (I) presented in Sect. 3.3 has been implemented so far.

To create an AST of a source code, JAbstractor uses the Recoder tool [9], which provides also an AST transformation framework. This is advantageously employed for the transformation of the provided methods (m to m^{inl}, Sect. 3.1) and autonomous activities (Sect. 3.2) – they are performed on their AST representations. Then, for each class A_i from $C^{Classes}$ a new Java class, $Merged^{Ai}$, is created. It represents the component's behavior exhibited through each interface I from $C^{Provided}$ implemented by the class A_i. The methods of the $Merged^{Ai}$ class correspond to the individual methods of the interface I.

Each $Merged^{Ai}$ class contains also initializing methods and fields for threads obtained in Sect. 3.2. In the source AST, threads are identified by invocation of the start method on the Thread class. The $Merged^{Ai}$ classes do not instantiate any other classes than threads, and do not contain other fields than those corresponding to $C^{Required}$. The final AST transformation translates the ASTs of $Merged^{Ai}$ classes into a BP AST to integrate the frame protocol in the form II introduced in Sect. 3.3.

The design of the tool is modular. In Sect. 3.1, it is suggested to use points-to analysis to improve results. Since we do not plan to provide an implementation of points-to analysis on our own, the tool just provides an interface to a general points-to analysis. Currently, there is just a naïve implementation based on type information; however, we plan to provide the points-to analysis implemented in the SOOT framework [11] through the general interface. Another modular aspect of JAbstractor is the way the architectural information is specified. There is an interface providing the information in the form of sets (Sect. 3) to the rest of the tool. The current implementation obtains the architectural information from Java annotations capturing the relation of declarations in the code to the abstractions of the SOFA component model.

5   Discussion and Related Work

In principle, an execution of a Java program on a specific computer can be modeled by FSM. The number of states, however, is extremely large bounded by 2^{memory_size}. In any case, such a FSM, besides being beyond the abilities of human comprehension, does not reflect the original structure of the Java program.

Nevertheless BP has the power of FSM. To make a BP specification useful, keeping the relation between the original structure of the component Java implementation and the extracted BP specification is very important both for human comprehension and for interpretation of results of a formal verification. To achieve this important property, certain degree of over-approximation via non-determinism is necessary despite loosing some details. In following paragraphs we focus on the effect of over-approximation employed in the extraction steps from Sect. 3.

Extraction of a reaction on a method call (Step1). A consequence of ignoring data and especially conditions in the extraction method proposed in Sect. 3.1 and Sect. 3.2 is the introduction of non-determinism into each control flow statement (over-approximation). Specifically, a loop with a number n of iterations is replaced by a finite number of iterations as well as bounded recursion. Similar comment goes to branching statements.

On the other hand, since the inlining is a straight-forward process, it always produces a result. Thus, there are no limits on the complexity of the interplay of activities on component's interfaces, however if the communication is really complex, the over-approximation can lead to spurious errors in a further formal verification (such as detection of communication errors as presented [14]).

Extraction of autonomous activities (Step 2). It has to deal with threads, their start and termination and also synchronization. Start is simple, but termination and synchronization relies on component state and method parameters ("data"), which are, however, ignored by inlining. Moreover, threads modeled in BP via parallel operator are limited to those which join in the context of the BP operator enclosing the parallel operator. For example in the protocol $?m\{t_1|\ t_2\}$ (i.e., $?m\uparrow;\ t_1|\ t_2;!m\downarrow$), neither t_1 nor t_2 can survive return from the method m. In consequence, a thread started in a method m and running beyond the return of m, can be modeled in BP only by dividing the thread into two sections – running inside m and another outside m. Similar issue is discussed in [15]. Also in this case, to reflect all possible divisions, the complexity of BP specification grows so that direct relation to the Java thread is blurred. Nevertheless, without considering data, it is hard to identify termination of Java threads. Thus, currently just the threads started during initialization and running indefinitely are supported.

Integration step (Step 3). The technique (a) inherently involves over-approximation. On the other hand, as mentioned in the conclusion of Sect. 3.3, combining the techniques (a) and (b) reduces the level of over-approximation. Nevertheless, the abstraction achieved by forming the frame protocol in the form (IV) is an important advantage in terms of explicitly specifying the required sequencing of methods calls when using the component. This is very important for an easy comprehension of the correct component usage, since this information is otherwise not apparent from Java interfaces (is hidden in the method code).

Overall. From the discussion above, it follows a need to reflect explicitly data in the extracted specification to lower the level of over-approximation while preserving a close relation to the Java code structure. There is already a candidate to replace BP extraction result form: the TBP specification [18] supports both, explicit notion of data (just enumeration types) and threads closer to Java capabilities (still a specific number).

Although introduction of data in the extraction process is a subject of future work, we have already identified individual steps and issues to be solved. First, it is necessary to identify data important for component "business" behavior. This typically means to identify member variables keeping the state of the component, method parameters significantly influencing the control flow of a method. Then, since TBP provides enumeration types only, a mapping of a source variable type into an enumeration type or replacement of a source variable by several variables of enumeration types have to be provided (introduces an abstraction). Identification of the important data and necessary mappings can be done manually by the user having a deep insight into the application structure. On the other hand, an automatized way seems to be possible: Quite promising is the idea of predicate abstraction.

When the information about important data is available it must be reflected by the extraction steps described in Sect. 3. In particular, inlining of methods implemented by different objects must also consider merging of those object's data. It is also desirable to employ again points-to analysis to identify the variables referencing the same instance. Also, statements and conditions referencing these important variables may not be considered as dead code.

Although whole paper considers extraction of a component's frame protocol in BP from the Java implementation, the overall idea, as well as individual steps, can be applied to different formalism of similar expressive power (FSM, resp. finite LTS) provided a suitable mapping of component model abstractions (provided/required interfaces, method call, autonomous activity) into the formalism is available.

Related work. A typical use case of a behavior specification extraction method is to make it easier to implement changes in legacy applications by describing desired interplay of calls on components interfaces and their relation to component autonomous activities. However, to enable the extraction and further formal verification, the architecture of a legacy application must also be provided. Here, the work [8] compares different approaches to static architecture extraction on general level. More specifically, the method [7] applies certain heuristics by means of static analysis of Java code to identify components and relations among them.

While the architecture extraction is a prerequisite to our method when dealing with legacy application, the following works aim at similar goal, even in a reduced form: They focus only on specification of method call acceptance (not considering required interfaces). None of them, however, deals with software components at such detail as we do (instead they deal with artifacts like classes and objects). Here, the approaches can be divided to several groups according to the technique used. The most straightforward technique is to employ monitoring of a running program to collect the information and then provide the specification capturing the monitored behavior. This is discussed in [3] where machine learning and stochastic methods are used to extract the behavior specification. Moreover, when the source code of the whole application is available, static analysis techniques can be used instead of monitoring. Quite advanced technique belonging to this other group is described in [5]. In particular, abstract interpretation is used to obtain abstract traces which are further transformed into a finite automaton. Obviously, this technique assumes correctness of the application. Another group form static analysis methods used on isolated classes; a representative can be found in [6], where, first, Boolean abstraction of the class is created using predicates provided by the user. The resulting abstraction is translated into the form required by the SMV model checker. Then, the model checker is queried by the L* algorithm to learn a finite machine model of the most general environment which does not allow the object to enter an invalid state.

Extraction of method effects from component implementation in Java via static analysis is presented in [17]. The technique is similar to our technique extracting method call reaction described in Sect 3.1. In addition, they focus on apparent relations between method parameters and branches and loops in the extracted method specification.

6 Conclusion and Future Work

In this paper we present a technique for an automated transformation of Java representation of SW components to their behavior specification in BP formalism. The technique is based on extraction of method reactions and extraction of autonomous activities. Results are integrated with the aim to maximize parallelism, to prevent the component to enter an invalid state by expressing the necessary call ordering. The technique was partially applied in the JAbstractor prototype tool.

In addition to propositions for future research mentioned in Sect. 5 (in particular replacing BP by TBP), more work has to be done on the JAbstractor tool. Currently, we are about to replace the Java representation provided by the Recoder tool by an EMF model. A long term goal is to develop a framework for evaluation of various extraction techniques able to exploit third party static analysis and model-checking tools.

References

[1] Plasil, F., Visnovsky, S.: Behavior Protocols for Software Components. IEEE Transactions on Software Engineering 28(11) (November 2002)
[2] Kofron, J.: Behavior Protocols Extensions, Ph.D. thesis, Charles University (September 2007), http://dsrg.mff.cuni.cz/~kofron/phd-thesis/
[3] Ammons, G., Bodík, R., Larus, J.R.: Mining specifications. In: Proc. of the 29th ACM SIGPLAN-SIGACT symposium on Principles of programming languages, Portland, Oregon (2002)
[4] Whaley, J., Martin, M.C., Lam, M.S.: Automatic extraction of object-oriented component interfaces. In: Proc. of the 2002 ACM SIGSOFT international symposium on Software testing and analysis, Roma, Italy (2002)
[5] Shoham, S., Yahav, E.: Fink. S., Pistoia M.: Static specification mining using automata-based abstractions. In: Proc. of the 2007 Int. Symposium on SW testing and analysis, London, United Kingdom (2007)
[6] Alur, R., Černý, P., Madhusudan, P., Nam, W.: Synthesis of interface specifications for Java Classes. In: Proc. of the 32nd ACM SIGPLAN-SIGACT symposium on Principles of programming languages (2005)
[7] Chouambe, L., Klatt, B., Krogmann, K.: Reverse Engineering Software-Models of Component-Based Systems. In: Proc. of CSMR 2008 (2008)

[8] Bowman, I.T., Godfrey, M.W., Holt, R.C.: Extracting source models from Java programs: Parse, disassemble, or profile? In: ACM SIGPLAN Workshop on Program Analysis for SW Tools and Engineering Toulouse, France (1999)

[9] Recoder Tool, http://apps.sourceforge.net/mediawiki/recoder/

[10] Schwartzbach, M.I.: Lecture Notes on Static Analysis (2008)

[11] Lhoták, O., Hendren, L.: Scaling Java Points-To Analysis using Spark. In: Hedin, G. (ed.) CC 2003. LNCS, vol. 2622, pp. 153–169. Springer, Heidelberg (2003)

[12] Hopcroft, J.E., Motwani, R., Ullman, J.D.: HUIntroduction to Automata Theory, Languages, and Computation. Addison-Wesley, Reading (2007)

[13] Giannakopoulou, D., Păsăreanu, C.: Interface Generation and Compositional Verification in JavaPathfinder. In: Chechik, M., Wirsing, M. (eds.) FASE 2009. LNCS, vol. 5503, pp. 93–107. Springer, Heidelberg (2009)

[14] Jezek, P., Kofron, J., Plasil, F.: Model Checking of Component Behavior Specification: A Real Life Experience. In: Electronic Notes in Theoretical Computer Science, vol. 160. Elsevier B.V., Amsterdam (2006)

[15] Parizek, P., Plasil, F.: Modeling of Component Environment in Presence of Callbacks and Autonomous Activities. In: Paige, R.F., Meyer, B. (eds.) TOOLS EUROPE 2008. LNBIP, vol. 11, pp. 3–22. Springer, Heidelberg (2008)

[16] Adamek, J.: Verification of Software Components: Addressing Unbounded Parallelism. Int. J. of Computer and Information Sci. 8(2) (2007)

[17] Kappler, T., Koziolek, H., Krogmann, K., Reussner, R.: Towards Automatic Construction of Reusable Prediction Models for Component-Based Performance Engineering. In: Proc. of Software Engineering (2008)

[18] Kofron, J., Poch, T., Sery, O.: TBP: Code-Oriented Component Behavior Specification. In: Proc. of SEW-32. IEEE, Los Alamitos (accepted for publication) (2009)

[19] Bures, T., Hnetynka, P., Plasil, F.: SOFA 2.0: Balancing Advanced Features in a Hierarchical Component Model. In: Proc. of SERA 2006. IEEE CS, Los Alamitos (2006)

Appendix A

Implementation of `SessionManager` and `RndGenerator` in Java. Annotations provide mapping of Java declarations into component model constructs.

```
1  @Provided interface Session {...}
2  @Provided interface RndGenerator {...}
3
4  public class SessionManager implements Session {
5    /* required interfaces */
6    @Required(name = "logic") BusinessLogic logic;
7    @Required(name = "hash") Hash hash;
8    @Required(name = "log") Log log;
9    @Required(name = "idGenerator")
10       RndGenerator idGenerator;
11   @Required(name = "uiNotify")
12       GUINotification uiNotify;
13   @Required(name = "db") Database db;
14
15   Map<Long, Date> activeSessions = new HashMap();
16   private DBCache dbCache;
```

```
17
18   private static class DBCache {
19     Map<String,String> userCache= new HashMap();
20     Database db;
21     public DBCache(Database database){
22         db = database;
23     }
24
25     public boolean loginQuery(String login,
26             String hashedPasswd){
27       String oldHashedPwd = userCache.get(login);
28       if (oldHashedPasswd==null){
29         if (db.loginQuery(login, hashedPasswd)){
30           userCache.put(login, hashedPasswd);
31           return true;
32         }
33         return false;
34       } else {
35           return hashedPasswd.equals(oldHashedPwd);
36       }
37     }
38   }
39
40   private void touchSession(long sessionId){
41     activeSessions.put(sessionId, new Date());
42   }
43
44   public synchronized long createSession(
45           String login,String passwd) {
46     String hashedPasswd = hash.getHash(passwd);
47     if (dbCache.loginQuery(login, hashedPasswd)){
48       long sessionId = idGenerator.generate();
49       log.log("User "+ login +" access granted");
50       touchSession(sessionId);
51       return sessionId;
52     } else {
53       log.log("User "+ login +" access denied");
54       return 0;
55     }
56   }
57
58   public synchronized String invokeCmd(
59           long sessionId, String command) {
60     String ret = null;
61     if (activeSessions.containsKey(sessionId)){
62       ret = logic.invokeCommand(command);
63       log.log("Command accepted: "+command);
64       touchSession(sessionId);
65     } else log.log("Command rejected: "+command);
66     return ret;
67   }
```

```
68
69    private Date getOldestTS(){…}
70
71    private void cleanupOldSessions(){
72      Date oldestTimestamp = getOldestTS();
73      Iterator it =
74          activeSessions.entrySet().iterator();
75      while (it.hasNext()) {
76        Entry<Long,Date> e = it.next();
77        Date entryDate = e.getValue();
78        if (oldestTimestamp.before(entryDate)){
79          it.remove();
80          uiNotify.sessionInvalidated(e.getKey());
81        }
82      }
83    }
84
85    @Start public void init(){
86      db.open("dbLogin", "dbLogin");
87      idGenerator.seed(1);//derived from time
88      dbCache = new DBCache(db);
89      Thread cleanupThread = new Thread(){
90        public synchronized void run() {
91          while (true) {wait(30000);}
92          cleanupOldSessions();
93          }
94        }
95      };
96      cleanupThread.start();
97    }
98  }
99
100 public class RandomGeneratorImpl
101     implements RndGenerator
102 {
103   long seed = -1;
104   public long generate() {
105     assert (seed!=-1);
106     return seed%13;//TODO: generate better
107   }
108   public void seed(long s) {
109     seed = s;
110   }
111 }
```

Towards Dynamic Component Isolation in a Service Oriented Platform

Kiev Gama and Didier Donsez

University of Grenoble, LIG, ADELE team
`kiev.gama@imag.fr, didier.donsez@imag.fr`

Abstract. When dealing with dynamic component environments such as the OSGi Service Platform, where components can come from different sources and may be known only during runtime, evaluating third party components trustworthiness at runtime is difficult. The traditional namespace based isolation and the security mechanisms provided in the Java platform (the base platform for OSGi) can restrict the access of such components but can not provide fault isolation. In this paper we present a dynamic component isolation approach for the OSGi platform, based on a recently standardized Java mechanism. When an untrusted component is activated during runtime, it is isolated in a fault contained environment but it can still collaborate with the application. If it is observed that the untrusted code does not bring any threat to the application, at runtime it can be dynamically promoted to the safe environment. Tests have been performed in a controlled environment where misbehaving components hosted in the sandbox were not able to disturb the main application.

1 Introduction

In Component Based Software Development (CBSD) one may not know in advance the impacts (e.g. runtime incompatibilities, errors leading to application crashes) of integrating third party components into an application. During development components can be tested (e.g. unit testing) as individual blackbox entities but component vendors may face combinatorial explosions when trying to validate their products against possible system configurations, and these combinations still grow if components can still be integrated after deployment of the system [39]. This is exactly the case of dynamic platforms where one may not predict which components are going to be deployed during application execution.

The OSGi Service Platform [29] is a component framework for the Java Platform, and is an example of such type of dynamic platform where components can be deployed, started, stopped or updated during runtime without stopping application execution. In dynamic environments as OSGi it is a frequent scenario having dependencies to service *interfaces* known at compile time but during runtime having the corresponding service *implementations* provided by possibly untrusted components dynamically deployed. The usage of OSGi in software industry has gained a strong momentum after the Eclipse Platform became one of its main adopters [10]. A large COTS market around OSGi is emerging [30] where third party components are becoming available increasingly, but defining their quality and trustworthiness is not a precise task. COTS quality models do exist, but they are difficult to be used due to the large quantity of attributes to be measured and the lack of information provided by component vendors [20]. The *reliability* characteristic (maturity, recoverability and fault tolerance as sub-characteristics) of those models is indirectly one of the attributes of component *trustworthiness*, which can be defined as measured and perceived dependability (a combination of reliability, safety, robustness, availability and security) [34].

As previously mentioned, fault isolation is an issue closely related to the reliability characteristic and can make composites stronger. It is indeed an essential theme in CBSD, since the strength of a composition is defined by its weakest component [39]. Since fault is a concept that has a very wide scope, we consider the concept from [23], which says that faults are the cause of errors (deviations from correct state) which may lead to system failures, thus being a threat to dependability. A detailed analysis [31] on component vulnerabilities in Java Service Oriented Platforms shows that some of them are caused by the lack of CPU and memory isolation between components, which is fundamental for fault isolation. OSGi uses class loader based namespace isolation, giving a sort of pseudo-isolation between components. However, namespace isolation is not robust enough for a multiple component vendor scenario where one cannot assure that such third party code behaves correctly. As all components and objects coexist in the same memory space without any mechanism that ensures object domains or other elaborate ways of isolation, components may introduce faults in applications:

- Inconsistencies and silent errors in the system when dynamicity is mishandled by components [7], caused by different factors such as incorrectly refactored applications and components.
- A component crash (e.g. stack overflow, out of memory exception) may bring the whole application down.

The objectives of this paper are: to provide a review on standard isolation mechanisms in the Java platform; and to present a component isolation approach for OSGi, based in one of the analyzed Java isolation mechanisms. The proposed mechanism allows untrusted components to execute in a fault contained sandbox that allows clean termination of components preventing any harm to the core (trusted) components environment enhancing applications' robustness and reliability. Our solution is based on a standardized Java Specification Request (JSR) that addresses isolation. However, by adding such isolation barriers, we are aware that a component communication overhead will be introduced. The intention is not to isolate each and every component since it would annihilate one of OSGi's main advantages, which is the fast communication between services and components.

The rest of this paper is organized as follows: section 2 details the standard isolation approaches in the Java Platform; section 3 analyzes the usage of those mechanisms for component isolation in different Java editions; section 4 highlights OSGi's isolation limitations; section 5 presents our proposed model and its implementation; section 6 describes related work; and finally, section 7 concludes and presents our perspectives.

2 Standard Isolation Mechanisms in Java

In this section we explore the standard isolation mechanisms that we have identified in the Java platform: namespace-based isolation, OS-based isolation and a relatively recent approach based on a sort of domain isolation.

2.1 Namespace-Based Isolation

As explained in [24], the class loader mechanism in Java provides the ability to dynamically load classes during application execution enabling features such as lazy loading; unloading of classes; multiple namespaces; and user extensibility through user defined class loading policies. These multiple namespaces are the standard form for achieving isolation in Java, where a class type is uniquely determined by the combination of class name and class loader. To better illustrate namespaces with class loaders, consider that two class loaders A and B co-existing in the same running application can load different versions of a foo.Bar class. Each class loader can apparently provide instances of the same class but in fact the provided foo.Bar objects are of different classes. By considering a fully qualified name notation to differentiate each class, as the one used in [24], we have something like <foo.Bar, A> and <foo.Bar, B> which visibly do not correspond to the same class.

The basic loading mechanism is based on a delegation principle inside a hierarchy. Before loading a given class, a child class loader asks its parent for that class. If the immediate parent can not find the class, this delegation continues until the top of the hierarchy. The hierarchy of class loaders defines that children can "see" the classes loaded by their parent, but not the contrary. Following that principle, sibling class loaders also can not share class definitions. However, this mechanism isolates code in different namespaces but does not ensure object instances living in isolated address spaces. Thus, namespaces do not bring the necessary robustness because faults in code residing in a class loader can affect other parts of the application.

2.2 OS-Based Isolation

This type of isolation is enforced by Operating System protection boundaries (e.g. processes in separated memory spaces). In Java this can be done with a combination of techniques by breaking a single application into multiple pieces running on different VMs (i.e. different processes) allowing application to be located in separate address spaces managed by the OS. Such type of isolation enables fault containment, thus a crash in a component would not bring the whole system down. However, using separate address spaces requires using relatively expensive inter-process communication in order to allow collaboration between the isolated components. In the case of Java it can be achieved either through sockets or higher level protocols such as RMI-IIOP. A significant disadvantage of such approach is exactly such type of cross-boundary communication overhead, as well as the memory footprint for each VM instance. Also, in the case of a component bringing a part of the application down, the restart of the crashed part would need to wait for the whole bootstrap of the VM and the component container/runtime. This solution may be resource consuming, especially in small devices, but in server application cases such as [22] the decision of isolating several web applications in different VMs had an acceptable performance overhead that was taken into account in their analysis.

2.3 Domain Isolation

The JSR 121 [15] is a relatively recent standardization effort for application isolation in Java. It defines the notion of Isolate, a first class representation of a strong isolation container with an API to control their lifecycle. The model proposed by the Isolate API does not specify how Isolates should be implemented. The strategy is implementation specific and could range, for example, from a per-isolate operating system process (e.g. using a standalone JVM) approach, to all-isolates in one process (i.e. same JVM) approach. The latter is used in the reference implementation provided by Sunlabs in the Multitasking Virtual Machine (MVM) [4], which realizes Isolates using a multitasking approach. The MVM allows several Java applications to run in the same OS process, where each isolate is a logical instance of the JVM, with logically separated heaps, and no objects that can be directly shared. A basic set of resources, like runtime classes and shared libraries, is shared by all isolates but applications run in complete isolation. In case of an application failure, only that application is impacted, not the JVM. Other applications are completely shielded from that application failure. Besides isolation, other advantages are the low memory footprint for multiple applications in the same VM and quick application startup.

The isolation achieved with Isolates is completely transparent. Legacy Java applications can be executed in Isolates without needing any additional changes. However, applications can be aware of the existence of Isolates and explicitly use the API. Although isolated, Java applications can achieve collaboration through previously existing mechanisms such as sockets and Remote Method Invocation (RMI), or through *Links*, which are part of the Isolate API. They provide a low-level layer for communication through basic data types such as byte arrays, buffers, serialized objects and sockets. The usage of isolates can make applications more robust by adding fault containment and clean application termination, serving also as a basis for enabling other features such as the Resource Consumption Management API [19].

3 Component Isolation in the Java Platform

Given the standardized mechanisms, we provide in this section a brief analysis of component isolation using such mechanisms in the Java Platform and the respective approaches for component collaboration across isolation boundaries. From the Java standard and enterprise editions we describe the isolation in Applets and Enterprise Java Beans (EJB), respectively; in the Java micro edition (ME) we show isolation in two application models: Midlets and the Xlets, from the CLDC[1] and the CDC[2], respectively; and finally we see the isolation approaches in Java Card Applets.

3.1 Applets

The isolation achieved with class loaders combined with security policies is fundamental for guaranteeing a sandbox where applets have restricted visibility of other applications and controlled access to system resources, enforced by security

---

[1] Connected Limited Device Configuration. http://java.sun.com/products/cldc/
[2] Connected Device Configuration. http://java.sun.com/javame/technology/cdc/index.jsp

verifications. This ensures that untrusted code (the applets) does not cause harm (e.g. accessing and damaging the file system) to the underlying system. The name-space based isolation through different class loaders guarantees that if a web page loads applets from different locations they do not have access to each other.

Applets are present in Java since the initial versions, when composition models were rudimentary and in the case of applets it could be done by placing the applets in the same web page [39] and letting them communicate via the AppletContext object. This can be possible only in the case of applets from the same code base, that is, the same directory on the server. Such rudimentary composition can not be possible when applets come from different locations.

3.2 Enterprise Java Beans

Isolation of EJBs is usually done in two flavors: either through class loaders name-spaces or by isolating components in different JVMs. In the former case, isolation fits in the class loading delegation principle previously described. Although there is no fixed structure for class loaders in Java EE, each vendor has its own implementation that follows the same principles. Fig. 1, based on an illustration from [1], illustrates a class loader hierarchy in Java EE.

Class loaders in grey, on the top of the hierarchy on Fig. 1, are the standard Java class loaders provided by the platform. The other class loaders represent a general Java EE class loading scheme. Every Enterprise Application Archive (EAR) will have its own class loader that will provide each application with its own namespace [1].

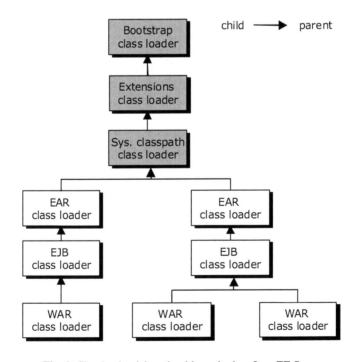

Fig. 1. Classloader delegation hierarchy in a Java EE Server

All EJBs of the EAR will be loaded by the same class loader, thus sharing the same namespace. Each Web Application Archive (WAR) is deployed with its own class loader and will not have class visibility to other sibling application.

The whole EJB model was conceived with distribution in mind, thus remote communication is supported by the component container. The infrastructure for EJB communication is based in a message based IPC approach that uses the RMI-IIOP protocol. Thus EJBs can also be isolated by separating them in different VMs. A crash in one component would not directly affect components hosted in other VMs. However, this choice leads to problems such as scalability and memory footprint. The cost of isolating components in separate VMs hosting heavyweight runtimes such as EJB containers would be expensive in terms of resources; communication overhead and coordination. An experimental isolation approach [14], which is detailed on the related work section, takes advantage of isolates for providing different levels of isolation in J2EE servers.

3.3 Midlets

The Mobile Information Device Profile (MIDP) for CLDC introduces the concept of MIDlets, which are managed applications with a life cycle similar to Java applets. MIDP has been conceived to execute in constrained devices where Java MIDlets would usually execute one at a time with security constraints concerning aspects such as visibility of types restricted to the same MIDlet suite. The MIDlet security model enforces that each MIDlet suite must run in isolation, but concerns were mostly related to type visibility since initial versions of MIDP executed one MIDlet at a time. Starting from MIDP 3.0 [18], parallel execution of MIDlets is specified. The Inter-MIDlet Communication (IMC) protocol, similar to sockets, would allow two MIDlets to establish communication by means of a channel, enabling communication and possibly some rudimentary composition such as in the case of applets. Although communication is possible using the IMC protocol, runtime isolation is enforced: MIDlets must not be able to have access to the variables or memory from each other, having their own executing spaces. They will always run in different contexts when executed. The isolation concept also applies to the usage of shared libraries (LIBlets), with the set of classes and resources of a LIBlet behaving (e.g. per-context static variable value) as if they were packaged with the MIDlet.

Multitasking is already being used as a way for isolating applications with less memory footprint [36] in CLDC devices. The Sqwak Virtual Machine [38] is another multitasking VM targeting the CLDC but for the Information Module Profile [16], which consists on a profile for devices without graphical display capabilities. Both of those approaches are based on Isolates, which appears to be the next generation standard for multitasking in upcoming JVMs.

3.4 Xlets

The Personal Basis Profile (PBP) [17] for CDC provides an application model based on Xlets which are managed applications originally defined for the Java TV API. The Xlet application model resembles Java applets and MIDlets, providing also small applications with life cycle (init, start, pause, destroy). PBP provides a means of communication between Xlets with the Inter-Xlet Communication (IXC) mechanism, which uses a subset of Java RMI. Xlets executing in the same virtual machine are able to exchange objects across class loader boundaries. Although such communication takes place in the same VM, it relies on RMI proxies. An Xlet can register an object in the IXC registry. Other Xlets running on the same VM can perform a lookup in the registry to retrieve the object that is bound to the queried name. The result is a dynamically generated stub that implements the same remote interface of that object. Since code is running in different class-loaders, the class definitions are not shared. The client Xlet must have the same interface type of the requested object packaged with its application so it can correctly retrieve the corresponding stub instances.

The approach above described fits in the initial CDC VM monolithic versions that provide class loader based namespace isolation. The CDC Application Management System (AMS) [37] introduces process-based application management, where all Java applications run in native processes coordinated by the AMS. The IXC would continue working as the communication mechanism between Xlets, but in a more robust environment with fault isolation and clean application removal.

3.5 Java Card Applets

In the Java Card platform, applications are called applets (*card applets* for disambiguation). A firewall mechanism isolates card applets from each other by mean of contexts, which are separate protected object spaces. It enforces security constraints and provides a secure environment where card applets may not access each other's functionality unless explicitly specified through shareable interfaces (SI). These contexts provide a sort of object domain in terms of data visibility, but do not provide fault isolation. The separate spaces and security mechanisms do not prevent an unhandled fault from halting the VM, as described in its specification: "As the Java Card virtual machine is single-threaded, uncaught exceptions or errors will cause the virtual machine to halt". Thus, a misprogrammed card applet that provokes a StackOverflowError, for example, affects all loaded applets. This applies also to the most recent Java Card specification (v. 3.0), which in addition to context isolation also provides *code isolation* in the connected edition. This type of isolation is implemented using the traditional class loader delegation hierarchy that provides separate class namespaces. Communication between card applets is still through SIs, but with the class loader hierarchy principle implies that the SI implementations be loaded by a higher level class loader so they can be visible to all card applets, which are all potential invokers of the shared object.

3.6 Summary

The predominant way for component isolation in Java is by means of class loaders, which allow separate namespaces that give less robust isolation. However a trend towards multitasking in the embedded market is observed as a means to enhance isolation. The utilization of Isolates allow programmatic access to an API for starting and controlling the execution of an application container that transparently provides strong isolation, enabling fault containment and a much more robust isolation mechanism than the one provided by class loaders. EJBs components can take advantage of isolation either with namespaces or in separate VMs, since these components where conceived for a distributed model where inter-VM communication is natural, but choosing to host individual EJBs in separate VMs leads to a rather complicated problem that would compromise scalability. Table 1 presents a summary of some isolation characteristics for each analyzed type of component approach.

Table 1. Isolation overview on the Java Platform

Component/Application Model	Isolation mechanism	Fault Containment	Collaboration
Java Applets	Namespace	No	Direct access
Local EJB	Namespace	No	Direct access
Remote EJB	OS based	Yes	RMI-IIOP
Midlets (MIDP 3)	Domain based[3]	Yes	Socket-like
Xlets[4]	OS based	Yes	IXC (RMI)
JavaCard V.2.x Applets	Domain-like[5]	No	Direct access
JavaCard V.3 Applets, Connected edition	Namespace	No	Direct access

4   Isolation in OSGi

The OSGi framework is a dynamic service platform for the construction of modular Java applications, allowing the installation, uninstallation, update and startup of components and services with no application reboot. OSGi components are called bundles, which are the platform's unit of deployment consisting of jar files with custom manifest attributes for defining, for example, information about versioning, package (type) dependencies and provided packages. Optionally bundles may provide services, which are published in a central registry that can be queried by service consumers, allowing component collaboration with loose coupling through service interfaces. After service binding, the consumer code directly references the servant object, without any proxies

The isolation level in OSGi is in fact a sort of enhanced namespace isolation by means of individual class loader instances provided for each bundle. The class loading mechanism follows some policies for loading types, basically considering the information provided by the Import-Package and Export-Package manifest attributes. Instead of a child to parent visibility in a tree hierarchy, the class loading in OSGi is rather a graph (Fig. 2), where sibling class loaders may provide classes between them.

Misprogrammed components are a concern since component developers that target the OSGi platform need to be aware of the dynamics in the environment, needing to appropriately release references to departed objects. When a service becomes unregistered, the referrer code is notified and must release the reference to the corresponding

---

[3] If utilizing the CLDC MVM.
[4] Considering the utilization of the CDC AMS.
[5] There is no traditional classloading in JavaCard v2.2.2, but its isolation model through firewalls does not provide fault isolation, as in JSR121 domain isolation.

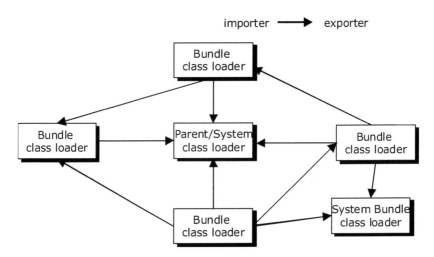

Fig. 2. Illustration of the classloading graph in OSGi

service. This unregistration may be due to a service implementation reacting (e.g. unregistering itself) to application or environment changes or due to the service providing bundle going to a process of deactivation (stopped, updated or uninstalled). Such type of dynamic events may happen frequently in such type of platform, and may incur problems known as stale references [7]. Static validation at load time would be a possibility for checking the occurrence of such problems, but that process is too costly, especially if the target platform runs on a resource limited device.

5   Dynamic Component Isolation

The OSGi specification tries to be as simple and lightweight as possible. Its direct object referencing brings the advantage of fast communication but it may impose problems if components do not handle correctly the inherent dynamicity of that platform. Other sorts of misbehavior, especially from untrusted third party components may also introduce faults, but such cases do not necessarily concern malicious components since a fault may happen due to lack of proper testing, or integration issues, for example. Security policies and class loading provide a limited level of isolation but no robustness.

Software-based isolation [40] introduces the concept of *sandboxes* for isolating in the process level untrusted modules and for providing fault containment, which is seen as a strategy for preventing error propagation across defined boundaries [27]. The term *sandboxing* has gained a wider sense throughout the years and now is often used to generally describe similar isolation techniques for preventing the underlying system to be harmed.

Therefore, in order to achieve such containment we needed to establish boundaries for separating components. Although there are custom VMs that provide object isolation in the Java platform through non-standard mechanisms, we wanted a solution focusing on technology that is standardized. We have chosen Java Isolates as our isolation boundaries for a few reasons: Isolates come from an official specification (JSR-121); its concepts are a trend for isolation and multitasking approaches that have been already tested with success in CLDC VMs; it continues to serve as an enabler for other features such as the ongoing effort of the resource consumption API [19] for Java.

Our component isolation mechanism for the OSGi platform tries to increase application robustness and dependability, in such a way that we can provide a sandbox where untrusted components are put in quarantine in a separate container where they can execute without harming (either intentionally or unintentionally) the application. In case a component misbehaves, or becomes stale, the sandbox can be restarted and the component can be safely terminated without needing to bring down the whole application. This type of isolation fills the well-isolated pre-condition for microrebooting [3] (individual rebooting of fine-grain application components). However, even if components are designed independently they are meant to collaborate as a part of a framework [28]. We have a means for isolating components but they still need to collaborate. Communication across boundaries is also provided in our approach, which is detailed in the next sub-sessions.

The implementation of the isolation solution described here was done in OpenSolaris with Sunlabs' Multitasking Virtual Machine[6] (MVM). We have patched the Apache Felix[7] v. 1.4.0 OSGi implementation for enabling the isolation solution using the JSR121 (Isolate API).

5.1 Isolation Mechanism

The solution provided in [8] uses services as the grain of isolation. The principle is also applied here, but in a coarser grain. While that solution focuses on service isolation via proxies in the same VM, the one described here focuses on separating components in isolated domains. The semantics is the same, as generalized in the meta-model from Fig. 3.

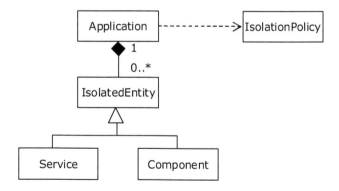

Fig. 3. Meta-model with the general isolation approach used either with services or components

---

[6] http://mvm.dev.java.net
[7] http://felix.apache.org

At runtime, when a given entity (i.e. a service or a component) is about to be activated (retrieved in the case of a service, and started in the case of a component) then the system verifies if that entity must be isolated, and proceeds with the isolation process if necessary.

Since OSGi consists of a dynamic platform, our isolation model also needs to be dynamic. The sandboxing is done selectively, and at runtime, only for untrusted components which are then grouped in the sandbox. Faults are quarantined in that isolated container, and can not interfere in the main environment. The mechanism also allows the component to be promoted from the quarantine to the main platform during application runtime, currently upon human decision based on application behavior observation. For the dynamic component isolation, upon installation of an OSGi bundle, the customized framework performs a policy verification against the bundle jar file in order to know if it must be isolated or not. Implementations for the policy verification may vary: it can be done based on signed jar files, CRC verification, etc.

Our current policy implementation simply verifies a list of known jar files to see if the deployed jar is known. If the jar does not pass the verification, it is installed in the main platform but marked as "untrusted". At startup time, when dependencies have been resolved, the platform will not start the untrusted jar in the main platform, but install that untrusted bundle and its dependencies on the sandbox and then perform the start up in the isolated environment, as illustrated in Fig. 4 showing that bundle C depends on types provided by bundle B which is also deployed in the sandbox but not started. As there is no dependency to Bunde A, there is no need to copy it to the sandbox. Thus, there are some rules concerning deployment:

- The main platform will always have all application bundles deployed, but no *untrusted* bundle in the *started* state;
- The sandbox will have untrusted bundles plus their dependencies, but no dependency in the *started* state, unless a dependency is also an untrusted bundle;
- No replicated bundle will be in the started state in both platforms at the same time.

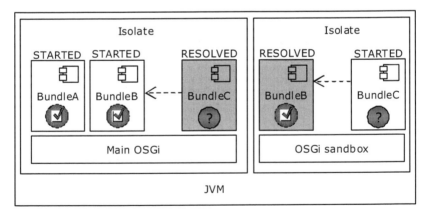

Fig. 4. Current deployment approach for dependency resolving in the sandbox. Untrusted bundles are also deployed in the main platform, but started only in the sandbox.

Although the duplication of components can increase memory footprint, and potentially load the same classes both in the main platform and in the sandbox, there are mechanisms that could reduce the cost of loading the same class representation multiple times in custom application class loaders [5], which is the case in OSGi. By hosting a component in a separate object domain (the sandbox) there will also be performance impact of the communication cost for trespassing the domain barrier if the sandboxed component needs to use services from a component in the main OSGi platform, and vice-versa.

5.2 Components Communication

In the OSGi platform, components establish communication through services which is done directly. In the case of our OSGi isolation mechanism, if an untrusted component needs to use a service provided by a trusted component, or vice-versa, the method calls need to cross the isolation boundaries that separate the service consumer and provider. This is done transparently by dynamic service proxies over a simple communication protocol which we have implemented. There is a two step process for retrieving a service instance in OSGi: query the service registry for a `ServiceReference` object, and then use that object for retrieving the actual service instance. In our implementation, if the requested service reference is not found in the local registry, the query is sent to the isolated platform. In case of a match the requestor gets an `IsolatedServiceReference` object, which is an instance of `ServiceReference`, and then requests the corresponding service which would be a dynamic proxy implementing the requested service interface. The proxy delegates the calls to the isolated platform using our protocol. The usage of service proxies evidently adds an overhead for proxy creation and subsequent method calls on the proxy. The service orientation without the communication overhead is one of the advantages of OSGi over other service oriented platforms. However, the goal of our proposed isolation mechanism is not to completely forbid the OSGi's standard proxyless service referencing. In the mechanism described here, the communication between services co-located in the same container is still done via direct object referencing.

This proof of concept has been implemented using `javax.isolate.Links`, a JSR-121 specific API for communicating between Isolates, but the communication layer has been abstracted in such a way that the details of the communication implementation can be easily changed to another approach. In doing so, the component isolation solution could be ported to non-multitasking VMs, but with the additional cost of a whole JVM footprint (besides its startup). The `Link` usage could be replaced by sockets, or even RMI. The protocol which we have written had a small set of messages for installing untrusted bundles in the sandbox; querying services in the isolated platform; invoking isolated services; sending framework events (Service and Bundle). This initial implementation focused on feasibility before giving any attention to performance. After performing simple microbenchmarks, we have identified that service calls using our protocol over the `Link` implementation did not perform better than ordinary RMI method calls outside the OSGi environment. More than 2/3 of the overhead was exactly in the synchronization of reading and writing on Links. Most likely this is due to the fact that the communication model used by Isolates is very simple and frequent transmission of messages may cause a large overhead [2]. Anyhow, optimizations can still be performed. Although it has outperformed our approach, if we choose to use RMI this implies in more complexity since it needs to add marker interfaces (`javax.rmi.Remote`) to the isolated services needing to be called across domain boundaries, methods need to throw a remote exepction and both isolated platforms (the main one and the sandbox) would need their own RMI object servers to be managed.

Crashes due to misbehaving code from untrusted component bring only the sandbox down, without any harm to the rest of the application. In such cases the platforms coordinator needs to bring back the sandbox and reestablish the communication channel that has been disrupted, by sending new and valid Link objects to the main platform. During this process, before restarting the sandbox and restablishing communication the main platform has to invalidate and to notify the departure of all isolated proxy clients and `IsolatedServiceReferences`.

In our controlled experiment we automatically deployed untrusted bundles in the remote platform after an attempt to install it in the main platform. The following test cases were performed on components providing services using primitive types:

- `StackOverflowErrors` intentionally fired have brought isolated components down along with the sandbox, but the sandbox could be automatically rebooted.
- Stale services (unregistered services that are still and erroneously being used by service consumers) would have their isolated proxies invalidated, similar to [8]. Misprogrammed sandboxed bundles did not prevent the unregistered services from the main platform from being appropriately released and garbage collected.
- Manual runtime promotion of sandboxed components to the main platform.

Although we have not addressed resource accounting, by using the sandboxing approach we can enable that in the component level if we consider isolate one component at a time. A multiple sandbox mechanism would add complexity concerning deployment and communication coordination, but would be a way to achieve fine grained isolation and resource accounting.

5.4 Current Limitations

As it was developed as a proof of concept, there are limitations in this isolation approach that were not yet addressed: policy implementation is just based on a file list, parameters and return types on proxied services are limited to primitives, Strings, and arrays of those types; the current isolation solution enables only one "shared" sandbox, where all untrusted components are executing. A misbehaving untrusted component will affect (e.g. stale services, stale threads, sandbox crash) all components that coexist in the sandbox. Only primitive, String attributes and properties map are available in `BundleEvent` and `ServiceReference` that come from an isolated platform. There is no unified identifier, that is, an untrusted bundle has a given id in the main platform, and most likely a different id in the sandbox platform.

6 Related Work

Other platforms already address the type of isolation we want to provide in OSGi applications. For instance, Microsoft COM components can be either loaded in the client application process or provided in an isolated process [25]. In the latter case, a surrogate process (dllhost.exe) can load the DLL and act as a server. Communication is transparently done via inter-process communication, bringing performance overhead but enabling fault isolation between the client and the component server. The Microsoft .NET platform addresses isolation as well, by means of Application Domains [35], which are like lightweight processes using the same concept that Java uses with Isolates. These domains have fault isolation: one domain can be terminated without interfering in the other domains' execution. Communication across domain boundaries is done in an RPC fashion where objects are sent via marshalling. Application domains can be dynamically loaded but would have unloading limitations if used for implementing a dynamic platform [6] such as OSGi.

Singularity [11] is a Microsoft research micro-kernel OS built with managed code. Instead of having processes isolation ensured by memory isolation, it uses software-isolated processes which have a communication overhead smaller than ordinary OS based process isolation. Secure object access is enforced by using static analysis (code is verified ahead of execution), and by not allowing run-time code generation.

A research [2] performed on alternatives for Java application isolation and resource accounting mentions component isolation as a means of preventing unwanted side effects and full resource reclamation. The paper provides an overview of the issue by presenting non-standard JVM solutions which try to tackle isolation and resource accounting. The custom isolation solutions presented would not be suitable to the dynamicity of OSGi, and even clash with its custom classloader approach. Our technique tries to be compliant with standardized VM mechanisms, such as JSR121 (which is also mentioned in that work) as well as enabling the architecture to work with multiple standard JVMs if no multitask VM is available. An experimental approach [14] uses the Isolate API and the MVM for improving isolation in a J2EE server. They evaluate different grains of isolation, like fine grained individual servlet isolation, and coarse grained isolation where they introduce J2EE application domains. Restructuring the code for isolating servlets individually was difficult, which lead them to discard the implementation of other fine grained isolation cases (e.g. EJBs). Coarse grain isolation of application domains combining the isolation of whole J2EE applications with the isolation of sub-servers (e.g. WebServer, Database, JMS) seemed to be a feasible choice for production servers.

Approaches like FreeBSD Jails [21] provide virtual environments that work as isolated compartments where a user have access only to processes and files from its own "jail" without having access to resources from other jails. Some approaches targeting isolation in the OSGi platform use virtualization [33, 26] as a way for isolating different customer platforms, that is, each provider would host their components and services in its own virtualized platform without accessing other providers' environment. Access to services from the underlying platform can be through a predefined subset [33] or transparently without restrictions [26]. However, the virtualization happens in the same JVM, where multiple OSGi platform instances execute. A malfunctioning component crashing in one platform would bring down all virtualized OSGi instances.

Another mechanism [9] combines JSR121 concepts with an extensible VM. They present JVM domains which allow lightweight isolation with the possibility to identify to what domain (i.e. a bundle) an object belongs to. They took the design decision of keeping direct object referencing as a way to keep the fast communication that exists in OSGi, however boundaries for fault containment are not mentioned.

R-OSGi [32] deals with the communication between services located in OSGi platforms in different machines, with the advantage of not being bound to any OSGi implementation. Service consumer proxy bytecode is dynamically generated and loaded as a bundle into the platform, which significantly increases the number of executing bundles, but it is managed by the R-OSGi core. R-OSGi could also be seen as a way of OSGi component isolation, but there is no complete unawareness of distribution in the client code, which in the most transparent case still needs wrapper code to adapt a system to distribution. In our approach we want to leave the isolation decision to the executing platform based on the isolation policies.

Security policies are also a form of isolating a component from having access to certain application APIs or system resources. Although security is an optional layer in OSGi implementations, it adds fine grained access to services and types. It is possible, for example, to prevent one component from having access to another by declaring that one of its provided services needs access permission. A practical implementation of OSGi application isolation enforced by security policies is presented in [12]. However, security policies would not provide fault containment in that case.

7 Conclusions and Perspectives

In this paper we have analyzed component isolation in the Java platform and in the OSGi service platform, a dynamic component platform for Java. We have described our dynamic component isolation approach for OSGi, implemented on top of a mechanism based on an official standard for isolated domains in Java. Our architecture allows its extension for working with multiple JVMs if no multitask VM is available. The isolation approach we propose adds a fault contained sandbox for the execution of untrusted components, enhancing application robustness and dependability. Isolated components that misbehave or become stale can be microrebooted by restarting only the sandbox, without bringing down the whole application. However, choosing to enhance isolation levels between components implies in a trade-off where the cost for components communication increase. The initial mechanism constructed on top of JSR121 Links did not perform as well as standard RMI calls (outside an OSGi environment). Our base tests using a controlled environment have validated the dynamic isolation without losing the collaboration between isolated components. Tests verified isolated faults, automatic sandbox reboot, correct reclamation of unregistered services and dynamic promotion of untrusted code to the trusted environment. This type of isolation could enable resource accounting in the component level.

Next activities consist in working on the current limitations, especially the improvement of the communication between isolates and the support to complex types in interface methods, as well as implementing a two-level isolation which combines the in-VM service isolation via proxies with the present component isolation approach. Automation of the component's promotion from the sandbox to the main platform is also desired and also tests outside the controlled environment in existing OSGi based applications are also necessary in order to validate our approach in a real scenario.

Acknowledgements. Individual thanks to the anonymous reviewers for their valuable feedback and Laurent Daynès from Sun Microsystems for his review, suggestions on the paper, and the discussions about Isolates. Part of this work has been carried out in the scope of the ASPIRE project (http://www.fp7-aspire.eu), co-funded by the European Commission in the scope of the FP7 programme under contract 215417. The authors acknowledge help and contributions from all partners of the project.

References

1. Allamaraju, S., et al.: Professional: Java Server Programming J2EE. Wrox Press (2001)
2. Binder, W.: Secure and Reliable Java-Based Middleware – Challenges and Solutions. In: 1st International Conference on Availability, Reliability and Security. ARES, pp. 662–669. IEEE Computer Society, Washington (2006)
3. Candea, G., Kawamoto, S., Fujiki, Y., Friedman, G., Fox, A.: Microreboot — A technique for cheap recovery. In: 6th Symposium on Operating Systems Design & Implementation (2004)
4. Czajkowski, G., Daynès, L.: Multitasking without Compromise: a Virtual Machine Evolution. In: The 16th conference on Object-oriented programming, systems, languages, and applications (OOPSLA), New York, USA, pp. 125–138 (2001)
5. Daynès, L., Czajkowski, G.: Sharing the runtime representation of classes across class loaders. In: The European Conf. on Obj. Oriented Progr., Glasgow, UK (2005)
6. Escoffier, C., Donsez, D., Hall, R.S.: Developing an OSGi-like service platform for.NET. In: Consumer Comm. and Networking Conf., USA, pp. 213–217 (2006)
7. Gama, K., Donsez, D.: A Practical Approach for Finding Stale References in a Dynamic Service Platform. In: Chaudron, M.R.V., Szyperski, C., Reussner, R. (eds.) CBSE 2008. LNCS, vol. 5282, pp. 246–261. Springer, Heidelberg (2008)
8. Gama, K., Rudametkin, W., Donsez, D.: Using Fail-stop Proxies for Enhancing Services Isolation in the OSGi Service Platform. In: MW4SOC 2008, pp. 7–12. ACM, New York (2008)
9. Geoffray, N., Thomas, G., Folliot, B., Clément, C.: Towards a new Isolation Abstraction for OSGi. In: Engel, M., Spinczyk, O. (eds.) The 1st Workshop on Isolation and integration in Embedded Systems. IIES 2008, pp. 41–45. ACM, New York (2008)
10. Gruber, O., Hargrave, B.J., McAffer, J., Rapicault, P., Watson, T.: The Eclipse 3. 0 platform: Adopting OSGi technology. IBM Systems Journal 44(2), 289–300 (2005)
11. Hunt, G., et al.: An Overview of the Singularity Project. Technical Report MSR-TR-2005-135, Microsoft Research (2005)
12. Jahn, M., Terzic, B., Gumbel, M.: Do not disturb my circles – Application isolation with OSGi. OSGi Community Event, Berlin (2008)
13. Java Card Technology, http://java.sun.com/javacard/
14. Jordan, M., Daynès, L., Jarzab, M., Bryce, C., Czajkowski, G.: Scaling J2EE™ application servers with the Multi-tasking Virtual Machine. Softw. Pract. Exper. 36(6), 557–580 (2006)
15. JSR 121: Application Isolation API Specification, http://jcp.org/en/jsr/detail?id=121
16. JSR 195: Information Module Profile, http://jcp.org/en/jsr/detail?id=195
17. JSR 217: Personal Basis Profile 1.1, http://jcp.org/en/jsr/detail?id=217

18. JSR 271: Mobile Information Device Profile 3,
    http://jcp.org/en/jsr/detail?id=271
19. JSR 284: Resource Consumption Management API,
    http://jcp.org/en/jsr/detail?id=284
20. Kalaimagal, S., Srinivasan, R.: A retrospective on software component quality models. SIGSOFT Software Engineering 33, 1–10 (2008)
21. Kamp, P.H., Watson, R.N.M.: Jails: Confining the omnipotent root. In: Proceedings of the 2nd International SANE Conference (2000)
22. Kwiatek, M.: Cluster Architecture for Java Web Hosting at CERN. In: The 15th International Conference on Computing In High Energy and Nuclear Physics, Mumbai, India, pp. 528–531 (2006)
23. Laprie, J., Randell, B.: Basic Concepts and Taxonomy of Dependable and Secure Computing. IEEE Trans. Dependable Secur. Comput. 1(1), 11–33 (2004)
24. Liang, S., Bracha, G.: Dynamic Class Loading in the Java Virtual Machine. In: OPSLA 1998, pp. 36–44 (1998)
25. Lowy, J.: 2001 COM and.NET Component Services, 1st edn. O'Reilly & Associates, Inc., Sebastopol (2001)
26. Matos, M., Sousa, A.: Dependable Distributed OSGi Environment. In: MW4SOC 2008, pp. 1–6. ACM, New York (2008)
27. Nelson, V.P.: Fault-Tolerant Computing: Fundamental Concepts. IEEE Computer 23(7), 19–25 (1990)
28. Nierstrasz, O., Dami, L.: Component-Oriented Software Technology. Object-Oriented Software Composition. Prentice-Hall, Englewood Cliffs (1995)
29. OSGi Alliance, http://www.osgi.org
30. OSGi Alliance. About the OSGi Service Platform, Technical Whitepaper Revision 4.1 (June 7, 2007), http://www.osgi.org/wiki/uploads/Links/OSGiTechnicalWhitePaper.pdf
31. Parrend, P., Frénot, S.: Classification of Component Vulnerabilities in Java Service Oriented Programming (SOP) Platforms. In: Chaudron, M.R.V., Szyperski, C., Reussner, R. (eds.) CBSE 2008. LNCS, vol. 5282, pp. 80–96. Springer, Heidelberg (2008)
32. Rellermeyer, J.S., Alonso, G., Roscoe, T.: R-OSGi: Distributed Applications through Software Modularization. In: The ACM/IFIP/USENIX 8th International Middleware Conference (2007)
33. Royon, Y., Frénot, S., Mouel, F.L.: Virtualization of Service Gateways in Multi-provider Environments. In: Gorton, I., Heineman, G.T., Crnković, I., Schmidt, H.W., Stafford, J.A., Szyperski, C., Wallnau, K. (eds.) CBSE 2006. LNCS, vol. 4063, pp. 385–392. Springer, Heidelberg (2006)
34. Schmidt, H.: Trustworthy components-compositionality and prediction. Journal of Systems Software 65(3), 215–225 (2003)
35. Stutz, D., Neward, T., Shilling, G.: Shared Source Cli Essentials. O'Reilly, Sebastopol (2002)
36. Sun Microsystems. Multitasking Guide-Sun Java Wireless Client Softw., Version 2.1, JME. 04/2008, http://java.sun.com/javame/reference/docs/sjwc-2.1/pdf-html/multitasking.pdf
37. Sun Microsystems. The CDC Application Management System. White Paper (June 2005), http://java.sun.com/j2me/docs/cdc_appmgmt_wp.pdf
38. Squawk Java ME VM, https://squawk.dev.java.net/
39. Szyperski, C., Gruntz, D., Murer, S.: Component Software: Beyond Object-Oriented Programming, 2nd edn. Addison-Wesley, Reading (2002)
40. Wahbe, R., Lucco, S., Anderson, T.E., Graham, S.L.: Efficient software-based fault isolation. In: The 14th ACM Symposium on Operating Systems Principles. SOSP 1993, pp. 203–216. ACM, New York (1993)

Control Encapsulation: A Calculus for Exogenous Composition of Software Components

Kung-Kiu Lau[1] and Mario Ornaghi[2]

[1] School of Computer Science, the University of Manchester
Manchester M13 9PL, United Kingdom
kung-kiu@cs.man.ac.uk
[2] Dipartimento di Scienze dell'Informazione, Universita' degli studi di Milano
Via Comelico 39/41, 20135 Milano, Italy
ornaghi@dsi.unimi.it

Abstract. In current software components models, components do not encapsulate control, and are composed by connection mechanisms which pass control from component to component. Connection mechanisms are not hierarchical in general, and therefore current component models do not support hierarchical system construction. In this paper we argue that control encapsulation by components, together with suitable composition mechanisms, can lead to a component model that supports hierarchical system construction. We show an example of such a model and present a calculus for its hierarchical composition mechanisms.

1 Introduction

In current software component models [10], components are either *objects* or *architectural units*. Such components do not encapsulate control (or computation), and are composed by *connection* mechanisms: delegation for objects (i.e. method call or event delegation), and port linking for architectural units. In general, connection as a composition mechanism does not support hierarchical system construction.

For hierarchical system construction, a composition mechanism should not be defined or applied in an *ad hoc* manner, and it should be compositional in the sense that connecting two components yields another component (of the same type) [1]. Object delegation is not defined in an *ad hoc* manner, since method calls are "hard-wired" in the caller objects, but it is not compositional: two objects connected by delegation do not yield a single object, but remains as two distinct objects (such a pair is not even a standard type).

On the other hand, architectural unit composition is compositional, but its application may be done in an *ad hoc* manner. Ports can be linked if they are compatible, and the resulting composite is another architectural unit; even the connectors can be generated automatically. However, there may be many possible combinations of compatible ports, and therefore a choice of connections has to be made on a case by case basis. Moreover, some ports may also be left unconnected, and the resulting composite unit can be defined in different ways, depending on whether and which of the unconnected ports are exported to the interface of the composite, or simply disposed of.

G.A. Lewis, I. Poernomo, and C. Hofmeister (Eds.): CBSE 2009, LNCS 5582, pp. 121–139, 2009.

We believe that control encapsulation in components, and composition mechanisms that are compositional with respect to, i.e. preserve, control encapsulation, can make a significant contribution to component-based development (CBD), by providing component models that support hierarchical system construction. In this paper, we discuss control encapsulation and its role in component models. In particular, we show how we achieve control encapsulation by composition mechanisms in a model that we have formulated [7,9]. By defining a calculus for these mechanisms, we show that they support hierarchical system construction.

2   Control Encapsulation

A software system consists of three elements: *control, computation* and *data*. The system's behaviour is the result of the interaction between these elements. In a component-based system, these elements can be distributed among the components, or they can be shared by the components, to varying degrees. However, the purpose of using components is to maximise distribution and to minimise sharing at the same time. That is, each component should encapsulate as much of these elements as possible, so as to minimise coupling between the components. By 'encapsulation' we mean 'enclosure in a capsule', as defined in the Oxford English Dictionary.

On the other hand, since the whole system is constructed by composing components, encapsulation in the components should not hinder their composition. Ideally it should be possible to do the construction in a hierarchical manner, so that it is easier to construct large systems systematically, and to reason about their properties. That is, ideally encapsulation should not hinder systematic or hierarchical composition.

Therefore an ideal approach to CBD should combine encapsulation and composition in such a way that composition *preserves* encapsulation. This is illustrated by Fig. 1, where two components C1 and C2, each with their own encapsulation, are composed into a composite C3, which also has its own encapsulation as a result of the composition. Such an approach would allow component-based systems to be constructed from decoupled components in a hierarchical fashion, with encapsulation at every level. However, it would require the components to be *compositional*, i.e. for a given definition of components, the result of composing two components is also a component (with encapsulation).

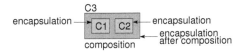

Fig. 1. Compositional encapsulation

Control encapsulation means that a component does not leak control. This means two things. First, it means that any control originated in a component does not leak out to another component. For example, in coordination languages [5], components are active, or have their own threads, i.e. originate their own control, but control never leaks out from components. Rather, components read input values from its (input) ports and outputs values to its (output) ports. The chosen coordination model then coordinates the distribution of the values on the output ports of the components to their input ports. Thus in coordination, components encapsulate control.

However, coordination is not concerned with preservation of encapsulation in composites, as in Fig. 1, because coordination does not build composites from sub-components. That is, coordination is not a composition mechanism for components: it leaves components 'as is'. Web service orchestration [17] is an example of such a coordination mechanism.

Secondly, control encapsulation means that when control is passed to a component, e.g. by a caller invoking a method in the component, the component returns the control to the caller upon completing its execution of the called method, without leaking it (to another component) during its execution of the call. Again, web services encapsulate control in this sense, but again, their orchestration does not compose components into composites.

In this section, we consider control encapsulation by composition mechanisms in current software component models [10]. In these models, components are either objects or architectural units. Exemplars of these models are EJB [4] and ADLs (architecture description languages) [11] respectively. In these models, components are composed by connection. We will show that components in these models do not encapsulate control, and connection does not support hierarchical system construction.

2.1   Connection

A generic view of a component is a composition unit with required services and provided services. Following UML2.0 [16], this is expressed as a box with lollipops (provided services) and sockets (required services), as shown in Fig. 2(a). An object normally does not have an interface, i.e. it does not specify its required services or its provided services (methods), but in component models like JavaBeans and EJB, beans are objects with an interface showing

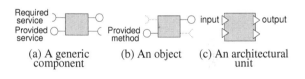

(a) A generic   (b) An object   (c) An architectural
    component   unit

Fig. 2. Components

its provided methods but usually not its required services (Fig. 2(b)). Architectural units have input ports as required services and output ports as provided services (Fig. 2(c).) Therefore, objects and architectural units can both be represented as components of the form in Fig. 2(a).

A required service represents an external dependency. A component with an external dependency is not encapsulated, in the sense of 'enclosure in a capsule'. Therefore, objects and architectural

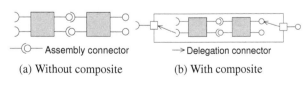

—Ⓞ— Assembly connector   —→ Delegation connector

(a) Without composite   (b) With composite

Fig. 3. Connection

units do not have encapsulation, in particular control encapsulation. We will show that control leaks out of these components.

Objects and architectural units are composed by connection (Fig. 3),[1] whereby matching provided and required services are connected by assembly connectors (Fig. 3(a)). We will show that connection does not always support hierarchical system construction.

In order to get a required service from another object, an object calls the appropriate method in that object. Thus objects are connected by method calls, i.e. by direct message passing (Fig. 4(a)). For architectural units, connectors between ports provide

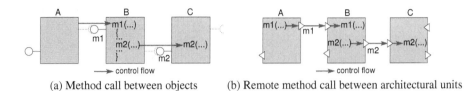

(a) Method call between objects   (b) Remote method call between architectural units

Fig. 4. Control flow in connection

communication channels for indirect message passing (Fig. 4(b)). In Fig. 4 it is clear that neither objects nor architectural units encapsulate control that either originates in them or is passed to them. When an object A makes a method call to another object B (Fig. 4(a)), it passes control to the callee object B; if during its execution the called method calls a method in another object C, then the object B passes control to C. C in turn may call a method in another object, and so on. The result is that control is leaked by B before it is (eventually if at all) passed back to A. When an architectural unit requires the service of another unit, it initiates control to invoke that service by passing control to that unit, albeit indirectly via their (connected) ports (Fig. 4(b)). Unlike objects, however, in an architectural unit, the required services are not necessarily invoked by provided services; rather, the unit can initiate control independently. For example, whereas in Fig. 4(a), in B the method m2 is invoked by m1, in Fig. 4(b), m2 is invoked not by m1 but by control initiated by B.

Connecting two components may or may not produce a composite. Object delegation does not result in a new (composite) object; rather, it produces a connection between two objects which retain their original identities (Fig. 3(a)). The unconnected services remain available for connecting to other objects. Clearly object delegation does not support hierarchical composition.

Architectural unit composition can produce a composite with its own ports (i.e. another architectural unit with its own identity), but the exact nature of this composite depends on whether and which of the unconnected ports are exported (by delegation connectors) to the composite's interface, or disposed of (Fig. 3(b)). In some component models, the notion of a composite is not clearly defined, and the unexported unconnected ports inside the composite can even remain available for connecting to other units. In general, therefore, architectural unit composition does not always support hierarchical composition.

---

[1] In [22] Szyperski classifies object delegation as object-oriented composition, and architectural unit composition as connection-oriented composition. We generalise both as connection.

3 Control Encapsulation in Exogenous Composition

We have formulated a component model [9, 7] in which components encapsulate control. In this section we briefly recall our model, and show how it achieves control encapsulation.

In our model, components are encapsulated: they encapsulate control, data as well as computation. Our components have no external dependencies, and can therefore be depicted as shown in Fig. 5(a), with just a lollipop, and no socket. There are two basic

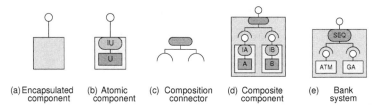

(a) Encapsulated component (b) Atomic component (c) Composition connector (d) Composite component (e) Bank system

Fig. 5. Encapsulated components and exogenous composition

types of components: (i) *atomic* and (ii) *composite*. Fig 5(b) shows an atomic component. This consists of a *computation* unit (U) and an *invocation connector* (IU). A computation unit contains a set of methods which do not invoke methods in the computation units of other components; it therefore encapsulates computation. An invocation connector passes control (and input parameters) received from outside the component to the computation unit to invoke a chosen method, and after the execution of method passes control (and results) back to whence it came, outside the component. It therefore encapsulates control.

A composite component is built from atomic components by using a *composition connector*. Fig. 5(c) shows a composition connector. This encapsulates a control structure, e.g. sequencing, branching, or looping, that connects the sub-components to the interface of the composite component (Fig. 5(d)). Since the atomic components encapsulate computation and control, so does the composite component. Our components therefore encapsulate control (and computation) at every level of composition. In fact they also encapsulate data at every level of computation [8] but we omit data encapsulation here for simplicity and for lack of space.

Our components are thus passive components that can be invoked. In typical software applications, a system consists of a 'main' component that initiates control in the system, as well as components that provide services when invoked, either by the 'main' component or by the other components. The 'main' component is active, while the other components are passive. Our components are the latter. They receive control from, and return it, to connectors. In a system, control flow starts from the top-level (composition) connector.

Fig. 5(e) shows a simplified bank system with two components *ATM* and *GA*, composed by a sequencer composition connector *SEQ*. Control starts when the customer keys in his PIN (and maybe also the operation he wishes to carry out). The connector *SEQ* passes control to *ATM*, which checks the customer's PIN; then it passes control to *GA* (get account), which gets hold of the customer *account* details (and possibly perform the requested operation). Control then passes back to the customer. Our composition connectors are *exogenous connectors* [9], encapsulating control as they do outside atomic components. Clearly, exogenous composition is hierarchical: components can be 'recursively' composed into larger composites. This is a consequence of control encapsulation.

3.1 Defining Control Encapsulation

So far we have defined control encapsulation informally. In this section we begin to define it formally. The basic mechanism used for exogenous composition is as shown in Fig. 5(d). We will elaborate on this.

The general picture of exogenous composition is given in Fig. 6, where a composition connector is connected to a component C (which may be atomic or composite). More precisely, a socket of the connector is connected to the lollipop of C. Control is passed from the connector to C via the socket, a method in C is invoked, and upon completion of its execution, control (and result) is passed back to the connector.

To define this control flow, we use $?C.q$ to denote a *request q* received by a component C, and $!C.r$ to denote a *result r* returned by C (Fig. 6(a)). Receiving a request ($?C.q$) and sending a result ($!C.r$) will be called "events". A request to C could be a method call, and a result returned by C the value(s) that result from the method execution. Fig. 6(b) shows a method $m(x : T) : R$ in C (with parameter x of type T and result of type R). A method call $m(v)$ to m is denoted by $?C.m(v)$,

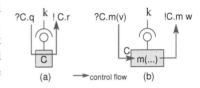

Fig. 6. Exogenous composition

which means the event "C receives the request $m(v)$". The corresponding result w returned by m is denoted by $!C.m\,w$, which means the event "C returns the result w of m". We write $?C.m(v) \preceq !C.m\,w$ to indicate that the request $?C.m(v)$ "causes" the result $!C.m\,w$, where $\preceq$ is a partial ordering on the events. The dot notation $C.m$ follows the object-oriented convention, whilst the punctuation marks ? and ! are often used in the above sense in CCS [13], while causality relations are typical of semantics based on *posets* (partially ordered sets) [21].

We will use the relation $\preceq$ in a weaker sense: $e_1 \preceq e_2$ indicates that the event e_1 must precede e_2 for some causal or non-causal reason, where an event may be a request or a result. That is, we relax the causal relationship to one of precedence. This allows us to express protocol requirements for the control flow. For example, an ATM terminal *ATM* may have the protocol:

$$\{?ATM.get(card, pin) \to_{ATM} !ATM.get\ ok, !ATM.get\ ok \to_{ATM} ?ATM.sel(op)\} \quad (1)$$

where we use $\to_{ATM}$ to denote the covering relation[2] of the protocol. That is, before asking the user u to select an operation, the login process must end successfully. Conversely, the user (caller) has to conform to the protocol with the following covering relation $\to_u$:

---

[2] A finite poset $\langle E, \preceq \rangle$ can be represented by a set of arcs $\{e_1 \to e_1', \ldots, e_n \to e_n'\}$, where $\to$ is the covering relation ($e \to e'$ if $e \neq e'$ and $e \preceq e'' \preceq e'$ entails $e'' = e$ or $e'' = e'$).

$$\{!ATM.get(card, pin) \rightarrow_u ?ATM.get\ ok,\ ?ATM.get\ ok \rightarrow_u !ATM.sel(op)\} \qquad (2)$$

i.e., send *card* and *pin* to the ATM, wait for the *ok*, and then select the operation. Each event in the *ATM* must synchronise with a dual one in the caller, where for a component C, the dual of $?C.q$ is $!C.q$ (the caller sends q and C receives it) while the dual of $!C.r$ is $?C.r$ (C returns r and the caller receives it). Our dual events correspond to complementary events in [14]. The main difference is that our model components and connectors do not behave symmetrically. Events will always refer to the component C and their duals to the connector or, more in general, to the environment interacting with C. The protocol requirements (1) and (2) together define the control flow for using the ATM to execute an ATM operation.

A protocol specifies the *expected behaviours* of a component C by posets of events such as (1), and a compatible connector k has dual behaviours such as (2). Compatibility means that the events of the expected behaviours of C synchronise with the dual ones in k, while respecting the partial ordering of the protocol (behaviours are related to the execution ordering, in general stricter than the one of the protocol). As for control encapsulation, we begin with a simplistic but very strong requirement, which will be weakened later. We say that:

> A behaviour of a component C has *control encapsulation* iff for every request $?C.q$ and result $!C.r$, $!C.r \rightarrow_C ?C.q$ does not belong to the behaviour.

It follows that:

> A component has *control encapsulation* if all its expected behaviours have control encapsulation.

Intuitively, $!C.r \rightarrow_C ?C.q$ is a "call back requirement": the result $!C.r$, sent to the environment of C, "pretends" that the environment will eventually call C again. We see this as a form of control exported from C to the environment. We show an example of control encapsulation and, then, a counterexample.

Example 1. Consider the component C in Fig. 6(b), with a single method $m(x : T) : T$. The expected behaviours of C are of the form

$$?C.m(v) \rightarrow_C !C.m\ w$$

for every call $m(v)$ and returned result w. Therefore C has control encapsulation. The compatible dual behaviours of the connector contains $!C.m(v) \rightarrow_k ?C.m\ w$. The control flows from the connector to C when $!C.m(v)$ and $?C.m(v)$ react,[3] i.e., when the connector makes the call $m(v)$. During the whole execution of m, control is encapsulated in C and comes back to the connector only when $?C.m\ w$ and $!C.m\ w$ react, i.e., when C returns w and the connector receives it. This is

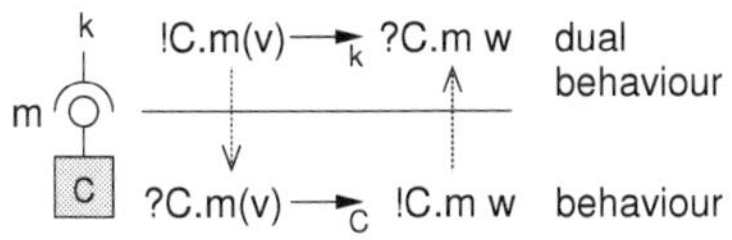

Fig. 7. Encapsulated control

depicted in Fig. 7, where the solid arrows correspond to the covering relation and the dotted arrows to the reaction between dual events.

---

[3] In the sense of CCS.

As counter examples to control encapsulation, consider objects and architectural units composed by connection (Fig. 4) again.

Example 2. Consider the objects A, B and C in Fig. 4(a). Suppose the method in B is $m1(x:T):T$ and the method in C is $m2$. A calls $m1$ in B, and while executing $m1$, B calls $m2$ in C. In this case, the behaviours of B and the dual ones of A and C are of the form depicted in Fig. 8. The objects A and B, together, form the environ-

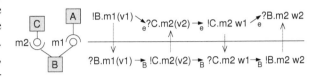

Fig. 8. Non-encapsulated control

ment e of B, and A starts the control flow as follows: (1) A calls $B.m1(v_1)$ and B starts; (2) B calls $C.m2(v_2)$ and C starts; (3) B obtains w_1 and uses it to get the final result w_2. The task (1) is performed inside B, (2) inside C and (3) again in B. B does not encapsulate control, because control flows to C before the call $m1(v_1)$ ends. This is reflected by the requirement $!C.m2(v_1) \rightarrow ?C.m2\ w_1$ where a request follows a result.

Similarly, we can show that the architectural unit B in Fig. 4(b) does not encapsulate control.

The above (informal) definition of control encapsulation is too strong, as the following example shows.

Example 3. Consider Example 1, but this time in a component B allowing C to be called by the connector k a number of times. Suppose we observe a behaviour of C of the form:

$$\{?C.m(v) \rightarrow_C !C.m\ w,\ !C.m\ w \rightarrow_C ?C.m(v'),\ ?C.m'(v') \rightarrow_C !C.m\ w'\}$$

In this case, in each of the calls $C.m(v)$ and $C.m(v')$, the control remains encapsulated in C until the end of the execution of m. However, according to our strong definition of control encapsulation, the behaviours of C violate control encapsulation, owing to $!C.m\ w \rightarrow ?C.m(v')$. The fact that we can observe this kind of behaviour is not a real lack of control encapsulation.

Indeed, the above observed behaviour is compatible with the requirements:

$$?C.m(v) \rightarrow !C.m\ w,\ \ ?C.m(v') \rightarrow !C.m\ w'$$

which are just two instances of the protocol considered in Example 3.1. Thus, according to our model, C has control encapsulation. In Fig. 9, we have used a dashed line for the arrow $!C.m\ w \rightarrow ?C.m(v')$, to put into evidence that it does not come from the protocol of the component C, but from the connector. We remark that the connector does not satisfy control encapsulation. In general, control is not encapsulated in a connector k, since it has to

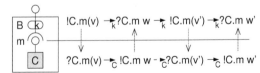

Fig. 9. Encapsulated control and connectors

connect the sub-components and coordinate their computation. A connector is only required to maintain the control encapsulated in the component containing it. In our example, k calls C a number of times, while maintaining control encapsulated in B.

We will relate control encapsulation to the interface behaviour specified by the protocol. In our example, C has control encapsulation since its interface protocol does not contain any "call back" requirement. In contrast, if the requirement $!C.m\ w \to\ ?C.m(v')$ belongs to the protocol of C, then the control *must* come back to C. This corresponds to the fact that we can use messages as a form of "control". For example, the result w may be a string containing the message "please, call me back again".

The example shows that we have to distinguish between the behaviour exhibited in an observation from the requirements of the protocol. Thus our weaker definition of control encapsulation:

> We say that a component violates control encapsulation *if its protocol does*.

Furthermore, when we compose components, we *compose their specifications* (which include protocols), i.e., we are looking for composition rules that allow us to reason at the specification level.

Having explained the notion of control encapsulation and how it can be defined using posets as *behaviour specifications*, we now show that exogenous composition (using exogenous connectors) is strictly hierarchical, by presenting a calculus for it.

4   A Generic Calculus for Exogenous Composition

In this section we outline a calculus for exogenous connectors, which allows us to build new components on top of already existing components (atomic or composite) in a hierarchical manner. First we define behaviour specifications (BSP) precisely, and then we introduce components, their specifications and their correctness.

Definition 1. A *BSP instance* with request alphabet Q and result alphabet R is a finite labelled poset $B(Q,R) = \langle E, \preceq, \lambda, Q, R \rangle$ with labelling function $\lambda : E \to Q \cup R$, where E is a finite set of "event indexes" and:

1. for every $i \in E$, if $\lambda(i) \in Q$, then there is an $i' \in E$ such that $i \preceq i'$ and $\lambda(i') \in R$;
2. for every $i \in E$, if $\lambda(i) \in R$, then there is $i' \in E$ such that $i' \preceq i$ and $\lambda(i') \in Q$;
3. for every $i, i' \in E$, if $\lambda(i) \in R$ and $\lambda(i') \in Q$ then $i \npreceq i'$.

In our approach, a BSP instance represents a "testable" requirement for the behaviour of a component C, so E is finite. Condition 1 says that if the control enters C with a request, it has to leave it with a result. Condition 2 says that every result is caused by a request, i.e., control cannot originate in C, while Condition 3 is our control encapsulation condition.

A label e of the alphabets $Q \cup R$ is called an event. Let i be an event index with label $\lambda(i) = e$. We call the pair $\langle e, i \rangle$ an *event occurrence* and we indicate it by e_i. When e_i has a unique index i, then i may be omitted. We use indexes just to distinguish different event occurrences. Thus behaviours are *equivalent up to reindexing*.[4] According to the

---

[4] A reindexing is an isomorphism $I : E_1 \to E_2$ preserving $\preceq$ and λ.

above section, we represent a behaviour instance by the labelled arcs $e_i \rightarrow e'_j$ of its covering relation, that we call requirement instances. We indicate by E_Q the subset of the indexes with label in Q, by E_R those with label in R, by $B(Q)$ the request part of $B(Q,R)$ (namely the restriction to E_Q) and by $B(R)$ the result part (namely the restriction to E_R). When we do not need to explicitly mention Q, R, we omit them.

Components are built on top of a repository of *computation units* (Fig. 5(b)). A computation unit U can be used by means of an *invocation connector IU*, giving rise to an *atomic component* also denoted by IU.[5] The connector IU defines the request and result alphabets Q_{IU} and R_{IU}. Furthermore, IU may have access to some permanent data. We model data access by means of a set of "access variables" $x_1, \ldots, x_n$ and we define a component state σ as a set of bindings $x_i \mapsto v_i$ associating each x_i with its accessed data value v_i. Finally, the BSP of IU is denoted by $[IU]$ and defines a set of behaviour triples of the form $\langle \sigma, B(Q,R), \sigma' \rangle$, where σ and σ' are states and $B(Q,R)$ is a behaviour with requests $Q \subseteq Q_{IU}$ and results $R \subseteq R_{IU}$. We will write

$$IU : \sigma \xrightarrow{B} \sigma' \tag{3}$$

to indicate that $\langle \sigma, B, \sigma' \rangle \in [IU]$, and we call (3) a BSP-requirement. We attach to each event occurrence of B an *expected property*, to be satisfied after the event occurrence. The expected property of a request concerns the external environment and the data flowing in, whilst that of a result concerns the state of IU and the data flowing out. A *test case* for $B(Q,R)$ is a sequence containing the requests of $B(Q)$ in an order consistent with $\preceq$. Similarly, a result sequence for $B(Q,R)$ is a sequence containing the results of $B(R)$ in an order consistent with $\preceq$. A behaviour triple $\langle \sigma, B(Q,R), \sigma' \rangle \in [C]$ specifies the following expected behaviour:

> if we start C in the state σ and we submit a test case T for $B(Q)$ while satisfying the expected properties of the requests, then C returns a result sequence for $B(Q,R)$ and reaches the state σ' while satisfying expected properties of the results.

We say that the test case T is successful iff C exhibits the expected behaviour. We say that C is *correct* iff for every $\langle \sigma, B(Q,R), \sigma' \rangle \in [C]$ and every test case T for $B(Q,R)$, T is successful.

Example 4. Here we give the BSP requirements of three atomic components. The *ATM* waits for a card c by $?ic(c)$ and a pin p by $?ip(p)$; if $p = pin(c)$ it gives the result ok, otherwise the result err.

It also updates the data access variable *card*. The event $ic(c)$ has the expected property "a card has been inserted, containing the data c", $ip(p)$ the property "p has been correctly composed", ok the property "*card* contains the data c of the inserted card the composed pin p coincides with $pin(c)$", and err the property "the card has been refused". *GA* waits for the ok event and then uses the data accessed by *card* to get the account number $num(card)$ and the bank $bank(card)$. It does not update any access variable. The expected properties should be evident from the signature. Finally, *EP* simply propagates the error event. The requirements are given in an open form, with the

---

[5] The invocation connector provides the interface, hence the overloading of names.

parameters c, p (the data access variables are not parameters). Each open requirement is to be considered as the set of its instances, obtained by grounding the parameters.

$$ATM : \text{if } p = pin(c) \ [card \mapsto \_] \xrightarrow[\twoheadrightarrow]{?ic(c)\to?ip(p),\,?ip(p)\to!ok} card \ [card \mapsto c];$$

$$\text{otherwise} \quad [card \mapsto \_] \xrightarrow[\twoheadrightarrow]{?ic(c)\to?ip(p),\,?ip(p)\to!err} [card \mapsto \_]$$

$$GA : \quad [card \mapsto c] \xrightarrow[\twoheadrightarrow]{?ok\to!acc\,(num(card),bank(card))} [card \mapsto c]$$

$$EP : \quad [] \xrightarrow[\twoheadrightarrow]{?err\to err} []$$

An alternative specification, where the information on *card* is passed using parameters rather than by data access is:

$$ATM : \text{if } p = pin(c) \ [] \xrightarrow[\twoheadrightarrow]{?ic(c)\to?ip(p),\,?ip(p)\to!ok(c)} [];$$

$$\text{otherwise} \quad [] \xrightarrow[\twoheadrightarrow]{?ic(c)\to?ip(p),\,?ip(p)\to!err} []$$

$$GA \quad [] \xrightarrow[\twoheadrightarrow]{?ok(c)\to!acc\,(num(c),bank(c))} []$$

$$EP \quad [] \xrightarrow[\twoheadrightarrow]{?err\to err} []$$

Now we define the semantics of the components and of the connectors by means of inference rules of the following form:

$$\frac{}{IU : \sigma \xrightarrow[\twoheadrightarrow]{B} \underline{w} \ \sigma'} IU \qquad \frac{C_1 : \sigma_1 \xrightarrow{B_1} \underline{w}_1\sigma_1' \quad \ldots \quad C_n : \sigma_1 \xrightarrow{B_n} \underline{w}_n\sigma_n'}{K(C_1,\ldots,C_n) : \sigma \xrightarrow[\twoheadrightarrow]{B} \underline{w} \ \sigma'} K$$

In the (IU)-rule, IU is an atomic unit, $\underline{w}$ is a subset of the access variables of IU and $IU : \sigma \xrightarrow[\twoheadrightarrow]{B} \underline{w} \ \sigma'$ means that (3) holds and that only the variables in $\underline{w}$ may have different values in σ, σ'. In (K), K is a connector, $K(C_1,\ldots,C_n)$ denotes the component obtained from $C_1,\ldots,C_n$ by means of K and $\sigma \xrightarrow[\twoheadrightarrow]{B} \underline{w} \ \sigma'$ is defined as a function of $\sigma_j \xrightarrow{B_j} \underline{w}_j \ \sigma_j'$. If invocation and composition connectors are introduced by rules of the above kind, the BSP semantic $[C]$ of an atomic or composite component C can be defined as follows:

$\langle \sigma, B, \sigma' \rangle \in [C]$ iff there is a judgement of the form $C : \sigma \xrightarrow[\twoheadrightarrow]{B} \underline{w} \ \sigma'$ provable by the connector rules.

We remark that we decouple the BSP semantics $[C]$ and the execution semantics of C. The former specifies the expected behaviours, expressed by behaviour triples, whilst the latter corresponds to the implemented behaviour. The two semantics are related by the notion of correctness introduced before. The correctness of the basic components is assumed. The one of the composed components is guaranteed as far as connectors are correctly implemented, i.e., their execution preserves correctness. We assume that a correct implementation is supplied by a *composition environment CE*, depending on the programming language(s), the run time environment and the supported communication mechanisms. We leave the notion of "successful test case" generic, to leave open the choice of *CE*. For example, we could use CCS or the π-calculus as a formal *CE*. In this case we can define both test cases and components as processes, and we can define successful test cases as particular kinds of "experiments" [13]. Alternatively, we could define our *CE* using Petri Nets [18], or we could choose an informal *CE* such as Net Beans. Finally, we could give an execution semantics based on our behaviours, in a way similar to [2] for the internal π-calculus.

$$\frac{C_1 : \sigma \xrightarrow{B_1} \underline{w}_1 \, \sigma', \quad C_2 : \sigma \xrightarrow{B_2} \underline{w}_2 \sigma'}{par(C_1,C_2) : \sigma \xrightarrow{B_1 \cup B_2} \underline{w}_1 \cup \underline{w}_2 \, \sigma'} \qquad \frac{C_1 : \sigma \xrightarrow{B_1} \underline{w} \, \sigma'}{sel(C_1,C_2) : \sigma \xrightarrow{1.B_1} \underline{w} \, \sigma'}$$

$$\frac{C_2 : \sigma \xrightarrow{B_2} \underline{w} \, \sigma'}{sel(C_1,C_2) : \sigma \xrightarrow{2.B_2} \underline{w} \, \sigma'} \qquad \frac{C_1 : \sigma \xrightarrow{B_1} \underline{w}_1 \, \sigma', \quad C_2 : \sigma' \xrightarrow{B_2} \underline{w}_2 \sigma'',}{pipe(p,C_1,C_2) : \sigma \xrightarrow{B_1|p|B_2} \underline{w}_1 \cup \underline{w}_2 \, \sigma''}$$

$$\frac{C : \sigma \xrightarrow{B} \underline{w} \, \sigma'}{ra(C,g) : \sigma \xrightarrow{B|g} \underline{w} \, \sigma'} \qquad \frac{C : \sigma \xrightarrow{B} \underline{w} \, \sigma'}{la(f,C) : \sigma \xrightarrow{f|B} \underline{w} \, \sigma'}$$

$$\frac{B \notin dom(p)}{loop(p,C) : \sigma \xrightarrow{B} \underline{w} \, \sigma} \qquad \frac{C : \sigma \xrightarrow{B_1} \underline{w} \, \sigma', \quad loop(p,C) : \sigma' \xrightarrow{B_2} \underline{w}\sigma''}{loop(p,C) : \sigma \xrightarrow{B_1|p|B_2} \underline{w} \, \sigma''}$$

Fig. 10. The basic connectors and their semantics

In Fig. 10 we show a set of basic rules, in part inspired by constructive logic, in particular by [12, 15]. In [15], information values are introduced. An information value $\alpha : A$ for a formula A can be seen as a constructive explanation of the (classical) truth of A and the rules of the related constructive calculus can be interpreted as truth preserving operations on the information values. Here, instead of information values we have behaviour instances (BI) with attached properties. The BI can be seen as an explanation of the attached properties in terms of the events making them true. The rules of the connectors define the BSP of the composite in terms of the BSP of the components and, according to the previous discussion on the *CE*, the connector execution is required to realise the behaviour of the composite while preserving the correctness. The composition operations used in the rules are the following. For conciseness, we will briefly comment on the similarity to the information-value logic (ivl) only for the first two.

- Disjoint Union (*par* rule). The disjoint union $B \cup B'$ is defined in the usual way [3]. The expected properties remain unchanged. In the *par* rule, we require also that $\underline{w}_1 \cap \underline{w}_2 = \emptyset$.

  The *par* rule is similar to the (ivl) $\wedge$-introduction rule. The latter takes two information values $\alpha : A$ and $\beta : B$ and builds $\langle \alpha, \beta \rangle : A \wedge B$. Similarly, *par* takes two BI B_1 for C_1 and B_2 for C_2 and builds $B_1 \cup B_2$ for $par(C_1,C_2)$. In the *par* composition the two components run independently, while preserving correctness. Indeed, no further ordering is imposed in $B_1 \cup B_2$ and the (possible) shared access variables are not updated. There are other forms of parallel composition, involving fork and join, not considered here for conciseness.

- Prefixing (*sel* rules). The behaviour $h.B(Q,R)$ is obtained by adding the prefix h to the labels (?q becomes ?$h.q$ and !r becomes !$h.r$). The *sel* rule is similar to the (ivl) $\vee$-elimination. An information value for $A \vee B$ is of the form $1.\alpha$, with $\alpha : A$, or $2.\beta$, with $\beta : B$. Roughly, $\vee$-elimination works as a case applying a suitable function $f_A(\alpha)$ or $f_B(\beta)$, depending on the index 1 or 2. Similarly, the selector uses the index h to choose the right component to execute while maintaining the correctness. If the signatures of the two components are disjoint, prefixing is not necessary. Furthermore, since the selection is based on the requests, one can apply prefixing only to the request part, as we will do in Section 4.1.
- Relabelling (left and right adapt $la(f,C)$ and $ra(C,g)$). Let $B(Q,R)$ be a behaviour. A left adaptor is based on an injective function $f : Q' \rightarrow Q$. It replaces every q in its range by the q' such that $f(q') = q$. The expected properties of q' must entail those of q. We indicate by $f|B$ the resulting behaviour. Dually, in $B|g$ the right adaptor relabels the results in the domain of g.
- Piping (pipe and loop rules). A pipe function p for $B_1(Q_1,R_1), B_2(Q_2,R_2)$ is a partial function $p : R_1 \rightarrow Q_2$. We require that $B_2(Q_2)$ is of the form $B_2(Q_2') \cup B_2(Q_2'')$, where Q_2' is the range of p. The function p is used to pipe the results $r \in dom(p)$ of R_1 into requests $p(r)$ of $B_2(Q_2')$, guaranteeing that if the expected property of r is satisfied, then so is that of $p(r)$. We say that p *can be applied* if for every linear extension S of $B_1(R_1)$, there is a linear extension T of $B_2(Q_2')$ such that $\lambda(T) = p(S)$, where $\lambda(T)$ is the sequence of the labels of T and $p(S)$ is that of the labels of $p(r)$ coming from the sub-sequence of S with labels from $dom(p)$. Intuitively, this means that the pipe connector sends the requests $p(S)$ to C_2. If p can be applied, then the latter are accepted, since they arrive in the right order. Otherwise, we get an abort result. The results with labels not in $dom(p)$ and the requests of $B_2(Q_2'')$ are not piped. To obtain the composite behaviour $B_1|p|B_2$ we *delete the piped events* (while reconstructing $\preceq$, details omitted) and we further impose that *the requests of $B_1(Q_1)$ precede those of $B_2(Q_2'')$ and the non-piped result of B_1 precede those of B_2.*
- Sequencing. Sequencing may be defined as $B_1 \cdot B_2 =_{def} B_1|u|B_2$, where u is the function with an empty domain or, more generally, a function such that $dom(u) \cap R_1 = \emptyset$. We remark that in piping (and hence in sequencing) the requests of B_1 precede those of B_2 and the results of B_1 precede those of B_2, but we do not require that the results of B_1 precede the requests of B_2 to preserve control encapsulation.
- The loop rule of Fig. 10 is only one of the possible iterations. It halts when no result belongs to the domain of p.

We conclude this section by briefly discussing the problem of the implementation in a composition environment *CE*. The latter plays an important role in our approach. The composition rules are used in the logical design phase, to meet the system's requirements. They work at a very high level of abstraction since they compose the BSP of components, rather than their implemented behaviours. The latter will be composed by the *CE*. This may lead to inefficiency. In particular, our strictly compositional approach may introduce a huge number of composition levels, and therefore long delegation chains, which may cause inefficiency. Our idea is that, once we have a satisfactory logical design, we can optimise it by transformations supported by the *CE*. An example of transformation is shown in Fig. 12, where we use hierarchical Petri Nets to implement the connection rules.

4.1 Typing Connectors

The rules of the previous section give a precise compositional semantics for the connectors. However, there are cases where the piping does not apply to any BSP instance B_2 of the second component. In this case, we say that the pipe aborts. We have a similar situation in the *loop* rule, when we are not in the base case and the pipe of the step aborts. To avoid aborts, we can type connectors. For simplicity, we do not consider here the data access and we show a simplified set of rules, which work in the simpler cases. Types are interpreted as sets of BSP instances and are built up from a family of basic types, which depends on the atomic components, using the following operations: [6]

- $\mathscr{B}_1 \times_p \mathscr{B}_2 = \{B_1 \cup B_2 \mid B_1 \in \mathscr{B}_1, B_2 \in \mathscr{B}_2\},$ [7] where we represent disjoint union by $1.\mathscr{B}_1 \cup 2.\mathscr{B}_2$.
- $\mathscr{B}_1 + \mathscr{B}_2 = \{1.B_1 \mid B_1 \in \mathscr{B}_1\} \cup \{2.B_2 \mid B_2 \in \mathscr{B}_2\}$
- $\mathscr{B}_1 \cdot \mathscr{B}_2 = \{B_1 \cdot B_2 \mid B_1 \in \mathscr{B}_1, B_2 \in \mathscr{B}_2\}$

Components are built starting from the atomic ones, using the connectors and the compositional semantics of the previous section. A judgement has the form $C : \mathscr{Q} \Rightarrow \mathscr{R}$, where C is a component, $\mathscr{Q}$ a request type, and $\mathscr{R}$ a result type. It means that for every $B(Q,R) \in [C]$, the request part $B(Q)$ belongs to $\mathscr{Q}$ and the result part $B(R)$ belongs $\mathscr{R}$, and for every $I \in \mathscr{Q}$, there is a $B(Q,R) \in [C]$ such that $B(Q) = I$ (= up to reindexing). The rules are given in Fig. 11, where:

$$\frac{C_1 : \mathscr{Q}_1 \Rightarrow \mathscr{R}_1 \quad C_2 : \mathscr{Q}_2 \Rightarrow \mathscr{R}_2}{par(C_1,C_2) : \mathscr{Q}_1 \times_p \mathscr{Q}_2 \Rightarrow \mathscr{R}_1 \times_p \mathscr{R}_2} \qquad \frac{C_1 : \mathscr{Q}_1 \Rightarrow \mathscr{R} \quad C_2 : \mathscr{Q}_2 \Rightarrow \mathscr{R}}{sel(C_1,C_2) : \mathscr{Q}_1 + \mathscr{Q}_2 \Rightarrow \mathscr{R}}$$

$$\frac{C_1 : \mathscr{Q}_1 \Rightarrow \mathscr{R}_1 \times_p \mathscr{R}_1' \quad C_2 : \mathscr{Q}_2 \times_p \mathscr{Q}_2' \Rightarrow \mathscr{R}_2 \quad p : \mathscr{R}_1' | \mathscr{Q}_2'}{pipe(p,C_1,C_2) : \mathscr{Q}_1 \cdot \mathscr{Q}_2 \Rightarrow \mathscr{R}_1 \cdot \mathscr{R}_2} \qquad \frac{C : \mathscr{Q} \Rightarrow \mathscr{R} + \mathscr{E} \quad p : \mathscr{R} | \mathscr{Q}}{while(p1,C) : \mathscr{Q} \Rightarrow \mathscr{E}}$$

$$\frac{C : \mathscr{Q} \Rightarrow \mathscr{R} \quad g : \mathscr{R} \to \mathscr{R}'}{ra(C,g) : \mathscr{Q} \Rightarrow \mathscr{R}'} \qquad \frac{C : \mathscr{Q} \Rightarrow \mathscr{R} \quad f : \mathscr{Q}' \to \mathscr{Q}}{la(f,C) : \mathscr{Q}' \Rightarrow \mathscr{R}}$$

Fig. 11. Typing connector composition

- The adaptors f and g are assumed to be chosen in a set of known adaptors such that $P(f(q))$ entails $P(q)$ and $P(r)$ entails $P(g(r))$, where $P(e)$ is the expected property attached to e. We have *problem domain adaptors* and *type adaptors*. The former transform basic types, the latter adapt the structure of the event terms of a BSP instance B, according to the type of B. Examples are $j1 : \mathscr{R} \to \mathscr{R} + \mathscr{R}'$ defined by $j1(!e) = !1.e$ and $j2 : \mathscr{R}' \to \mathscr{R} + \mathscr{R}'$ defined by $j2(!e) = !2.e$.

---

[6] For conciseness, we mix syntax and semantics.
[7] Different kinds of parallel compositors C have different $\times_C$.

– The pipe function $p : \mathscr{R}_1'|\mathscr{Q}_2'$ is such that for every $R' \in \mathscr{R}_1'$, there is $Q' \in \mathscr{Q}_2'$ such that R' pipes to Q'. It is chosen in a set of known pipes for the types $\mathscr{R}_1', \mathscr{Q}_2'$. Like adaptors, pipe functions are required to maintain the expected properties. We may have problem domain and type pipes. Examples of type pipes are $e1 :$ $!\mathscr{B}+!\mathscr{B}' \rightarrow ?\mathscr{B}$, defined by $e1(!1.e) = ?e$ and $is1 :!\mathscr{B}+!\mathscr{B}' \rightarrow ?\mathscr{B}+?\mathscr{B}'$, defined by $is1(X) = j1(e1(X))$. Both are partial (only the labels of the form $1.e$ are piped), but $e1$ destructures $1.e$ into e while $is1$ leaves $1.e$ unchanged.
– The while connector is a special case of loop, defined by:

$$while(p,C) =_{def} ra(loop(p1,C),e2)$$

The pipe function $p1$ is defined by $p1(1.r) = p(r)$, while $p1(2.r)$ is undefined. This guarantees that the loop halts when we get a result of the form $2.B$, with $B \in \mathscr{E}$. The adaptor $e2$ eliminates the prefix 2, giving rise to $B \in \mathscr{E}$. There are other specialisation of $loop$, giving rise to components that transform an input stream into an output stream. Here we do not discuss the issue of termination.

Now we discuss the application of typed rules in a hierarchical top-down or bottom-up development. Let $\mathscr{Q} \Rightarrow \mathscr{R}$ be a problem specification and CR be a component repository. To get a composed component C solving our problem, we look for a proof tree applying the inference rules, with conclusion $C : \mathscr{Q} \Rightarrow \mathscr{R}$ and assumptions containing components of CR. In the bottom-up approach we start by applying the rules to components chosen in CR, in such a way that the behaviour of the composites becomes "nearer and nearer" to the wanted one. We stop when we reach it. Here the problem is that it is difficult to establish what is "nearer". On the other hand, in simple cases a brute-force approach could work. The top-down approach is goal oriented. To solve $\mathscr{Q} \Rightarrow \mathscr{R}$ we have to choose one of the rules with a conclusion $C : \mathscr{Q}' \Rightarrow \mathscr{R}'$ matching $\mathscr{Q} \Rightarrow \mathscr{R}$. The premises of the rule contain the sub-problems. We stop the decomposition process when we reach a sub-problem solved by a component of the repository. Rules sel and par are top-down deterministic, i.e., the types of the premises are uniquely determined by the one of the conclusion. The adaptor and while rules are top-down non deterministic, because the types of the of the premises are determined by those of the consequence and by the non-deterministic choice of the adaptor (f, g) or type pipe (p) function. Finally, the pipe rule is not purely top-down. Indeed, the types of the premises depend also on the components we want to pipe. On the other hand, if we are looking for a pipe, likely we have an idea of the components we want to pipe. We illustrate the above discussion by an example.

Example 5. Let ATM and GA be the atomic components of Example 4 and let us assume that we have to solve the problem specified by

$$ic(c) \rightarrow ip(p) \Rightarrow err + acc(num(c), bank(c)) \tag{4}$$

i.e., the user inserts card c and pin p and the component returns either err (operation refused) or $acc(num(c), bank(c))$ (account number and bank of c). The types of ATM and GA are shown below, where we omit ?, ! since on the left hand side of $\Rightarrow$ we have requests, and results on the right hand side:

$$ATM : ic(c) \rightarrow ip(p) \Rightarrow err + ok(c)$$
$$GA : \quad ok(c) \Rightarrow acc(num(c), bank(c))$$

We observe that: the request type of the problem coincides with the one of the *ATM* component; $ok(c)$ pipes to $ok(c)$ by the identity pipe $I : \mathscr{2}|\mathscr{2}$; and the result type of *GA* entails the one of the problem. Thus it is reasonable to look for the following pipe

$$\frac{ATM : ic(c) \rightarrow ip(p) \Rightarrow err + ok(c), \quad C : err + ok(c) \Rightarrow err + acc(num(c), bank(c)), \quad I}{pipe(I, ATM, C) : ic(c) \rightarrow ip(p) \Rightarrow err + acc(num(c), bank(c))}$$

where *C* can be likely obtained from *GA* by the *sel* rule, as suggested by the + in its result type. Indeed, our top down process can be continued until we reach the following solution for *C*:

$$\frac{EP : err \Rightarrow err \qquad\qquad\qquad GA : ok(c) \Rightarrow acc(num(c), bank(c))}{\dfrac{ra(EP, j1) : err \Rightarrow err + acc(num(c), bank(c)) \quad ra(GA, j2) : ok(c) \Rightarrow err + acc(num(c), bank(c))}{sel(ra(EP, j1), ra(GA, j2)) : err + ok(c) \Rightarrow err + acc(num(c), bank(c))}}$$

where $EP : err \Rightarrow err$ is a propagator. With request $?1.err$, the selector sends $?err$ to $ra(EP, j1)$, which returns $j1(!err) = !1.err$. With request $?2.ok(c)$, $?ok(c)$ is sent to $ra(GA, j2)$, which returns $!2.acc(n, b)$ (where $n = num(c)$ and $b = bank(c)$).

As already remarked, our approach may introduce redundancies and many composition levels and this problem is to be solved at the composition environment level. We conclude this section by an example on this issue.

Example 6. Let us assume to use Petri Nets as a *EC*. We label transitions by request types (to fire, a transition waits for a mark) and places by result types (a place receives a mark). A component is represented by a unique transition with an input place waiting for requests and an output place receiving the results, as shown in Fig. 12. If a

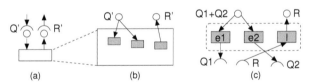

Fig. 12. Petri-net components and connectors

component is not atomic, its place can be exploded into type sub-nets, i.e., we have a hierarchical representation of composites (Fig. 12 (b)). Connectors are net schemas, with plugs for the components they connect. In Fig. 12 we show a plug (a) and the *sel* connector (b). Composing means plugging the input and output places in the corresponding connectors. Connectors and components are typed. The types of a connector are parametric and a component can be plugged in only it its types match those of the connector. For example, the type $acc(db, c) + err$ matches $Q_1 + Q_2$, where Q_1, Q_2 are type variables.

Fig. 13(a) is the net representation of the proof-tree of (4). In Fig. 13(b) we show a simplification of the net in (a), based on the fact that the pipe function *I* (for Identity) maps *x* into *x*, *EP* is a propagator, and transitions $e1(1.x) = x$ and $j1(x) = 1.x$ compose into $is1(1.x) = 1.x$ (the latter simply controls that the form of the token is $1....$).

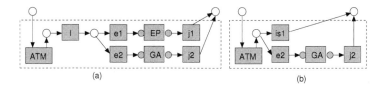

Fig. 13. Petri-net simplification

5   Discussion and Concluding Remarks

The calculus for exogenous composition in Section 4 shows that exogenous composition supports hierarchical system construction. Control encapsulation allows us to consider the request and result types separately. This facilitates both hierarchical decomposition and composition of the functions of the system, while offering the facility for specifying protocols. Types and inference rules for them make the calculus non *ad hoc*. Indeed, we say that exogenous composition is both *functional,* i.e. it can be defined explicitly as a function, and *algebraic*, i.e. it results in a unit of the same type as the sub-units. A composition mechanism that is functional can be fully automated as a composition operator, since it is fully defined. By contrast, a non-functional mechanism can only be applied manually, since it requires glue. A composition mechanism that is algebraic supports hierarchical (recursive) composition, since each composition step yields a construct of the same type. Such mechanisms are most desirable since they can constitute a component algebra [1]. By contrast, a non-algebraic mechanism cannot support hierarchical composition, since each composition step may yield a construct of a different type.

The calculus for software composition in [1] is also based on the π-calculus. However, it is not based on control encapsulation, and the composition mechanism is connection. Units (called *forms*) are linked by scripts via their services. So the composition mechanism is like architectural unit composition, using connection (with glue); it is algebraic but non-functional.

In our calculus, we have chosen to stay at a very abstract level, to decouple the calculus (meant to be used in the design phase) from the composition environment (in the deployment phase) for implementing a design expressed in the calculus. Our study of the latter is only at an initial stage. Some ideas come from [6], where connectors are implemented in the formalism of hierarchical Petri nets [19]. Using Petri nets we do not have a natural representation of streams, which can be treated in the calculus by means of a special kind of loop connector. So we are considering the π-calculus as a candidate for building a formal model of a composition environment. The advantage is that our behaviours fit with a a restricted form of π-calculus. The fact that restricted forms of process calculi give rise to a compositional semantics is not new [20, 2]. An example is the *internal π-calculus* [2], which admits *event structures* [23] as a compositional semantics [2], and has a simpler notion of equivalence than the full π-calculus. Interestingly, the internal π-calculus comes with the idea of formalising internal mobility. Our approach comes with the idea of control encapsulation, which allows us to give a calculus for typed components where types have a "request-result" form $\mathscr{Q} \Rightarrow \mathscr{R}$, highlighting the functional behaviour of components. Event structures are posets with a conflict relation. In our case, we have a further simplification and we use only posets. We have not yet studied the possibility of extending our approach to event structures.

Our system is Turing complete using *pipe*, *sel* and *while*, and atomic units for *succ* and '=', over natural numbers. This shows that our calculus is powerful but undecidable. In particular, termination is undecidable and must be treated *ad hoc*. Iteration rules that are not *ad hoc* and more controlled can be given, and we could argue that they are sufficient for the purpose of building applications from components at a high granularity level.

Finally, using the calculus will naturally lead to multiple levels of composition. So it is important to be able to optimise such a design by simplifying the composition at a particular level, or even reducing the number of levels. Here, the typed inference rules should be able to offer useful help. For instance, ideas from proof-theory (in particular, cut elimination) would seem to be able to offer strategies for optimising a pipe composition.

Acknowledgements

We wish to thank the reviewers for their detailed and constructive comments that have helped us to improve the paper.

References

1. Achermann, F., Nierstrasz, O.: A calculus for reasoning about software composition. Theoretical Computer Science 331(2-3), 367–396 (2005)
2. Crafa, S., Varacca, D., Yoshida, N.: Compositional event structure semantics for the internal *pi*-calculus. In: Caires, L., Vasconcelos, V.T. (eds.) CONCUR 2007. LNCS, vol. 4703, pp. 317–332. Springer, Heidelberg (2007)
3. Davey, B.A., Priestley, H.A.: Introduction to Lattices and Order, 2nd edn. Cambridge University Press, Cambridge (2002)
4. DeMichiel, L., Keith, M.: Enterprise JavaBeans, Version 3.0. Sun Microsystems (2006)
5. Gelernter, D., Carriero, N.: Coordination languages and their significance. Comm. ACM 35(2), 97–107 (1992)
6. Lau, K.-K., Ntalamagkas, I., Tran, C.: Composite software composition operators using coloured Petri-nets. Technical report, Computer Science, Univ. Manchester (in preparation)
7. Lau, K.-K., Ornaghi, M., Wang, Z.: A software component model and its preliminary formalisation. In: de Boer, F.S., Bonsangue, M.M., Graf, S., de Roever, W.-P. (eds.) FMCO 2005. LNCS, vol. 4111, pp. 1–21. Springer, Heidelberg (2006)
8. Lau, K.-K., Taweel, F.: Data encapsulation in software components. In: Schmidt, H.W., Crnković, I., Heineman, G.T., Stafford, J.A. (eds.) CBSE 2007. LNCS, vol. 4608, pp. 1–16. Springer, Heidelberg (2007)
9. Lau, K.-K., Velasco Elizondo, P., Wang, Z.: Exogenous connectors for software components. In: Heineman, G.T., Crnković, I., Schmidt, H.W., Stafford, J.A., Szyperski, C., Wallnau, K. (eds.) CBSE 2005. LNCS, vol. 3489, pp. 90–106. Springer, Heidelberg (2005)
10. Lau, K.-K., Wang, Z.: Software component models. IEEE Trans. on Soft. Eng. 33(10), 709–724 (2007)

11. Medvidovic, N., Taylor, R.N.: A classification and comparison framework for software architecture description languages. IEEE Trans. on Soft. Eng. 26(1), 70–93 (2000)
12. Miglioli, P., Moscato, U., Ornaghi, M., Usberti, G.: A constructivism based on classical truth. Notre Dame Journal of Formal Logic 30(1), 67–90 (1989)
13. Milner, R.: A Calculus of Communicating Systems. Springer, Heidelberg (1980)
14. Milner, R.: Communicating and Mobile Systems: the π-Calculus. Cambridge University Press, Cambridge (1999)
15. Ornaghi, M., Benini, M., Ferrari, M., Fiorentini, C., Momigliano, A.: A constructive object oriented modeling language for information systems. ENTCS 153(1), 67–90 (2006)
16. OMG. UML 2.0 Infrastructure Final Adopted Specifcation (2003)
17. Peltz, C.: Web services orchestration and choreography. Computer 36(10), 46–52 (2003)
18. Petri, C.A.: Kommunikation mit Automaten. PhD thesis, University of Bonn (1962)
19. Reisig, W., Rozenberg, G. (eds.): APN 1998. LNCS, vol. 1492. Springer, Heidelberg (1998)
20. Sangiorgi, D.: π-calculus, internal mobility, and agent-passing calculi. Theoretical Computer Science 167(1&2), 235–274 (1996)
21. Schröder, B.S.W.: Ordered Sets: An Introduction. Birkhäuser, Basel (2003)
22. Szyperski, C.: Universe of composition. Software Development (August 2002)
23. Winskel, G., Nielsen, M.: Models for concurrency. In: Handbook of Logic in Computer Science. Semantic Modelling, vol. 4, pp. 1–148. Oxford University Press, Oxford (1995)

Component Specification Using Event Classes

Mark Bickford

Cornell University Computer Science
and ATC-NY
33 Thornwood Dr. Suite 500, Ithaca, NY, USA
markb@cs.cornell.edu

Abstract. Working in a higher-order, abstract *logic of events*, we define *event classes*, a generalization of interfaces, and *propagation rules* that specify information flow between event classes. We propose a general definition of a *component* as a scheme, parameterized by a set of input classes, that defines a set of output classes and propagation rules. The specification of a component is a relation between its input classes and defined output classes that follows from its propagation rules and definitions.

We define a subset of *programmable* event classes that can be compiled and executed and a language, called $E^\#$, for specifying components. Components specified in $E^\#$ preserve programmability–if the component's input classes are programmable then its output classes and propagation rules are programmable.

Thus a component specified in $E^\#$ is a higher-order object: given programs for its input classes, it produces a distributed program for propagating information and programs for its output classes. These programs can be passed as inputs to other components so that components can be composed.

1 Introduction

We may view all computing as information processing: a computation receives information, initially or through an on-going interaction with its environment, and produces some information, on exit or interactively. From this viewpoint, specification of a computational process will naturally focus on *information associated with events*. A specification must define how the process recognizes its input events and reads the associated input information and must also define how the environment will recognize the output events produced by the process and read the information associated with them. In addition, the specification defines the relation between the input and output events and their associated information.

The specification of the input (output) events and associated information is usually called the *interface* specification, while the relation between the interfaces might be called the *functional* specification. The interface specification and functional specification are often written separately but, when this is done, important properties of the process may become difficult or impossible to specify.

For example, a separate functional specification may express the relation between the input information and the output information but be unable to express relations that depend on the temporal ordering of the input and output events. Conversely, an interface specification may be unable to express that the information coded by an input event

G.A. Lewis, I. Poernomo, and C. Hofmeister (Eds.): CBSE 2009, LNCS 5582, pp. 140–155, 2009.
© Springer-Verlag Berlin Heidelberg 2009

depends on the state of the process, which, in turn, is a function of the prior history of input and output events.

In this paper we define the concept of an *event class* as a generalization of an interface. An event class is a set of events together with a function that assigns information to each event in the class. The concept of event class combines aspects of both interface and functional specification: determining which events are in the class could be an interface issue, while the function that assigns information to the event can depend on state (a function of the past history of events) in ways that would be part of the functional specification.

Using event classes we factor a specification into components where each component is parameterized by a set of input classes. A component defines auxiliary classes and output classes in terms of the input parameters and also imposes information flow constraints called *propagation rules*. A component is a *program scheme* rather than a program: it describes how to *construct* programs for its output classes and information flow rules from programs for its input classes.

2 Constructive Methods

Our work is in the area of automated program construction referred to as the *proofs-as-programs paradigm*[2,6]. The idea is that certain logical statements can be regarded as specifications and constructive proofs of such statements can be transformed into programs that satisfy the specifications.

For example, a constructive proof of the statement

$$\forall x\colon T.\ \exists y\colon S.\ R(x,y)$$

can be transformed into a functional program F, of type $T \to S$ such that, $R(x, F(x))$ is true, for any $x \in T$. Constructive theorem proving systems such as NuPrl and Coq *extract* the *constructive content* of proofs and produce such functions automatically.

As another example, for any type Σ of symbols, Σ^* is the same as the type $list(\Sigma)$, and we can also define the type $Reg(\Sigma)$ of regular grammars over Σ and the relation $w \in Lang(G)$ for $G \in Reg(\Sigma)$ and $w \in \Sigma^*$. The constructive content of $w \in Lang(G)$ is a *parse tree* for w as a member $Lang(G)$. The constructive content of the following *decidability theorem*

$$\forall G\colon Reg(\Sigma).\ \forall w\colon \Sigma^*.\ w \in Lang(G)\ \lor\ w \notin Lang(G)$$

is a *parser generator*. Given a grammar G it produces a parser P which, when given word w, produces either a parse tree for w or determines that $w \notin Lang(G)$.

A parser generator is clearly a useful tool, but the efficiency of the parsers generated by this method depends on the proof of the decidability theorem. If we merely prove that it is possible to generate all possible parse trees of w and check each one for conformance with the grammar G, then the parsers extracted from this proof will use this infeasible algorithm. If, on the other hand, we develop the theory of finite state automata and prove the decidability theorem by showing that every regular grammar is recognized by an automaton, then the extracted parsers will be efficient.

Over the last several years, we have developed constructive methods that extend the proofs-as-programs paradigm to the generation of distributed systems. The programs we generate are not purely functional, they have state, they have multiple agents or threads, and agents send messages to one another. To extract such programs from proofs of specifications, the specifications must be logical properties of inherently distributed structures, the *event structures* discussed in section 3.

The concept of *event classes* has arisen, in the context of this work, as a useful abstraction with which to write specifications. Event classes combine some of the features of the examples just mentioned. Recognizing when an event is in an event class is analogous to deciding whether $w \in Lang(G)$–with primitive *kinds* of events (e.g. receipt of a message with a particular header) corresponding to the basic symbols Σ, and the history of prior events corresponding to the word w. Computing the value of an event in the class is like computing a functional program. These two aspects are woven together. The events are recognized not merely on the basis of the primitive kinds of prior events, but on the values computed for them. The value computed for an event can be a function of some state variables, where state variables are expressed abstractly as the most recent value of some event class.

Event classes are useful because we can combine them using *combinators* that encode programming patterns. We prove general abstract properties of these combinators, and use them to derive further properties of specifications that use the combinators.

Equally important is the fact that we can define a subset of event classes that we call *programmable*. A programmable class can be implemented by an efficient program, one that uses a finite number of threads, has a finite set of state variables, and handles a finite set of primitive kinds of events. Such a program is analogous to the finite state automata that recognize regular languages.

We will describe a language, $E^{\#}$, for defining components in which all classes are programmable. $E^{\#}$ achieves this property by limiting the definition of event classes to a certain general form that preserves programmability. Because of this, correct-by-construction programs can be automatically generated from specifications written in $E^{\#}$.

It is probably obvious, from this, that $E^{\#}$ can specify only a limited range of distributed systems. One major limitation is that $E^{\#}$ can express only the temporal ordering between events, not explicit time bounds between events. The reason is that generating correct-by-construction programs for specifications with explicit time bounds would require an algorithm to decide whether the time bounds are feasible and produce a schedule when they are. It is a goal for future work to find a restricted class of programs and specifications for which the scheduling problem is decidable, so that the constructive approach can be applied.

Another current limitation of $E^{\#}$ is that messages can only be sent on links with known endpoints. More flexible message passing methods can be added to a future version of $E^{\#}$ provided that we can give precise logical specifications for them and correctly implement the specifications with efficient programs.

Even with these limitations, $E^{\#}$ is expressive enough to specify a variety of distributed algorithms, such as leader election and consensus protocols, or authentication protocols. The concepts, event class and programmable event class, may also be useful for other component specification models, even if the goal is not program synthesis.

All of our concepts and definitions are expressed in a logical language that we call the *logic of events*. We begin with a brief overview of this language.

3   Logic of Events

An *event language* $\mathcal{L}$ is any language extending $\langle E, loc, < \rangle$, where loc is a function on E, and $<$ is a relation on E. For an event $e \in E$, $loc(e)$ is the *location* of the event and $e_1 < e_2$ means event e_1 causally precedes event e_2. Locations represent agents, processes, or threads. An *event structure*[1] is a model for $\mathcal{L}$ that satisfies the axioms

- $\leq$ is a locally-finite partial order (every e has finitely many predecessors)
- *Local order*, defined by $e_1 <_{loc} e_2 \equiv e_1 < e_2 \wedge loc(e_1) = loc(e_2)$, is a total ordering on any set of events whose members all have the same location.

There is an analogy between event structures and space-time: events correspond to points, locations to spatial coordinates, and $<$ and $<_{loc}$ to temporal ordering. We have also added an operator, $time(e)$, to the event language that provides a temporal coordinate, but, since the methods described here construct programs only for asynchronous systems, our specifications will use only the temporal ordering relations.

To make a connection between abstract events and programs we must make clear what attributes of an event a program can recognize. Some events are receipts of messages while others represent internal events such as a timer expiring or a random number being generated. We therefore add two operators, $kind(e)$, and $val(e)$ to the event language. When an event e occurs, a program that has access to $kind(e)$, and $val(e)$ can pass $val(e)$ to an appropriate handler, based on $kind(e)$.

We use a model of message passing in which messages are sent reliably on named, fifo, *links* from one location, the *source* of the link, to another location, the *destination* of the link. Each message has an associated *tag*, which can be thought of as a header, and is included in the kind. Thus, one kind of event is **rcv**(l, tg). An event e of this kind is the receipt of a message with tag tg on link l. In this case, $val(e)$ is the remaining data in the received message.

Any other event e is called an internal event and has a kind of the form **internal**(nm), where nm is a token. In this case, $val(e)$ may have whatever meaning is appropriate for the internal action. In particular, it provides a convenient way to represent nondeterministic choice: the value of an internal event can be chosen nondeterministically.

4   Using the Logic of Events

We use the logic of events within a higher-order logic so that we can define and quantify over functions from events to events, and functions from events to other types. In particular, we use the constructive type theory of NuPrl, but our methods are compatible with any higher-order logic, such as the logics (classical or constructive) used formal systems like Isabelle/HOL, PVS, and Coq.

---

[1] The event structures defined here differ from those defined by Winskel [7]. See section 12 for a comparison.

For example, we will need the concept of an *event proposition*, a proposition about events. In a classical higher-order logic, event propositions are just sets of events, so they have type[2] $E \to \mathbb{B}$. In constructive type theory, a proposition about events is a member of the type[3] $E \to \mathbb{P}$. In fact, since the type, E, of events, depends on the event structure we are talking about, this definition, and all the definitions mentioned in this paper, include another parameter, es, of type ES, the type of event structures. Our notation consistently hides the parameter es.

As an example of the expressiveness of event logic we define the operators of linear temporal logic. If P and Q are event propositions, then the following are also event propositions:

$$P \wedge Q =_{def} \lambda e.\, P(e) \wedge Q(e)$$
$$P \Rightarrow Q =_{def} \lambda e.\, P(e) \Rightarrow Q(e)$$
$$\neg P =_{def} \lambda e.\, \neg P(e)$$
$$\Box P =_{def} \lambda e.\, \forall e': E.\ e \leq_{loc} e' \Rightarrow P(e')$$
$$\Diamond P =_{def} \lambda e.\, \exists e': E.\ e \leq_{loc} e' \wedge P(e')$$
$$P \mathbf{U} Q =_{def} \lambda e.\, \exists e': E.\ e \leq_{loc} e' \wedge Q(e') \wedge$$
$$\forall e'': E.\ (e \leq_{loc} e'' <_{loc} e') \Rightarrow P(e'')$$

We easily prove identities such as:

$$\Box\Box P \equiv \Box P$$
$$\Diamond\Diamond P \equiv \Diamond P$$
$$\Diamond P \equiv \mathrm{TR}\ \mathbf{U}\ P$$

where

$$P \equiv Q =_{def} \forall e: E.\ P(e) \Leftrightarrow Q(e)$$
$$\mathrm{TR} =_{def} \lambda e.\ \mathrm{True}$$

The logic of events is more general than linear temporal logic for several reasons. The set of locations can be arbitrary, so there are many disjoint sets of linearly ordered events, but these events may be related by the causal order. Higher-order logic over a model that includes events allows us to define functions from events to events, and express useful properties of such functions.

For example, suppose that   ($*$) $\forall e: E.\ P(e) \Rightarrow \exists e': E.\ Q(e') \wedge R(e, e')$
This means that there is a function $f: \{e: E \mid P(e)\} \to \{e': E \mid Q(e')\}$ that satisfies $\forall e: E.\ P(e) \Rightarrow R(e, f(e))$. This property merely states that f is a Skolem function for ($*$), but we can express additional properties of a function like f that do not follow from f being a Skolem function. For example, we can state that f is *local order preserving*:

$$\forall e_1, e_2: E.\ e_1 <_{loc} e_2 \Rightarrow f(e_1) <_{loc} f(e_2)$$

---

[2] $\mathbb{B}$ is the type of Boolean values $\{T, F\}$.

[3] In constructive logic, the propositions $\mathbb{P}$ are identified with the universe of types. A nonempty type is "true" and members of the type are witnesses to its truth.

5   Event Classes

An *event class* (of type T) is simply a partial function from events to values of type T. If X is an event class[4], then we write $E(X)$ for the set of events in the domain of X and say that events in $E(X)$ are *in* the class X. For an event $e \in E(X)$, $X(e)$ is the value (of type T) assigned to e by class X.

Thus, class X partitions the events and for those events e that are in $E(X)$ assigns a value of type T.

Notation: We write[5] $X(e) = \omega$ to mean $e \notin E(X)$.

Notation: If $t(X, \ldots, Y)$ is an expression mentioning event classes $X, \ldots, Y$ define $[t(X, \ldots, Y)]$ to be

$$\lambda e.\ e \in E(X) \wedge\ \ldots\ \wedge e \in E(Y)\ \wedge\ t(X(e), \ldots, Y(e))$$

So, for example, $[X = 5](e)$ means $e \in E(X)\ \wedge\ X(e) = 5$. Note that an event e may be in any number of different event classes.

The class $f(X)$: If f is a function from $T \to S$, we may define a class $Y = f(X)$ by stipulating that

$$E(Y) \subseteq E(X)\ \wedge\ \forall e\colon E.\ \forall v.\ [X = v](e)\ \Rightarrow\ [Y = f(v)](e)$$

This says that an event is in class Y if and only if it is in class X, and its Y-value is computed from its X-value by applying function f.

The class $(X|p)$: Similarly, if p is a predicate $T \to \mathbb{B}$, we may define a class $Y = (X|p)$ by stipulating that

$$\forall e\colon E.\ \forall v.\ [X = v\ \wedge\ p(v)](e)\ \Leftrightarrow\ [Y = v](e)$$

This says that an event is in class Y if and only if it is in class X and its X-value passes the test p.

The class $(X)'$: Class $Y = (X)'$ (of great importance to us) is defined by the property that, for any event e, the value $(X)'(e)$ is the X-value of the most recent X-event occurring prior to e, if there is one, and otherwise, e is not in class $(X)'$. Formally, for all events e, and values v:

$$[Y = v](e) \Leftrightarrow \exists e'\colon E.\ e' <_{loc} e\ \wedge\ [X = v](e')\ \wedge$$
$$\forall e''\colon E.\ e' <_{loc} e'' <_{loc} e$$
$$\Rightarrow\ e'' \notin E(X)$$

---

[4] In classical logic, the domain $E(X)$ and the values $X(e), e \in E(X)$ completely characterize the event class X. In constructive logic, we will need an additional property: the domain $E(X)$ is *decidable*–there is an effective procedure to decide whether or not an event e is in $E(X)$. Thus, in constructive type theory an event class is represented by a function of type $E \to (T + Unit)$.

[5] We use ω rather than $\perp$ because $X(e) = \perp$ would indicate a computation compatible with all possible results, rather than a computation that has *decided* that e is not in the domain of X.

6   Programmable Event Classes

An event class X is *programmable* if there is a program, possibly a distributed program, that recognizes the events in X and computes their values. Since we assume that programs can directly access only the kind and val of events, a program for class X must decide whether event e is in class X, and, if so, compute $X(e)$ as a function of the history

$$\{\langle kind(e'), val(e') \rangle | e' \leq_{loc} e\}$$

An efficient program will not store the entire history, it will instead accumulate a function of the history. Also, the program for a class should depend on the history of only a fixed, finite set of kinds of events. Without this restriction, a program's behavior could change when composed with another program that introduced other kinds of events. Finally, the events in a programmable class should occur at only finitely many locations, so that a distributed program for the class will require only a finite set of agents.

We therefore define a *class program* (of type T) to be

1. a finite list of locations, $locs$, and for each $i \in locs$:
2. an initial state, $s_0(i)$
3. a finite list of event kinds, $ks(i)$
4. a function $update_i(s, k, v)$ for updating the state s when an event with kind $k \in ks(i)$ and val v occurs at location i
5. a function $test_i(s, k, v)$ that returns a member of the disjoint union $(T + \text{Unit})$

Type $T + S$ is the disjoint union of types T and S. Its members are values of the form $inl(t)$, where $t \in T$, or the form $inr(s)$, where $s \in S$. Thus the type $(T + \text{Unit})$ represents values from T (as $inl(t)$) and ω (as $inr()$).

The run of a class program initializes, at each of its locations, i, a state variable s_i to $s_0(i)$, and sets the state variable $s_i := update_i(s_i, k, v)$ whenever an event of kind $k \in ks(i)$ and val v occurs at location i.

The value returned by test function, $test_i$, is a member of a disjoint union– either $inl(t)$, for some $t \in T$, or else $inr()$. Event e with $loc(e) = i$ is in the class computed by the program if and only if $i \in locs$, and $kind(e) \in ks(i)$, and $test_i(s_i, kind(e), val(e))$ returns $inl(t)$. In this case, t is the value assigned to e by the class program.

Definition. An event class is *programmable* if it is the class computed by a class program.

Examples

- The class VAL(k) where $[\text{VAL}(k) = v](e) \Leftrightarrow (kind(e) = k \land val(e) = v)$, is programmable.
- If X is programmable then the classes $f(X)$ and $X|p$ are programmable.
- The class $(X)'$ is not programmable since events of any kind may occur after an X-event, so there is no finite list of kinds for all $(X)'$-events.

7   Closure Properties of Event Classes

The event classes $f(X)$ and $X|p$ are simple examples of a class defined as a function of other classes. In fact, event classes are closed under a very general definition scheme. We illustrate this with a few more examples, before discussing the general case.

The class $(X + Y)$: Suppose that X is a class of type T, and Y is a class of type S. We can define a class $X + Y$, of type $T + S$, so that

$$[X = t](e) \Rightarrow [(X + Y) = inl(t)](e)$$
$$e \notin E(X) \wedge [Y = s](e) \Rightarrow [(X + Y) = inr(s)](e)$$
$$E(X + Y) \subseteq E(X) \cup E(Y)$$

For this, it suffices to define[6]

$$X + Y = \lambda e.\ F(X(e), Y(e))$$
$$\text{where: } F(\omega, \omega) = \omega$$
$$F(t, -) = inl(t)$$
$$F(\omega, s) = inr(s)$$

The clause, $F(\omega, \omega) = \omega$ implies that an event in $X + Y$ must be in at least one of the classes X or Y.

The class $(X; Y)$: Suppose that X is a class of type T, and Y is a class of type S. The class $X; Y$, of type $T \times S$, includes only Y-events, e, that have been preceded by an X-event. The value, $(X; Y)(e)$, of such an event is the pair $\langle t, s \rangle$ where $Y(e) = s$ and t is the value of the most recent X-event before e.

Recalling our definition of the class $(X)'$, we see that

$$X; Y = \lambda e.\ G(Y(e), (X)'(e))$$
$$\text{where: } G(\omega, -) = \omega$$
$$G(s, \omega) = \omega$$
$$G(s, t) = \langle t, s \rangle$$

The clause, $G(\omega, -) = \omega$ implies that an event in $X; Y$ must be in class Y. The clause, $G(s, \omega) = \omega$ implies that an event in $X; Y$ must also be in class $(X)'$.

The class $\mathbf{accum}(h, b, X)$: When an event e in class X occurs, we can assign it not only its X-value, v, but a "running total" of v and the values of all prior X-events. The running total is defined by the parameters h and b: b is the total when no X-events have occurred, and $h(t, v)$ is the new total when an X-event of value v occurs when the previous total is t. The class that contains the same events as class X but assigns them this running total, we name $\mathbf{accum}(h, b, X)$. It can be defined by:

$$\mathbf{accum}(h, b, X) = \lambda e.\ H(X(e), (\mathbf{accum}(h, b, X))'(e))$$
$$\text{where: } H(\omega, -) = \omega$$
$$H(v, \omega) = h(b, v)$$
$$H(v, t) = h(t, v)$$

---

[6] If classes X and Y have an event e in common, then the definition of $(X + Y)(e)$ is asymmetric–it treats e only as an X-event. A slightly more complicated definition of the class would have type $T + S + (T \times S)$ and handle this case symmetrically.

This definition is recursive since it defines **accum**(h, b, X) as a function of itself. The recursion is well-founded because the occurrence of **accum**(h, b, X) on the righthand side of the definition is inside of a "prime". The value of **accum**(h, b, X) at event e is defined in terms of the prior values of **accum**(h, b, X). The ordering $<_{loc}$ is well-founded, so the recursion is well-founded and defines a unique event class.

Example: Request/Ack Suppose we want to design a component that enforces the requirement

> After a request is made, no request is made until after an acknowledgment is received.

One design that implements this requirement is to remember the last relevant event and when "a request is requested" make the request if the last event was an ack and ignore the request otherwise.

We can parameterize our component design with two input classes W (for *wants* to request) and A (for *acknowledge*). The relevant events are in class $W + A$, and remembering the last relevant event corresponds to the class $(W + A)'$. If we define

$$Req = \lambda e.\ H(W(e), (W + A)'(e))$$
$$\text{where:}\ H(\omega, -) = \omega$$
$$H(x, inl(x')) = \omega$$
$$H(x, \text{otherwise}) = x$$

Then the clause $H(\omega, -) = \omega$ implies that a *Req*-event must be a W-event, and the second clause, $H(x, inl(x')) = \omega$ implies that a W-event is not a *Req*-event when the last relevant event was a W-event. Otherwise, either there was no prior relevant event or the prior event was an A-event, so the W-event is also a *Req*-event (with the same value).

It is now easy to show that, *no matter what the classes W and A are*, the class *Req* satisfies

$$\forall e \colon E(Req).\ \forall e' \colon E(Req).\ (e <_{loc} e') \Rightarrow$$
$$\exists e'' \colon E(A).\ (e <_{loc} e'' <_{loc} e')$$

This is a formal statement of the original requirement.

This example illustrates (part of) our general concept of a component: in terms of a set of input classes, it defines a set of output classes and a guaranteed relation between the input classes and defined output classes. The need for something more can be seen from the fact that merely defining the class of events that are "allowed to make a request" does not force any requests to actually be made (and our specification was trivially satisfied when there are no requests). To state that events in a class cause some action to be taken, we will use *propagation rules* (see section 9).

General class combinator: The classes $X + Y$, $X; Y$, **accum**(h, b, X), and *Req* share a common definition form under which the set of event classes is closed. The general form, which we call a *class combinator*, is a function

$$H(U_1, \ldots, U_m; P_1, \ldots, P_n; S)$$

of $m > 0$ *unprimed* class arguments, $n \geq 0$ *primed* class arguments, and one, optional, *self* argument, that is *strict in its unprimed arguments*:

$$H(\omega, \ldots, \omega; -, \ldots, -, -) = \omega$$

Theorem 1. *If H is a class combinator, then for any event classes*

$$U_1, \ldots, U_m; P_1, \ldots, P_n$$

there is a unique event class C such that for every event e,

$$C(e) = H(U_1(e), \ldots, U_m(e); (P_1)'(e), \ldots, (P_n)'(e); (C)'(e))$$

Proof. Let[7] $C =_{rec} \lambda e.\, H(U_1(e), \ldots, U_m(e), (P_1)'(e), \ldots, (P_n)'(e), (C)'(e))$
To show that C is an event class, we must prove that, for every event e, $C(e)$ is defined–either ω or some value x. We prove this by induction on $<_{loc}$. Assuming that $C(e')$ is defined for all $e' <_{loc} e$ we see that $(C)'(e)$ is defined and hence $C(e)$ is defined. The uniqueness of C is easy to prove. □

Notation: Let $C_H(U_1, \ldots, U_m, P_1, \ldots, P_n)$ be the class defined by combinator H and classes $U_1, \ldots, U_m; P_1, \ldots, P_n$.

In fact, Theorem 1, is an instance of a more general theorem that allows class definitions with mutual recursion.

8   Closure Properties of Programmable Event Classes

The programmable event classes are also closed under the class combinators.

Theorem 2. *If H is a class combinator, and event classes $U_1, \ldots, U_m; P_1, \ldots, P_n$ are programmable, then the event class $C_H(U_1, \ldots, U_m, P_1, \ldots, P_n)$ is programmable.*

Proof. We give a sketch of the proof. We proved the full version of the theorem, constructively, in NuPrl.

Each of the classes U_i and P_j has a program; let these be

$$Pgs = \ldots, Pgm(U_i), \ldots, Pgm(P_j), \ldots$$

We describe the program for $C_H(U_1, \ldots, U_m, P_1, \ldots, P_n)$, first for the case where the combinator H does not mention the optional "self" argument. The program has:

1. the list of locations, *locs* formed from the union of the locations in Pgs. And has, for each $i \in locs$:

---

[7] In NuPrl, recursive definitions of the form $f =_{rec} \lambda x.\, F(f, x)$ are made using the Y-*combinator*, for which $Y(F) = F(Y(F))$. We prove that functions defined by recursion are total by an induction on some well-founded ordering (in this case, $<_{loc}$). Other logical systems, such as Coq, and PVS do not include the Y-combinator or general recursion, but do have strong enough induction/definition principle to carry out our argument, or will support a simple fixed point argument in domain theory.

2. the initial state, $\langle s_0^1(i), s_0^2(i), \dots, \omega, \dots, \omega \rangle$ consisting of the tuple of initial states of all programs in Pgs that include location i and extra state components, pr_j, with initial state ω, for each of the primed arguments P_j that contain location i. The extra state pr_j will remember the most recent value of class P_j.
3. the list of kinds, $ks(i)$ is the union of the kinds from each program in Pgs that includes location i.
4. the update function $update_i(s, k, v)$ updates each component of the state just as the corresponding program in Pgs would (if k is not one of the kinds for that program, the corresponding component is unchanged). The extra state component pr_j corresponding to argument P_j is updated as follows: If k is one of the kinds for program $Pgm(P_j)$ and s_j is the component of the state for P_j, and t_{ij} is the test function from program $Pgm(P_j)$ for location i, then if $t_{ij}(s_j, k, v) = inl(x)$ for some x, pr_j is set to x. Otherwise p_j is unchanged.
5. the test function $test_i(s, k, v)$ is

$$H(t_{i1}(s_1, k, v), \dots, t_{im}(s_m, k, v), pr_1, \dots, pr_n)$$

If the combinator H does mention the optional "self" argument, then each location will include one more state component, *self*, initially ω. This component is updated to x when the test function of the program returns $inl(x)$, and the test function itself is

$$H(t_{i1}(s_1, k, v), \dots, t_{im}(s_m, k, v), pr_1, \dots, pr_n, self) \qquad \square$$

Our constructive proof of theorem 2 provides the basis for a verified compiler for the language $E^{\#}$ described below.

9   Propagation Rules

Starting with basic programmable classes like VAL(k) and applying $(X + Y)$, $(X; Y)$, **accum**(h, b, X), and other definable class combinators, we can define complex programmable event classes. The program that implements such a class accumulates state information needed for the test function to decide whether an event is in the class and, if so, compute its value. But how is this information to be used by components of a distributed system?

Distributed systems must propagate information from one location to another, and this is not done by the programs for event classes. So, we need one more ingredient to complete our language for specifying components of distributed systems: *propagation rules*.

The *forward propagation rule* $X \xrightarrow{R} Y$ states that the information associated with an event in class X should propagate to related information associated with an event in class Y. Expressed in the logic of events, part of the formal meaning of this rule is:

$$\forall e \colon E.\ \forall v.\ [X = v](e) \Rightarrow$$
$$\exists e' \colon E.\ e \le e' \wedge [R(Y, v)](e')$$

This says that for every event e in class X, with X-value v, there will be a Y-event e', *causally after or equal to* e, with a value related to v by relation R.

Recall that such a $(\forall e.\exists e')$-property can also be expressed using a Skolem function, f, and that we can also assert that f is *local order preserving*. We want the meaning of $X \xrightarrow{R} Y$ to include the order-preserving property, so, accordingly, our full definition of the propagation rule is:

$$\exists f\colon E \to E.\ (\forall e\colon E.\ e \le f(e)) \ \wedge$$
$$(\forall e_1, e_2\colon E.\ e_1 <_{loc} e_2 \Rightarrow f(e_1) <_{loc} f(e_2)) \ \wedge$$
$$(\forall e\colon E.\ \forall v.\ [X = v](e) \Rightarrow [R(Y, v)](f(e)))$$

When the relation $R(v, v')$ is $v = v'$, then we omit R and write simply $X \to Y$; in this case the last clause of the definition is

$$\forall e\colon E.\ \forall v.\ [X = v](e) \Rightarrow [Y = v](f(e))$$

This says that the value of every X-event will occur later as the value of a Y-event.

Propagation rule for simple send: When $Y = \text{VAL}(\mathbf{rcv}(l, tg))$ then $X \to Y$ means that the X-value of every event in X must be sent (in order) on link l with tag tg. If all of the events in class X occur at the source[8] of l, then this is easily accomplished by adding "send statements" to the program for class X, so that, when the test function returns $inl(x)$, the program sends message $\langle tg, x \rangle$ on link l.

10   The $E^{\#}$ Language

We have built a prototype executable specification language, called $E^{\#}$, based on the concepts of event classes and propagation rules. It provides an ML-like syntax for defining basic items: locations, links, and kinds, and for declaring the types of basic kinds of events. For example, this $E^{\#}$ fragment:

```
let l1 = link(a,b,1);; let l2 = link(b,a,1);;
let r = rcv(l1,req);;  let a = rcv(l2,ack);;
r,a: int
```

defines locations, a and b, links l1 and l2, and kinds r and a. Link l1 goes from a to b (and it is link number 1 of possibly more links from a to b). Kind r is the kind of a receipt on link l1 of a message with tag req. Because of the declaration r: int, the message received will be an integer (the message types are closed under union, product, and list, and include base types of strings, booleans, and integers).

$E^{\#}$ has a syntax for defining event classes and propagation rules. For example:

```
let +(X,Y) = f(X,Y) where f(x,none) = inl(x)
                           f(x,y) = inl(x)
                           f(none,y) = inr(y) end;;
```

---

[8] If events in class X can occur at locations other than the source of link l, then to implement $X \to \text{VAL}(\mathbf{rcv}(l, tg))$ requires a distributed program that sends the values of X-events to a "proxy" at the source of link l that forwards the values it receives on link l with tag tg.

```
let accum(h,b,X) = g(X, self')
                   where g(a,none) = h(b,a)
                         g(a,t) = h(t,a) end;;
let ;(X,Y) = f(Y, X') where f(b, none) = none
                            f(b,a) = pair(a,b) end ;;
```

defines the combinators $(X + Y)$, **accum**(h, b, X), and $(X; Y)$ defined in section 7. Note that the ascii syntax for ω is none, note also that the "strictness clause" like f(none,none) = none is supplied automatically and does not need to be written.

A "module" combinators.esh, containing general-purpose combinators can be created and then imported into other modules. Our Request/Ackknowledge example could be written:

```
import combinators.esh
let Req(W,A) = h(W,(W+A)')
    where h(x,d) = if isl(d) then none else x  end;;
```

Here the input class parameters W and A have been made into arguments of a combinator. We plan to extend $E^{\#}$ to declare type and class parameters so that we could write:

```
import combinators.esh
T : type
class W, A : T
let Req = h(W,(W+A)')
      where h(x,d) = if isl(d) then none else x end;;
```

If this were a module req_comp.esh then we would use it as follows:

```
class W : int
let l1 = link(a,b,1);; let l2 = link(b,a,1);;
let r = rcv(l1,req);;  let a = rcv(l2,ack);;
r,a: int
let A = val(a);;
let R = val(r);;
import req_comp.esh with (int for T, A for A, W for W)
Req => R
```

This $E^{\#}$ program includes definitions of A and R as basic classes VAL(**rcv**(l2, ack)) VAL(**rcv**(l1, req)). It also includes a propagation rule Req => R. The current prototype supports only the "simple send" propagation rules, so the class on the righthand side must be a "basic receive class".

11   Compilation of $E^{\#}$

The $E^{\#}$ compiler parses the input module and then generates two things, a logical specification and a program. The logical specification is a proposition in the logic of events. It states a property that is true in any event structure that is consistent with (i.e. could result from a run of) the program. Our prototype places the generated logical specification into the NuPrl library so that we can use it to derive other properties of the program.

The generated program is a simple *distributed state machine* (DSM). This is similar to the class programs described earlier except that they also contain "send statements". More precisely, a DSM is:

1. a finite list of locations, $locs$, and for each $i \in locs$:
2. a list of state variables with types and initial values.
3. a finite list of event kinds, $ks(i)$
4. handlers for each of these kinds, k: the handler for k is a list of expressions, in the state variables and the variable val, that define the next states for all the state variables when evaluated with val set to the value of the event of kind k. In addition, the handler includes a list of pairs of a link and an expression in the state variables and val. The expressions evaluate to a list of messages (a header tag and a value) that should be sent on the given link.

Verified compiler. The core of our prototype $E^{\#}$ compiler is correct-by-construction because we use the constructive proof of Theorem 2 to assemble the programs for all event classes in the $E^{\#}$ program being compiled. The NuPrl system can *extract* an executable witness term from a proof. The extract of Theorem 2 is a function that takes programs for input classes and produces a program for the class defined by the combinator. We have programs for the basic classes of the form $VAL(k)$ (these come from the extract of a very simple theorem). Thus the $E^{\#}$ compiler simply applies these extracts repeatedly to compute the program for each class.

Compilation of the propagation rules is currently implemented with "hand written" ML code. For the "simple send" propagation rules this is fairly straightforward, but we plan to prove a theorem about the "programmability" of propagation rules and implement this part of the compiler with a "correct-by-construction" witness term, as well.

12   Related Work

We developed the logic of events and the theory of event classes out of our needs for abstraction in the formal verification and/or synthesis of distributed systems. Because of our somewhat confined world view, it is likely that there are many connections between our ideas and existing software engineering methods that we are unaware of. Here are some connections that we are aware of:

de Alfaro and Henzinger [3] use *interface automata* to specify assumptions about the temporal ordering of input events and guarantees on the temporal ordering of output events. They use a game theoretic algorithm to compute a new set of assumptions on the environment when components are composed. The interface assumptions expressed by interface automata can clearly be expressed in the logic of events, and moreover by programmable event classes. We expect that the interface automata composition rule can be made into a combinator on event classes, and this is a topic for further research.

The AsmL specification language [1] developed at Microsoft Research is based on Gurevitch's Abstract State Machine model. The distributed version [5] of this model, Distributed ASM's has a semantics similar to our event structures. In particular, actions are partially ordered with the actions of a single agent linearly ordered. AsmL specifications focus on evolving states while our methods focus on events and associated information and we make state a derived quantity.

Our use of the name *event structure* is misleading to readers familiar with Winskel's event structures[7]. Our event structures are formal model of what might be called *extended message sequence charts* because the events and their locations and ordering form a message sequence chart, while the kinds and values are an extension. Thus our event structures simply model the observed behavior (or a *run*) of a distributed system. The causal ordering between events is merely the ordering in which the events in the run occurred. In contrast, Winskel's event structures are a generalization of Petri-nets, an abstract model of the processes themselves. The ordering relation is an *enabling relation* and the additional *conflict relation* specifies events that can not occur in the same run. For example, a Winskel event structure might have events that have time, location, and value, and the conflict relation contains pairs of events with the same time and location but with different values. This would say that events with the same time and location but different values cannot occur in the same run. We would prove the same result by showing that, in any event structure (in our model, this is a single run) events with the same location and time must be equal, in which case they must have the same value.

The conflict relation in Winskel event structures can be used to model the choice of *fresh* values, such as *nonces* used in authentication protocols. Two events that choose the same nonce can be in conflict, and this models the assumption that all nonces are fresh. In our model, we state such assumptions as logical constraints on the event structures.

13   Ongoing Work

We are currently building "back end" translators from the DSM intermediate language, produced by the $E^\#$ compiler, into target languages such as Java, C#, and F#. The Java version should be ready by June, 2009.

We are using the $E^\#$ tools (collectively called "Elan"–the Event Logic Assistant) to specify and generate consensus algorithms. We have a complete proof of a simple consensus algorithm[9] that tolerates t crash failures and uses $3t + 1$ voters, and we have specified the algorithm in $E^\#$ and generated the intermediate DSM for it. Within another year or two we plan to have correct-by-construction versions of real-world consensus algorithms such as Paxos (Lamport), and the randomized consensus algorithm of Ben-Or.

Another focus of our work is to have the ability to generate *diverse* code from $E^\#$ specifications. Having back ends for several languages is one factor for diversification, but we can also use different representations for the state in our generated programs (e.g. arrays, linked lists, etc. for abstract lists, hash tables, balanced trees, etc for sets).

---

[9] The FLP[4] theorem states that no safe consensus algorithm is guaranteed to terminate. We prove the safety of the consensus algorithm and a weaker liveness property, *non-blocking*, "from any reachable state it is *possible* to reach termination".

Acknowledgments

We would like to thank: David Guaspari for editing and reorganizing several drafts of this report; Bob Constable for enthusiastic technical and financial support for this work and collaboration.

References

1. Barnett, M., Schulte, W.: The abcs of specification: Asml, behavior, and components. Informatica 25, 517–526 (2001)
2. Bates, J., Constable, R.: Proofs as programs. ACM Transactions on Programming Languages and Systems 7, 113–136 (1985)
3. de Alfaro, L., Henzinger, T.: Interface automata. In: Proceedings of the, ACM Press, New York (2001)
4. Fischer, M.J., Lynch, N.A., Paterson, M.S.: Impossibility of distributed consensus with one faulty process. In: PODS 1983: Proceedings of the 2nd ACM SIGACT-SIGMOD symposium on Principles of database systems, pp. 1–7. ACM, New York (1983)
5. Gurevitch, Y., Rosenzweig, D.: Partially Ordered Runs: A Case Study. Microsoft Research MSR-TR-99-88 (1999)
6. Martin-Lof, P.: Constructive mathematics and computer programming. In: Mathematical Logic and Programming Languages, pp. 167–184. Prentice-Hall, London (1985)
7. Winskel, G.: Event structures. In: Brauer, W., Reisig, W., Rozenberg, G. (eds.) APN 1986. LNCS, vol. 255, pp. 325–392. Springer, Heidelberg (1987)

Integrating Functional and Architectural Views of Reactive Systems

Jewgenij Botaschanjan and Alexander Harhurin

Institut für Informatik, TU München, Germany
{botascha,harhurin}@in.tum.de

Abstract. An integrated model-based development approach has to capture the relationship between requirements, design, and implementation models. In the requirements engineering phase, the most important view is the functional one, which specifies functionalities offered by the system and relationships between them. In the design phase, the component-based view describes the system as a network of interacting components. Via their interaction, they realize the black-box behavior specified in the functional view. To ensure the consistency between both views, a formal integration of them is necessary.

The presented formal framework captures and interrelates both function- and component-based models. In particular, we provide a correct-by-construction procedure, which transforms a functional specification into a component-based architecture. Applicability of the method is evaluated in an industrial case study with the help of a CASE tool.

1 Introduction

Rapid increase in the amount and importance of different software-based functions as well as their extensive interaction are just some of the challenges that are faced during the development of embedded reactive systems. As a consequence, the focus of concerns in software engineering shifts from individual software components to the cross-cutting functions these components offer.

The service-oriented approach is an efficient way to manage the complexity in large-scale model-based development involving many distributed subsystems and teams. Thereby, functions (services), rather than structural entities (components), are emphasized as the basic building blocks for system composition [11]. In contrast to components, services are partial models which describe only fragmented aspects of the overall system behavior. Following the separation-of-concerns principle, a stakeholder can describe a single purpose as a service independent of other services.

A significant factor behind the difficulty of model-based developing complex software is the wide conceptual gap between the problem (function/service) and the implementation (component) domains of discourse [17]. Currently, the step from service-oriented specifications to component-based architectures requires a *manual* transformation. Testing is the main method for consistency checking between both models.

In light of this observation, we introduce a mathematical framework to model multi-functional reactive systems during the early phases of a model-based development process. Thereby, we focus on the formal definitions of services provided by a system,

G.A. Lewis, I. Poernomo, and C. Hofmeister (Eds.): CBSE 2009, LNCS 5582, pp. 156–172, 2009.
© Springer-Verlag Berlin Heidelberg 2009

and show how our service-oriented specification can be transformed into a component-based architecture. The term "service" is used in a variety of meanings, and on various levels of abstraction in the software engineering community. Our notion of service captures functional requirements on a system.

Our approach provides two interrelated views of a software system. *Service-Based Specification* (*SBS*) specifies the system functionality as a set of partial black-box models of the overall behavior. In other words, the overall behavior is specified from different viewpoints [16] by a set of scenarios – causal relations between input and output messages from/to actors in the system environment. We call such scenarios *services* and formalize them by means of I/O automata. Scenarios/services are in certain relationships with each other. The combination of these services according to their relationships yields the overall specification of the system. A further view of the system is the component-based *Logical Architecture*. It decomposes the system behavior into a network of communicating components. Via their interaction, they have to realize the black-box behavior specified by the SBS [10].

The presented framework forms the basis for the comprehensive development process. On the one hand, both views establish a clean separation between the services provided by the system and the software architecture implementing the services. On the other hand, based on the formal foundation, various correct-by-construction methods for the transition between both models can be defined. The fact that our service- and component-based models are based on the same notation and implemented in the same CASE tool facilitates this process. In particular, we present a property preserving procedure, which transforms an SBS into a network of components automatically. Thereby, several services together with their functional dependencies (relationships) are mapped to a component in a schematic manner. Furthermore, special synchronization components are synthesized to preserve the semantics of the SBS. Subsequently, the resulting components can be regrouped arbitrarily and distributed according to quality requirements [4]. However, this is out of the scope of this paper.

Contributions. Our contributions in this paper are twofold. First, in the presented operational framework both function- and component-based views of the system can be modeled in an integrated manner. On the one hand, the total behavior of a component can be specified from different viewpoints by a set of partial services. On the other hand, a (hierarchical) service can be realized by a component network. The consistency between both models can formally be proved. Furthermore, due to a clear link between services and components, it is possible to identify the components which are affected by the changes in the service-based specification and vice versa.

Second, the presented approach bridges the conceptual gap in our model-based development framework. The development process introduced in [18] consists of three phases: requirements analysis yielding a consistent service-based specification [9,20], transformation from specifications to component-based architectures, and deployment of components onto a network of communicating electronic control units [7]. The transition procedure proposed in this paper guarantees a seamless integration of our models at the top of a model chain closing the gap between requirements and design.

Running Example. The concepts introduced in the remainder of the paper will be illustrated on a fragment of a specification originally written and implemented for

"Advanced Technologies and Standards" of Siemens, Sector Industry. The considered bottling plant system comprises several distributed subsystems: to transport empty bottles from a storehouse to the bottling plant, fill bottles with items, seal them, and transport them back to the storehouse. All these systems are operated by a central control unit (CU) which provides a user interface to receive commands and display the system status as well as a device interface to send/receive control signals to/from the subsystems. Although there are over 70 scenarios of system behavior, in this paper we consider only a small subset concerning the interplay between the CU and the conveyor belt. Among other things, the user can start and stop the conveyor. There is also an emergency brake available. When the emergency brake is activated, the CU immediately switches the conveyor off. In this case, the CU is not allowed to switch the system on and the emergency lamp flashes red until an abolition of the emergency command is received.

Outline. The remainder of this paper is organized as follows. In Section 2, we compare our work to related approaches. Section 3 introduces the notion of a component and that of a service and explains the methodological difference between the service-based specification and component-based architecture. In Section 4, a formal framework for modeling specifications and software architectures is presented. In Section 5, we show how a service-based specification can be transformed into a component-based architecture. Finally, we show how our formal approach is implemented in a CASE tool in Section 6 before we conclude the paper in Section 7.

2 Related Work

The presented work is based on a theoretical framework introduced by Broy et al. [11] where the notion of service, decomposition, and refinement are formally defined. This framework proposes to model services as partial stream processing functions. However, it does not cover several relevant issues such as an operational semantics, behavior extension by new aspects, or automatic combination of services into components. In [23], Krüger et al. introduce a methodological approach to defining services and mapping them to component configurations. From use cases, roles and services as interaction patterns among roles are derived. Subsequently, the roles are refined into a component configuration, onto which services are mapped to yield an architectural configuration. Due to the applied algorithm for the synthesis of state machines from MSCs [22], this approach assumes the services to be complete descriptions of the system behavior. This completeness assumption is limiting, considering that interaction-based specifications are inherently partial [30]. Our approach, in contrast, supports a combination of *partial* aspects of the same system behavior.

   Several approaches study the model merging in specific domains including requirements [28] and software architecture [2]. Also, a wide range of techniques for supporting synthesis of component models from declarative requirements [14] or scenarios [19] exist. In the last years, SCESM community has studied a number of further synthesis approaches that turn scenario descriptions into state machines [24]. The closest approach to our work is the framework introduced by Uchitel and Chechik [30], who defined the combination of partial descriptions of the same system. In contrast to this work, where different automata are merged into a global one, we aim at a network of components, which can be grouped and distributed according to given quality requirements and organizational issues.

The relationship between requirements and the architecture has received increased attention recently [5]. The goal-oriented approach, proposed by van Lamsweerde [31] aims at refining high-level goals to requirements and modeling architectures based on underlying system goals. This process relies on a set of predefined refinement patterns, and is not automated. Use Case Maps, introduced by Buhr [12], combine behavior and structure into one view by allocating use cases (responsibilities) to architectural components. This approach requires human intervention for the allocation of use cases.

The combination of services has traditionally been studied in the telecommunication domain [13]. In this field, services (known as features) are considered as increments of the basic functionality. Approaches to this problem (e.g., by Jackson and Zave [21]) propose analytical techniques to detect and to eliminate feature interactions in the implementation domain. Here, in contrast, we propose a correct-by-construction approach to bridging the gap between requirements and architecture models.

Current approaches in the domain of aspect-oriented modeling [29] are concerned with specifying features in modeling views and analyzing interactions across the views at high levels of abstractions (e.g., [3,27]). However, in contrast to our work, these approaches do not take the semantical combination of aspects into consideration, and do not support overlapping aspects based on shared messages.

3   Functional and Architectural Views of the System Behavior

In this section, we introduce the notion of a service and that of a component and explain the methodological difference between the service-based specification and component-based architecture.

A central question in software engineering is how to adequately structure the functionalities of the system at different levels of abstraction. A specification consists of a set of requirements, which usually deal with only fragmented aspects of the system behavior. Different scenarios and system modes (e.g., initialization, shutdown, or normal-case behavior) are usually described by separate requirements. Each further requirement adds a new aspect of the specified behavior. Specifications relate functionalities to each other, e.g., a scenario should always precede another one, or it has a higher priority than the other one. These relationships exclusively determine the structure of the functional specification. On the other hand, the functionality has to be realized by a software architecture, which is typically structured into components. There may be many possible component-based architectures that implement the given functionality. Such architectures may be based on various architectural styles such as layered architecture or client-server. The pure functional structure has usually to be redistributed according to quality requirements and other criteria.

In light of this observation, we propose two orthogonal concepts for structuring and decomposing functionality of the system under consideration (cf. Figure 1).

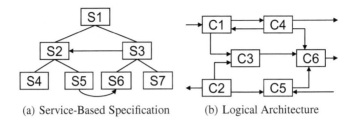

(a) Service-Based Specification   (b) Logical Architecture

Fig. 1. Different Views of the System Behavior

Service-Based Specification. The Service-Based Specification defines the *function view* of the system and structures the user functionality into services without any architectural details. The specification consists of a set of services and relationships between them. A service specifies a partial and non-deterministic relation between certain inputs and outputs of the system, which interacts with its environment within a number of scenarios. In other words, a service is a fragmented aspect of the system behavior. The specification does not define the internal data flow within a system – every service obtains inputs from and sends outputs directly to the environment. Usually, services describe system reactions for only a certain subset of the inputs. This partial description allows the distribution of the system functionality over different services and/or leaving the reaction to certain inputs unspecified.

Logical Architecture. This model defines the *architectural view* of the system and decomposes the functionality into a network of communicating components. Typically, the collaboration between the components realizes the black-box behavior specified at the functional level. The Logical Architecture forms the basis for grouping and distribution of the system functionality over components according to quality constraints rather than functional relationships. Here, structuring is done by means of the most diverse criteria. Besides functional decomposition the architecture might be structured according to the organizational structure within the company, or according to other non-functional requirements.

Specification vs. Architecture. There are three main differences between both views. First, it is the methodological difference between the black-box and white-box views of the system. While the SBS provides a hierarchy of functions observable at the outer boundaries of the system, the Logical Architecture focuses on the internal component-based structure of the system. Second, the structuring of the system functionality in both views follows radically different decomposition and grouping principles. While the structuring into services is platform-independent, the structuring into components is usually platform specific (cf. Model Driven Architecture). Finally, the formal difference between both views lies in the relationships between their building-blocks. In general, inter-service relationships are non-associative, which makes regrouping of services very limited. In Section 5 we realize the inter-service relationships by the commutative and associative inter-component communication, that allows us arbitrary restructuring of the component-based architecture.

4   Service-Oriented Development

This section introduces a formal framework for modeling specifications and software architectures of a system. Thereby, the basic building block of both models is a service – a formal representation of a system functionality. Mathematically, a total component is a special case of a partial service. Both models differ in the combination operator only. In the following, we show how services can be *combined* to service-based specifications and *composed* to component-based architectures.

4.1   Service

A service has a *syntactic interface* consisting of the sets of typed input and output ports, which represent the system's I/O devices (sensors and actuators) according to Parnas et al. [26]. Figure 2(a) depicts the syntactic interface of a service from our running example. There, input and output ports are depicted by empty and filled cycles, respectively.

The semantics of a service is described by an I/O automaton. This is a tuple $S = (V, \mathcal{I}, T)$ consisting of variables V, initial states $\mathcal{I}$, and a transition relation T. V consists of mutually disjoint sets of typed variables I, O, L. The type of a variable $v \in V$ is denoted by the function $ty(v)$, which maps v to the set of all possible valuations. The variables from I and O are the input and output ports of the service interface, respectively. L is a set of local variables. A *state* of S is a valuation α that maps every variable from V to a value of its type. $\Lambda(V)$ is the set of all type-correct valuations for a set of variables V, i.e., for all $\alpha \in \Lambda(V)$ and all $v \in V$ holds $\alpha(v) \in ty(v)$.

We define the following relations on variable valuations: for $\alpha, \beta \in \Lambda(V)$ and $Z \subseteq V$, $\alpha \stackrel{z}{=} \beta$ denotes the equality of variable valuations from Z, i.e., $\forall v \in Z : \alpha(v) = \beta(v)$. For an assertion Φ with free variables from V and $\alpha \in \Lambda(V)$, we say that α *satisfies* Φ, written as $\alpha \vdash \Phi$, iff Φ yields true after replacing its free variables with values from α. Finally, the priming operation on a variable name v yields a new variable v' (the same applies for variable sets). Priming of valuation functions yields a mapping of equally valued primed variables, i.e., for given $\alpha \in \Lambda(V)$, α' is defined by $\forall v \in V : \alpha(v) = \alpha'(v')$. Priming is used to argue about the current and next state within the same logical assertion. For Φ with free variables from $V \cup V'$ and $\alpha, \beta \in \Lambda(V)$ we also write $\alpha, \beta' \vdash \Phi$ to denote that Φ yields true after replacing free unprimed variables by values from α and primed ones by values from β.

$\mathcal{I}$ is an assertion over $O \cup L$ characterizing the *initial states* of the system.

T is a set of transition assertions over $V \cup V'$. In a transition $t \in T$ the satisfying valuations of unprimed variables describe the current state while the valuations of the primed ones constrain the possible successor states. By enabling several satisfying successor state valuations for one current state, we can model non-determinism. A transition is not allowed to constrain primed input and unprimed output variables. By this, we disallow a service to constrain its own future inputs, and enforce the clear separation between the local state (read/write) and the outputs (write only).

We instantiated the above service model for an extended version of I/O automata used in our CASE tool. As in the classical I/O automata [25], a transition leads from one control state to another and might consist of four logical parts: precondition, input

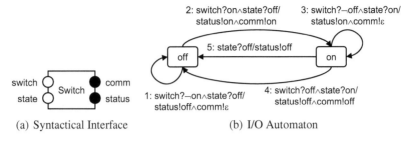

(a) Syntactical Interface   (b) I/O Automaton

Fig. 2. Service `Switch`

pattern, post-condition and output pattern. In our concrete syntax `i?v` denotes an input
pattern, which evaluates to true if the variable $i \in I$ has the value v and `o!v` an output
pattern, which is satisfied by an assignment of value v to the output variable $o' \in O'$.
Figure 2 shows the specification of service `Switch` from our running example, which
formalizes the following scenario of the CU. The user can switch the conveyor on/off,
by putting one of the two commands (`on` or `off`) in. Additionally, the CU receives
the state of the conveyor through the port `state`. If the conveyor is in state `off` and
the user switches it on, in the next step the CU sends command `on` through its port
`comm` to the conveyor, as well as message `on` through port `status` to the user display
(cf. Transition 2). Note, Transition 5 does only reference two of the four existing ports.
This means that the remaining ports are allowed to have arbitrary values within their
respective type domains when the automaton executes this transition.

In order to be able to reason about transition steps, we define the successor state
of some valuation α as $\mathrm{Succ}(\alpha) \stackrel{\mathrm{def}}{=} \{\beta \mid \exists t \in T : \alpha, \beta' \vdash t\}$. The complementary
predicate En yields true if a service can make a step: $\mathrm{En}(\alpha) \stackrel{\mathrm{def}}{\Leftrightarrow} \mathrm{Succ}(\alpha) \neq \emptyset$. If $\mathrm{En}(\alpha)$
holds, we say that the service is *enabled* in state α.

The language of a service automation consists of valuation sequences $\alpha_0\alpha_1 \ldots$, called
runs, such that $\alpha_0 \vdash \mathcal{I}$ holds and for all $i \in \mathbb{N}$ either $\alpha_{i+1} \in \mathrm{Succ}(\alpha_i)$ or $\neg \mathrm{En}(\alpha_i)$ and α_i
is the last element in the sequence. By this, the semantics of our service is *input-disabled*.

4.2   Service Combination

Single services can be combined to a composite service. This directly reflects the idea
that each further requirement/scenario adds a new aspect of the specified behavior. The
combination of these fragmented aspects yields the overall system behavior.

Unlike the classical notion of composition (e.g., [15,25]), which reduces the number
of possible behaviors of individual automata, we are interested in obtaining a mechanism for the *extension* of the system behavior. The service combination accepts all
inputs, which the single services can deal with as long as the outputs produced by these
services are unifiable (not contradictory). The reaction of the combination accords with
the reactions specified by the single services.

The combination of two services is defined only if input ports of one service and the
output ports of the other do not coincide: $(I_1 \cup L_1) \cap (O_2 \cup L_2) = (O_1 \cup L_1) \cap (I_2 \cup L_2) =$
$\emptyset$ and their common variables $V_1 \cap V_2$ have the same type. Then, we speak of *combinable*
services.

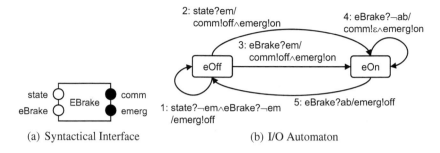

(a) Syntactical Interface   (b) I/O Automaton

Fig. 3. Service EBrake

For two combinable services S_1 and S_2, their combination $C \stackrel{\text{def}}{=} S_1 \parallel S_2$ is defined by $C \stackrel{\text{def}}{=} (V_C, \mathcal{I}_C, T_C)$, where $I_C \stackrel{\text{def}}{=} I_1 \cup I_2$, $O_C \stackrel{\text{def}}{=} O_1 \cup O_2$, $L_C \stackrel{\text{def}}{=} L_1 \cup L_2$, $V_C \stackrel{\text{def}}{=} I_C \cup L_C \cup O_C$, $\mathcal{I}_C \stackrel{\text{def}}{=} \mathcal{I}_1 \wedge \mathcal{I}_2$. T_C is described by the successor function below. The combined automaton makes a step if either the current input can be accepted by both single services, and their reactions are not contradictory, or the input can be accepted by one of both services only. In the latter case, the local variables of the not enabled service (i.e., the service with $\neg \text{En}(\alpha)$) are not modified, and its output variables (not common with the first service) are unrestricted. Formally, the set of successors of the combination is defined for all $i, j \in \{1, 2\}$, $i \neq j$ as follows:

$$\text{Succ}(\alpha) \stackrel{\text{def}}{=} \{\beta \mid \exists t_1 \in T_1, t_2 \in T_2 : \alpha, \beta' \vdash t_1 \wedge t_2\}$$

$$\cup \{\beta \mid \exists t_i \in T_i : \alpha, \beta' \vdash t_i \wedge \neg \text{En}_j(\alpha) \wedge \alpha \stackrel{L_j}{=} \beta\},$$

where $\text{En}_i(\alpha)$ is true iff S_i is enabled in state α.

To illustrate the concept of combination, we consider a further scenario concerning the emergency brake from our example. The CU switches the system off if the user puts the emergency brake on (message em on port eBrake) or a critical state message is received from the conveyor (message em on port state). The CU is not allowed to

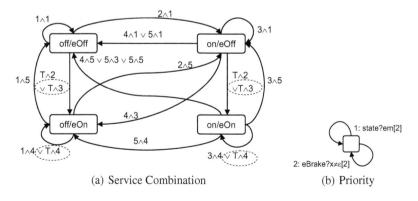

(a) Service Combination   (b) Priority

Fig. 4. Behavior Specifications

switch the system on and the emergency lamp flashes until an abolition of the emergency (ab) is received on eBrake. The service in Figure 3 formalizes this scenario.

The combination of services Switch and EBrake results in the automaton in Figure 4(a) (without transitions marked by dashed ovals). There, the labels of transitions are of the form $t_s \wedge t_e$, where t_s and t_e are the transition numbers from Figures 2(b) and 3(b), respectively. A label of the form $\top \wedge t_e$ identifies situations where service Switch is not enabled. A transition with a label $l_1 \vee l_2$ is an abbreviation of two transitions with labels l_1 and l_2, respectively.

4.3 Prioritized Combination

Usually, some events or scenarios explicitly have a higher priority in specifications than others. For example, the system reaction in the case of emergency has higher priority than the normal-case behavior. In order to be able to reflect this in our service model, we introduce the notion of a *prioritized combination*. It allows an individual service to take control over other services depending on specific input histories. Thereby, we can express different relationships between services without any modifications on them.

The prioritized combination temporally allows a service to take priority over another service. Thereby, the prioritized combination is controlled by a special service S_P with the interface consisting of all input ports of both services and no output ports. Transitions of S_P might prioritize one of both services. If the current input enables a transition of S_P and this transition prioritizes service S_2, only S_2 is *executing* – the local state of S_1 remains unmodified, the output variables exclusively controlled by S_1 are not subject to any restrictions. If the current input does not enable any transition of S_P or the enabled transition prioritizes no service, the combination behaves like the un-prioritized one. Thus, the priority determines certain inputs for which the system behavior should coincide with the behavior of one of both services only.

The prioritized combination $PC \overset{\text{def}}{=} S_1 \parallel^{S_P} S_2$ is defined for a pair of combinable services S_1, S_2 and a special priority service $S_P \overset{\text{def}}{=} (I_P \uplus L_P, \mathcal{I}_P, T_P, p)$ by $PC \overset{\text{def}}{=} (V_{PC}, \mathcal{I}_{PC}, T_{PC})$, where $I_P \overset{\text{def}}{=} I_{PC} \overset{\text{def}}{=} I_1 \cup I_2, O_{PC} \overset{\text{def}}{=} O_1 \cup O_2, L_{PC} \overset{\text{def}}{=} L_1 \cup L_2 \cup L_P$, $V_{PC} \overset{\text{def}}{=} I_{PC} \cup L_{PC} \cup O_{PC}, \mathcal{I}_{PC} \overset{\text{def}}{=} \mathcal{I}_P \wedge \mathcal{I}_1 \wedge \mathcal{I}_2$. The function $p \colon T_P \to \{0,1,2\}$ defines whether S_1, S_2 or no service is prioritized by a certain transition from T_P. T_{PC} is described by the successor function below. It is defined over the transition set T_C of the unprioritized combination of S_1 and S_2 for all $i, j \in \{1,2\}, i \neq j$:

$$\text{Succ}(\alpha) \overset{\text{def}}{=} \{\beta \mid \exists t \in T_C : \forall t_P \in T_P : (\alpha, \beta' \vdash t \wedge \neg t_P) \wedge \alpha \overset{L_P}{=} \beta\}$$
$$\cup \{\beta \mid \exists t \in T_C, t_P \in T_P : (\alpha, \beta' \vdash t \wedge t_P) \wedge p(t_P) = 0\}$$
$$\cup \{\beta \mid \exists t_i \in T_i, t_P \in T_P : (\alpha, \beta' \vdash t_i \wedge t_P) \wedge p(t_P) = i \wedge \alpha \overset{L_j}{=} \beta\}.$$

The first subset describes the case when no transition of S_P is enabled, the second one – when the enabled transition of S_P prioritizes none of both services. In both cases, the behavior of $S_1 \parallel^{S_P} S_2$ coincides with the behavior of $S_1 \parallel S_2$. The last subset contains the common behaviors of prioritized service S_i and S_P, i.e., the behavior of service S_1 or S_2 which is temporally prioritized by a currently enabled transition of S_P.

In our running example, it makes sense to prioritize the emergency break signals `eBrake?em` and `state?em`. We require that the combined system must behave like service `EBrake` if one of these signals arrives. The priority service which prioritizes emergency signals is depicted in Figure 4(b) (both transitions prioritize service `EBrake`). The prioritized combination of `Switch` and `EBrake` with regard to the priority service results in the automaton in Figure 4(a) (including formulas enclosed in dashed ovals). Whenever an emergency signal has arrived, this combination behaves like service `EBrake` (transitions marked by dashed ovals), otherwise the behavior is identical to the unprioritized combination from the last section.

The un-prioritized combination from the previous section is a special case of the prioritized one. The prioritized combination is in general non-associative, however, it is commutative[1] and distributive. These properties are shown in [9].

4.4 Composition

A component – the architectural building block – can be specified by a set of services combined according to their interrelationships as described above. In the architectural view, a system is usually described by a network of communicating components. The inter-component communication is not supported by the combination operators. Consequently, we define a *composition* operator on services and, thus, integrate the architectural view into our framework. As a reminder, mathematically, the total component is a special case of the partial service.

The composition operator permits two services to communicate directly via homonymous input/output port pairs. Two services are composable if $L_1 \cap V_2 = L_2 \cap V_1 = I_1 \cap I_2 = O_1 \cap O_2 = \emptyset$ and their shared variables $V_1 \cap V_2$ have the same type.

For two composable services S_1 and S_2, the composition $C \stackrel{\text{def}}{=} S_1 \oplus S_2$ is defined by $C \stackrel{\text{def}}{=} (V_C, \mathcal{I}_C, T_C)$, where $I_C \stackrel{\text{def}}{=} (I_1 \cup I_2) \setminus (O_1 \cup O_2)$, $O_C \stackrel{\text{def}}{=} (O_1 \cup O_2) \setminus (I_1 \cup I_2)$, $L_C \stackrel{\text{def}}{=} L_1 \cup L_2 \cup (V_1 \cap V_2)$, $V_C \stackrel{\text{def}}{=} I_C \cup L_C \cup O_C$, $\mathcal{I}_C \stackrel{\text{def}}{=} \mathcal{I}_1 \wedge \mathcal{I}_2$. T_C is described by the successor function below. The composite automaton makes a step if both services accept their current inputs:

$$\text{Succ}(\alpha) \stackrel{\text{def}}{=} \{\beta \mid \exists t_1 \in T_1, t_2 \in T_2 \wedge \alpha, \beta' \vdash t_1 \wedge t_2\}.$$

The composite service C is enabled if both services in the composition are enabled, i.e., $\text{En}(\alpha) \stackrel{\text{def}}{=} \text{En}_1(\alpha) \wedge \text{En}_2(\alpha)$. The service composition is very similar to those introduced in [15] and, therefore, sketched very briefly. The composition is synchronous, strong causal as well as associative and commutative as shown in [6].

4.5 Requirements Analysis

The formalization of functional requirements by an SBS makes it possible to analyze them automatically and thus to detect and solve inconsistencies (known as *feature interaction*). The SBS allows us to abstract from a complex component-based structure and focus on the consistency between system functions.

---

[1] Provided that priority function p uniquely identifies every transition with combined services.

According to our definition, the service combination accepts all inputs, which the individual services can deal with as long as their outputs are unifiable. The combination does not contain transition combinations with contradictory outputs to the same input. Thus, the combined service is not able to react to an input if all possible outputs specified by the services in isolation are mutually contradictory. An inconsistency between two services exists when a service in the presence of other services is prevented from reacting to all inputs which can be suitably processed by the services in isolation. A subclass of these inconsistencies are deadlocks (if the combination is not able to react to any input in a certain local state). We refer to [9] for detail.

Based on our model, further important properties as determinism or input coverage can be checked. However, this is not in scope of this paper.

5   From Specification to Logical Architecture

In this section we show how a service-based specification can be transformed into a component-based architecture. Therefore we propose a property preserving transition procedure. This means, the presented procedure transforms a given service specification $S = S_1 \|^{SP} S_2$ (a combination of services) into its realizing network of components C_S (a composition of components), which provably preserves the behavior of S. The procedure relies on translating the partial services onto total components and introducing synchronization components to preserve the semantics of the (prioritized) combination.

Figure 5 depicts a synthesized network of components whose overall behavior coincides with the behavior specified by the prioritized combination of services Switch and EBrake from Section 4. In contrast to services, components are not allowed to share common input ports. Therefore, the values on each port of the overall system interface, which are read by more than one component, have to be split up into several identical values. Component Demux (for demultiplexer) splits up the values on the input ports and forwards them to components Switch$^\perp$, EBrake$^\perp$ and Priority$^\perp$. Components Priority$^\perp$ and P-Coord temporally disable Switch$^\perp$ according to the semantics of the prioritized service combination from Section 4.3. Finally, since an output port can not be written by more than one component, the outputs of Switch$^\perp$ and EBrake$^\perp$ are merged to common values by component Mux (for multiplexer).

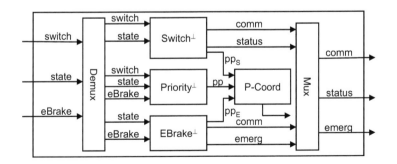

Fig. 5. Logical Architecture

According to our strong-causal semantics [6], the processing of messages in a component causes a unit delay. Thus, in order to keep inputs and outputs in-sync, each of them are processed by a (de-)mux. The main advantage of the presented solution is that `Priority`$^\perp$ immediately disables/enables `Switch`$^\perp$, i.e., without a delay between current inputs and the prioritization effect (see below). Therefore, we make use of our input-disabled semantics to enforce the correct behavior of (un-)prioritized components.

The transition procedure consists of the following steps[2]:

1. Partial services are totalized to components;
2. to ensure a correct composition of components, the homonymous variables of the original services are renamed in a schematic manner;
3. to preserve the behavior of the service combination, new coordinating components are synthesized;
4. renamed components and synthesized coordinators are composed to a network.

In the following the transition steps are explained in detail.

Totalization. A component cannot be partial – to each input there must be a defined reaction. However, the reaction of a service is defined for a subset of inputs only. Thus, the first step of our procedure is the totalization of the service behavior. A component has to react by a dedicated value $\perp$ to all inputs, for which there is no defined reaction of the accordant service. Formally, to totalize a partial service $S = (V, \mathcal{I}, T)$ to a component $S^\perp = (V, \mathcal{I}, T^\perp)$ by the value $\perp$, all variable types from V are extended by $\perp$ and $T^\perp$ is defined by $\mathrm{Succ}_{S^\perp}(\alpha) \stackrel{\text{def}}{=} \mathrm{Succ}_S(\alpha) \cup \{\beta \mid \neg\mathrm{En}_S(\alpha) \wedge \alpha \stackrel{L}{=} \beta \wedge \forall o \in O : \beta(o) = \perp\}$. The behavior of $S^\perp$ coincides with the behavior of S for all defined inputs, otherwise $S^\perp$ makes a "stuttering step": issues $\perp$ and preserves the local variables valuations.

Renaming. In contrast to the combination, in the composition, components are not allowed to share a common input or output port (this ensures the associativity of the composition). In order to establish the required composability between components, their ports are renamed in a uniform manner. Thus, we aim at indexing all ports of a component by the name of the accordant service. For this purpose we define the renaming operator $[./.]$. Formally, the renamed component $S[w/v] = (V_w, \mathcal{I}_w, T_w)$ is defined by $V_w \stackrel{\text{def}}{=} (V \setminus \{v\}) \cup \{w\}$, $\mathcal{I}_w \stackrel{\text{def}}{=} \mathcal{I}[w/v]$, and $T_w \stackrel{\text{def}}{=} \{t[w/v] \mid t \in T\}$, where $v \in V$ and $w \notin V$ is a pair of equal-typed variables. $\Phi[w/v]$ denotes the replacement of all occurrences of v by w and v' by w' in a given assertion Φ. Obviously, the behaviors of S and $S[w/v]$ are equal up to renaming. We lift the renaming operator for variable sets by $S[v_i/v]_{v \in U}$ for some subset $U \subseteq V$, and define it as a successive renaming of all variables in U by new ones.

I/O Coordination. Using the operator defined above we rename a common port p shared by a pair of services S_1, S_2 as two ports p_1 and p_2 contained in the interfaces of $S_1[p_1/p]$ and $S_2[p_2/p]$, respectively. However, this procedure causes a valuation desynchronization of the new ports p_1 and p_2. According to the SBS semantics, they must

---

[2] This automated procedure supports only a many-to-one mapping of services to components.

always have the same value. To synchronize the values on these ports, a *mux/demux* is synthesized for each input/output port (in Figure 5 three single demuxes are composed to Demux and three muxes are composed to Mux).

For a pair (S_1, S_2) and their common input port ip, the interface of the demux $dem(S_1, S_2, ip, \bot) \stackrel{\text{def}}{=} (V_d, \mathcal{I}_d, T_d)$ contains one input port $I_d \stackrel{\text{def}}{=} \{ip\}$ and two output ports $O_d \stackrel{\text{def}}{=} \{ip_1, ip_2\}$, where $ip_1, ip_2 \notin (V_1 \cup V_2)$ and $ty(ip) = ty(ip_1) = ty(ip_2)$. Thus, $V_d \stackrel{\text{def}}{=} I_d \uplus O_d$. The semantics of a demux is very simple. It copies each value on the input port to both output ports: $T_d \stackrel{\text{def}}{=} \{ip'_1 = ip'_2 = ip\}$ and $\mathcal{I}_d \stackrel{\text{def}}{=} ip_1 = ip_2 = \bot$.

For a pair (S_1, S_2) and their common output port op, the interface of the mux $mux(S_1, S_2, op, \bot) \stackrel{\text{def}}{=} (V_m, \mathcal{I}_m, T_m)$ is defined by $V_m \stackrel{\text{def}}{=} I_m \uplus O_m$, $I_m \stackrel{\text{def}}{=} \{op_1, op_2\}$, and $O_m \stackrel{\text{def}}{=} \{op\}$. Thereby, $op_1, op_2 \notin (V_1 \cup V_2)$, $ty(op) = ty(op_1) = ty(op_2)$. The mux forwards the input values to the output port only if both values are equal or one of them is $\bot$. Formally, $T_m \stackrel{\text{def}}{=} \{(op' = op_1 = op_2) \vee (op' = op_1 \wedge op_2 = \bot) \vee (op' = op_2 \wedge op_1 = \bot)\}$. For $\mathcal{I}_m$ we demand that the valuation of op in the mux and in the service combination must be equal: $\alpha \vdash \mathcal{I}_m \stackrel{\text{def}}{\Leftrightarrow} \exists \beta \vdash \mathcal{I}_1 \wedge \mathcal{I}_2 : \beta(op) = \alpha(op)$. Since the reaction to unequal inputs is not specified, the behavior of a mux is not total.

The above synthesis procedures are easily generalized for an arbitrary number of services sharing a common I/O port or for non-common ports contained in the interface of only one service. In the latter case the coordinators become simple unit-delay identity functions.

Synthesis. In the following the synthesis procedure is explained in detail. The service combination $S = S_1 \| S_2$ is transformed into the following component composition (cf. Figure 5 without components $\texttt{Priority}^\bot$ and $\texttt{P-Coord}$):

$$C_S \stackrel{\text{def}}{=} DE \oplus S_1^\bot[v_1/v]_{v \in V_1} \oplus S_2^\bot[v_2/v]_{v \in V_2} \oplus MU,$$

where $S_i^\bot[v_1/v]_{v \in V_i}$ is the totalization of S_i with variables indexed by $i \in \{1, 2\}$;

$$DE \stackrel{\text{def}}{=} \bigoplus_{ip \in I_1 \cup I_2} dem(S_1, S_2, ip, \bot) \quad \text{and} \quad MU \stackrel{\text{def}}{=} \bigoplus_{op \in O_1 \cup O_2} mux(S_1, S_2, op, \bot)$$

are the compositions of (de-)muxes for all I/O ports, respectively. Obviously, all components in C_S are mutually composable. As already explained, the composition of demultiplexers DE splits up the values on the common input ports and forwards them to the components $S_1^\bot$ and $S_2^\bot$. The outputs of both components are merged to common values by the composition of multiplexers MU.

Regarding the prioritized combination, it is important to ensure that the priority component immediately disables/enables one of both affected components, i.e., without a unit delay between current inputs and the prioritization effect. Otherwise, the prioritization is based on outdated inputs and the composition behavior does not coincide with the combination behavior. For example, if components $\texttt{Switch}^\bot$, $\texttt{EBrake}^\bot$ and $\texttt{Priority}^\bot$ are connected directly, the prioritization signal generated by $\texttt{Priority}^\bot$ arrives at the components one unit later than the inputs this signal is based on. Therefore, two components are connected with their priority via an additional coordinator (cf. $\texttt{P-Coord}$ in Figure 5). Due to the input-disabled semantics of our components,

Switch$^\perp$ and EBrake$^\perp$ can execute a transition only if their outputs can be consumed by P-Coord. It consumes the outputs from a component only if it receives the prioritization signal for this component from Priority$^\perp$. By this, we realize the *immediate* prioritization of components without any delays.

Formally, for a combined service $S = S_1 \|^{S_P} S_2$ with priority $S_P = (I_P \uplus L_P, \mathcal{I}_P, T_P, p)$ we construct a component $S_P^{ext} \stackrel{\text{def}}{=} (I \uplus L \uplus \{pp\}, \mathcal{I}_P, \overline{T}_P)$ with a new output port $pp \notin (I \cup L)$ and $ty(pp) = \{0, 1, 2, \perp\}$. S_P^{ext} behaves like the original service S_P and, additionally, sends its current prioritization decision through the new port pp. According to the semantics from Section 4.3, this decision is defined by the function $p(t)$. If the component S_P^{ext} executes a transition and this transition prioritizes one of both components ($p(t) \in \{1, 2\}$), value $p(t)$ is sent through pp. If no component is prioritized ($p(t) = 0$), a $\perp$ is sent through the port. Formally, $\overline{T}_P \stackrel{\text{def}}{=} \{t \wedge pp' = p(t) \mid t \in T_P \wedge p(t) \in \{1, 2\}\} \cup \{t \wedge pp' = \perp \mid t \in T_P \wedge p(t) = 0\}$. Note, after totalization S_P^{ext} also sends a $\perp$ if S_P is not enabled.

Corresponding output ports are added to the interfaces of S_1 and S_2 to connect them with their priority via a priority coordinator. For $S_i = (V_i, \mathcal{I}_i, T_i)$ with $i \in \{1, 2\}$ we obtain $S_i^{ext} \stackrel{\text{def}}{=} (V_i \uplus \{pp\}, \mathcal{I}_i, \overline{T}_i)$. Each transition of S_i^{ext} can non-deterministically send the index i or the value 0 through the port pp: $\overline{T}_i \stackrel{\text{def}}{=} \{t \wedge (pp' = i \vee pp' = 0) \mid t \in T\}$.

The priority coordinator is a mux $mux(S_1, S_P, S_2, pp, \perp)$ with three input ports pp, pp_1, and pp_2. As a reminder, a mux can execute a transition only if all inputs except for $\perp$ are equal. Thus, the coordinator executes a transition in the following cases. (a) The mux receives value 1 through ports pp and pp_1 and a $\perp$ through pp_2. This means, component S_1 is prioritized and executes a transition. The unprioritized component S_2 is not able to execute a transition because values 2 or 0 on its port pp_2 can not be consumed by the mux. Thus, it sends a $\perp$ and does not modify its local variables. (b) The same goes for $pp = 2$, $pp_1 = \perp$ and $pp_2 = 2$. Here, component S_2 is prioritized. (c) The mux receives a $\perp$ through pp, and 0 through both pp_1 and pp_2. This means, no component is prioritized. S_1 and S_2 execute their transitions and send 0 through pp_1 and pp_2, respectively. In all other cases, the priority coordinator can not execute a transition. Thus, due to the input-disabled semantics, the coordinator prevents other components from executing transitions which are not in accordance with the service combination semantics.

The prioritized service combination $S = S_1 \|^{S_P} S_2$ is transformed into the following component composition (cf. Figure 5):

$$C_S \stackrel{\text{def}}{=} DE \oplus \bigoplus_{i \in \{1,2,P\}} (S_i^{ext})^\perp [v_i/v]_{v \in V_i} \oplus mux(S_1, S_P, S_2, pp, \perp) \oplus MU.$$

The (de-)multiplexers DE and MU have the same role as in the unprioritized composition. The prioritization between both components S_1^{ext} and S_2^{ext} is coordinated by the component S_P^{ext}. To assure a prioritization without delays the three components are connected via the coordinator $mux(S_1, S_P, S_2, pp, \perp)$.

The behavior of the synthesized component network simulates the behavior of the service-based specification. Furthermore, due to the commutativity and associativity of the composition operator, the components can subsequently be regrouped and distributed according to further quality requirements.

For the reasons of limited space we omit the formal definition of the simulation relation and the correctness proofs. We refer to [8] for detail.

6 Tool Support

Both service- and component-based perspectives are integrated in a CASE tool. AutoFOCUS [1] is a tool for the model-based development of reactive systems. It supports graphical description of the developed system in both functional and architectural perspectives. Each perspective consists of three views (cf. Figure 6). In the *Project Explorer*

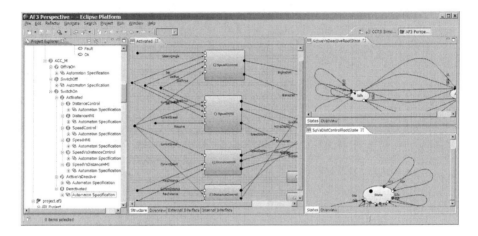

Fig. 6. Different AutoFOCUS Views for SBS Approach

view services/components are structured hierarchically. In the *Structure Diagrams* view syntactical interfaces are defined. *State Transition Diagrams* describe the behavior of services/components using our I/O automata. The simulation environment allows us to validate service-based as well as component-based models. We are currently working on an automatic transformation of service-based specifications into logical architectures using the transition procedure from Section 5.

7 Conclusion and Outlook

We have presented an automata-based framework for modeling multi-functional reactive systems during the early phases of a model-based development process. Two orthogonal perspectives (functional and architectural) on the system behavior are formally defined. The proposed Service-Based Specification combines single (fragmented and incomplete) scenarios, formalized as services, to an overall system behavior. Thereby, we focus on a combination of partial behaviors concerning the same (sub-)system but specified from different viewpoints. The Logical Architecture defines the architectural view and decomposes the functionality into collaborating components. Via their interaction, the components realize the black-box behavior specified at the functional level. The formal integration of service- and component-based models in a mathematical framework is the main contribution of our work. The proposed property-preserving step from service-based specifications to logical architectures forms the basis for the comprehensive development process that can be supported by a tool in the sense of model transformation techniques. Thus, our models integrate seamlessly at the top of a model chain closing the formal gap between requirements and design.

We see the application area of the proposed approach in the model-based development of reactive systems. With a scenario-based specification as an input, this specification is checked for consistency by verification and simulation [9,20]. Subsequently, the specification is transformed into a component-based architecture. Finally, the components are deployed onto a network of electronic control units [7]. We are currently working on automating the second step. The fact that both specification and architecture models have the same mathematical foundation facilitates this process. Beyond this, our future work includes the development of the methodically important mapping of one service to several components ($n : m$ mapping).

Acknowledgments. We are grateful to Judith Hartmann, Benjamin Hummel, Leo Kof, Christian Leuxner, Sabine Rittmann and Bernd Spanfelner for their advice on early versions of the paper.

References

1. AutoFOCUS 3, http://af3.in.tum.de/
2. Abi-Antoun, M., Aldrich, J., Nahas, N., Schmerl, B., Garlan, D.: Differencing and merging of architectural views. In: Proceedings of ASE 2006. IEEE Computer Society Press, Los Alamitos (2006)
3. Baniassad, E., Clarke, S.: Theme: an approach for aspect-oriented analysis and design. In: Proceedings of ICSE 2004 (2004)
4. Bass, L., Clements, P., Kazman, R.: Software Architecture in Practice. Addison-Wesley, Reading (1998)
5. Berry, D.M., Kazman, R., Wieringa, R.: Second international workshop on from software requirements to architectures (STRAW 2003). SIGSOFT Softw. Eng. Notes 29(3) (2004)
6. Botaschanjan, J.: Techniques for Property Preservation in the Development of Real-Time Systems. PhD thesis, TU München (2008)
7. Botaschanjan, J., Gruler, A., Harhurin, A., Kof, L., Spichkova, M., Trachtenherz, D.: Towards Modularized Verification of Distributed Time-Triggered Systems. In: Misra, J., Nipkow, T., Sekerinski, E. (eds.) FM 2006. LNCS, vol. 4085, pp. 163–178. Springer, Heidelberg (2006)
8. Botaschanjan, J., Harhurin, A.: A Formal Framework for Integrating Functional and Architectural Views of Reactive Systems. Technical Report TUM-I0904, TU München (2009)
9. Botaschanjan, J., Harhurin, A., Kof, L.: Service-based Specification of Reactive Systems. Technical Report TUM-I0815, Technische Universität München (2008)
10. Broy, M., Krüger, I., Pretschner, A., Salzmann, C.: Engineering automotive software. Proceedings of the IEEE 95(2) (2007)
11. Broy, M., Krüger, I.H., Meisinger, M.: A formal model of services. ACM Trans. Softw. Eng. Methodol. 16(1) (2007)

172 J. Botaschanjan and A. Harhurin

12. Buhr, R.J.A.: Use case maps as architectural entities for complex systems. IEEE Trans. Softw. Eng. 24(12) (1998)
13. Calder, M., Kolberg, M., Magill, E.H., Reiff-Marganiec, S.: Feature interaction: a critical review and considered forecast. Comput. Networks 41(1) (2003)
14. Damas, C., Lambeau, B., van Lamsweerde, A.: Scenarios, goals, and state machines: a win-win partnership for model synthesis. In: Proceedings of FSE14. ACM Press, New York (2006)
15. de Alfaro, L., Henzinger, T.A.: Interface automata. SIGSOFT Softw. Eng. Notes 26(5) (2001)
16. Finkelstein, A., Kramer, J., Nuseibeh, B., Finkelstein, L., Goedicke, M.: Viewpoints: A framework for integrating multiple perspectives in system development. International Journal of Software Engineering and Knowledge Engineering 2(1) (1992)
17. France, R., Rumpe, B.: Model-driven development of complex software: A research roadmap. In: Proceedings of FOSE 2007. IEEE Computer Society Press, Los Alamitos (2007)
18. Gruler, A., Harhurin, A., Hartmann, J.: Development and configuration of service-based product lines. In: Proceedings of SPLC 2007. IEEE Computer Society Press, Los Alamitos (2007)
19. Harel, D., Kugler, H.: Synthesizing state-based object systems from LSC specifications. In: Yu, S., Păun, A. (eds.) CIAA 2000. LNCS, vol. 2088, pp. 1–33. Springer, Heidelberg (2001)
20. Harhurin, A., Hartmann, J.: Towards consistent specifications of product families. In: Cuellar, J., Maibaum, T., Sere, K. (eds.) FM 2008. LNCS, vol. 5014, pp. 390–405. Springer, Heidelberg (2008)
21. Jackson, M., Zave, P.: Distributed feature composition: A virtual architecture for telecommunications services. IEEE Trans. Softw. Eng. 24(10) (1998)
22. Krüger, I., Grosu, R., Scholz, P., Broy, M.: From MSCs to statecharts. In: Proceedings of the Distributed and Parallel Embedded Systems. Kluwer Academic Publishers, Dordrecht (1999)
23. Krüger, I.H., Mathew, R.: Systematic development and exploration of service-oriented software architectures. In: Proceedings of WICSA 2004 (2004)
24. Liang, H., Dingel, J., Diskin, Z.: A comparative survey of scenario-based to state-based model synthesis approaches. In: Proceedings of SCESM 2006. ACM Press, New York (2006)
25. Lynch, N.A., Tuttle, M.R.: An introduction to input/output automata. CWI-Quarterly, 2(3) (1989)
26. Parnas, D.L., Madey, J.: Functional documents for computer systems. Science of Computer Programming 25(1) (1995)
27. Rashid, A., Moreira, A., Araújo, J.: Modularisation and composition of aspectual requirements. In: Proceedings of AOSD 2003: Aspect-oriented Software Development. ACM Press, New York (2003)
28. Sabetzadeh, M., Easterbrook, S.: View merging in the presence of incompleteness and inconsistency. Requir. Eng. 11(3) (2006)
29. Solberg, A., Simmonds, D.M., Reddy, R., Ghosh, S., France, R.B.: Using aspect oriented techniques to support separation of concerns in model driven development. In: Proceedings of COMPSAC 2005. IEEE Computer Society Press, Los Alamitos (2005)
30. Uchitel, S., Chechik, M.: Merging partial behavioural models. SIGSOFT Softw. Eng. Notes 29(6) (2004)
31. van Lamsweerde, A.: From system goals to software architecture. In: Bernardo, M., Inverardi, P. (eds.) SFM 2003. LNCS, vol. 2804, pp. 25–43. Springer, Heidelberg (2003)

Integration of Extra-Functional Properties in Component Models*

Séverine Sentilles, Petr Štěpán, Jan Carlson, and Ivica Crnković

Mälardalen Research and Technology Centre, Mälardalen University, Västerås, Sweden
{severine.sentilles,jan.carlson,ivica.crnkovic}@mdh.se
psn08003@student.mdh.se

Abstract. Management of extra-functional properties in component models is one of the main challenges in the component-based software engineering community. Still, the starting point in their management, namely their specification in a context of component models is not addressed in a systematic way. Extra-functional properties can be expressed as attributes (or combinations of them) of components, or of a system, but also as attributes of other elements, such as interfaces and connectors. Attributes can be defined as estimations, or can be measured, or modelled; this means that an attribute can be expressed through multiple values valid under different conditions. This paper addresses how this diversity in attribute specifications and their relations to component model can be expressed, by proposing a model for attribute specifications and their integrations in component models. A format for attribute specification is proposed, discussed and analyzed, and the approach is exemplified through its integration both in the ProCom component model and its integrated development environment.

1 Introduction

One of the core challenges still remaining in component-based software engineering (CBSE) is the management of extra-functional properties, often expressed in terms of attributes of components or of systems as a whole. In CBSE, one desired feature is the integration of components in an automatic and efficient way. The integration process is achieved by "wiring" components through their interfaces. The second aspect of the integration is the composition of extra-functional properties and this part is significantly more complex. The problem already appears in the specifications of attributes. While component models precisely define interfaces as a means of functional specification, specifications of attributes in relation to component specification is either not defined, or unclear. Is an attribute a property of a component or the result of interaction between components, or maybe the result of performing a function that is part of the component interface, or the result of combining a component and its environment? So far these questions have not been addressed in a systematic way.

This paper addresses the question of attribute specification in component models. The specification of attributes has several aspects that we discuss and demonstrate on a component model.

---

* This work was partially supported by the Swedish Foundation for Strategic Research via the strategic research centre PROGRESS, and by the EU FP7 Project Q-ImPrESS.

G.A. Lewis, I. Poernomo, and C. Hofmeister (Eds.): CBSE 2009, LNCS 5582, pp. 173–190, 2009.

First, we address the question of the form of attribute specifications. Our starting points are related to Shaw's specification which identifies the specification of attributes as a triple containing attribute name, value and credibility information [1]. We refine this definition in extension of values and credibility.

The second aspect of attribute specification that we address is related to the component and system lifecycle. During the lifecycle of a component an attribute changes with respect to how the value is obtained and the accuracy (credibility) of its value. In early phases of the component lifecycle a component is being modelled and then the attribute value can be an estimation or even a requirement. The accuracy of the estimation during the development process can be changed, as a result of an increasing amount of information or a change in the way the value is obtained. In the run-time phase (or even in the development phase in some cases), the attribute value can be measured.

The third aspect of the attribute specifications concerns the variations of the values — not only as a result of different ways of obtaining the value, but also different values depending on the external context. Some attributes are directly related to the system context — for example, the execution time of a component does not only depend on the component behaviour and input parameters, but also on the platform characteristics. For such cases it is obvious that we need to be able to specify these different values and the conditions under which the attribute value is valid.

There are also other aspects of integration of component models and their attributes. By nature the attributes are parts of (i.e., they characterize) components, but they also can be related to a particular element of a component or a system. For example, an attribute can be annotated to a component directly, or to a port in the interface of a component, or to a connector. In general, a component model that supports the management of attributes should have the possibility to relate attributes to different architectural elements of the component model.

The aim of this paper is to analyze the different aspects of attribute specifications to formalize their form and their integration with component models. A formal specification of an attribute format makes it easier to manage component and system properties. It also catalyzes the process of integrating extra-functional properties into component models.

Since attributes are very different, the concrete results can be shown on particular classes of attributes integrated with particular component models. To illustrate the attribute specifications in a component model, we use ProCom [2,3], and annotations of attributes as an immanent part of the model. We also provide implementation examples.

The rest of the paper is organized as follows. Section 2 defines the attribute specifications. Section 3 discuses the attribute specifications of composite components in relation to the attributes of composable components. Since an attribute can include different values, i.e., different versions of an attribute can exist, in a system analysis or verification process it is important to select a particular version of an attribute. The selection principles and a possible support is discussed in Section 4. The principles of attribute specifications are exemplified in the ProCom component model, and a prototype tool that manages attributes is demonstrated in Section 5. Section 6 surveys related work, followed by a short discussion in Section 7, before the paper concludes with a summary and future work.

2   Annotation of Attributes in Component Models

The purpose of attributes is to provide additional information about the components, complementing the structural information that is provided by the component model.

This additional information is intended to give a better insight in the behaviour and capability of the component in terms of reliability, safety, security, maintainability, accuracy, compliance to a standard, resource consumption, and timing capabilities, among many others. In that sense, attributes bridge the gap between the knowledge of what a component does and its actually capabilities.

2.1   Attributes in a Component Model

As mentioned in [4], the additional information provided by attributes does not necessarily concern the component as a whole, but in fact often points more precisely to some parts of a component such as an interface or an operation of an interface. In our view, this relation should not be limited to components, interfaces and operations, but be extended so that attributes can be associated with other elements of a component model, including for example ports, connectors or more notably component instances. For instance, having an extra-functional property on connectors to capture communication latency, makes it possible to reason about the response time of complex operations that involve communication between components.

Following this standpoint, we define as *attributable* an element of a component model (*component, interface, component instance, connector,* etc.) to which extra-functional properties (*attributes*) can be attached. By this means, all attributable entities are treated in similar way with regards to the definition and usage of attributes. Fig. 1 depicts these relations.

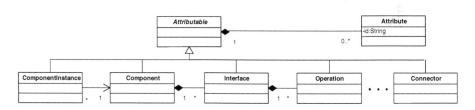

Fig. 1. The relation between attributes and the elements of a component model

2.2   Attribute Definition

The exhaustive list of possible attributes to consider is endless and, as stated in [5], there is no a priori, logical or conceptual method to determine which properties exist in a system or in components. Furthermore, a single property can have a multitude of possible representations. This problem inheres in one of the fundamental characteristics of extra-functional properties and properties in general: they are issued by humans. Therefore, different users will consider different types of information important for the development of the software system, and for the same property they might associate a different meaning and representation.

Consequently, the definition of a suitable format specification for extra-functional properties able to deal with the great variety of properties possibly of interest remains a challenge. This definition should be generic and flexible enough to handle the heterogeneity of properties while being extensible to support the emergence of new ones. This means that the specification format must be able to cope with different formats and different levels of formalism.

An informal way to specify these properties is to use annotations. However, it gives too much freedom concerning the definition and this brings problems to manage extra-functional properties at a large scale or in automated processes such as composition or analysis.

In order to move towards a precise formalisation of extra-functional properties, which allows an unambiguous understanding and a precise semantics both with respect to meaning and valid specification format of the value, we define the concept of *Attribute* as:

$$Attribute = \langle TypeIdentifier, \ Value^+ \rangle$$
$$Value = \langle Data, \ Metadata, \ ValidityCondition^* \rangle$$

where:

- *TypeIdentifier* defines the extra-functional property (i.e. the identifier property in Fig. 1);
- *Data* contains the concrete value for the property;
- *Metadata* provides complementary information on data and allows to distinguish between them; and
- *ValidityConditions* describe the conditions under which the value is valid.

The remaining of this section details these concepts, based on diagrams issued from the meta-model of our attribute framework (the full meta-model is given in Appendix 8). However, an important aspect of this definition, which is worth noting already at this point, is the possibility for an attribute to have a several values. This is further explained in Section 2.5.

2.3   Attribute Type

Similarly to the concept of "class" in object oriented programming, an *attribute type* designates a class of attributes. In this respect, an attribute is then comparable to a class instance, and must comply with the specific structure imposed by the attribute type. An attribute type specifies thus an *identifier* which is a condensed significative name describing the principal characteristics of the attributes (e.g., "Worst Case Execution Time", "Static Memory Usage", etc.), a list of *attributable* elements to which the property can be attached, and a specification of the *data format* that the attribute instances must conform to. As illustrated in Fig. 1, the identifier of the attribute type is shared by all the attributes of the same attribute type, and an attribute belongs to a single attribute type only.

Consequently, the uniqueness of the attribute types must be ensured so that it is not possible to have two attributes with the same identifier but different value formats. This requires techniques outside the definition of the attribute concept itself. A simple technique is to keep a *registry* of attribute types, where all the declaration of attribute

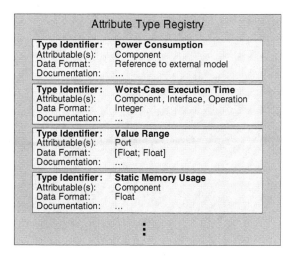

Fig. 2. Attribute type registry

types are stored to ensure their uniqueness. Fig. 2 illustrates an attribute type registry containing several attribute types.

Although this way of specifying attributes types (or attributes, in a broader sense) provides the great advantages of being open and extensible so that it can fit the multitude of extra-functional properties which need to be defined, it still requires users to have an intuitive and common understanding of what the meaning and intended usage of the attributes were when they were created. Therefore it is important to provide proper attribute type *documentation*. This documentation is stored in the attribute type registry and consists of an informal text written in natural language. Nevertheless, it must supply enough information to primarily clarify the meaning of the attribute type as well as its intended usage.

It is reasonable to assume that hundreds of attribute types or more will be introduced. Several classification schemes (e.g., [6] and [7]) have been proposed which can be used as basis to identify groups of attribute types such as "resource usage", "reliability", "timing", etc. These categories could allow navigation across attributes more easily and possibly hide the whole set of attribute types that are uninteresting for a particular project. A remaining challenge is in this case to determine appropriate categories, as the proposed classifications are distinct and often non-orthogonal as mentioned in [5]. However, this is not within the scope of this paper.

2.4 Attribute Data

To elicit information on the element of the component model they are associated with, the part of attributes concerned with expressing data must be represented in an unambiguous and well-tailored format. This implies that in addition to supporting primitive types such as integers, floats, etc., and structured types such as arrays, complex types must also be covered. These complex types include representation of value distributions, various external models, images, etc.

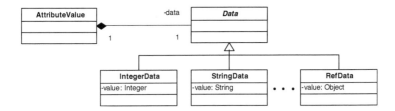

Fig. 3. Attribute data

For this, we define a generic data structure, called *data*, which is specialized into a number of simple data types and a reference to any complex object, as illustrated in Fig. 3. This structure can be extended to build more complex data structure such as records or tuples.

2.5   Multiple Attribute Values

Attributes emerge during the software development process as additional information needs to be easily available either to guide the development, to make decisions on the next step to follow, to provide appropriate (early) analysis and tests of the components, or to give feedbacks on the current status. This need for information starts already in early phases of the development, in which extra-functional properties are considered as constraints to be met and expected to be satisfied later on, thus becoming an intrinsic part of the component or system description.

This implies that through the development process, (i) the meaning of an attribute typically changes from a required property to a provided/exhibited property, and (ii) its value changes too as the knowledge and the amount of information about the system increases. Thus the actual data as well as the appropriate metadata needs to be successively refined to be replaced by the latest and most accurate value. For example, an attribute, estimated in a design phase, is replaced with a new value coming from a measurement after the implementation phase is completed, or with more information available the analysis become more efficient and reliable and therefore the confidence in the property, expressed by the accuracy metadata, increases.

However, the gradual refinement of an attribute towards its most accurate value is not always the expected way to deal with extra-functional properties. Often, values which are equally valid in the current development phase, need to exist simultaneously. In other words, this means that the latest value must not replace the previous one. This requires an ability for an attribute to have multiple values to cope with information coming from various context of utilization, to keep different values obtained through different methods, to keep the required value and a provided value for verifying the

Fig. 4. Multiple attribute values

conformity to the initial requirement, or to compare a range of possible values to make a decision. This ability of an attribute to have multiple values is depicted in Fig. 4.

2.6 Attribute Value Metadata

Introducing the possibility to have multiple values for attributes also requires the ability to distinguish between them. Furthermore, it is important to document the way an attribute value has been obtained to ensure that information about a component (or another element of a component model) is correct and up-to-date. These two functions are provided by the *attribute value metadata*, or simply *metadata*, which role is to capture the context in which the corresponding attribute value has been obtained: when, how and possibly by whom. However, the question of determining the complete list of elements that metadata should cover remains.

We define a partial list of metadata that we consider indispensable to provide a basic support for the concepts around the attribute definition (see Fig. 5). The list consists of the version of the current attribute value, the timestamp indicating when the attribute value was created or updated, the source of the value ("requirement", "estimation", "measurement", "formal analysis with the tool X", "simulation", "generated from model", "generated from implementation", etc.). Other metadata are optional; for example the accuracy of the value or some informal comments about the attribute value.

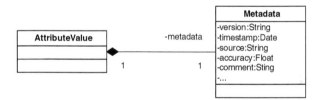

Fig. 5. Attribute value metadata

2.7 Validity Conditions of Attribute Values

Reusability is a desired feature of component-based software engineering, which implies that a component is assumed to be (re-)useable in many different contexts. As an intrinsic part of components, revealing what the component is capable of, attributes are intended to be reusable too. This means that the validity of their information must still be accurate in the new context in which the component is reused. Hence, to keep consistent all the information concerning the component, both its expected behaviour and capabilities, and the actual ones, it is necessary to specify in what type of contexts an attribute value is valid, i.e., fully or partially reusable.

We refer to these specifications of context restrictions as *validity conditions*. The validity conditions explicitly describe the particular contexts in which an attribute value can be trusted. Different types of contexts exist and, as with attribute types, an attempt to identify them all is bound to fail. They include, at least, constraints on the underlying platform, specification of usage profile, and dependencies towards other attributes, as illustrated in Fig. 6.

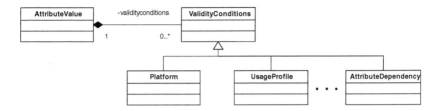

Fig. 6. Validity conditions of attribute values

With the intentions of developing an automated process to select only valid values for the current context, the validity conditions must be defined in a strict manner and it is important that they are publicly exposed. However, strictly ensuring the respect of all the validity conditions is a too restrictive approach since in this case, only the attribute values for which the validity conditions are fully satisfied would be reusable. For instance, a component might be reused even though some of its attribute values are not trustworthy for the current design. This reuse might require a manual intervention to lower the confidence in the provided values. We envision that, as a conscious decision, some attribute values could be reused regardless of their validity conditions not being satisfied, but it would typically affect the values. For example, the value might be reused with a lower accuracy, or with the data modified to add some safety margins.

3   Attribute Composition

So far, the attributes has been in focus, and the attributable elements have simply been viewed as black-box units of design or implementation, to which attributes can be attached. However, the existence of hierarchical component models that also include composite components — components built out of other components — influences the ways in which the values of attributes can be established.

Ideally, all attributes of a composite component should be directly derivable from the attributes of its sub-components. While this is easily achievable for some attribute types, e.g., static memory usage, others depend on a combination of many attributes of the sub-components, or on software architecture details [5].

Even for composable attributes, we argue that it is beneficial to allow them to also be stated explicitly for the composite component as such. In particular, this allows analysis of the system also at an early stage of the development when the internals of a composite component under construction are not fully known, or not fully analyzed with respect to all attributes required to derive the attributes of the composite component.

The ability of the proposed attribute framework to store multiple values for a single attribute permits explicitly assigned information to co-exist with information generated by composition. To distinguish between them, the metadata field *source* can be given the value *composition* to indicate that the value was derived from the sub-components.

Specification of attributes of a composite is illustrated in Fig. 7. The composite component has been explicitly given an estimated value for the attribute representing static memory usage, and another value is provided by composition, which for this attribute simply means a summation over the sub-components.

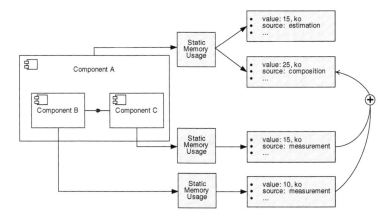

Fig. 7. A composite component with co-existing explicit and derived attribute values

Attribute composition can be viewed as the responsibility of the development process, i.e., it should specify when and how attribute values should be derived for composite components, possibly supported by automated functions in the development tools. An interesting alternative, in particular for easily composable attributes such as static memory usage, is to include the specification of a composition operator in the attribute type registry.

4   Attribute Configuration and Selection

From the previous sections we realize that an attribute can have many values. The question is which value of an attribute is of interest for a particular analysis, and what is the criteria to select it? The second question, related to the consistency of definition when using several attributes, reads: Which values of different attributes belong together?

This problem is addressed in version- and configuration management, and we apply the principles from Software Configuration Management (SCM). SCM distinguishes two types of versioning: (i) *versions* (also called revisions) that identify evolution of an item in time. Usually the latest version of an item is selected by default, but also an old version can be selected, for example using a time stamp (select the latest version created before a specific time); and (ii) *variants* which allow existence of different versions of the same item at the same time. The versions and variants can be selected according to certain selection principles, such as: *state* (select the latest version with the specified state), *version name*, also called label or tag (select a version designed by a particular name). The latter is explicit since version names are unique, while states are not.

We adopt these principles in management of attributes. Since an attribute can have many values, each value is treated as an attribute version. A developer has two possibilities of managing attribute versions.

Attribute navigation. The possibility to navigate through different versions of an attribute (i.e., through different values), and update the selected value (changing data, or metadata information, or modifying the validity conditions).

Configuration. Values are selected, for one or several attributes, according to a given
  selection principle (e.g., based on version name or timestamp).

The *configuration filter* is important as it can be applied to the entire system, or to
a set of components, and then all architectural elements expose particular versions of
the attributes that match the filter. This is important when some system properties are
analyzed using consistent versions of several attributes (for example in an analysis of a
response time of a scenario performed on a particular platform).

The configuration filter is defined as a combination of attribute metadata and validity
conditions, and the use of the following keywords:

Latest. The latest version.
Timestamp. The latest version created before the specified date.
Versionname. A particular version designated by a name.

Metadata and validity conditions are equivalent from the selection point of view. In the
selection process the filter defines constraints over metadata or validity conditions in the
same way. The difference is however in understanding the filtering mechanism and in
helping the developer in recording possible problems if the validity conditions that are
filtered are contradictory (for example if the developer specifies to use attribute values
valid for "platform X" and "platform Y").

The configuration filter is defined as a sequence of matching conditions combined
with AND or OR operators. The conditions are tested in order, and if a condition is not

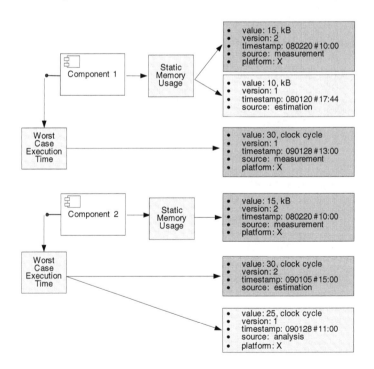

Fig. 8. Attribute value selection

fulfilled the next one is examined. The configuration filter is specified in the following format:

$$Condition_1 \text{ [AND } Condition_2 \dots] \quad \text{OR}$$
$$Condition_3 \text{ [AND } Condition_4 \dots] \quad \text{OR}$$
$$\vdots$$

The conditions within a line are combined by AND operator, while lines are combined with the OR operator. A concrete example of the configuration filter is the following:

(Platform: X) AND (Source: Measurement)   OR
(Release 2.0)   OR
Latest

In this example the configuration filter will select first all values with validity conditions matching "Platform: X" and with "Source: Measurement" in the metadata. If such values exist, the latest one is selected; if not, the filter will select the latest version labeled with "Release 2.0". If no such version was found, simply the latest version of the attribute will be selected. The selected attributes values are shown as gray boxes in Fig. 8.

5   A Prototype for ProCom and the PROGRESS IDE

This section concretizes and exemplifies the proposed attribute framework in the context of *ProCom*, a component model for distributed embedded systems [2,3]. The characteristics of this domain make component-based development particularly challenging. For example, the tight coupling between hardware and platform, and high demands on resource efficiency, are to some extent conflicting with the notion of general-purpose reusable components.

ProCom applies the component-based approach also in early phases of development, when components are not necessarily fully implemented. Already at this point, however, it is beneficial that the components are treated as reusable entities to which properties, models and analysis results can be associated. Safety and real-time demands are addressed by a variety of analysis techniques, in early stages based on models and estimates, and later based on measurements, source code and structural information. Efficiency is achieved by a deployment process in which the component-based system design is transformed into executables that require only a lightweight component framework at runtime.

This extensive analysis support throughout the design and deployment process requires a large amount of information to be associated with various entities at different stages of the development. Information that is of interest to more than one type of analysis, or which should be reused together with the entity, is captured by attributes. Concretely, ProCom is based around two main structural entities — components and subsystems — both of which are *attributable* (as defined in Section 2.1). The attributable elements also include component services, message ports, and communication channels, among others.

The initial set of attribute types is influenced by the envisioned analysis of timing and resource consumption, and includes information about execution times, static and

Table 1. Examples of attributes in ProCom

Identifier	Attributable(s)	Data format	Documentation (short)
Static memory	Component, Subsystem	Int	The amount of memory (in kB) statically allocated by the component or subsystem.
WCET	Service	Int	The maximum number of clock cycles the service can consume before terminating.
Value range	Port	[Int;Int]	Upper and lower bounds on the values appearing on the port.
Resource model	Subsystem	External file	A REMES model specifying resource consumption.

dynamic memory usage, and complex behavioral models handled by external model checking tools. Table 1 lists some of the attribute types used in ProCom.

To ease the development in ProCom, an integrated development environment called PROGRESS IDE is being developed. It is a stand-alone application built on top of the Eclipse Rich Client Platform, and includes a component repository, architectural editors to independently design components and systems, a C development environment, and editors to specify behaviour and resource utilization.

A variant of the proposed attribute framework is included in the PROGRESS IDE, in the form of two plugins: one for the core concepts that are required e.g., by analysis tools interested in, or producing, attribute values; and one for the graphical user interface through which the developer can view and edit attributes. In its current version, the prototype does not support validity conditions, nor is the selection mechanism fully implemented. For a detailed presentation of the attribute framework prototype, see [8].

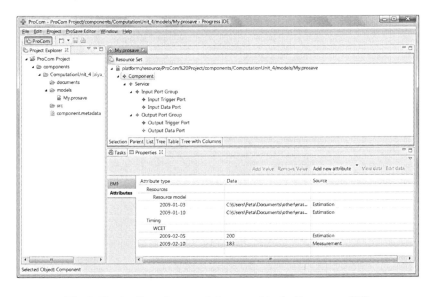

Fig. 9. The Attribute framework integrated in the PROGRESS IDE

The graphical part of the framework consists of an additional tab in the property view, where the attributes of the currently selected entity are presented. In Fig. 9, a component is selected in the top editor, and its attributes (*Resource model* and *WCET*) are shown in the property view below. In the depicted scenario, each attribute has two values, distinguished by the metadata timestamp.

The attribute type registry is realized by an extension point that allows other plug-ins to contribute new attribute types. In addition to the information specified in Section 2.3 (e.g., data format and documentation), the extension can also define how the new attribute type is handled by the graphical interface, by defining classes for viewing, editing and validating its data.

6 Related Work

Although a lot of work has been done studying extra-functional properties in general, few component models actually integrate support for specifying and managing extra-functional properties. When this support exists, it concerns specific types of extra-functional properties such as temporal properties or resource-related properties and is intended for reasoning and predictability purposes.

The relation between extra-functional properties and functional specifications of component models was first explicitly addressed in the Prediction-Enabled Component Technology project (PECT) [9]. In PECT, extra-functional properties are handled through "analytical interfaces" conjointly with analytical models to both describes what are the properties that a component must have and the theory that should support the property analysis.

In Robocop [10] the management of extra-functionality is done through the creation of models: a resource model describes the resource consumption of components in terms of mathematical cost functions and a behavioural model specifies the sequence in which their operations must be invoked. Additional models can be created.

The support for extra-functional property proposed by Koala [11] handles only static memory usage of components. The information about this property is provided through an additional analytic interface which must be created and filled for every components existing in the design. It is not possible to add information about this property to already existing components. Moreover, through diversity spreadsheets, Koala proposes a mechanism outside the analytical interface to deal with dependencies between attributes.

Contrary to our approach, which allows various elements of a component model to have attributes, these components models manage extra-functional properties on component- or system-scale only.

The closest approaches to our concept of attributes are those which define extra-functional properties as a series of name-value pairs; for example Palladio [12] and SaveCCM [13]. Palladio uses annotations and contracts to specify extra-functional properties concerned with performance prediction of the system under design. SaveCCM follows the concept of credentials proposed by Shaw [1], where extra-functional properties are represented as triples $\langle Attribute, \ Value, \ Credibility \rangle$ where Attribute describes the component property, Value the corresponding data, and Credibility specifies the source of the value. Similarly to our registry of attribute types, these credentials should be used conjointly with techniques to manage the creation of new credentials.

Other approaches not related to a particular component model have also been proposed. Zschaler [14] proposes a formal specification for extra-functional properties with the aim to investigate architectural elements and low-level mechanisms such as tasks and scheduling policies that influence particular extra-functional properties. In this specification, extra-functional properties are split between intrinsic properties which are inherited from the implementation and are fixed, and extrinsic properties which are properties which depend on the context. In [15], a specification language for specifying the quality of service of component-based systems is proposed. The language supports specification of derived attributes for composites, and links between attribute specification and measurement.

Comparing with what exists for UML, our approach relates to the MARTE subprofile for non-functional properties [16] which extends UML with various constructs to annotate selected UML elements. Similarly, extra-functional properties are defined in a "library" as types with qualifiers and used in the models. Attribute values can be specified through a Value Specification Language, which also defines value dependencies between attributes through symbolic variables and complex expressions. Dependencies involving more than one element are expressed through constraints. MARTE also acknowledges the need for co-exisiting values from different sources, but the associated information is not as rich as our metadata concept, and the selection mechanism is not elaborated. However, MARTE does not support component-based development and design space exploration, nor provide means to manage refinement of non-functional properties. Our work could gain in integrating the generic data type system and also in integrating the value specification language for supporting the specification of the attribute values, which are now left to the creator of the attributes.

Our approach also relates to work on service level agreements (SLA) in service-oriented systems [17], although our motivation for capturing non-functional properties comes mainly from the need to perform analysis, rather than as the basis for negotiation of quality of service between a service provider and consumer. In the context of SLA, non-functional properties are used in the formal specification of services, defining, e.g., the availability of a service or the maximum response time, while we associate non-functional properties with architectural entities to facilitate predictable reuse.

In summary, our approach differs from previous in focusing on reuse of attribute values, proposing an attribute concept allowing to have multiple values and a mechanism to select among them, and encompassing context dependencies that must be satisfied for a value to be valid in a new context.

7   Discussion

Our purpose with this attribute model is to provide a structure for managing extra-functional properties closely interconnected to the component model elements with the long-term vision of supporting a seamless integration and assessment of extra-functional properties in an automatized and efficient way. This structure is intended to be used throughout a component-based development process from early modelling to deployment steps (for an overview of this development process, see [18]). In particular, it should be possible for reused components with extensive, detailed information to co-exist with components in an early stage of development, and for analysis to treat the two transparently.

With regards to other models, our proposition is characterized by the support for multiple attribute values. Although for some simple attributes such as *number of lines of code*, one and only one value is correct at a given point in time, for other attributes the value vary according to the methods or techniques used to obtain it, and it is not always possible to say that one value is more correct than another. An example of such attributes is the *worst-case execution time* for which different analysis techniques give different values, all of which can be considered equally true in the characterization of the attribute. For instance, a "safe" static analysis technique gives a higher number than a probabilistic method but the confidence in the fact that the value cannot be exceeded is higher. For components in an early stage of development, even a simple attribute such as *lines of code* could be estimated by several approaches, and thus have multiple values that are equally correct at the time.

One possible way to manage multiple property sources would be to create a separate attribute type for each variant of the property, treating e.g., *estimated worst case execution time* and *measured worst case execution time* as two separate attribute types. However, viewing them as a single attribute with multiple values facilitates analysis that use attributes as input. For example, analysis that derives the response time of an operation can be based on the execution time attribute without having to deal with the different possible sources of this information. Thus, the same response time analysis can be performed based on early execution time estimates, safe values from static code analysis, or measurements. Multiple values also significantly reduces the amount of properties types which can be defined (in the case in which the methods provide results for the same property) while preserving the source of information through the metadata and the usage context through the ValidityConditions.

Another noticeable characteristic of our model is the specification of validity conditions for individual attribute values. Many attributes depend on factors external to the entity, such as underlying middleware or hardware. When a component is reused in the same, or similar, context, the attribute value can also be reused without restrictions. If, on the other hand, the component is reused in a context that does not match the validity condition, the value will not be used (e.g., in analysis) unless proceeded by a conscious decision by the developer. For example, the value can be used with lower confidence as an early estimate, or fully reused if the developer believe that it still applies in the new context.

The approach presented in the papers aims for increasing analysability and predictability of component-based systems. It however introduces a complexity in the design process. By having many attribute types and different versions of attributes, there is a need for a selection of a "proper" attribute version. There is also a need for ensuring consistency between attributes of different types. We propose that this is handled outside the attributable entity, by a configuration management-like mechanism in the development environment. This allows the developer to specify which attribute version, from a number of currently "correct" ones, that should be used in the analysis performed at this point. The attribute version can be determined by different parameters, such as specification of the context (identified by ValidityConditions).

The defined infrastructure for attributes facilitates a complete analysis that includes analysis of different properties and relations between them, including a trade-off analysis. For example, by simple changes of the configuration filters, the process of the analysis and presentation of the results for all attributes is simpler, and consistent.

8   Conclusion

Providing a systematic way of attribute specifications and their integration into a component model is important for an efficient development process; it enables building tools for attribute management, such as specification, analysis, verification, and first of all efficient management of different attributes, or the same attributes attached to different components. It also facilitates integration of different analysis tools. This paper proposes a model for attribute specification which is expandable in the sense of allowing specification of new attribute types or new formats of attribute presentations. The model distinguishes attribute types (defined by a name and a data type), attribute values which include metadata and specification of the conditions under which the attribute value is valid. The main challenge in the attribute specification formalization is to provide a flexible mechanism to cover a large variety of attribute types and their values, and keeping them manageable. This is the reason why the model is extensible.

The proposed model has been integrated into ProCom, a component model aimed for development of component-based embedded systems for which the modeling, estimation and prediction of extra-functional properties are of crucial importance. The prototype, developed and integrated in the PROGRESS IDE, covers both introduction of new attribute types and specification of attributes for components and other modeling entities, with data formats ranging from primitive types to complex models handled by external tools.

Our plan is to further develop the model and the tool. The validity conditions can be further formalized to enable automatic selection of attribute values depending on the context in the development process. The same is true for the filter selection mechanism that should enable the developers an easy selection process. Further, we plan to develop an attribute navigation tool that will be able to show differences between different attribute values and validity conditions. Finally, a set of predefined attributes will be specified for the ProCom component model, which will improve the efficiency and simplicity of attribute management.

References

1. Shaw, M.: Truth vs Knowledge: The Difference Between What a Component Does and What We Know It Does. In: International Workshop on Software Specification and Design, p. 181 (1996)
2. Sentilles, S., Vulgarakis, A., Bureš, T., Carlson, J., Crnković, I.: A component model for control-intensive distributed embedded systems. In: Chaudron, M.R.V., Szyperski, C., Reussner, R. (eds.) CBSE 2008. LNCS, vol. 5282, pp. 310–317. Springer, Heidelberg (2008)
3. Bureš, T., Carlson, J., Crnković, I., Sentilles, S., Vulgarakis, A.: ProCom – the Progress Component Model Reference Manual, version 1.0. Technical Report MDH-MRTC-230/2008-1-SE, Mälardalen University (June 2008)
4. Crnković, I., Larsson, M.: Building Reliable Component-Based Software Systems. Artech House, Inc., Norwood (2002)

5. Crnkovic, I., Larsson, M., Preiss, O.: Concerning Predictability in Dependable Component-Based Systems: Classification of Quality Attributes. In: de Lemos, R., Gacek, C., Romanovsky, A. (eds.) Architecting Dependable Systems III. LNCS, vol. 3549, pp. 257–278. Springer, Heidelberg (2005)
6. ISO/IEC: Information Technology - Software product quality - Part 1: Quality model. Report: ISO/IEC FDIS 9126-1:2000 (2000)
7. Bertoa, M.F., Vallecillo, A.: Quality attributes for COTS components. In: 6th International Workshop on Quantitative Approaches in Object-Oriented Software Engineering (QAOOSE 2002) (2002)
8. Štěpán, P.: An extensible attribute framework for ProCom. Master's thesis, Mälardalen University, Sweden (2009)
9. Hissam, S., Moreno, G., Stafford, J., Wallnau, K.: Packaging predictable assembly with prediction-enabled component technology. Technical Report: CMU/SEI-2001-TR-024 (2001)
10. Maaskant, H.: A Robust Component Model for Consumer Electronic Products. Philips Research, vol. 3, pp. 167–192. Springer, Heidelberg (2005)
11. van Ommering, R., van der Linden, F., Kramer, J., Magee, J.: The Koala component model for consumer electronics software. Computer 33(3), 78–85 (2000)
12. Koziolek, H.: Parameter dependencies for reusable performance specifications of software components. PhD thesis, Oldenburg, University (2008)
13. Åkerholm, M., Carlson, J., Fredriksson, J., Hansson, H., Håkansson, J., Möller, A., Pettersson, P., Tivoli, M.: The SAVE approach to component-based development of vehicular systems. Journal of Systems and Software 80(5), 655–667 (2007)
14. Zschaler, S.: Formal specification of non-functional properties of component-based software. In: Proc. Workshop on Models for Non-functional Aspects of Component-Based Systems (2004)
15. Aagedal, J.Ø.: Quality of Service Support in Development of Distributed Systems. PhD thesis, Faculty of Mathematics and Natural Sciences, University of Oslo (2001)
16. Espinoza, H., Dubois, H., Gérard, S., Pasaje, J.L.M., Petriu, D.C., Woodside, C.M.: Annotating UML models with non-functional properties for quantitative analysis. In: Bruel, J.-M. (ed.) MoDELS 2005. LNCS, vol. 3844, pp. 79–90. Springer, Heidelberg (2006)
17. Bianco, P., Lewis, G.A., Merson, P.: Service level agreements in service-oriented architecture environments. Technical Report CMU/SEI-2008-TN-021, Carnegie Mellon (2008)
18. Land, R., Carlson, J., Larsson, S., Crnković, I.: Towards guidelines for a development process for component-based embedded systems. In: Gervasi, O., et al. (eds.) ICCSA 2009, Part I, LNCS, vol. 5592. Springer, Heidelberg (2009)

Appendix A: Attribute Framework Meta-model

Below, the full attribute framework meta-model is presented.

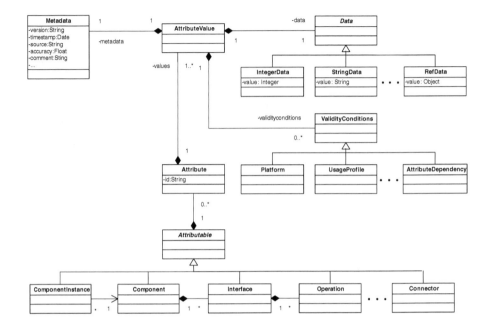

Modelling Layered Component Execution Environments for Performance Prediction

Michael Hauck[1], Michael Kuperberg[2], Klaus Krogmann[2], and Ralf Reussner[2]

[1] FZI Research Center for Information Technology
Karlsruhe, Germany
hauck@fzi.de
[2] Software Design and Quality Group,
Universität Karlsruhe (TH), Germany
{mkuper,krogmann,reussner}@ipd.uka.de

Abstract. Software architects often use model-based techniques to analyse performance (e.g. response times), reliability and other extra-functional properties of software systems. These techniques operate on models of software architecture and execution environment, and are applied at design time for early evaluation of design alternatives, especially to avoid implementing systems with insufficient quality. Virtualisation (such as operating system hypervisors or virtual machines) and multiple layers in execution environments (e.g. RAID disk array controllers on top of hard disks) are becoming increasingly popular in reality and need to be reflected in the models of execution environments. However, current component meta-models do not support virtualisation and cannot model individual layers of execution environments. This means that the entire monolithic model must be recreated when different implementations of a layer must be compared to make a design decision, e.g. when comparing different Java Virtual Machines. In this paper, we present an extension of an established model-based performance prediction approach and associated tools which allow to model and predict state-of-the-art layered execution environments, such as disk arrays, virtual machines, and application servers. The evaluation of the presented approach shows its applicability and the resulting accuracy of the performance prediction while respecting the structure of the modelled resource environment.

1 Introduction

Extra-functional properties are becoming increasingly important: Users are concurrently accessing complex distributed software systems and the scale of applications grows constantly, which makes it hard to provide high Quality of Service (QoS) as expected by users. In this setting, early design-time model-based prediction approaches help to develop software which fulfills QoS requirements such as a low response time. Most state-of-the-art design-time prediction approaches operate on component-oriented models, because components allow to structure an application and simplify its analysis. These design-time prediction approaches also help to avoid creating implementations which suffer from bottlenecks introduced in the design phase, by analysing the design models before the implementation is started. Thus, the design-time QoS prediction saves costs for adapting implemented software in order to meet QoS requirements.

G.A. Lewis, I. Poernomo, and C. Hofmeister (Eds.): CBSE 2009, LNCS 5582, pp. 191–208, 2009.

To control the increasing complexity of large-scale applications, the use of middleware such as application servers and architecture frameworks is gaining popularity. Additionally, software and hardware virtualisations like Java Virtual Machine and Xen are becoming popular as they increase the flexibility of execution environments. These additional software and hardware layers[1] have significant impact on extra-functional properties of software systems, which makes it desirable to capture them during design-time modelling.

Still, current component-oriented modelling approaches lack explicit support of layering of both software and hardware, as we will lay out in related work in Section 4. This shortcoming limits the expressiveness of the models because the structure of the application and the access limitations imposed by layering cannot be expressed faithfully, and it becomes impossible to account for the performance impact introduced by virtualisation layers. Ignoring layers also means that the entire model of the execution environment must be exchanged even if a single layer is changed, for example when different Java Virtual Machines are to be compared on the same hardware.

The contribution of this paper is a working solution for modelling layers and virtualisation. It is implemented as an extension of the Palladio Component Model (PCM) [1], its model of the execution environment, and its tools. Our solution increases the expressiveness and the performance prediction capabilities of the PCM, and is the first component model to provide support for bytecode-based performance prediction. The extended PCM is capable of capturing detailed information on usage of software resources such as operating system calls or virtual machine calls, but also of hardware resource usage like RAID array accesses and CPU demands. Each resource modelled by the PCM provides explicit resource interfaces which can have multiple services, thus enabling the distinction of services that may cause resource contention from services that can be executed in parallel without impacting each other. For example, concurrent write accesses to a RAID array compete, while concurrent read accesses can run in parallel without causing contention. Furthermore, the extended PCM specifies well-defined communication among models of layers, avoiding overlapping modelling artifacts and allowing to change a layer and its model without side effects on other layers. By maintaining a clean division of modelling tasks and artefacts in the PCM, our approach supports division of labour across different roles such as component developer, system architect and application deployer, which is beneficial for modelling large-scale and heterogeneous applications.

We successfully evaluated the extended Palladio Component Model and performance prediction approach in a case study that modelled a multi-layered application running on a Java virtual machine. We show that the performance of components in this application can be successfully modelled and predicted using the extended PCM and its tools.

The remainder of this paper is structured as follows: Section 2 presents the foundations of this work, Section 3 details on requirements of layer modelling the application to large-scale software systems and Section 4 highlights related work. Section 5 presents

---

[1] The term *layer* will hereafter be used to describe a grouping and abstraction mechanism for software components, where primarily components of adjacent layers communicate with each other. Components reside in layers.

the realised model extensions and simulation enhancements while Section 6 presents an evaluation of the extended Palladio Component Model and its performance prediction capabilities. Section 7 summarises the paper and discusses future work.

2 Foundations

The Palladio Component Model (PCM) [1] is a domain-specific language for modelling component-based software architectures and corresponding execution environments. Technically, the PCM is a meta-model, as its instances are models of concrete components and applications; the meta-model is described in detail in [1].

The PCM allows for modelling components including their behaviour, their relations, their deployments, and their assembly into software architectures. The resulting models can be transformed into analytical and simulation models for performance prediction to enable the evaluation of design decisions. Other transformations can be written for being applied to the PCM model instances to predict other QoS properties, such as reliability or maintainability. The PCM comes with an Eclipse-based PCM workbench for creating architectural application models, models of execution environments and for parametrically modelling the usage (workload) of the modelled application.

A component can be a basic component or a composite component. A *basic component* cannot encapsulate further components, whereas a *composite component* contains other components (which can be basic components or composite components). A PCM model of a component must have at least one *provided interface* and can have *required interfaces*. These interfaces are modelled as first-class entities and put into relation to components by *provided roles* or *required roles*; each interface has at least one *service* which can have input parameters and can have at most one output parameter.

To enable the prediction of the performance of a software system, additional information on the performance can be attached to provided services of a component. This information is an *abstracted* specification of a service's behaviour, called Resource Demanding Service Effect Specification (*RD-SEFF*). RD-SEFFs are being modelled as automata with two main types of elements: *internal actions* (which also specify resource demands a service itself causes, e.g. CPU usage) and *external actions* (which model the calls to required services, using the required interfaces of the component). The resources (whose usage is specified in internal RD-SEFF actions) are specified in the execution environment that a component is deployed on and executed in.

The PCM defines different models of a software system, which together make up a full PCM instance to allow for division of labour. These models are provided by different developer roles summarised in Fig. 1 (see [12] for an in-depth description).

In Fig. 1, the different developer roles and the artefacts they work with are shown:

- the *component developer* is responsible for providing specifications of basic and composed components, which he stores in component repositories,
- the *system architect* assembles components into a complete software system by specifying how components are connected and how they interact with each other,
- the *system deployer* installs and configures the software system on the execution environment's nodes (in context of the PCM-based modelling, the system deployer

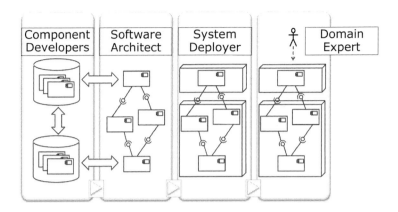

Fig. 1. PCM Developer Roles and Artefacts

also provides a model of the execution environment, on which a software system is deployed),

– and the *domain expert* provides a usage model which describes the workload of the software system (i.e. an aggregated, stochastic description of the end-user behaviour, incl. the number of concurrent users; the PCM breaks this information down into the usage and input parameters of individual component services [11]). The usage model describing the workload is denoted by the stickman icon in the right part of Fig. 1.

The last PCM role is the *QoS analyst* who performs the QoS analysis and interprets its results, and makes the results available to the other roles and stakeholders. The *QoS analyst* is not shown in Fig. 1 since it is a cross-cutting role which interacts with all other roles.

3   Requirements for Modelling Layered Execution Environments

This section describes three scenarios from which we derive six requirements for the modelling of execution environments in component-oriented meta-models. We also point out why existing concepts and component models do not fulfill these requirements, before we discuss how these requirements map specifically to the Palladio Component Model (PCM). The scenarios and the resulting requirements serve as the preparations for the contribution described in Section 5 and its evaluation in Section 6.

The following three scenarios enjoy increasing popularity in today's software systems, so it is desirable to support them in component-oriented modelling approaches:

SC1 Layered execution environments that consist of multiple *software layers* (e.g. virtual machines running on top of operating system hypervisors) and of *layers of hardware resources* like RAID array controllers on top of single disks. In this scenario, single hard disks are hidden by the RAID controller and thus they cannot be accessed directly anymore. Of course, multiple virtualisation layers are possible, and in some cases a layer can use all layers below it, not only the layer directly underneath it.

SC2 Bytecode components, for example Java components that are compiled to platform-independent bytecode. Java bytecode components are comprised of bytecode instructions which are executed on Java Virtual Machines and not directly by an operating system on a hardware CPU. Bytecode components include elementary (i.e. non-method) bytecode instructions like `IADD` for integer addition as well as invocations of the platform APIs provided by the virtual machine.

SC3 Complex parts of the execution environment, for example Windows/Linux schedulers or hardware controllers like RAID controllers, for which third-party, non-PCM behaviour models or performance models already exist. The effort of re-modelling these existing complex models in the PCM is too high, while their runnable implementation (e.g. Java code) is a candidate for integration with the prediction tooling in the PCM or other meta-models.

It is important to stress that the first scenario cannot be modelled satisfactory using only conventional components. To see why, consider Fig. 2 where the component `VIRTUALPC` virtualises the component `WINDOWS` (which models the Windows operating system, which in turn accesses the CPU that is not shown in the figure). In the left part of the figure, the business component `B` can access both `VIRTUALPC` and `WINDOWS`, because they have the same interface `osInterface`. This modelling would contradict the reality, where the host OS cannot be accessed bypassing the virtualiser. A solution to this problem is to encapsulate the `WINDOWS` component in the `VIRTUALPC` component, making the latter a composite component, as illustrated by the right part of Fig. 2.

However, the solution using composite components for encapsulation is also problematic: it means that if `WINDOWS` is to be replaced by another component `WINDOWS2`

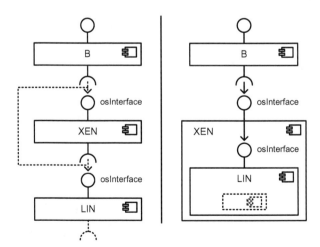

Fig. 2. Counterexample showing the impact caused by absence of well-defined layering: Undesired bypassing of a resource virtualiser (left); restricted reuse of virtualisers modelled as composite components (right). Further possible component connections indicated by dashed line.

(e.g. a different Windows OS), the `VIRTUALPC` composite component has to be replaced with another composite component `VIRTUALPC'` which encapsulates `WINDOWS2`. Clearly, the encapsulation does not support the interchangeability of the different layers: `WINDOWS` and `WINDOWS2` should be interchangeable while maintaining `VIRTUALPC`. Besides, this model does not reflect reality, since the `VIRTUALPC` executable does not encapsulate the underlying operating system in practice.

Both ways of modelling show that features of infrastructure environments containing layers cannot be captured by models containing traditional components only. This results in the requirement to support strict layering in the component model, where a layer can only be deployed on the adjacent lower layer.

Besides the above practical scenarios, components should hold important properties that are highlighted in the component definition of Szyperski [23]:

> "*A software component is a unit of composition with contractually specified interfaces and explicit context dependencies only. A software component can be deployed independently and is subject to composition by third parties.*"

In the following subsection, we derive requirements for the modelling of execution environments, using the above scenarios and Szyperski's definition as motivation.

3.1 Derived Requirements for the Modelling of Execution Environments

The above scenarios **SC1–SC3** and the component definition lead to the following six requirements for advancing the modelling of execution environments:

R1 "explicit layering": Introduction of explicit, well-defined support for layering of software and hardware parts of the software system and the execution environment (cf. **SC1**).

R2 "explicit assumptions": Components should not make assumptions on their environment that are not stated in their required interface(s), cf. Szyperski's component definition, this should also be reflected in the component model. For example, a component cannot know whether it is run directly on hardware or on a virtualiser of it. Only the interface of the execution environment can be known (e.g. a component can only run in a Java virtual machine; cf. **SC1** and **SC2**). Thus, explicit resource interfaces need to be introduced to capture the assumptions of a component.

R3 "environment parametrisation": Component behaviour specifications need to be parameterised over resource services to support the interchangeability in **SC1**. For example, hard disk read and write can have a different response time which cannot be known by a component, whose behaviour thus must be explicitly parameterised over read and write resource access.

R4 "third-party models": Support for existing third-party, source-code level behaviour models of complex parts of execution environments like operating system schedulers [7] to increase precision of analyses (cf. **SC3**). The integration of these source code models should be seamless and supported by meta-model.

R5 "division of work": Components should allow for division of labour which is implied by third-party composition (cf. Szyperski's component definition). The same holds for layers, which should support dividing responsibilities along with layers. For managing large-scale applications, dividing modelling among roles is desirable.

R6 "lower complexity": To lower users' learning curve, existing modelling concepts and principles should be maintained. For example, complexity of models can be lowered if modelling constructs are reused for different concepts (e.g. if basic and composite components share the same relations to interfaces).

In the following subsection, we study how far these requirements are fulfilled by current component (meta-)models.

3.2 Implementation of Requirements in Current Component Models

Before the work described in this paper was started, the PCM allowed for hardware resources only, for example CPUs, HDDs, or network connections. These resources were accessed implicitly, i.e. not through interfaces. The *software* parts of the execution environment (e.g. software layers that virtualise the hardware resources) would have to be modelled as components. Distinct hardware layers were not supported at all.

Other component models such as ROBOCOP [2], SOFA [3] or KLAPER [5] also only support structuring applications mostly by basic and composite components. If also components of the execution environment (e.g. middleware and applications servers) are captured, these models result in a very large *single* layer that captures *both* business *and* technical aspects. In some models, other elements of the execution environment like virtual machines, or hardware servers can be captured in a distinct layer, but remain as a *monolithic block*, only. For example, resource demands are given as fixed time in ms, or can only be mapped to a single resource layer, which itself cannot be composed. Exchanging a single element of execution environment requires *re-modelling* the entire monolithic block. Therefore, estimating the impact of the execution environment on component properties is not possible as it would be necessary to re-model them to enable "what-if" analyses.

We detail on related approaches in the next section. After that, Section 5 describes our extension of the PCM that fulfills the requirements described above and that overcomes the limitations found in the "old" PCM and also in the related approaches.

4   Related Work

The most widespread **standard for modelling software systems** is the Unified Modeling Language (UML) [16], but it does not support modelling of software layers or resource access through interfaces. Specific enhancements such as the UML Profile for Schedulability, Performance and Time (UML-SPT) [15] contain a resource model including resource usage, resource management and deployment modelling, but do not provide layers for software components. The UML Profile for Modelling and Analysis of Real-time and Embedded Systems (MARTE) [17], contains a more sophisticated resource model, but its specification is still under development. All UML-based approaches share the loose semantics of UML, which make them hard to analyse and simulate.

Transformations into analysis models include the Core Scenario Model (CSM) [18], which can be considered as a bridge between the UML-SPT profile and performance models like layered queueing networks. The CSM allows for modelling the behaviour of software, but comprehensive resources like composite resources cannot be modelled. Modelling of active resources is limited to the specification of attributes like "time per operation" and "scheduling policy". The intermediary language KLAPER of Grassi et al. [5] focuses on component-based systems and allows to transform them into analysis models like queueing networks, or Petri nets. A resource is associated with offered services, which may contain specifications of the service execution time or the failure probability. KLAPER is designed to be simple, and resources are not distinguished from components. Thus, KLAPER cannot distinguish between component services and resource services and this results in a single component/resource layer.

Component models with support of performance prediction include PCM [1], SOFA [3], PACC [9], ROBOCOP [2] and CUTS [20]. SOFA was designed to support dynamic component reconfiguration and controllers, which are a specific part of a component. Controllers are accessed through a special interface that provides features like life-cycle management or reconfiguration. In SOFA, component business logic can interact with its control part. While the SOFA execution platform supports detailed distribution aspects, its meta-model only supports a *ResourceDeploymentDescription* (cf. [10]) to allocate resources by a component. The PACC approach [9] provides a framework for assembling components and analysing such assemblies, for example with regard to performance properties. However, resource demands of a component can only be specified in milliseconds, not in a platform-independent way. ROBOCOP [2] is a middleware architecture and execution framework for embedded real-time component-based applications. It allows to predict the performance of such embedded applications and contains an execution framework which abstracts the underlying platform [4]. Resources in ROBOCOP include, among others, CPU, memory, and bus. Component specifications may contain a resource-usage specification, for example the claimed CPU time in milliseconds. Again, it is not possible to specify the resource demand in a platform-independent way and the ROBOCOP publications do not disclose a resource meta-model. CUTS [20] is a tool that allows for creating models of component-based systems, which can then be used for early system integration tests. As for ROBOCOP, CUTS mainly aims at QoS evaluation of real-time and embedded systems.

Software Performance Models have been pioneered in Software Performance Engineering (SPE), which is a quantitative software engineering approach that aims at meeting performance requirements [22], but focuses on monolithic systems instead of component-based software systems. The resulting meta-model in SPE is generic and strongly relates to queuing networks [21]. A resource can only be modelled as a *Server* or *WorkUnitServer* element. Possible resource attributes are limited to "quantity", "schedulingPolicy", "timeUnits", and "serviceTime". Another performance model is presented by Woodside et al. in [25], where Resource Functions are used to model resource demands of components. These functions can be determined by measurements, but only resource demands that occur on CPU or hard disk resources are considered. The approach of [25] does not deal with a complex layered execution environments through which resources are accessed.

Layering is discussed in several publications. Sharma et al. [19] are concerned with the performance of layered architectures in which layers cannot be distinguished from components and support no composition. They capture average resource demands per service and limit the approach to two resource types (CPU, HDD). Resource demands cannot be transformed across layers (beyond simple additions per layer), and no explicit meta-model exists. Gupta and Shirole [6] focus on the performance of collaboration products like groupware applications. To estimate the impact of single layers, they require benchmarks per layer but do not support design-time prediction – instead they provide a development process for meeting requirements. Their approach does not deal with components nor explicit interfaces. Maly and Woodside [14] use LQNs as design model and focus on modelling networks. No architecture meta-model is provided in [14], thus neither layers nor explicit interfaces exist. Verdickt et al. [24] follow an MDA approach and estimate the performance impact of middleware (layers). In their approach, such specific information is added to a flattened system model, which is not supporting layers.

5   Modelling Layered Execution Environments in the PCM

This section describes extensions of the Palladio Component Model (PCM; as described in [1]) that fulfill the requirements **R1** through **R6** defined in Section 3. Section 6 evaluates this extensions in a case study.

The extensions made to the PCM will be explained using the example of a multi-layered application from Fig. 3. In the example, newly introduced resource interfaces are distinguished from business interfaces by the use of "square" instead of "rounded" balls (cf. the interface of the CPU in Fig. 3). We will detail on the interfaces after introducing the new layers which are also present in Fig. 3.

Layers. According to **R1** ("explicit layering"), layering was introduced in the PCM. In the example, a `ResourceContainer` is the model of a node of the execution environment, where the node is a physical computer incl. hardware resources such as CPU. On the `ResourceContainer` multiple layers are deployed. These layers are classified in four types (from bottom to top in Fig. 3): Resources, controllers, infrastructure components, and business components. The layers are presented in the following.

The computer runs an operating system hypervisor (e.g. a Xen Virtual Machine, "HostOSController") which hosts an operating system (e.g. a Linux distribution, "GuestOSController"). The hypervisor and the guest OS are modelled as controllers, where a controller is a novel feature introduced into PCM to support modelling of complex logic that is not available as a PCM component or resource (for example where only Java code that simulates the modelled logic exists; **R4** "third-party models"). The controllers are layered (with the guest OS on top) to express that the JVMComponent cannot access the provided interface of the HostOSController anymore, but has to access the provided interface of the GuestOSController instead.

The JVMComponent is a component that models the JVM, which is part of the execution environment. Therefore, the JVMComponent is an infrastructure component that resides in a so-called `InfrastructureComponentScope` of the extended PCM to differentiate business logic from technical components (cf. **R5**, "division of work"). Within a single `InfrastructureComponentScope`, multiple components connected through provided and required interfaces can be deployed.

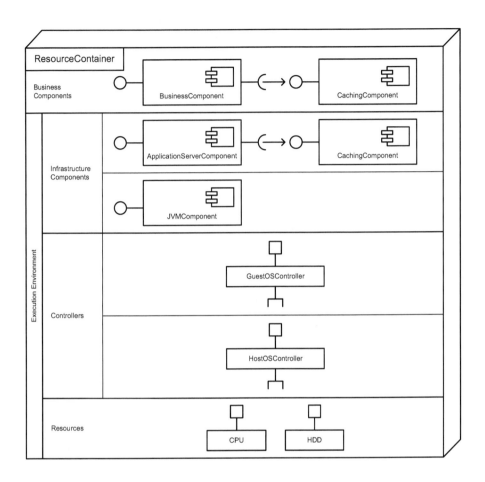

Fig. 3. A Resource Container Example

While for example an application server component is business logic for the manufacturer, it is a technical component for all users of the application server. Thus, infrastructure components have the same structure like all components and only differ in the `InfrastructureComponentScope` they are deployed in.

The final business logic layer of an application resides in the uppermost layer and is formed from usual business components.

Further model extensions. Beyond the extensions introduced above, the PCM was extended in the following areas. For accessing the execution environment, e.g. CPU and HDD resources or controllers, explicit `ResourceInterfaces` have been introduced (cf. **R2**, "explicit assumptions"). In the PCM, resources now are entities that offer `ResourceInterfaces` which itself contain `ResourceServices`. The same holds for the newly introduced controller elements, which can, like components, also require `ResourceInterfaces`.

Resources are the bottommost layer and do not contain RD-SEFFs for their provided resource services and cannot have required interfaces. Instead, resources are accompanied by Java code that integrates with the Palladio tooling and provides behaviour for the simulation. Resource usage in upper layers is in the simulation translated by this Java code into timing values using implementations of queues that form a (layered) queuing network. Therefore, for each service of a resource as specified by the `ResourceInterface` of it, basic timing values (for non-concurrent resource access) must be specified.

The introduction of explicit `ResourceServices` means that resource demands in internal actions of RD-SEFFs can reference single services of a resource (cf. **R3** "environment parametrisation"). It also means that the components have explicit required `ResourceInterfaces` and thus explicitly state requirements to the execution environment (e.g. that they can run only on a JVM and a Java EE application server).

Infrastructure components and controllers can provide and require `Resource-Interfaces` and hence can forward resource demands from upper to lower layers. As introduced above, infrastructure components use RD-SEFFs as behavioural specification which is also used to propagate resource demands to lower layer, while controller use Java code for this.

`ResourceInterfaces` are bound at deployment time (and not at system assembly time as usual interfaces). By using layers, binding of `ResourceInterfaces` can be automated as it is non-unambiguous. Required `ResourceInterfaces` are automatically bound to an interface of the next lower layer that provides a compatible interface. While these bindings of `ResourceInterfaces` are explicit in the model, tooling can hide them in the concrete syntax (e.g. graphical representation) to hide unnecessary complexity (cf. **R6** "lower complexity"). In Fig. 3, the bindings of the resource interfaces are thus not shown (e.g. between JVMComponent and Guest-OSController). Although introducing explicit `ResourceInterfaces`, complexity of modelling does not significantly increase due to automations enabled by layering. For *non*-layered component models, binding is *not* unambiguous, as potentially an infinite number of possible `ResourceInterfaces` exists for binding. In general, no automation is possible in such models.

Excerpts from the meta-model. In the following, we present the part of the PCM meta-model that deals with the modelling of layered controllers of the execution environment. The meta-model part for infrastructure component allocation is not shown here and can be found in [8]. However, infrastructure components share the same meta-model elements as business components. Hence, infrastructure components are modelled in the same way as business components and only allocated in a different way. To model parts of the execution environment with components, the component concepts can be reused (cf. **R6**, "lower complexity").

Fig. 4 shows the part of the PCM meta-model that deals with the modelling of controllers. A controller always refers to a specific `ControllerType`. The `ControllerType` specifies which controller code has to be used during simulation. Similar to resources, `ControllerTypes` are made available to the PCM deployer in a `ResourceRepository`. Since a PCM deployer only uses controllers that are already

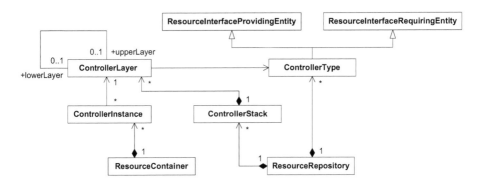

Fig. 4. PCM Meta-Model: Controllers

available, he does not have to create own instances of the `ControllerType` element.
A `ControllerType` inherits from `ResourceInterfaceProvidingEntity`
and `ResourceInterfaceRequiringEntity`, hence it can provide and require
`ResourceInterfaces` (the `ResourceInterface` and corresponding roles are
not shown in the figure, for the sake of clarity). To allow for a modelling of layered
controllers, every controller is deployed in its own `ControllerLayer`. Multiple
`ControllerLayers` are strictly ordered by means of associations which reference
the next upper `ControllerLayer` ("upperLayer") or the next lower `Controller-`
`Layer` ("lowerLayer"), respectively. Since controllers of the same `Controller`
`Type` can be deployed on several `ResourceContainers` (in fact, even one
`Resource-Container` may contain several controllers of the same `Controller`
`Type`, e.g. Linux running in a virtualised Linux), the `ControllerInstance` denotes the actual instance of the controller. A `ResourceContainer` has a reference
to all `Control-lerInstances` that are deployed on this `ResourceContainer`.
Thus, resource demands can be mapped unambiguously to a deployed controller.

To allow for reuse of a previously modelled set of `ControllerLayers`, a `Re-`
`sourceContainer` may also optionally reference a `ControllerStack` (e.g. a
Linux with Sun JVM). A `ControllerStack` serves as a container for predefined
`ControllerLayers` and is contained in a `ResourceRepository`, which makes
the reuse of a `ControllerStack` possible. However, a `ResourceContainer`
does not need to reference a predefined `ControllerStack`. In any case, for every
deployed controller, the `ResourceContainer` has to reference a `Controller-`
`Instance` element.

Limitations of the extended PCM model. The resource and execution environment access only allows for specifying one parameter, i.e. the demand, to keep the PCM simulation slim and force abstractions. Supporting multiple parameters also could force
Component Developers to specify parameter values that cannot be known. For example, a HDD interface might provide a `"read"` service whose demand specifies the
number of bytes to be read. A second parameter which specifies the probability of hit-
ting a HDD cache (which strongly influences performance) cannot be guessed by a
Component Developer as the actual size of the HDD cache cannot be known.

Furthermore, in the current version, we concentrated on processing resource types like a CPU or a HDD. A network resource type has not been considered yet.

6   Evaluation

In this section, we evaluate the new meta-model presented in this paper. We show how the extensions support explicit layering and investigate the ability to accurately model scenarios.

In this section, we use the new extended meta-model to predict the performance of the component-based FileShare application [13] whose Java bytecode implementation runs on a Java Virtual Machine (JVM for Java SE). The FileShare application allows users to share files by uploading and downloading them. Before a file can be uploaded, FileShare checks in two databases that (i) the file is not yet uploaded and (ii) it is not copyrighted (i.e. is eligible for sharing). The files are compressed before being stored to save server space, and the file hash (digest) is used for lookup in the two aforementioned databases. Thus, the FileShare application involves business components and execution environment (JVM, CPU). In this paper, we only consider the components for compressing and for hashing because they already cover the two types of operations found in Java bytecode: primitive instructions (e.g. IADD integer addition) and method invocations (e.g. java.lang.ArrayList.add).

6.1   Objective

The objective of this case study is to show that the new meta-model is appropriate for modelling realistic scenarios, such as bytecode components executed on JVMs. For estimating the impact of a specific JVM on application performance or to predict the performance of the FileShare application for other execution environments, the JVM must be modelled as an explicit component that can be exchanged. To demonstrate the power of the extended model, we will focus on the JVM component in the following, while the case study covers the whole scenario.

The old Palladio meta-model did not support appropriate modelling of the JVM and of business components that run on it: the JVM had to be modelled as a *business* component that provided an interface for executing Java API methods and bytecode instructions, and itself used the CPU and other resources. All components therefore resided at the same single layer. Also, each bytecode or API instruction had to be modelled as a single external service call. As outlined in Section 5, the new extended meta-model allows to specify several ResourceServices in a ResourceInterface which then can be provided by resources or infrastructure components. In the new model, accesses to the execution environment can be distinguished from calls to components.

6.2   Scenario

To understand the case study, we will briefly go through the basics of bytecode-based performance prediction that we will apply to the compression and hashing components in FileShare. For the approach, business components (hashing, compression), infrastructure components (JVM), and resources (CPU) need to be treated as distinct layers to capture their individual performance impact. The approach works in four steps (which were described in detail in [13])

1. Obtain the resource demand of business components, i.e. to collect the number of bytecode instructions and methods executed at runtime (dynamic) which are issued to the JVM per provided service of the business component. For example, how often IADD etc. are executed for files to be hashed.
2. Obtain the resource demand of infrastructure components, i.e. the resources used by the JVM per individual instruction/method. For example, the JVM "delegates" CPU usage down to the "lower" resource CPU. Here, to obtain the CPU usage of an instruction/method (i.e. number of CPU cycles) we divide its benchmarked duration through the duration of one CPU cycle.
3. Combine the results of Steps 1 and 2, where for each instruction/method, its runtime count is multiplied with its resource demands. The resulting total (aggregated) per-resource demands are delegated to the "lower" resources.
4. The Palladio tooling computes performance metrics from the aggregated resource demands, e.g. response times or resource utilisation.

Dynamic instruction/method counts for a component service depend on that service's input parameters (i.e. the usage profile). Thus, in a correct JVM model, the CPU-independent JVM resource demands in the service's RD-SEFF must be expressed parametrically. Building on results of [13] where these dependencies were machine-learned using genetic programming, the JVM resource demands (e.g. the number of IADD instructions) of the component services have been specified in the internal actions of RD-SEFF as illustrated by an excerpt in Fig. 5.

For the JVM infrastructure component, the mapping from the offered resource services (e.g. IADD) to the process resource service of the CPU is CPU-specific. In this case study, we used a platform with a dual-core Intel T2400 1.83 GHz CPU with 1.5 GB of main memory, running Windows XP Pro with Sun JDK 1.6.0_06. Thus, one CPU cycle takes 0.5464 ns, and the ICONST_1 instruction that was microbenchmarked to take 1.68 ns is specified in the ICONST_1's RD-SEFF to consume 3.07 CPU instructions. We also assume that Garbage Collection does not interrupt the execution of a bytecode instruction; the impact of the Garbage Collection on execution of entire algorithms/methods is complex to estimate and we consider it future work.

The model of the JVM must also account for complex optimisations of the real JVM like JIT speedup. So we have reused the results of [13], which indicate that the average JIT speedup for the compression component is 12.9. To model the effects of JIT speedup on the compression component, we have divided the CPU resource demands

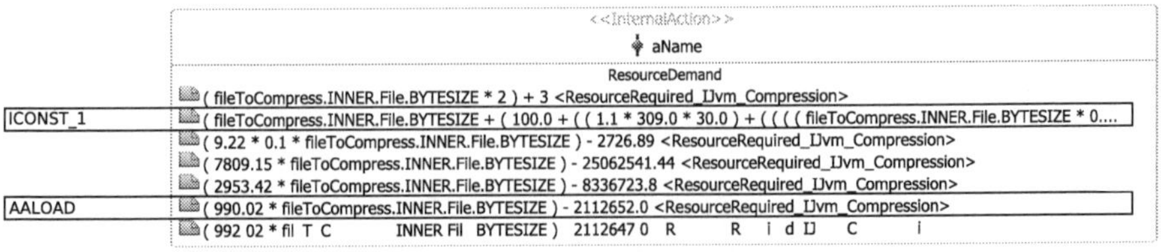

Fig. 5. An excerpt of the RD-SEFF for the infrastructure component modelling the JVM

in its RD-SEFF by 12.9 for the used combination of JVM, CPU and for the used algorithm. While this pragmatic solution is not universal, it applies pretty well [13] for 20 different input files given to compression FileShare, which included variously-sized, both uncompressed textual and compressed image (JPEG) files. Though we realise that the inclusion of the speedup factor into the RD-SEFF may make that RD-SEFF specific for the combination of the JVM, CPU and the algorithm, there is not enough evidence in literature on JIT speedup. However, the concepts of the new meta-model in Palladio will allow to parameterise the JIT speedup once more evidence on the latter becomes available, e.g. using a JIT compiler component that is layered between the JVM component and the CPU resource.

After the instruction/method counts have been specified in RD-SEFFs of the compression and hashing components, and the JVM's CPU usage has been specified in its RD-SEFF, we have performed the actual performance prediction.

6.3   Results

Although we have taken only 18 most frequent bytecode instructions (to reduce manual effort of creating the RD-SEFFs), the prediction results for the "compression and hashing" part of FileShare were at most 10% off.

Figure 6 shows a comparison of the predicted and measured results for an uncompressed 25 KB file: Compression and hashing together were predicted to take 112 ms, while 123 ms were measured. The resulting underestimation of $< 9\%$ originates in the consideration of "only" the 18 most frequent bytecode instructions, and in the interpolation that was cast into the mathematic expressions used in the RD-SEFFs' resource demands.

This bytecode scenario shows that concepts which could not be expressed using the old meta-model can now be expressed with the new one, and that the performance can be successfully predicted for the new scenario. We note that since our example used the CPU as the (lowest-level) resource, the full power of Palladio simulation and tools is available: for example, specification of a parameterised usage profile, simulation of contention, evaluation of the CPU utilisation but also the visualisation and the repositories for components and resources.

Due to the explicit layering and components with explicit environmental dependencies only, we could also have exchanged parts of the software stack (e.g. to simulate

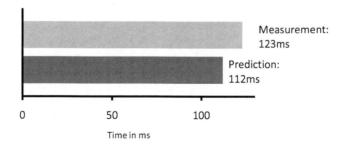

Fig. 6. An excerpt of the results for the infrastructure component modelling the JVM

replacing the Sun JVM by an IBM JVM). To enable simulations of the new software stack model, only the JVM component needs to be changed. Thus, the extended component model supports well what-if scenarios for all layers of components.

In the case study, we only modelled the CPU as resource. This simplification is warranted, since no hard disk activity during benchmarking could be observed, and the fact that the CPU usage and memory usage are impossible to disentangle and to measure separately at the level of individual bytecode instructions. The current approach still is limited as there is no automation for constructing the RD-SEFFs for the JVM.

7   Conclusion

In this paper, we have presented an evaluated solution for modelling state-of-the-art layered execution environments, such as disk arrays, virtual machines, and application servers. Our contribution includes support for model-based performance prediction of components running in these (virtualised) execution environments, as we have successfully shown in a case study where Java bytecode components were executed on a virtual machine. The presented solution introduces explicit interfaces for resource access, thus parameterising models of components over the used resource types, so that adding additional middleware or virtualisation layers does not lead to re-modelling of components.

We have applied our approach to the Palladio Component Model (PCM) and its tools, which is now the first component model to support well-defined layering of execution environments to separate business components (e.g. customer management) from infrastructure components (e.g. application servers), but also from hardware resources (e.g. CPUs and hard disks), and controllers (e.g. RAID controllers). The extended PCM simplifies working on large modelling projects by supporting the division of labour: layering of components and controllers allows for better isolation, avoiding overlapping modelling artifacts and allowing to change a layer and its model without side effects on other layers. Also, the PCM roles such as application deployer or software architect continue to be supported in the extended PCM, further supporting division of labour among developers.

Our approach introduces only a limited additional complexity to the component model as the extensions make use of pre-existing structures. The GUI of the PCM tools hides the low-level details of the introduced model extensions from the user, making the approach intuitive to use.

During our studies we found out that the same component is an infrastructure component to some developers, while others see it as a business component. For example, for a JVM developer the JVM is business logic, while for a developer of a user management component it is infrastructure. This is reflected in the extended PCM by having one type of components, which must only be deployed differently. If other component models should start adopting the principle of layering, they must be aware of varying assignments of components to layers.

For future work, we plan to integrate controllers into the PCM simulation and to study the scalability of our approach. For usability reasons, we would like to integrate further automation aspects into the PCM workbench: for example, in many cases, resource connectors can be derived automatically from given infrastructure component and controller layers. To enhance the applicability of performance prediction for byte-code components, we plan to integrate tools for bytecode counting and benchmarking into the PCM workbench.

Acknowledgments. This work was partially funded in the context of the Q-ImPrESS research project (http://www.q-impress.eu) by the European Union under the ICT priority of the 7th Research Framework Programme.

References

1. Becker, S., Koziolek, H., Reussner, R.: The Palladio component model for model-driven performance prediction. Journal of Systems and Software 82, 3–22 (2009)
2. Bondarev, E., de With, Peter, H.N., Chaudron, M.: Predicting Real-Time Properties of Component-Based Applications. In: Proc. of RTCSA (2004)
3. Bures, T., Hnetynka, P., Plasil, F.: Sofa 2.0: Balancing advanced features in a hierarchical component model. In: SERA 2006: Proceedings of the Fourth International Conference on Software Engineering Research, Management and Applications, pp. 40–48. IEEE Computer Society Press, Washington (2006)
4. Gelissen, J., Laverty, R.M.: Robocop: Revised specification of framework and models (deliverable 1.5). Technical report, Information Technology for European Advancement (2003)
5. Grassi, V., Mirandola, R., Sabetta, A.: From Design to Analysis Models: a Kernel Language for Performance and Reliability Analysis of Component-based Systems. In: WOSP 2005: Proceedings of the 5th international workshop on Software and performance, pp. 25–36. ACM Press, New York (2005)
6. Gupta, S., Shirole, J.V.: Architecting, Developing and Testing for Performance of Tiered Collaboration Products. In: WOSP 2008: Proceedings of the 7th international workshop on Software and performance, pp. 25–32. ACM Press, New York (2008)
7. Happe, J.: Concurrency Modelling for Performance and Reliability Prediction of Component-Based Software Architectures. PhD Thesis, University of Oldenburg, Germany (2008)
8. Hauck, M.: Extending Performance-Oriented Resource Modelling in the Palladio Component Model. Master's thesis, University of Karlsruhe (TH), Germany (February 2009)
9. Hissam, S.A., Moreno, G.A., Stafford, J.A., Wallnau, K.C.: Packaging Predictable Assembly. In: Bishop, J.M. (ed.) CD 2002. LNCS, vol. 2370, pp. 108–124. Springer, Heidelberg (2002)
10. Hnětynka, P.: Making Deployment Process of Distributed Component-Based Software Unified. PhD Thesis, Charles University in Prague (September 2005)
11. Koziolek, H., Becker, S., Happe, J.: Predicting the Performance of Component-based Software Architectures with different Usage Profiles. In: Overhage, S., Szyperski, C., Reussner, R., Stafford, J.A. (eds.) QoSA 2007. LNCS, vol. 4880, pp. 145–163. Springer, Heidelberg (2008)
12. Koziolek, H., Happe, J.: A Quality of Service Driven Development Process Model for Component-based Software Systems. In: Gorton, I., Heineman, G.T., Crnković, I., Schmidt, H.W., Stafford, J.A., Szyperski, C., Wallnau, K. (eds.) CBSE 2006. LNCS, vol. 4063, pp. 336–343. Springer, Heidelberg (2006)
13. Kuperberg, M., Krogmann, K., Reussner, R.: Performance Prediction for Black-Box Components using Reengineered Parametric Behaviour Models. In: Chaudron, M.R.V., Szyperski, C., Reussner, R. (eds.) CBSE 2008. LNCS, vol. 5282, pp. 48–63. Springer, Heidelberg (2008)

14. Maly, P., Woodside, C.M.: Layered Modeling of Hardware and Software, with Application to a LAN Extension Router. In: Haverkort, B.R., Bohnenkamp, H.C., Smith, C.U. (eds.) TOOLS 2000. LNCS, vol. 1786, pp. 10–24. Springer, Heidelberg (2000)
15. Object Management Group (OMG). UML Profile for Schedulability, Performance and Time (January 2005)
16. Object Management Group (OMG). Unified Modeling Language Specification: Version 2, Revised Final Adopted Specification, ptc/05-07-04 (2005)
17. Object Management Group (OMG). UML Profile for Modeling and Analysis of Real-Time and Embedded systems (MARTE) RFP (realtime/05-02-06) (2006)
18. Petriu, D.B., Woodside, M.: A Metamodel for Generating Performance Models from UML Designs. In: Baar, T., Strohmeier, A., Moreira, A., Mellor, S.J. (eds.) UML 2004. LNCS, vol. 3273, pp. 41–53. Springer, Heidelberg (2004)
19. Sharma, V.S., Jalote, P., Trivedi, K.S.: Evaluating Performance Attributes of Layered Software Architecture. In: Heineman, G.T., Crnković, I., Schmidt, H.W., Stafford, J.A., Szyperski, C., Wallnau, K. (eds.) CBSE 2005. LNCS, vol. 3489, pp. 66–81. Springer, Heidelberg (2005)
20. Slaby, J.M., Baker, S., Hill, J., Schmidt, D.C.: Applying system execution modeling tools to evaluate enterprise distributed real-time and embedded system qos. In: RTCSA 2006: Proceedings of the 12th IEEE International Conference on Embedded and Real-Time Computing Systems and Applications, Washington, DC, USA, pp. 350–362. IEEE Computer Society, Los Alamitos (2006)
21. Smith, C.U., Llado, C.M.: Performance Model Interchange Format (PMIF 2.0): XML Definition and Implementation. In: QEST 2004: Proceedings of the The Quantitative Evaluation of Systems, First International Conference, Washington, DC, USA, pp. 38–47. IEEE Computer Society, Los Alamitos (2004)
22. Smith, C.U., Williams, L.G.: Performance Solutions: A Practical Guide to Creating Responsive, Scalable Software. Addison-Wesley, Reading (2002)
23. Szyperski, C., Gruntz, D., Murer, S.: Component Software: Beyond Object-Oriented Programming, 2nd edn. ACM Press/ Addison-Wesley, New York (2002)
24. Verdickt, T., Dhoedt, B., Gielen, F.: Incorporating SPE into MDA: Including Middleware Performance Details into System Models. SIGSOFT Softw. Eng. Notes 29(1), 120–124 (2004)
25. Woodside, M., Vetland, V., Courtois, M., Bayarov, S.: Resource Function Capture for Performance Aspects of Software Components and Sub-Systems. In: Dumke, R.R., Rautenstrauch, C., Schmietendorf, A., Scholz, A. (eds.) WOSP 2000 and GWPESD 2000. LNCS, vol. 2047, pp. 239–256. Springer, Heidelberg (2001)

Component-Based Real-Time Operating System for Embedded Applications

Frédéric Loiret[1], Juan Navas[2], Jean-Philippe Babau[3], and Olivier Lobry[2]

[1] INRIA-Lille, Nord Europe, Project ADAM
USTL-LIFL CNRS UMR 8022, France
frederic.loiret@inria.fr
[2] Orange Labs
{juanfernando.navasmantilla,olivier.lobry}@orange-ftgroup.com
[3] Université Européenne de Bretagne
jean-philippe.babau@univ-brest.fr

Abstract. As embedded systems must constantly integrate new function-alities, their developement cycles must be based on high-level abstractions, making the software design more flexible. CBSE provides an approach to these new requirements. However, low-level services provided by operat-ing systems are an integral part of embedded applications, furthermore deployed on resource-limited devices. Therefore, the expected benefits of CBSE must not impact on the constraints imposed by the targetted do-main, such as memory footprint, energy consumption, and execution time. In this paper, we present the componentization of a legacy industry-established Real-Time Operating System, and how component-based ap-plications are built on top of it. We use the Think framework that allows to produce flexible systems while paying for flexibility only where desired. Performed experiments show that the induced overhead is negligeable.

1 Introduction

Until recently, embedded systems were defined as resource constrained, dedicated and closed computing systems buried within an electro-mechanical structure they interact with. Much of the embedded systems are also real-time systems, i.e. systems in which *temporal predictability* is a key issue.

While limited resources constraint remains, paradigms like *Everyware* [13] boosted embedded systems development; growing demand in embedded devices market imposes new preoccupations such as Time to Market, industrial stan-dards compliance, and adaptability to dynamic operation context. Consequently, embedded systems can no longer be closed and specific-task systems, since they must adapt themselves to the surrounding environment. System's design, devel-opment, deployment, and maintenance complexity has increased and traditional code-centric methodologies are no longer suitable, not only at application level, but also at operating system level since the latter is integral part of embedded applications.

Component-Based Software Engineering (CBSE) [27] addresses several aspects in today's embedded systems development. Systems are designed by assembling

G.A. Lewis, I. Poernomo, and C. Hofmeister (Eds.): CBSE 2009, LNCS 5582, pp. 209–226, 2009.
© Springer-Verlag Berlin Heidelberg 2009

software and *system* components [15] and may evolve at execution time through dynamic reconfiguration [24]. CBSE is particularly useful in handling the multiple variants of a same product line, as components can be treated as independent, arbitrary fine-grained entities to be deployed in heterogeneus devices. Several approaches, some of them inspired by CBSE paradigm, have been applied to obtain similar design and run-time benefits in the resources-constrained systems domain:

- Virtual machines and bytecode/script interpreters [17,22,30] allow run-time flexibility in very resource-limited platforms such as sensor networks *motes*. However, peformance penalty increases as virtual machines are designed to be less application-specific, making this approach not scalable for more general real-time embedded systems product lines.
- Real-time embedded systems can be built by compiling component-based architecture descriptions [29,18]. By this way, design-time CBSE benefits are preserved but the notion of *component* disappears at run-time, failing to take advantage of a global CBSE approach. Also, existing framework programming models make difficult the introduction of real-time specific concepts and prior developements.
- Component-based versions of executive parts can be integrated to real-time component-based applications that means to assemble OS-related services or to componentize existing RTOS source code. This approach globally preserves CBSE benefits, but may induce a significant overhead concerning critical metrics of embedded systems such as memory footprint, real-time responsiveness and execution time. However, recent studies [20] show that it is possible to control and to limit the possible overheads caused by flexibility support.

The contribution of this paper follows this last approach. It presents how an existing real-time operating system, μC/OS-II, is componentized, as well as the considerations that shall be respected in this re-engineering task. We use the THINK component framework [8,4], an implementation of the FRACTAL component model [6] that fullfills the constraints of embedded-systems. This component model is used in a homogeneous way at both application and operating system levels. A THINK component is an entity that is preserved during the whole system life cycle with minimal performance overhead.

The paper is organized as follows: Section 2 briefly describes μC/OS-II RTOS, THINK framework and its underlying FRACTAL component model. Section 3 identifies challenges to be faced in a RTOS componentization task; Section 4 details the componentization scheme. Section 5 presents a use-case benchmark that demonstrates the benefits of our approach. Section 6 describes related work. Section 7 concludes the paper.

2   Background

This section presents the features of the μC/OS-II kernel and the THINK component framework. We stress in Section 2.3 the reasons that led us to conduct our work grounded on these two projects.

2.1   The μC/OS-II RTOS

μC/OS-II is a preemptive, real-time multitasking kernel for microprocessors and microcontrollers. It is implemented in ANSI C and certified by the FAA[1] for use in software intended to be deployed in avionics equipment. It has been massively used in many embedded and safety critical systems products worldwide.

The main services provided by μC as an RTOS are sketched out in Fig. 1, which gives the module structure of the kernel distribution. The main services are implemented within the `Core`, the `Task` and the `Port` modules. The latter implements the hardware-dependent services.

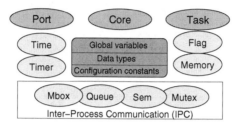

Fig. 1. μC Modules

μC/OS is implemented as a monolithic kernel, i.e. it is built from a number of *functions* that share common *global variables* and *data types* (such as *task control block, event control block*, etc).

It is a highly configurable kernel, whose configuration relies on more than 70 parameters. Since the kernel is provided in source form, configurability is done via conditional compilation at precompilation time, based on `#define` constants. μC allows to scale down, the main objective being to reduce the memory footprint of the final executable (up to several KBytes, depending on the processor). Hence, it is possible to avoid code generation of non required services, or to reduce the size of data structures used by the kernel. Several parameters allow developers to configure essential properties of the kernel, e.g. the *tick* frequency.

The execution time for most of these services is both constant and deterministic, which is a compulsory requirement for real-time systems in order to avoid unpredictable *kernel jitter* [3].

For a full description of the features, the design and the internals of μC/OS-II, we refer the interested reader to the book [2][2].

2.2   The Think component Framework

THINK is an implementation of the FRACTAL component model that aims to take into account the specific constraints of embedded systems development. The FRACTAL specifications [6] define a hierarchical, reflective and general-purpose

---

[1] Federal Aviation Administration.

[2] In this paper, we refer to the version 2.86 of μC/OS.

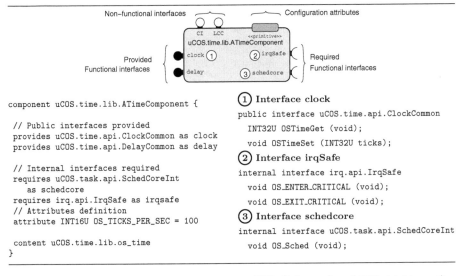

Fig. 2. Definition of a primitive component: ADL (left part) and IDL (right part)

component model. A *component* definition exports *functional interfaces* (provided or required), configuration *attributes*, and may also provide *non-functional interfaces* implementing introspection and architectural reconfiguration services at run-time.

The THINK framework allows developers to build embedded systems made out of FRACTAL components. A system architecture is described using an Architecture Description Language (ADL), interfaces are defined using an Interface Description Language (IDL). The code that implements the method of server interfaces is written in regular C (or wrapped assembler language) where ADL symbols are represented by convenient C symbols. The mapping between ADL symbols and C symbols can be specified using annotations in commentary section of the C files which facilitates the encapsulation of legacy code. An example of a THINK component definition is given in Figure 2[3].

The THINK compiler maps architectural elements to C variables in implementation code, transforms existing functional code and produces meta-data and implementation of non-functional interfaces. The meta-data typically allow to retrieve an attribute, the descriptor of a bound-to server interface of the component context of a bound-to component. The resulting C code is then passed to traditional C compilers and linkers to generate the final binary file.

Since applying the component paradigm can easily impacts on performances, the THINK compiler provides tools to produce, from a same architectural description, different binary images with different performance versus flexibilty trade-offs. Architectural elements can be tagged with flexibility-oriented properties in an Aspect-Oriented-Programming manner. These properties will be

---

[3] By convention, the *functional interfaces* are graphically placed on the left and right sides of the component, the *non-functional interfaces* on the top side.

interpreted by the compiler to generate an optimized binary image that only embeds flexibility where actually desired. For example:

– The address of the context of a *single* component is known at compile-time and need not be passed in calls;
– A *constant* attribute is implemented as a compile-time constant and no meta-data is generated;
– A *static* binding does not generate meta-data and calls to the corresponding client interface are implemented as direct function calls;
– The implementation code of the server interface can even be inlined in the caller;
– no meta-data is generated for a server interface to which all bindings are static.

2.3 μC/OS-II and Think Are Good Canditates

Regarding our experiment, μC/OS is a good candidate for the following reasons:

– It is a mature real-time operating system used in many industrial projects.
– A fundamental particularity of μC/OS resides in its determinist nature, which is a basic property to consider, and to preserve in a reengineering of its internal structure.
– Its highly configurable capability is an interesting property that can help to compare with a component-based approach for which only the required services of the application are linked by composition within the final binary.
– μC/OS was designed to be portable, and a special attention has been paid to clearly distinguish between the generic code and the hardware dependent code. This eases the separation of concerns applied to an implementation designed with the component paradigm.

Considering the THINK framework and its underlying component model, we can highlight the following points:

– The component paradigm adopted by the THINK framework provides a high degree of flexibility, which combined with the genericity and configurability of the FRACTAL component model, allows the construction of dedicated and fully configurable operating systems.
– Architecture-oriented optimizations make THINK specially well suited for resource-limited embedded systems, as they allow to specify where flexibility capabilities should be added and which FRACTAL non-functional interfaces should be provided by components.
– Several case studies have been conducted with THINK to design minimal operating systems for various embedded platforms[4] (ARM, PowerPC, AVR, Xscale, etc). These experiments demonstrate the robustness of the tools constituing the THINK framework.

---

[4] See http://think.objectweb.org/

3   Challenges Considering a μC Componentization

Since a component is a basic first-class reuse entity, the separation of concerns is a key concept of CBSE. Improving this separation implies maximizing the decoupling between components in terms of encapsulated data and services. As a first challenge, considering that our experiment is based on an RTOS which was not initially designed as a component-based architecture, an important re-engineering effort of the μC/OS's implementation should be considered.

The component paradigm is based on abstractions which are well-suited to address flexibility requirements for complex systems. In our approach, we are interested in providing such a flexibility not only at application level but also at RTOS level.

From a design point of view, we want to provide a framework to build both an application-dedicated executive part and also reusable parts of executive off-the-shelf components. Since the component is a configurability unit for the developer, the granularity of components is a crucial point to consider according to these flexibility requirements. Furthermore, we have to provide the ability to choose and tune existing components. It should be possible within the design process to tailor the components according to various execution contexts. For example, to provide several implementations of a given component without changing its specifications, or to implement various parts of a complex communication protocol, etc. These aspects play a major role in the design and the developement of embedded systems. At the end, to mitigate the constraints of resource limited platforms, only the strictly required RTOS components should be embedded in the deployed system.

A third challenge appears when considering flexibility at runtime. Indeed, since the basic reconfiguration units are the components, their attributes and their assemblies are specified via bindings, and these concepts should thus be reified at runtime. Moreover, considering that our experiment tackles several very low-level RTOS services which will not be adapted at runtime, it is not compulsorily required to provide such reconfiguration capabilities for any components of the architecture. This requirement is a basic aspect to tackle considering the targetted application domain.

Last, but not least, the impact on execution time and memory footprint must be considered. An RTOS implementation designed following the component paradigm and the aforementionned flexibility requirements should not involve unbounded overheads in term of performance. Moreover, the component framework should not introduce indeterminism in the execution of the RTOS services.

4 μC/OS Componentization

4.1   Motivations for a μC/OS's Reengineering

The modular structure of μC is a good starting point for our componentization process since the core functionalities of the OS are clearly identified. However,

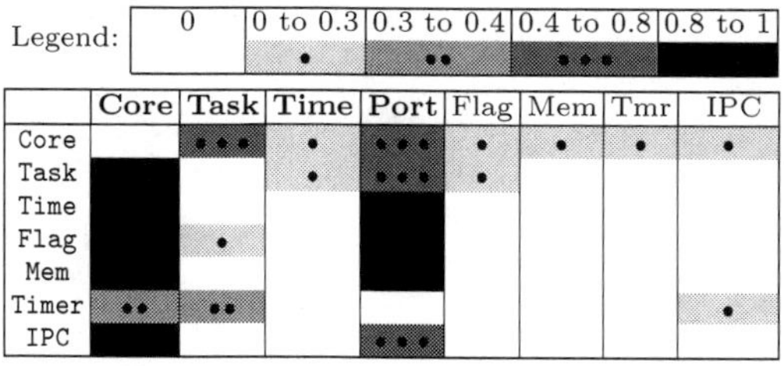

Fig. 3. Coupling between μC modules based on function dependencies

we considered several parameters in order to improve the separation of concerns in the resulting component-based infrastructure proposed in the next section.

First, we considered the basic aspects usually defined within a real-time kernel [7,26]. The two main aspects of an RTOS are the *Task Management*, for scheduling and the dispatching of tasks, and the *Event Management*, mainly for hardware events processing. Because these two aspects expose key features of an RTOS, we considered as a requirement the reification of them at architectural level. Moreover, since they are tangled over several μC modules, a reengineering of the kernel source code has been performed.

Second, we have conducted several coupling analysis within the original μC/OS implementation. The Fig. 3 presents a coarse-grained coupling between μC modules[5] based on the function *dependencies*. To compute the coupling metric between modules **A** and **B**, the number of function calls between them is divided by the total number of function call between **A** and the other modules[6]. This analysis highlights for example a tightly coupling between the **Task** and the **Core** modules. Indeed, the latter implements several functions related to *Task Management*. The **Port** module provides the functions to enable/disable hardware interrupts necessary for global variables protection. This explains the thightly coupling between all the modules to these functions. We have also conducted this coupling analysis with the global variables access, the data types definition and the configuration constants. This analysis helped us to propose the fine-grained component-based design of μC presented in the next section.

4.2   Description of the Componentization Process

The componentization process of the operating system has been conducted in the following steps:

1. Interface Definitions.   The μC function definitions are specified with the THINK IDL. For each type of service (e.g. *timer management*, *task management*, etc), a set of interfaces are defined according to their nature – creation or deletion of a resource, commonly or rarely used functions – and ordered within packages

---

[5] The **Mbox**, **Queue**, **Sem** and **Mutex** modules are gathered under the **IPC** appellation (for *Inter-Process Communication*).

[6] For example, the **Core** module makes 28 function calls to the **Task** module, and sums a total of 36 calls with all the modules. The result is a coupling metric of 0.77.

(e.g. see Fig. 2). Furthermore, we make a distinction between *internal interfaces* which are used only between µC modules, and *public interfaces* which provide all services visible at the application level following a set of system calls that may be invoked by application tasks.

2. Componentization.   As a first componentization level, we define an architecture structured as the original µC implementation: each module sketched in Fig. 1 is reified as a primitive component using the THINK ADL. The architectural artifacts of these ADL descriptions are expressed within source code using annotations to inform the THINK compiler of this mapping. These components are encapsulated into a top-level composite that exposes the public interfaces available for the application tasks.

From this componentization level, and following the reengeneering motivations exposed in Section 4.1, the architecture is refined. RTOS key-features scattered over the modules were reified as components, and resulting tighly-coupled functions are merged.

3. Global Variables Expressed at Architectural Level.   Within our componentization process, each µC/OS' global variable is defined as private data of primitive component (i.e. "task-related variables" defined within the `TaskManager Component`). Getter/setter functions are specified according to the data type definition of each variable and mapped to internal interfaces. The access to these variables between components are then expressed at architectural level via basic bindings.

4. Resources Components.   From our point of view, within a CBSE design process, the resources of the operating system used by the application (such as a semaphore, a mailbox or a timer) should be reified at the architectural level. Therefore, µC/OS resources are represented by primitive components, called *resource wrappers*. Application components access these resources using basic bindings. This approach allows the developer to configure these resources from their exported configuration attributes (e.g. the task priority, the initial value of a semaphore, etc). Examples of such *resource wrappers* are given in Fig. 6.

5. Attribute Definitions.   From the configuration parameters defined by µC/OS, we isolate two kinds of *attributes*. First, those which let the architect configure essential properties of the RTOS, such as the tick frequency, the priority assigned to the task managing the timer. Second, those which specify the thresholds for the use of ressources managed by the RTOS, e.g. the maximum number of tasks or semaphores supported by the kernel, the size of strings for event names, etc. Attribute signatures are thus defined (with naming conventions according to their kind) and attached to component definitions.

6. Component Library.   Finally, we provide a library of ready-to-use RTOS, as a set of composite components, according to the services that they provide to the application (via their public interfaces).

An example of such a componentized RTOS is presented Fig. 4. It corresponds to the minimal operating system required by the application presented in the

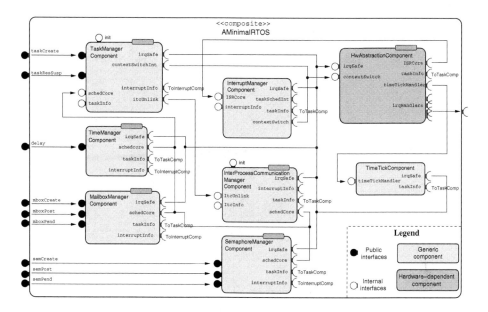

Fig. 4. Architecture's Example of a μC RTOS

next section. The non-functional interface `init` (e.g. for the TaskManager Component) is invoqued by a THINK-generated life-cycle-controller component that manages, among others, system initialization.

5 Evaluation

In this section, we evaluate our component-based design of μC/OS in comparison with its original implementation. As a qualitative evaluation in Section 5.2, we present how a classical multi-task application is designed using functional and resource components compared to a "pure C" implementation. We show how design time and runtime flexibility is addressed within our approach. Finally, we conduct benchmark tests in Section 5.3 to measure performance and memory footprint overheads introduced by the component-based design.

5.1 Motivation Example

To better illustrate several aspects of the following evaluation, we introduce in Fig. 5 a typical real-time and embedded application scenario that will be revisited throughout the course of this section. This example is composed of three tasks. The tasks `Task1` and `Task2` read and write a shared data which is protected by a binary semaphore (execution steps ① -③). A task pending on the semaphore (via the `acquire` service) can not be blocked more than 4 time units (which corresponds to a timeout specified by the semaphore). `Task2` is activated periodically by a timer, while Task1 is activated in response to an

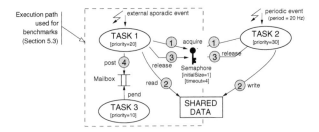

Fig. 5. A real-time application example

external interrupt event. At the end of its execution cycle, `Task1` sends the content of the read data to the `Task3` using a mailbox (execution step ④). This example illustrates the basic concepts used to design a real-time application.

5.2 Qualitative Evaluation

Design space provided to the application developer. Within our approach, the application is designed as interconnected components. The high-level design space provided to the application developer is based on the same architectural concepts used at RTOS level. Indeed, we use the THINK component model in a homogeneous way at these two abstraction levels (application and OS). As an illustration, the architecture of the application presented above is sketched out in Fig. 6. It shows a set of functional and resource components that require services provided by the operating system configuration in Fig. 4.

Each application task given in Fig. 5 is represented by a composition between a *Task resource component* and a *functional component* which implements the task's entry point (via the **runner** interface). Resource components are instances of already existing components found in previously built components library; developers simply configure their attributes according to desired behavior (e.g. the *priority* for the tasks, the *timeout* for the semaphore, etc). The bindings between resource or functional components and the RTOS are generated automatically by our framework from interface signatures.

Bottom line, we provide the application developer a higher-level design procedure, compared to commonly used plain C language mechanisms. Besides, the operating system resources used by the application are reified as basic components. First, this feature offers a clear view, at architectural level, of the resources used by the system, and it reifies via bindings how they are shared by the functional components. Second, it makes easier their configuration since each instance exports its configuration attributes at the architectural level, simply accessible by the developer.

Flexibility at Design Time. Within the original implementation of μC/OS-II , compilation options allow to configure essential properties of the RTOS and to scale down the final executive using precompilation directives. Within our approach, these configuration capabilities are managed at architectural level:

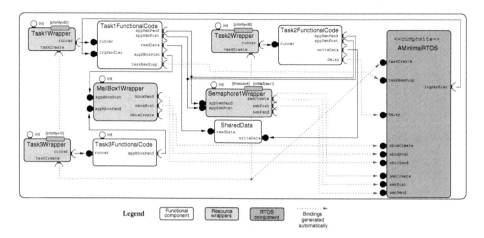

Fig. 6. A componentized example

- The configuration of the RTOS' essential properties is addressed using components configuration attributes. These attributes are defined at architectural level, as for instance the OS_TICKS_PER_SEC attribute defined for ATimeComponent definition given in Fig. 2. Moreover, we implemented a simple tool which returns, from a given architecture description, the whole set of component attributes configurable by the developer.
- The capability to scale down the final executive is addressed using the RTOS components stored in the library provided to the developer. For a given primitive component, several ADL definitions are stored in the library, differing by the number of interfaces – and thus the kind of services – they provide. A set of RTOS composite component definitions are then built, exporting their public interfaces according to the interfaces provided by different combinations of subcomponents[7].

Finally, the RTOS componentization does not restrict the configuration capabilities supported by the original μC/OS-II implementation. Moreover, we can emphasize a feature arising from our approach. Since the application components export the services that they require from the RTOS, it is possible to automatically retrieve from the component library the corresponding composite definition which fits strictly the needs of the application. This feature is well-suited to address the constraints of resource-limited platforms, and represents a significant benefit of our approach compared to the manual configuration of original μC constants.

Flexibility at Runtime. As it has been presented in Section 2.2, the THINK compiler generates meta-data that describes the FRACTAL component model architectural concepts at the C source-code level and consequently in final binary file.

---

[7] The THINK ADL supports inheritance relationships between architectural definitions which facilitates that procedure.

This meta-data provides the necessary infrastructure to enable flexibility from *inside* components. The standard FRACTAL API [6] that enables introspection and reconfiguration from *outside* components can be generated over these meta-data. Note however that THINK only injects these control interfaces (and their respective implementations) only where it has been specifically specified, none being injected by default.

As run-time flexibility may not be necessary for all system components, the THINK framework provides mechanisms to specify whether a single component or a subset of system components is not likely to evolve at execution time. Using flexibility-oriented *properties* the architect can instruct the THINK compiler whether to generate the meta-data that make these components flexible. This feature allows to apply flexibility only where needed, and the way it is effectively needed, producing substantial reductions in memory footprint size and execution times, as it is presented in the following quantitative evaluation.

5.3   Quantitative Evaluation

As it has been described in Section 4.2, the componentization process led us to a reengineering of the μC's internal structure. Besides, we propose to reify the kernel resource instances as components, introducing a level of indirection between the functional and the operating system components. Finally, the tools provided by the THINK framework allow to introduce several level of flexibility at runtime. In the following sections, we measure how this impacts the resulting executable in term of memory footprint and execution time. The evaluation is based on the RTOS and the application example presented respectively in Fig. 4 and Fig. 6.

Memory Footprint. The Fig. 7 presents the memory footprints for a monolithic implementation used as a reference, compared to its component-based design[8]. We measure the overhead in code (i.e. .text section) and data, including initialized (i.e. .data section) and uninitialized (i.e. .bss section) data. We make this distinction as code is usually placed in ROM, whereas data are generally placed in RAM. For the component-based design, we propose three different configuration scenarios for the RTOS and the application presented in the preceding sections: the *highly flexible*, where components' meta-data allowing run-time flexibility are conserved at execution time, the *not flexible* scenario for which a completely static system is generated, and the *partially flexible*, for which only two functional components (Task3FunctionalCode and SharedData given in Fig. 2) are made flexible.

The systems generated in these scenarios do not include the non-functional FRACTAL interfaces that allow components to export FRACTAL's introspection and reconfiguration capabilities. This means that flexibility can only be exploited from inside components. In many cases, this basic flexibility level is enough to modify attributes or outgoing bindings according to internal component events.

---

[8] These experiments have been conducted using GCC with the -Os option that optimizes the binary image size.

			Reference	Component-Based Design		
			(a)	(b)	(c)	(d)
				highly flexible	not flexible	partially flexible
(1)	RTOS	Code	13508	+16.8 %	+0 %	–
		Data	14072	+3.26 %	+0 %	–
(2)	Complete System	Code	14003	+20.6 %	+1.8 %	+2.3 %
		Data	20252	+4.59 %	+0 %	+0.5 %

Fig. 7. Memory footprint sizes (in Bytes) and overheads, **(1)** for the RTOS level from Fig. 4, and **(2)** for the complete system from Fig. 6

			Reference	Component-Based Design	
			(a)	(b)	(c)
				highly flexible	partially flexible
				with FRACTAL APIs	with FRACTAL APIs
(3)	RTOS	Code	13508	+32.2 %	–
		Data	14072	+16.8 %	–
(4)	Complete System	Code	14003	+47.8 %	+4.1 %
		Data	20252	+20.9 %	+1.1 %

Fig. 8. Memory footprint sizes (in Bytes) and overheads, with the FRACTAL APIs, **(3)** for the RTOS level from Fig. 4, and **(4)** for the complete system from Fig. 6

From these results, we highlight the significative overhead implied by the *highly flexible* configuration (Fig. 7 (1)b and (2)b). This reflects the widespread use of interfaces and attributes within the component-based design that lead to the generation of the meta-data that enable flexibility, and confirms that optimization is an important issue. The *not flexible* configuration shows that such optimizations are feasible and they actually lead to an expected close to null overhead[9] (Fig. 7 (1)c). These results hence demonstrate the capability of the THINK approach to benefit from CBSE at design time, without having to pay any overhead if no flexibility is required. The *partially flexible* configuration's overheads (Fig. 7 (2)d) show how runtime flexibility could be configured for only a dedicated subset of components at a reasonable cost.

The Fig. 8 shows the memory footprint overheads for the *highly flexible* and *partially flexible* scenarios when FRACTAL introspection and reconfiguration APIs implementations are injected into the systems. The *highly flexible* scenario (Fig. 8 (3)b and (4)b) shows the significative overheads resulting in both Code and Data sections. This is explained by the meta-data required to control the many bindings introduced by the encapsulation of the whole system into small components. Again, the *partially flexible* scenario (Fig. 8 (4)c) shows that this overhead can be considerably reduced if these control interfaces are only injected where actually desired, as permitted by the THINK compiler.

[9] The light overhead observed in Code section (Fig. 7 (2)c) corresponds to the encapsulation of the *resource components* presented in Sec.5.2, overhead that may be eliminated in a near release of the THINK compiler.

Measures at RunTime. Considering the performance, the Fig. 9 presents the comparison between the monolithic and the component-based design which has been conducted considering the execution path given in Fig. 5. It traverses more than ten components of the architecture, from the application level as well as the RTOS level (since semaphore and mailbox services provided by the RTOS are involved), and includes a context switch between Task1 and Task2 implemented by the hardware-dependent component. The testing environment consists of a Pentium 4 monoprocessor at 2.0 GHz. The scenario was simulated under a Linux 2.6 kernel (using a Linux port of μC) patched by Rt-Preempt. The latter converts the kernel into a fully preemptible one with high resolution clock support, allowing precise performance measures. The results show that even for the *highly-flexible* configuration, the impact on performance is small, and becomes negligible when considering the optimized configuration. The figure also shows that the maximal amount of memory which is dynamically allocated at runtime remains unchanged within our component-based design compared to the monolithic one.

	Monolithic Design	Component-Based Design	
	reference	highly flexible	not flexible
Execution Path (μs)	45.97	**+2.8 %**	**+1.3 %**
Memory usage (*Bytes*)	49200	49200	49200

Fig. 9. Performance overheads and memory allocated dynamically

6   Related Work

Several approaches have been proposed to satisfy actual needs of fast development cycles and dynamic adaptation to changing work contexts. In the very resource-constrained domain of wireless sensor networks, Virtual Machines (VM) or similar approaches such as MATÉ [17], TAPPER [30] and DAVIM [22] provide support for run-time flexibility and low energy consumption at communication tasks. VM's implementations are strongly bound to the application hence hardly scalable to more general real-time embedded systems. DAVIM provides support for more complex dynamic reconfiguration by adding or removing operation libraries and so modify a running VM.

Applying modularity benefits into OS executives development process, OS-KIT [10] and ECOS [21] provide a set of operating system components that can be used as building blocks to configure an operating system. Component definition and binding languages such as KNIT [25] can be used to assist the assemblage of components. While producing efficient applications, these frameworks do not support dynamic reconfiguration and flexibility control. OSKIT is also more oriented to non-embedded hardware platforms.

Following a CBSE approach, TINYOS [18] and KOALA [29] define component models and allow to build a whole system, i.e. an application bound to a particular executive, compiling component architectures.

TINYOS is a component-based operating system and programming framework focused to *motes* in sensor networks domain. It reduces the penalty of fine-grained components by imposing a component-programming language, NESC [11], a dialect of C that facilitates functional code analysis and inlining. The use of this language introduces some significant limitations: besides making difficult the use of legacy code, a TINYOS application must be statically declared, as dynamic memory allocation is not supported. Dynamic reconfiguration at applicative and executive level is hence not supported, although.

KOALA is a component-based development framework and a component model oriented to consumer electronic (CE) devices. The component paradigm is exploited at design time, bindings and other model abstractions are translated to traditional C programming language structures and compiled. Consequently KOALA-based systems do not suffer from components-related performance overheads, but lack dynamic reconfiguration support.

ROBOCOP project [1] enriched KOALA component model offering, among others, component discovery and instantiation services and dynamic bindings features achieving CE devices requirements. Resources consumption is exhibited by *IResource* interfaces and is considered constant per operation [23]. An evaluation mechanism to measure static memory consumption had been developed for KOALA [9].

ROBOCOP and KOALA propose a similar approach to THINK and QINNA, a QoS framework for THINK [28,12]. It has been tested in many industrial experiments and accepted as an ISO standard under the name of M3W. However, we have not found enough information about how the component model is compiled, neither comparison with legacy code performance.

CAMKES [16] is a general embedded-systems oriented component model. Component-based applications run on top on a L4 micro-kernel [19] and a set of basic operating-system services provided by IGUANA [14]. Produced glue code is agressivily optimized from compile-time available information. If flexibility at run-time is required, extension layers can be added to the application. This approach is flexible as it allows to minimize memory size overhead in a basic application and to add additional functionnalities if required. Nevertheless, the extension layers strongly rely on services provided by L4 micro-kernel and IGUANA, creating a tight dependence between the component model, the component-based application and the operating system.

HARTEX [5] is a component-based framework dedicated to real-time kernels. The RTOS is designed as a composite component encapsulating the kernel primitives which are structured as interconnected sub-components. From a library of basic kernel components implemented from scratch, the framework allows to derive kernel configurations depending on the functionalities needed by the application. However, as far as we know, HARTEX is not based on an ADL, providing a higher-level representation of the component dependencies and kernel configurations. It is unclear how composition is managed by their compilation process and the framework do not support dynamic reconfiguration as well.

7   Conclusions

Component-based Software Engineering has emerged as a technology for the rapid assembly of flexible software systems, where the main benefits are reuse and separation of concerns. However, applying CBSE in the context of embedded systems implies to master the flexibility cost in term of performance, since they rely on low-level operating system services and are deployed on resource-limited devices.

This paper brings the following contributions to tackle these issues. First, we propose a componentization from an existing and mature Real-Time Operating System, μC/OS-II, based on the THINK component framework. From the RTOS resources reified as components, we present how component-based applications are designed on top of it. At design time, within our component-based approach, we fully address the configuration capabilities proposed by the original μC implementation. Furthermore, we can highlight an improvement arising from our approach, which fulfill a constraint imposed by resource-limited platforms: from the application architecture which express its dependencies towards the RTOS services, we can retrieve automatically from the component library the operating system component which fits stricly the needs of that application.

Second, the THINK component framework allows to introduce runtime flexibility, for RTOS components, as well as for application components, since we use its component model in a homogeneous way at these two abstraction levels. From a quantitative evaluation, and based on the THINK features allowing to apply flexibility only when desired, we show that overheads involved by our component-based design in term of performance are reasonables, and negligeables when considering a completely static version of the executable.

Relevant future work concerns improving configurability features of the RTOS at design time. Firstly, we are investigating a predicate-based ADL support within the THINK framework to provide a precompilation feature at architectural level. Secondly, the extensibility capabilities of our component-based design could be improved by exporting basic data type definitions used by the RTOS (such as *task control block, event control block*) at architectural level.

References

1. Robocop ITEA Project. Robocop: Robust Open component-based software architecture for configurable devices project,
   http://www.hitech-projects.com/euprojects/robocop/
2. MicroC/OS-II: The Real-Time Kernel. CMP Media, Inc., USA (2002)
3. Angelov, C., Berthing, J.: A Jitter-Free Kernel for Hard Real-Time Systems. In: Wu, Z., Chen, C., Guo, M., Bu, J. (eds.) ICESS 2004. LNCS, vol. 3605, pp. 388–394. Springer, Heidelberg (2005)
4. Anne, M., He, R., Jarboui, T., Lacoste, M., Lobry, O., Lorant, G., Louvel, M., Navas, J., Olive, V., Polajovic, J., Pulou, J., Poulhies, M., Seyvoz, S., Tous, J., Watteyne, T.: Think: View-Based Support of Non-Functional Properties in Embedded Systems. In: Proceedings of the 6th International Conference on Embedded Software and Systems (ICESS 2009) (2009)

5. Berthing, J., Angelov, C.: Component-Based Design of Safe Real-Time Kernels for Embedded Systems. In: EUROMICRO Conference, pp. 129–136 (2007)

6. Bruneton, E., Coupaye, T., Stefani, J.-B.: The Fractal Component Model, Version 2.0-3 (2004)

7. Buttazzo, G.C.: Hard Real-Time Computing Systems, 2nd edn. Springer, Heidelberg (2005)

8. Fassino, J.-P., Stefani, J.-B., Lawall, J., Muller, G.: Think: A software framework for component-based operating system kernels. In: Proceedings of the USENIX Annual Technical Conference, pp. 73–86 (June 2002)

9. Fioukov, A., Eskenazi, E., Hammer, D., Chaudron, M.: Evaluation of static properties for component-based architectures. pp. 33–39 (2002)

10. Ford, B., Back, G., Benson, G., Lepreau, J., Lin, A., Shivers, O.: The Flux OSKit A Substrate for Kernel and Language Research. In: Proceedings of the sixteenth ACM symposium on Operating systems principles, pp. 38–51 (1997)

11. Gay, D., Levis, P., von Behren, R., Welsh, M., Brewer, E., Culler, D.: The nesC Language: A Holistic Approach to Networked Embedded Systems. In: ACM Conference on Programming language design and implementation (PLDI) (2003)

12. Gonnord, L., Babau, J.-P.: Quantity of Resource Properties Expression and Runtime Assurance for Embedded Systems. In: ACS/IEEE International Conference on Computer Systems and Applications, AICCSA 2009, Rabbat, Morocco (to be published) (May 2009)

13. Greenfield, A.: Everyware: The Dawning Age of Ubiquitous Computing. Peachpit Press, Berkeley (2006)

14. Heiser, G.: Secure Embedded Systems need microkernels. USENIX 30(6), 9–13 (2005)

15. Kopetz, H., Suri, N.: Compositional Design of RT Systems: A Conceptual Basis for Specification of Linking Interfaces. In: Proceedings of the Sixth IEEE International Symposium on Object-Oriented Real-Time Distributed Computing (ISORC 2003), Washington, DC, USA, p. 51. IEEE Computer Society, Los Alamitos (2003)

16. Kuz, I., Liu, Y., Gorton, I., Heiser, G.: CAmkES: A Component Model for Secure Microkernel-based Embedded Systems. J. Syst. Softw. 80(5), 687–699 (2007)

17. Levis, P., Culler, D.: Maté: A Tiny Virtual Machine for Sensor Networks. In: ASPLOS-X: Proceedings of the 10th international conference on Architectural support for programming languages and operating systems, pp. 85–95. ACM, New York (2002)

18. Levis, P., Madden, S., Polastre, J., Szewczyk, R., Whitehouse, K., Woo, A., Gay, D., Hill, J., Welsh, M., Brewer, E., Culler, D.: TinyOS: An Operating System for Sensor Networks. Ambient Intelligence, 115–148 (2005)

19. Liedtke, J.: On Micro-Kernel Construction. In: SOSP 1995: Proceedings of the fifteenth ACM symposium on Operating systems principles, pp. 237–250. ACM, New York (1995)

20. Lobry, O., Polakovic, J.: Controlling the Performance Overhead of Component-Based Systems. In: Pautasso, C., Tanter, É. (eds.) SC 2008. LNCS, vol. 4954, pp. 149–156. Springer, Heidelberg (2008)

21. Massa, A.: Embedded Software Development with eCos. Prentice-Hall, Englewood Cliffs (2002)

22. Michiels, S., Horré, W., Joosen, W., Verbaeten, P.: DAViM: a Dynamically Adaptable Virtual Machine for Sensor Networks. In: MidSens 2006: Proceedings of the international workshop on Middleware for sensor networks, pp. 7–12. ACM, New York (2006)

23. Muskens, J., Chaudron, M.R.V.: Prediction of Run-Time Resource Consumption in Multi-task Component-Based Software Systems. In: Crnković, I., Stafford, J.A., Schmidt, H.W., Wallnau, K. (eds.) CBSE 2004. LNCS, vol. 3054, pp. 162–177. Springer, Heidelberg (2004)
24. Polakovic, J., Ozcan, A.E., Stefani, J.-B.: Building Reconfigurable Component-Based OS with THINK. In: EUROMICRO Conference on Software Engineering and Advanced Applications (2006)
25. Reid, A., Flatt, M., Stoller, L., Lepreau, J., Eide, E.: Knit: Component composition for systems software. In: Proc. of the Fourth Symposium on Operating Systems Design and Implementation, pp. 347–360 (2000)
26. Stankovic, J.A., Rajkumar, R.: Real-Time Operating Systems. Real-Time Systems 28(2-3), 237–253 (2004)
27. Szypersky, C., Gruntz, D., Murer, S.: Component Software. Beyong Object-Oriented Programming, 2nd edn. ACM Press, New York (2002)
28. Tournier, J.-C., Olive, V., Babau, J.-P.: Qinna, an Component-Based QoS Architecture. In: Heineman, G.T., Crnković, I., Schmidt, H.W., Stafford, J.A., Szyperski, C., Wallnau, K. (eds.) CBSE 2005. LNCS, vol. 3489, pp. 107–122. Springer, Heidelberg (2005)
29. van Ommering, R., van der Linden, F., Kramer, J., Magee, J.: The Koala Component Model for Consumer Electronics Software. Computer 33(3), 78–85 (2000)
30. Xie, Q., Liu, J., Chou, P.H.: Tapper: a Lightweight Scripting Engine for Highly Constrained Wireless Sensor Nodes. In: IPSN 2006, pp. 342–349. ACM, New York (2006)

Services + Components = Data Intensive Scientific Workflow Applications with MeDICi

Ian Gorton, Jared Chase, Adam Wynne, Justin Almquist, and Alan Chappell

Pacific Northwest National Lab
Richland, WA 99352, USA

Abstract. Scientific applications are often structured as workflows that execute a series of distributed software modules to analyze large data sets. Such workflows are typically constructed using general-purpose scripting languages to coordinate the execution of the various modules and to exchange data sets between them. While such scripts provide a cost-effective approach for simple workflows, as the workflow structure becomes complex and evolves, the scripts quickly become complex and difficult to modify. This makes them a major barrier to easily and quickly deploying new algorithms and exploiting new, scalable hardware platforms. In this paper, we describe the MeDICi Workflow technology that is specifically designed to reduce the complexity of workflow application development, and to efficiently handle data intensive workflow applications. MeDICi integrates standard component-based and service-based technologies, and employs an efficient integration mechanism to ensure large data sets can be efficiently processed. We illustrate the use of MeDICi with a climate data processing example that we have built, and describe some of the new features we are creating to further enhance MeDICi Workflow applications.

Keywords: workflow, middleware, components, services.

1 Introduction

The continued exponential growth of computational power, data generation sources, and communication technologies is giving rise to a new era in information processing – data intensive computing (DIC) [1]. Data intensive scientific applications facilitate human understanding of complex problems and provide timely, meaningful analytical results in response to the exponentially growing data complexity and associated analysis requirement. Scientific domains such as biology, astronomy and climatology abound with data intensive problems, and the amount of data produced by sensors and experiments is ever-growing.

Regardless of scientific domain, many data intensive applications are structured as pipelines, or workflows, comprising a number of distinct computations. In general, workflow applications gather data sets from one or more data sources, transform the data into a format amenable for processing, analyze the data to produce useful results, and store the data in a repository where scientists can access it. Many of the steps in the processing and the data sets that are accessed are distributed across different execution sites, requiring data to be moved across the network for subsequent processing by the next step(s) in the workflow.

G.A. Lewis, I. Poernomo, and C. Hofmeister (Eds.): CBSE 2009, LNCS 5582, pp. 227–241, 2009.
© Springer-Verlag Berlin Heidelberg 2009

Not surprisingly, the development of these applications often employs similar approaches and software tools. The control flow logic needed for an application is commonly created using scripting languages, such as PERL, Python or shell scripting environments. The scripts control the order of execution of the software modules in the workflow, pass the data from the output of one module to the input of the next, and launch the modules on distributed execution platforms.

For anything more than a trivial application, the script for a workflow must control branches and loops in the workflow execution. For example, in order to scale processing for serial modules, workflows need to run multiple replicas of modules in parallel. This creates considerable complexity in the execution scripts themselves, making them especially difficult to maintain and evolve. To address this, some recent applications are exploring using dedicated scientific workflow technologies such as Kepler [2] and Taverna [3]. These technologies provide a proprietary, visual language that can be used instead of an execution script, and considerably raise the level of abstraction employed in a workflow application solution.

At the Pacific Northwest National Lab (PNNL), we have worked with many scientists in domains such as climatology, biology [4] and hydrology, who rely on script-controlled workflow applications to perform their science. These applications are data intensive [5], with a common theme being the rapid growth of the data sets that must be processed. To handle larger data sets, the coordinating execution script for the workflow must be modified to create more parallelism and to execute the data analysis modules on higher performance hardware. As these workflow scripts can be hundreds or sometimes thousands of lines of code, making these modifications is a slow, expensive task that creates a road block in scientific discovery.

In response to the challenges of building high performance, data intensive computing, we have created MeDICi (Middleware for Data Intensive Computing) [6]. MeDICi is designed to address the scalability, reliability and ease of use issues that arise when existing scientific workflow technologies are used [7]. MeDICi integrates component-based and service-oriented approaches to provide a flexible development and deployment environment for scientific workflows. MeDICi has been built to reuse and leverage standards-based workflow and integration technologies used widely in commercial applications. This has created a highly robust and low friction platform that can rapidly exploit on-going enhancements in commercial standards and their supporting platforms.

The contributions of this paper are as follows:

- Describes the loosely coupled MeDICi architecture, which provides a unique, *mix-and-match* solution for scientific workflow applications
- Describes the MeDICi Workflow design notation, and how it is mapped to standard BPEL (Business Process Execution Language)
- Shows how MeDICi efficiently integrates service-based and component-based approaches to minimize data transfer overheads in data intensive applications

The paper describes the MeDICi architecture and associated tools, and briefly illustrates the use of MeDICi for a climate data processing application we have built. The paper concludes by analyzing the strengths and weaknesses of our approach, and describing areas of future research.

2   MeDICi Overview

MeDICi is a middleware platform for building complex, high performance analytical applications. These applications are structured as workflows (sometimes called pipelines) of software components, each of which perform some analysis on incoming data and pass on their results to the next step in the workflow.

The MeDICi project comprises three, loosely-coupled sub-projects, as depicted in Fig. 1.

- MeDICi Integration Framework (MIF) – a component-based, asynchronous messaging platform for distributed component integration.
- MeDICi Workflow – a BPEL-based design and execution environment that integrates with MIF components or standard Web services to provide workflow definition tools and a standards-based recoverable workflow execution engine.
- MeDICi Provenance – a Java API, RDF-based store and content management system for capturing and querying important metadata that can be used for forensic investigations and reconstruction of application results.

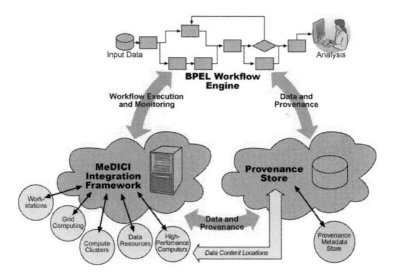

Fig. 1. MeDICi Architecture Overview

In a MeDICi Workflow application, the application designer creates a workflow graphically using our DWF language. Each task in the workflow calls an associated Web service, which may be a standard service located somewhere on the Internet, or a Web service supported by a MIF component deployed in the MIF container. MIF components wrap computational codes that require complex integration, and support a protocol that is designed to minimize the data transfer overheads between elements of the workflow. Optionally, MIF components can record metadata (known as provenance) about the data they receive/produce and the processing carried out. The metadata is passed transparently from a component to the MIF container, and this sends a message to a message queue called *ProvenanceListener*. MeDICi Provenance takes these messages from the queue, and stores them in an RDF store for subsequent analysis by scientists.

The next sections describe MeDICi Workflow and MIF in more detail. However, MeDICi Provenance is beyond the scope of this paper.

3 MeDICi Workflow

MeDICi Workflow is built upon standard BPEL (Business Process Execution Language) workflow engine technology. The user describes the steps in a workflow graphically using our MeDICi DWF design tool, which defines a visual workflow design language to abstract away much of the complexity of BPEL [8,9], and automatically generates a corresponding BPEL representation of the DWF workflow.

In the DWF design tool, designers select icons from a palette that contains a list of all MIF components available for the application. Each icon is associated with an XML description of the properties of the MIF components that must be configured in order to use the component in DWF. These properties also specify the Web service endpoints that the BPEL engine must call to asynchronously invoke each MIF component. (MeDICi Workflow applications can also call external Web services that are not MIF components). Designers then connect the icons together into a workflow, add any necessary configuration properties, incorporate control constructs such as loops, branches and parallel executions, and finally generate and deploy the BPEL to execute the application.

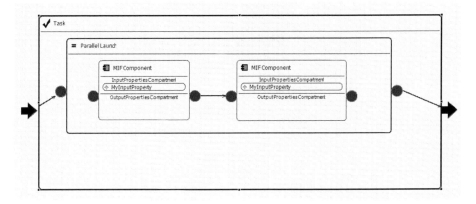

Fig. 2. Example DWF Workflow

A simple DWF workflow is shown in Fig. 2. The top level structure of the workflow is the *Task*. Within a *Task*, the designer defines the workflow. The designer drags MIF components from the palette into a *Task* and defines input and output properties for each component. Properties represent the input values that must be passed to the MIF component. These can be constants that the designer sets, or variables that are derived from the outputs of a previous step in the workflow. Global variables can also be defined in DWF and simple expressions can be created by the designer to manipulate global variable values between workflow steps. The workflow designer then connects the components together in a sequence.

In addition to sequences of components, DWF supports iteration, selection and parallel control constructs. For example, in Fig. 2, a *ParallelLaunch* construct specifies that the contained sequence of components should be replicated and executed concurrently. A *Data Array Key* property of the *ParallelLaunch* specifies the name of a variable that contains an array of data items to be processed by the concurrent components. Each item in the array is passed to its corresponding component instance within the *ParallelLaunch*, giving a simple mechanism for passing data to concurrent component instances. An equivalent mechanism is available for collecting the outputs from each concurrent component for subsequent merging and processing.

The DWF Builder exploits the Eclipse Modeling Framework (EMF) and Graphical Modeling Framework (GMF), and hence all DWF workflows conform to the defined DWF metamodel. Any DWF workflow can therefore be represented in a model file, as in Fig. 3.

```
<?xml version="1.0" encoding="UTF-8"?>
<dwf:workflow xmi:version="2.0" xmlns:xmi="http://www.omg.org/XMI"
xmlns:xsi="http://www.w3.org/2001/XMLSchema-instance"
xmlns:dwf="http://dwf.pnl.gov/" label="sdaf">
  <tasks>
    <components xsi:type="dwf:parallellaunch">
      <outputs taskoutputconnection="//@tasks.0/@outputs.0"/>
      <inputs/>
      <subcomponents xsi:type="dwf:mifcomponent">
        <outputs connec-
tion="//@tasks.0/@components.0/@subcomponents.1/@inputs.0"/>
        <inputs/>
        <inputProperties key="MyInputProperty" value="MyInputPropertyValue"/>
      </subcomponents>
      <subcomponents xsi:type="dwf:mifcomponent">
        <outputs/>
        <inputs/>
        <inputProperties key="MyInputProperty" value="MyInputPropertyValue"/>
      </subcomponents>
    </components>
    <inputs taskinputconnection="//@tasks.0/@components.0/@inputs.0"/>
    <outputs/>
  </tasks>
```

Fig. 3. Example Model File in DWF Language

We have built a translation and deployment service in the DWF Builder. These convert the DWF model file into standard BPEL, and then deploy the generated BPEL to a BPEL Server. As an example, the BPEL generated for the DWF workflow in Fig. 2 is shown in the ActiveBPEL Designer tool in Fig. 4. As can be seen from this example, the BPEL equivalent is much more verbose than the DWF version. This illustrates one of the goals of DWF, namely to create a workflow modeling environment that is conceptually much simpler for scientists than BPEL, but that can still exploit standard BPEL technology.

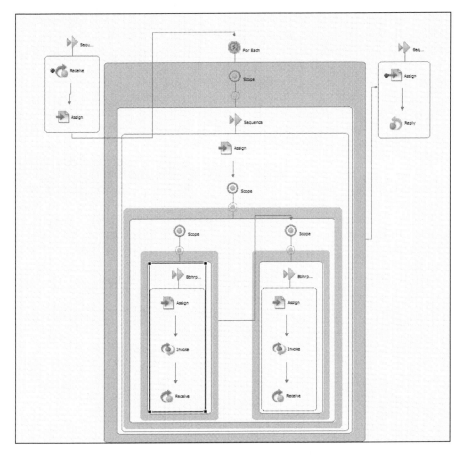

Fig. 4. BPEL Workflow generated from simple DWF example

4 MeDICi Integration Framework

The MIF is designed as the core of a MeDICi workflow application. The MIF architecture leverages open source middleware technologies and defines a component-based programming model for wrapping and connecting (legacy and new) distributed software modules into a component-based workflow. The codes that are encapsulated as MIF components can be written in any programming language (e.g. we have experience with C++, FORTRAN, Java, R, Haskell, C#, Matlab) and be distributed across a cluster or a network of processing nodes. A simple caricature of a MIF application architecture is depicted in Fig. 5.

MIF components are constructed using a Java API that supports inter-component communication using asynchronous messaging. Local components execute inside the MIF container, executing Java-based application components that are defined in the workflow application. Remote components are wrapped in the same programmatic interface, but utilize a component proxy in MIF that facilities executing the

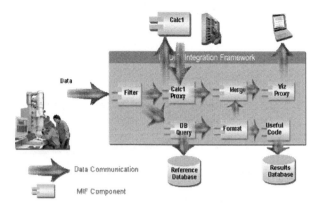

Fig. 5. The MeDICi Integration Framework

component code outside the MIF container. Remote components are used to implement distributed workflows and to integrate with non-Java codes and high-performance computing platforms. Further, MIF components can be hierarchically structured, allowing more complex functionality to be composed internally within a component. More details on the MIF API and component model are in [6].

Messages can be passed between components by copy or by reference. Copying occurs when a message contains a data payload, and reference passing occurs when the payload contains a reference to a data item in the MIF disk cache which is located, usually locally, with each MIF container instance. The cache, illustrated in Fig. 6, is visible to all components in a container, and cache data is referenced with a URI.

By default, the MIF container mechanism for exchanging messages between components uses Java method calls. Messages can also be exchanged using the Java Messaging Service (JMS) or Web services to enhance reliability and scalability. This is simply achieved by configuring the endpoints used by components for communication within the MIF container. No code changes are needed and the components themselves are oblivious to the transport that is used.

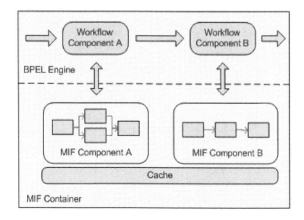

Fig. 6. MIF Components and the MIF Cache

The MIF container environment is provided by Mule, an open source messaging platform (http://mulesource.org/). MIF extends the Mule API to make application construction simpler and to create an encapsulation mechanism for component creation. Our current implementation uses the JBoss JMS for messaging and Apache's CXF for Web services, but the MIF API is agnostic to the underlying messaging platform. This allows deployments to configure MIF applications using specific technologies that meet their quality of service requirements. In addition, if the provenance and JMS options are not used in a MIF application, then the deployed application does not need these platforms to be started, thus releasing resources within the MIF container.

We have designed the MIF API to be regular and simple to learn. Still, to further ease the burden of MIF application development, we have built the MIF Component Builder (see Fig. 7). This allows application developers to graphically wire together the components in a MIF application and configure each component with a number of properties, including the underlying application code to execute. The tool then generates all of the MIF API code needed for an executable MIF application. Components can also be stored in an XML representation in a component library for subsequent use in different MIF applications. Generated components can also optionally expose an asynchronous Web service (WSDL) interface so that they can be orchestrated by an external orchestration engine, such as MeDICi Workflow. The use of the WSDL interface in workflow applications is described later in this paper.

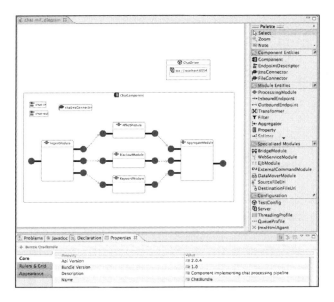

Fig. 7. MIF Component Builder Example

5   MeDICi Workflow Applications

MIF applications can execute standalone, and in our experience this is common when an application processes relatively small, frequent messages, such as those encountered in a cybersecurity application [10]. However, in scientific workflow applications, the processing of individual components and applications can take from hours to weeks, depending on the input data size and algorithmic complexity. In these applications, MeDICi Workflow is employed in conjunction with the MIF to orchestrate the execution of the MIF components.

Essentially, the MeDICi Workflow DWF description specifies the order of execution of the components in the application. The DWF components simply call the corresponding MIF components using their WSDL interface. The MIF components ensure the computations in the workflow are executed efficiently, and return control to the DWF layer when each completes. As the workflow executes, the MeDICi Workflow engine provides the necessary run-time monitoring and recovery capabilities so that the workflow execution can be tracked and restarted should failures occur.

Further, data intensive MeDICi applications must be able to efficiently process and exchange very large data sets. To make this possible, the interface between the MeDICi Workflow engine and MIF components is designed to exchange only references to data sets, and simple value parameters. To this end, each MIF component exposes an identical WSDL interface, which simply takes a single parameter as an argument. The parameter contains a collection of key-value pairs that are required to instantiate the MIF component. These key-value pair entries are initialized by the DWF component from the properties set in the DWF workflow and passed to the Web service for the MIF component. The values specify initialization parameters, including references to the input files needed by the component. When the MIF component returns, it also passes a single parameter containing key-value pairs back to the DWF workflow. These values typically contain references to the output files produced by the execution of the component. Part of the generated WSDL for invoking a MIF component is illustrated below:

```
<wsdl:message name="run">
  <wsdl:part element="tns:run" name="parameters">
  </wsdl:part>
</wsdl:message>
<wsdl:portType name="MifServiceInterface">
  <wsdl:operation name="run">
    <wsdl:input message="tns:run" name="run">
    </wsdl:input>
  </wsdl:operation>
</wsdl:portType>
<wsdl:binding name="MifServiceSoapBinding"
type="tns:MifServiceInterface">
  <soap:binding style="document" trans-
port="http://schemas.xmlsoap.org/soap/http" />
  <wsdl:operation name="run">
    <soap:operation soapAction="" style="document" />
    <wsdl:input name="run">
      <soap:body use="literal" />
    </wsdl:input>
  </wsdl:operation>
</wsdl:binding>
<wsdl:service name="MifService">
  <wsdl:port binding="tns:MifServiceSoapBinding"
name="MifServicePort">
    <soap:address location="not needed" />
  </wsdl:port>
</wsdl:service>
```

In addition, MIF components can be designed to store their results in a file-based cache that is visible to all distributed MIF components in an application within the same security domain. This scheme, illustrated in Fig. 8, works as follows:

1. When a MIF component produces a file as output, it is stored in the cache and the cache reference is returned from the component to MeDICi Workflow as one of its outputs.
2. In the workflow engine, the file reference is then passed as an input parameter to the next step in the workflow.
3. The workflow engine invokes the associated MIF component, which uses the cache reference to find its input data.

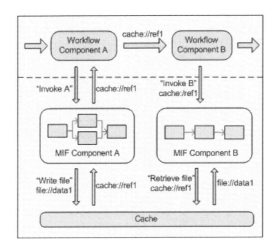

Fig. 8. Efficient data set exchange between components in MeDICi Workflow

The cache is not effective however when a workflow incorporates distributed legacy codes that cannot be modified. These codes expect their inputs to be located locally, and write their outputs to a local file system. This means the workflow must move the data to the remote system so that the computation can execute, and then copy the results from the remote system to where the next computation in the work-flow expects its inputs. When these files are massive, the workflow must minimize the costs of this data movement to ensure the application executes as efficiently as possible. Specifically, a naïve implementation that moves a file from the remote sys-tem to the MeDICi cache, and then to the next remote system in the workflow is not acceptable, as the cost of two copy operations will be too high.

MeDICi addresses this problem using *DataMover* components in MIF. These take a source host address and file as input, and a target host and location, and move the input file directly to the target location. The default implementation logs in to the target host using *ssh* and executes a secure copy (*scp*) command to directly perform the data movement. (This requires the security certificates to be correctly configured before the workflow executes). This scheme is depicted in Fig. 9 and en-sures that no additional data movement costs are incurred in the workflow execution.

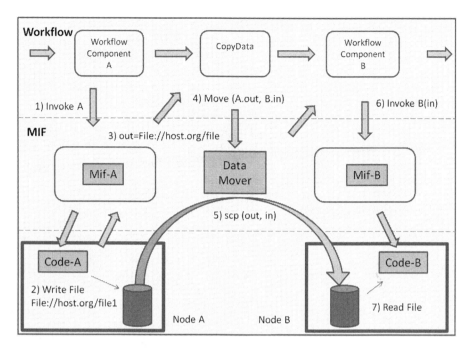

Fig. 9. Efficient Data Movement in MeDICi Workflow

6 MeDICi Workflow Example

The Atmospheric Radiation Measurement (ARM) Program is a major research atmospheric research program supported by the U.S. Department of Energy. ARM scientists and researchers use continuous data obtained from multiple sensors around the world in their science. Data from these sensors is processed at PNNL and then made available to workflow applications known as Value Added Processes (VAPs), which process various subsets of the data and produce results for scientists to analyze. At the heart of each VAP are serial codes written in FORTRAN or C that perform a different scientific analysis on some subset of the ARM data

In general, each VAP has three stages in its workflow, namely data pre-processing, analysis and post-processing. Pre-processing involves retrieving data from the ARM data store and transforming it into a format that can be input into the scientific analysis code that is the centerpiece of each VAP. Processing involves executing the scientific code on the prepared input data. As the input data represents one or more years of sensor data, and the codes work on much smaller timescales (e.g. minutes/hours), the code has to be executed multiple times, once for each time period in the input data. Post-processing involves merging the multiple outputs from the analysis code, executing visualization and statistic routines, and transforming the outputs into the format required by the ARM database.

BBHRP (Broadband Heating Rate Profile) is an ARM VAP which provides critical evaluations of radiation measurements. The workflow for the VAP is controlled by a shell script which coordinates the execution of the multiple processes in each of the

VAP phases. The script implements a workflow that was written over the course of several years, and has evolved over time to more than 500 lines of complex logic. It was therefore decided to re-implement the BBHRP workflow with MeDICi. Using MeDICi's visual programming tools and component-based architecture, the resulting system should be considerably simpler to modify to incorporate new processing modules, and easier to scale by executing the workflow on larger clusters.

The first step in implementing the BBHRP VAP in MeDICi was to break apart the existing script into independent modules that could be wrapped as MIF components. This required working closely with the BBHRP script developer to understand how the workflow functioned and the many implicit assumptions in the code. The end result was a collection of MIF components, each of which encapsulates a simple script that launches a single process involved in the BBHRP workflow. Each component also exposes a Web service interface so that the MeDICi Workflow engine can invoke it.

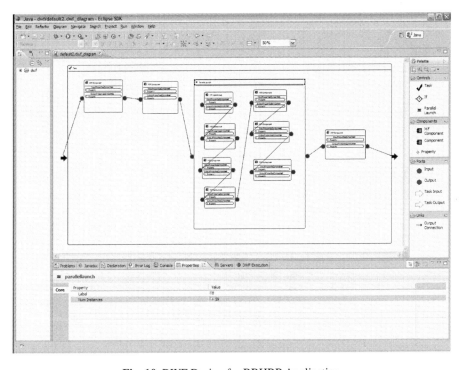

Fig. 10. DWF Design for BBHRP Application

Next, the BBHRP workflow was created as a DWF workflow, as depicted in Fig. 10. The *ParallelLaunch* is used to execute concurrent instances of MIF components on multiple nodes in a cluster in order to reduce the time needed to execute the VAP. The 7 MIF components contained within the *ParallelLaunch* scope represent the BBHRP analysis code, and execute sequentially on each node to process the set of input values that are passed for processing. After all the inputs are processed, a post-processing component gathers together all the results files into a single file so that further calculations can be carried out.

7 Related Work

Technologies to support scientific workflows are many and varied. Prominent in scientific computing are Kepler [2], Pegasus [11] and GridNexus[12]. Kepler provides a comprehensive desktop-based, visual workflow design and execution tool based on Ptolemy II [13]. Workflows compose actors, which are reusable independent computation blocks. Actors communicate with external services, processes and data to enact a workflow. Kepler provides a set of control structures that a workflow designer uses to explicitly coordinate workflow execution. In contrast, Pegasus takes an abstract workflow application design and maps the composed computations to available resources on a computational grid. The mapping is achieved used AI planning techniques to generate a concrete execution plan that can be interpreted by Condor's DAG-Man [14] workflow engine. Like Kepler, GridNexus is based on Ptolomy II as a graphical design tool that can be used to specify workflow applications. The resulting workflows are transformed into an XML-based scripting language, JXPL, which is interpreted by a suitable engine which can be co-located with the design environment, or, in contrast to Kepler, run remotely. Again, each of these tools employs proprietary design notations and proprietary workflow engines, and has a strong focus on Grid-based computational environments.

MeDICi has much in common with these tools, but employs a very different design philosophy to existing tools. MeDICi is designed to leverage widely used, standardized, open source middleware and workflow tools (e.g. BPEL, JEE) that are widely used in commercial applications. These technologies are robust and continuously evolved and improved by a broad development community. This greatly reduces the effort needed to build and extend MeDICi with new features, as we can exploit new features and tools produced by the associated communities.

BPEL has been successfully used previously for scientific workflows [15], and as in MeDICi, efforts have been made to provide a simpler design notation for scientists that can be transformed to an underlying BPEL representation [8]. Scientific workflow applications based purely on BPEL technologies are however unable to scale to orchestrate data-intensive applications. This is because when a BPEL workflow manipulates and transfers GB-TB-sized data sets, these data sets are passed across the network and through the BPEL engine, effectively doubling overhead of data transfer [16] (and in reality, breaking the BPEL engine).

MeDICi addresses this problem by extending and improving on the solution described in [17], which is limited in the way it can handle branches in workflows and ignores security. This is achieved by introducing a dedicated integration layer, the MeDICi Integration Framework (MIF) that underpins the BPEL engine, optimizes data transfers between computational tasks using a cache and dedicated *DataMover* components, and provides a scalable, component-based development environment that promotes code reuse. The resulting two-layer workflow execution architecture employs asynchronous communications between the BPEL and MIF layers, and ensures only references to data sets are communicated between the two layers. This greatly reduces execution overheads.

8 Further Work

We are actively working on two areas to enhance the development and execution of MeDICi Workflow applications. These are more flexible and efficient data movement components, and application monitoring, as described below.

File transfer over *ssh* and *scp* protocols perform well within a LAN but do not scale to larger files and slower WAN connections. Therefore, we have designed the *DataMover* MIF component to be extensible in order to utilize faster, secure file transfer protocols such as *bbcp*, which encrypts the authentication channel, but not the file transfer channel, or GridFTP. Initially, a collection of *DataMover* components will be available in MIF, and these can be included in MeDICi Workflow applications. The eventual aim is that the particular file transfer protocol to be used can be selected at runtime, based on execution environment characteristics.

As MeDICi Workflow applications may take days or weeks to execute, it is essential that application monitoring tools are available. As a MeDICi Workflow application is executed by a BPEL engine, we are initially utilizing BPEL monitoring technologies that are supplied with the BPEL engine. This provides a simple way to monitor applications. Ideally however, we wish monitoring to be based on the DWF description of the workflow, not the more verbose BPEL representation that is generated from DWF. This is being addressed by calling the BPEL administrative API from the DWF design tool and mapping the execution state to the DWF components. The DWF design can then provide a simplified graphical representation of the BPEL workflow and visually indicates the state of the workflow during execution, in order to monitor workflow progress. If more details are needed, the native BPEL design tool can be used to graphically examine the BPEL operations that are in flight at any moment, set breakpoints and examine intermediate data. This debugging capability is another 'out of the box' BPEL feature that we freely exploit.

9 Conclusions

MeDICi demonstrates how robust, powerful, standards-based, open source technologies from commercial applications can be leveraged and tailored for scientific workflow applications. The MeDICi architecture is specifically designed for efficient handling of large data sets for data intensive workflow applications. It encourages the creation of components that encapsulate scientific application codes, and simplifies workflow application construction with the DWF workflow description language. MeDICi provides design tools to simplify component and workflow design. The design tools are built using Eclipse-based model-driven development technologies, and generate standard Java and BPEL respectively.

We are encouraged by our initial experiences using MeDICi in several different application domains. By gaining more experience with the technologies, we hope to continue to improve its ease of use and range of capabilities. MeDICi is open source and freely downloadable from http://medici.pnl.gov

References

1. Kouzes, R.T., Anderson, G.A., Elbert, S.T., Gorton, I., Gracio, D.K.: The Changing Paradigm of Data-Intensive Computing. Computer 42(1), 26–34 (2009)
2. Ludäscher, B., Altintas, I., Berkley, C., Higgins, D., Jaeger, E., Jones, M., Lee, E.A., Tao, J., Zhao, Y.: Scientific workflow management and the Kepler system. Concurrency and Computation: Practice and Experience 18(10), 1039–1065 (2006)
3. Goble, C.A., Oinn, T., Greenwood, M., Addis, M.: Taverna: Lessons in creating a workflow environment for the life sciences. Concurrency and Computation: Practice and Experience (Special Issue on Workflow in Grid Systems) 18(10), 1067–1100 (2005)
4. Shah, A.R., Singhal, M., Gibson, T.D., Sivaramakrishnan, C., Waters, K.M., Gorton, I.: An Extensible, Scalable Architecture for Managing Bioinformatics Data and Analyses. In: IEEE Fourth International Conference on eScience 2008, December 7-12 , pp. 190–197 (2008)
5. Gorton, I., Greenfield, P., Szalay, A., Williams, R.: Data-Intensive Computing in the 21st Century. Computer 41(4), 30–32 (2008)
6. Gorton, I., Wynne, A., Almquist, J., Chatterton, J.: The MeDICi Integration Framework: A Platform for High Performance Data Streaming Applications. In: Seventh Working IEEE/IFIP Conference on Software Architecture (WICSA 2008), Vancouver, Canada, pp. 95–104 (2008)
7. Barker, A., van Hemert, J.: Scientific Workflow: A Survey and Research Directions. In: Wyrzykowski, R., Dongarra, J., Karczewski, K., Wasniewski, J. (eds.) PPAM 2007. LNCS, vol. 4967, pp. 746–753. Springer, Heidelberg (2008)
8. Butchart, B., Cameron, N., Chen, L., Wassermann, B., Emmerich, W., Patel, J.: Sedna: A BPEL-based environment for visual scientific workflow modeling. In: Workflows for eScience. Springer, Heidelberg (2007)
9. Akram, A., Meredith, D., Allan, R.: Evaluation of BPEL to Scientific Workflows. In: CCGRID 2006. Sixth IEEE International Symposium on Cluster Computing and the Grid, vol. 1, pp. 269–274 (2006)
10. Wynne, A., Gorton, I., Almquist, J., Chatterton, J., Thurman, D.: A Flexible, High Performance Service-Oriented Architecture for Detecting Cyber Attacks. In: Hawaiian International Conference on Systems Science (HICSS 2008). IEEE, Los Alamitos (2008)
11. Lee, K., Paton, N.W., Sakellariou, R., Deelman, E., Fernandes, A., Mehta, G.: Adaptive Workflow Processing and Execution. In: Pegasus 3rd International Workshop on Workflow Management and Applications in Grid Environments (WaGe08), Proceedings of the Third International Conference on Grid and Pervasive Computing Symposia/Workshops, Kunming, China, May 25-28, pp. 99–106 (2008)
12. Brown, J., Ferner, C., Hudson, T., Stapleton, A., Vetter, R., Carland, T., Martin, A., Martin, J., Rawls, A., Shipman, W., Wood, M.: GridNexus: A Grid Services Scientific Workflow System. International Journal of Computer Information Science (IJCIS) 6(2), 72–82 (2005)
13. http://ptolemy.berkeley.edu/ptolemyII
14. Couvares, P., et al.: Workflow Management in Condor. In: Taylor, I., et al. (eds.) Workflows in e-Science. Springer, Heidelberg (2006)
15. Emmerich, W., Butchart, B., Chen, L., Wassermann, B., Price, S.: Grid Service Orchestration Using the Business Process Execution Language (BPEL). J. Grid Comput. 3(3-4), 283–304 (2005)
16. Barker, A., Weissman, J.B., van Hemert, J.I.: Orchestrating Data-Centric Workflows. In: Procs. Int. Sym. On Cluster Computer and the Grid, pp. 210–217. IEEE, Los Alamitos (2008)
17. Barker, A., Weissman, J.B., van Hemert, J.: Eliminating the Middle Man: Peer-to-Peer Dataflow. In: HPDC 2008: Proceedings of the 17th International Symposium on High Performance Distributed Computing, pp. 55–64 (June 2008)

Ensuring Consistency between Designs, Documentation, Formal Specifications, and Implementations

Joseph R. Kiniry and Fintan Fairmichael

School of Computer Science and Informatics and
CASL: The Complex & Adaptive Systems Laboratory,
University College Dublin,Belfield, Dublin 4, Ireland
kiniry@acm.org, fintan.fairmichael@ucd.ie

.

Abstract. Software engineering experts and textbooks insist that all of the artifacts related to a system, (e.g., its design, documentation, and implementation), must be kept in-sync. Unfortunately, in the real world, it is a very rare case that any two of these are kept consistent, let alone all three. In general, as an implementation changes, its source code documentation, like that of Javadoc, is only occasionally updated at some later date. Unsurprisingly, most design documents, like those written in UML, are created as a read-only medium—they reflect what the designers *thought* they were building at one point in the past, but have little to do with the actual running system. Even those using formal methods make this mistake, sometimes updating an implementation and forgetting to make some subtle change to a related specification. The critical problem inherent in this approach is that abstraction levels, while theoretically inter-dependent, are actually completely independent in semantics and from the point of view of the tools in pervasive use. Entities in different layers have no formal relationship; at best, informal relations are maintained by ad hoc approaches like code markers, or code is generated once and never touched again. This paper presents a new approach to system design, documentation, implementation, specification, and verification that imposes a formal refinement relationship between abstraction levels that is invisible to the programmer and automatically maintained by an integrated set of tools. The new concept that enables this approach is called a *semantic property*, and their use is discussed in detail with a set of examples using the high-level specification language EBON, the detailed design and specification language JML, and the Java programming language as the implementation language.

1 Introduction

Ad hoc constructs and local conventions have been used to annotate program code since the invention of programming languages. The purpose of these annotations is to convey "extra" programmer knowledge to other system developers and future maintainers. These comments usually fall into that grey region between completely unstructured natural language and formal specification. For example, an ad hoc convention promoted by Eclipse are the FIXME, TODO, and XXX task tags that cause errors or warnings to appear in Eclipse's *Problems* view.

G.A. Lewis, I. Poernomo, and C. Hofmeister (Eds.): CBSE 2009, LNCS 5582, pp. 242–261, 2009.
© Springer-Verlag Berlin Heidelberg 2009

Invariably, such program comments rapidly exhibit "bit rot". Over time, these comments and the implementation to which they refer diverge to an inconsistent state (a process often referred to as erosion or drift [1]). Unless they are well maintained by documentation specialists, rigorous process, or other extra-mile development efforts, they quickly become out-of-date. They are the focus for the software engineering mantra: an incorrect comment is worse than no comment at all.

Recently, with the adoption and popularization of lightweight documentation tools in the literate programming tradition [2,3], an ecology of semi-structured comments is flourishing. The rapid adoption and popularity of Java primed interest in semi-structured comment use via the Javadoc tool. Other similar code-to-documentation transformation tools have since followed in volume, including Jakarta's Alexandria, Doxygen, and Apple's HeaderDoc. SourceForge reports dozens of projects with "Javadoc" in the project summary, and FreshMeat reports several dozen more, with some overlap.

While most of these systems are significantly simpler than Knuth and Levy's original CWEB, they share two key features.

Firstly, they are easy to learn, since they necessitate only a small change in *convention* and *process*. Rather than forcing the programmer to learn a new language, complex tool, or imposing some other significant barrier to use, these tools actually *reward* the programmer for documenting their code.

Secondly, a culture of documentation is engendered. Prompted by the example of vendors like Sun, programmers enjoy (or, at least, do not abhor) the creation and use of the attractive automatically-generated documentation in a web page format. This documentation-centric style is only strengthened by the exhibitionist nature of the Web. Having the most complete documentation is now a point of pride in some Open Source projects—a state of affairs unguessable a decade ago.

The primary problem with these systems, and the documentation and code written using them, is that *even semi-structured comments have no semantics*. Programmers are attempting to state (sometimes quite complex) knowledge, but are not given the language and tools with which to communicate this knowledge. And since the vast majority of developers are unwilling to learn a new, especially formal, language with which to convey such information, a happy-medium of *informal formality* is necessary.

That compromise, the delicate balance between informality and formality, is the core principle behind *semantic properties*, the core conceptual contribution of this paper.

Informally, semantic properties are nothing more than what today's programmers call *annotations*, and what are known as *pragmas* in the non-OO world. Javadoc tags, gcc's #defines, and C#'s XML comments are three examples of (potential) semantic properties. Of course, none of these specific technologies were created with semantic properties in mind—support for them is engineered into the design of semantic properties. This decision is taken to ensure that programmers do not need to learn new technologies or languages to use and take advantage of semantic properties.

More formally, semantic properties are *general-purpose* annotations that have a *domain-independent* formal semantics. For a given domain (e.g., a programming or specification language), semantic properties' semantics are mapped into the semantic domain of their application via a refinement relation. These refinement relations are *semantics preserving*—they are defined in such a way that their meaning is preserved between refinement levels.

As mentioned earlier, semantic properties look just like comments, annotations, or design notes—they are used as if they were normal semi-structured documentation. But, rather than being ignored by compilers and development environments as comments typically are, they have the attention of augmented versions of such tools. Semantic properties permit one to embed a tremendous amount of concise information wherever they are used without imposing the often insurmountable overhead seen in the introduction of new languages and formalisms for similar purposes.

Semantic properties are not a newly-invented idea. They have been used in several research groups, in the classroom, as well as in corporate settings for over a decade. We are now using them also in a software product lines setting. Over the years, semantic properties, via its underlying logic, called kind theory, have integrated several formal methods in practical, pragmatic fashion, unbeknownst to collaborators, students, and employees. In the following pages several examples of semantic properties are described. We will focus this explanation via the use of a concrete example.

2   Running Example

Our running example comes from an advanced tutorial on JML from 2006 [4]. The focus of that tutorial is the detailed specification and verification of an alarm clock using the Java Modeling Language (JML) and Java. The refinement relationship between JML and Java in this example is depicted diagrammatically in Figure 1. We extend this example to include high-level specifications written in the Extended Business Object Notation language (EBON), for which we are responsible. BON is a textual and graphical domain-independent specification language akin to UML [5], but which focuses on all software engineering stages from domain analysis to architecture to contract-centric component design. EBON is simply the BON language plus semantic properties.

To illustrate the use of semantic properties in more detail, consider the task of modeling a logical clock, like those used in concurrent and distributed algorithms.

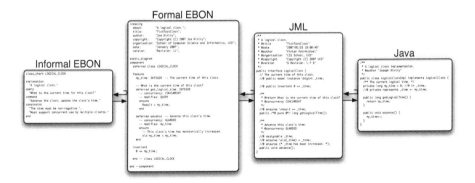

Fig. 1. A diagrammatic representation of refinement from EBON to Java

The first stage of our verification-centric software development process involves concept identification. (A full description of this process is found elsewhere [6].) Concepts, called *classes* (as in *classifiers*) in EBON, are named, described with single sentences, and their high-level relations (*is-a*, *has-a*, and *is-a-kind-of*) are identified.

```
static_diagram CONCEPTS_AND_RELATIONS
  component
    deferred class LOGICAL_CLOCK
    deferred class ALARM
    effective class CLOCK persistent
    effective class ALARM_CLOCK persistent

    ALARM_CLOCK inherit CLOCK
    ALARM_CLOCK inherit ALARM
  end
```

Listing 1. An EBON static diagram describing the core concepts of the running example

In this example, the concepts identified through domain analysis are *alarm*, *alarm clock*, and *logical clock*. Their relationships are summarized in the EBON static diagram CONCEPTS_AND_RELATIONS in Listing 1. Their definitions are elided in this example.

Each concept is summarized with an *informal diagram*. An informal diagram describes the concept and its interfaces in terms of *queries*, *commands*, and *constraints*. Queries and commands are collectively known as *features*.

For example, the logical clock must store a time value and, in EBON terminology, support a *query* to determine the current time stored in the clock. A *command* is also necessary to monotonically advance the time stored in the clock. Furthermore, a *constraint* states that the time stored in the clock is always non-negative. Finally, the logical clock must also behave correctly while being used by multiple concurrent clients.

```
class_chart LOGICAL_CLOCK
  explanation
    "A logical clock."
  query
    "What is the current time of this clock?"
  command
    "Advance the clock; update the clock's time."
  constraint
    "The time must be non-negative.",
    "Must support concurrent use by multiple clients."
end
```

Listing 2. An EBON class chart for LOGICAL_CLOCK

This interface and requirements are expressed using an EBON informal chart. Like most requirement languages, informal EBON uses structured English to denote analysis concepts and requirements. The EBON class chart shown in Listing 2 captures this information.

Classical software engineering *requirements* are expressed as *constraints* in EBON. Likewise, *features* (as in formal feature models from the area of software product lines [7]) are expressed via EBON features.

```
indexing
  about:          "A logical clock.";
  title:          "TickTockClock";
  author:         "Joe Kiniry";
  copyright:      "Copyright (C) 2008 Joe Kiniry";
  organisation:   "School of Computer Science and Informatics, UCD";
  date:           "January 2008";
  version:        "Revision: 11";

static_diagram
component
  deferred class LOGICAL_CLOCK

    feature
      my_time: INTEGER   -- The current time of this clock.

      -- What is the current time of this clock?
      deferred get_logical_time: INTEGER
        -- concurrency: CONCURRENT
        -- modifies: QUERY
        ensure
          Result = my_time;
        end

      deferred advance   -- Advance the clock; update the clock's time.
        -- concurrency: GUARDED
        -- modifies: my_time
        ensure
          -- This clock's time has monotonically increased.
          old my_time < my_time;
        end

    invariant
      my_time >= 0; -- The time must be non-negative.

    end -- class LOGICAL_CLOCK

end --component
```

Listing 3. An EBON formal specification for LOGICAL_CLOCK

This model is refined, mapping informal specifications into something more formal and concrete, as seen in Listing 3. For example, the constraint "The time must be non-negative." is refined to an invariant of the form: $my\_time \leq 0$. A feature *time* of type *INTEGER* is defined that represents the current time of this clock. The clock's query and command are also refined into appropriate features (function types). Also, note that the concept "time" is refined to a property having the EBON type *INTEGER*, a mathematical integer.

This diagram contains uses of two semantic properties, one called *concurrency* and the other *modifies*. In order to achieve our desired concurrency property, the informal constraint is refined by annotating the features with the *concurrency* semantic property whose labels denote the concurrency semantics of their feature. The query get_logical_time is labelled CONCURRENT (multiple calls may proceed at the same time), and the command advance as concurrency GUARDED (additional calls block until the original call has completed). This specification models a standard multiple reader, single writer pattern.

Additionally, a frame condition is stated for these two features. Frame conditions specify what parts of the model may be changed when a function is invoked. These two annotations make explicit that the function `get_logical_time` is indeed a `QUERY`, and the function `advance` may only modify the value of the field `my_time`.

```
/**
 * A logical clock.  This realization uses a integral representation,
 * rather than a continuous one.
 * @title          "TickTockClock"
 * @date           "2009/01/23 18:00:49"
 * @author         "Fintan Fairmichael"
 * @organisation   "CSI School, UCD"
 * @copyright      "Copyright (C) 2009 UCD"
 * @version        "$ Revision: 1.7 $"
 */
public interface LogicalClock {
  // The current time of this clock.
  //@ public model instance \bigint _time;

  //@ public invariant (* The time must be non-negative. *);
  //@ public invariant 0 <= _time;

  /**
   * @return What is the current time of this clock?
   * @concurrency CONCURRENT
   */
  //@ ensures \result == _time;
  public /*@ pure @*/ long getLogicalTime();

  /**
   * Advance the clock; update the clock's time.
   * Note that time may increase by more than one.
   * @concurrency GUARDED
   */
  //@ assignable _time;
  //@ ensures \old(_time) < _time;
  //@ ensures (* _time has been increased. *);
  public void advance();
}
```

Listing 4. A JML formal specification of the EBON class `LOGICAL_CLOCK`

For the reader familiar with JML, this formal specification of `LOGICAL_CLOCK` looks syntactically familiar. A JML refinement of this EBON class is found in Listing 4.

A JML specification is a JML-annotated Java module (a class or an interface). `LogicalClock.java` contains a Javadoc-annotated Java interface which contains two methods. Each method is, in turn, also annotated with Javadoc comments. Some of the Javadoc tags are standard (e.g., `@return` and `@author`), and others are not. All of the tags, standard and non-standard (`title`, `date`, `organisation`, `copyright`, `version`, and the aforementioned `concurrency`), are all semantic properties.

The JML specification also contains, of course, JML annotations. In this particular case, these annotations capture the formal meaning of the idea of a logical clock, as embodied by this Java type. In particular, a model (specification-only) field called `_time` of type `\bigint` (the type representing mathematical integers, i.e., $\mathbb{Z}$) is defined, complemented by an invariant stating that the value of that field is always non-negative.

Furthermore, both methods have contracts. The contract `getLogicalTime` states that the value returned by the method is always identical to that held in the model field `_time`. The contract for `advance` states that the method may only change the value of the model field _time (and *nothing* else) and that calling this method causes time to move monotonically forward, as embodied by the formal postcondition \old(_time) > _time (the new value of _time is strictly greater than its old value before the call). The informal postcondition, contained in the JML comment block (* ... *), reminds us of the meaning of its sister specification.

```
/**
 * A logical clock implementation.
 * @author "Joseph Kiniry"
 */
public class LogicalClockImpl implements LogicalClock {
  /** The current logical time. */
  private long my_time = 0; //@ in _time;
  //@ private represents _time <- my_time;

  public synchronized long getLogicalTime() {
    return my_time;
  }

  public void advance() {
    my_time++;
  }
}
```

Listing 5. A Java implementation of the EBON class LOGICAL_CLOCK

One possible implementation of this type is in Listing 5. Time is represented by a long field that refines the corresponding model field in the JML specification. This means that the invariants of the model field apply to the concrete one through the refinement, as denoted by the represents clause, where the arrow denotes functional data refinement.

2.1 Modifications

We will now consider some short examples of ways that we could modify our example, causing the design and implementation to become inconsistent.

One oft-performed change is renaming a class or feature in a system. If we were to perform a rename at one abstraction-level of our system the other levels will not be in-sync, with regards to naming. This is of course easily remedied by performing a renaming on the related artifacts over all levels. Note that the real name of an entity is independent of a particular naming style. For instance the names LOGICAL_CLOCK (Eiffel style) and LogicalClock (Java style) are equivalent. Naming styles can easily be applied or removed when mapping to or from particular domains.

Another interesting change to our system would be to modify the advance feature of the logical clock to take an integer argument, a measure of the amount with which to increase the time. This change might involve adding an argument of type int to the advance method signature in the LogicalClock interface and LogicalClock Impl class, as well as adding a parameter of type INTEGER to the LOGICAL_CLOCK formal model. The postcondition must also be changed to reflect that the time has increased by the provided amount, but we will ignore this for the moment. Again, if we make the change at one refinement level, the levels will become inconsistent. To maintain consistency the relevant changes must be made at all levels that detail the parameters for the `advance` feature. Thus, the signature of the `advance` feature in the formal EBON specification changes from `deferred advance` to `deferred advance -> INTEGER`.

Consider the case where the postcondition of the `advance` feature/method is to be strengthened, such that the time cannot increase by more than 100 from its old value. As a JML `ensures` clause, one might write this as `_time-\old(_time)<=100`. Once more, a change to the system at one level (JML specification) causes other levels to become inconsistent. The required change to the formal EBON model is the addition of the `ensure` clause `my_time-old my_time<=100`.

There are a many more changes that could be made to our example that require modifications on other abstraction levels to maintain consistency. The levels affected can be above and/or below the original modification's level. There are also changes that do not affect other levels, for instance a change to the author property.

3   Subtleties of Refinement

There are a number of subtleties to examine in this simple example. They relate to the support for inheritance and structure in the refinement semantics of semantic properties.

3.1   Inheritance

First, note that the implementation contains far less documentation that the previous examples. For example, there is no denotation of project or version particulars, and methods do not have comments or contract clauses. This is the case because many semantic properties have a *semantics for inheritance*. Thus, some of the semantic properties that annotate the higher-level specifications, like the Javadoc comments in the `LogicalClock` interface or those in the EBON formal specification, are automatically inherited by their children. The realization of a semantics for inheritance is sometimes quite simple and other times is not. Regardless, it is always concretely shown to the user in a simple fashion.

For example, compare the comments on the feature `advance` in the JML and EBON formal specifications, or the class comments in both specifications. The content of the EBON annotation is exactly the *first sentence* of the content of the JML annotation. The inheritance semantics of natural language comments (which are simply semantic properties with no tag) is *structural* in nature and relies upon the structure of natural language.

Other documentation refinements are subtle. For example, notice that the annotation on a query in formal EBON maps to the `@return` annotation in Java. Likewise, the annotation on a EBON command maps to the first line of the Java method comment. Likewise, the informal constraint "`The time must be non-negative.`" is refined into an informal JML comment. As a reminder to the reader: there is a formal semantics for all of these refinements (discussed below) and consistency is automatically maintained between all of these artifacts.

Another example is seen in the realization of the `getLogicalTime` method. This method is a query in the informal model (since it is in the `query` section), it is marked as a QUERY in the formal EBON model, and it is realized as a pure method in the JML model.

Concurrency is topic that makes for more interesting semantics. Since the get_log ical_time feature in the EBON formal model was annotated with a CONCURRENT tag, its realization in Java is a normal method that is threadsafe. On the other hand, the GUARDED annotation on advance indicates that the method must be synchronized in its realization.

Type refinement is also interesting. A set of built-in base types exist in EBON. Value types like INTEGER and REAL are unsurprisingly mapped to mathematical integers and reals in JML (respectively). But other mappings are more subtle. EBON includes a set of basic mathematical abstractions like SET, SEQUENCE, and RELATION. Each of these is mapped to the appropriate JML model (e.g., org.jmlspecs.models.JMLSet), and thence to Java, usually via Java collections. The validity of data refinements is maintained by EBON and JML's refinement semantics—for example, the refinement from the VALUE type to INTEGER in EBON, or the bigint model field to the long concrete field in JML.

Finally, note that refinement of formal specifications need not be syntactic equality when mapped across syntaxes, but instead semantic equivalence. Note, for example, the difference between the formal invariant in the EBON formal diagram and the JML formal specification to which it refines.

3.2 Structure

Structural refinement has its share of straightforward and subtle aspects as well. Annotations, like those seen in the indexing block in Listing 3 and in the class Javadoc comment in Listing 4 are substructures of the EBON and JML specification respectively. These substructures are maintained in structural refinement between levels, in this case EBON and JML, and can be augmented, refined, replaced, or deleted as one moves down the refinement chain. For example, the @title semantic property must match exactly across refinement levels, whereas the @author property need not. Likewise, the class comment must match, but only partially—the first sentence of the refinement (the Javadoc class comment) must be identical to the contents of the about property.

Naming is another structural property. For example, the standard convention in EBON is to name classes using capitalized underbar-separated words, much like the standard convention used to name constants in Java programs, whereas the standard convention for Java class names is to capitalize the first character of each word, with no separators between words. The substructures of identifiers are thus automatically mapped in refinement, as see in the example: LOGICAL_CLOCK refines to LogicalClock. Likewise, there is support for refining EBON features to Java constants, fields, and methods (as appropriate).

Feature ordering is a seemingly uninteresting structural property that sometimes has a non-trivial impact on refinement. In particular, in some development groups the declaration order of method calls and fields is tightly constrained and checked with tools like CheckStyle. If this is the case, the refinement relationship between a Java class and, say, an EBON specification, must respect these constraints. For example, when one adds a feature to a EBON formal chart, the automatic addition of the appropriate method at the

Java level must occur at exactly the right position in the source so as to respect local conventions.

Another obvious structural relationship maintained by refinement is between classes and features. Obviously, if a Java class contains a method that may be used by clients, it must be captured in the refinement up the chain (in the JML, EBON, etc.). What is less clear is what happens when visibility comes into play.

EBON has a notion of feature visibility. Each feature is either public, and visible to any client class, or is restricted, and available only to a certain group of other classes. The semantics of feature restriction in EBON are more rich than that available in Java, where one only has *public*, *protected*, *package*, and *private* class and method visibility. Consequently, each of Java's visibility levels is mapped to the appropriate EBON selective export specification.

Note that the inverse refinement, from EBON to Java, is not total: some selective export specifications in EBON do not naturally map to Java's visibility constructs. This situation, that of a higher-level being *more* expressive than a lower-level one occasionally happens and our current solution is to detect and flag such situations as an error.

A similar situation exists with regards to naming. EBON, much like Eiffel, supports feature renaming during inheritance—Java does not. Thus, any use of renaming in an EBON specification that relates to a JML or Java refinements triggers an error.

3.3 Semantics and Tools

As one can see, there are subtleties in the interplay between refinements of inheritance and structures and the preexisting tools that operate on artifacts at the various refinement levels. *We must be careful to ensure that all refinements respect tool semantics.* For example, if a refinement of documentation from EBON to Java contradicts the standard use of Javadoc, then the refinement is not very useful.

In the current EBON/JML/Java-centric system there are seven different kinds of tools that we must respect. All of these tools are integrated into the Mobius Program Verification Environment (PVE), which is discussed in more detail later in this paper.

1. Documentation tools (e.g., Javadoc and Doxygen) interpret semantic properties in the *documentation* and *usage* categories.
2. Specification tools (e.g., the JML tool suite, ESC/Java2) interpret the semantic properties in the *contract* category.
3. IDEs (like Eclipse and Emacs) interpret semantic properties in the *process* category.
4. Bug/feature trackers (we use Trac, GForge, and Bugzilla) understand some of the semantic properties in the *meta-info* and *process* categories.
5. Configuration management and revision control tools (e.g., CVS and subversion) process semantic properties in the *meta-info* category.
6. The Java compiler and some static checkers interpret Java annotations that are refinements of the *inheritance* category of semantic properties.
7. And finally, static checkers (like CheckStyle, FindBugs, PMD, and ESC/Java2) interpret a mixed subset of semantic properties across many categories.

By virtue of the manner in which we specify semantic properties' semantics below, and coupled with the precise way that we configure and use the aforementioned tools, it is guaranteed that tools' behavior does not contradict the automatic upkeep of refinements in our system.

4 Expressing Semantics

The meaning of semantic properties is expressed in a formalism called *kind theory* [8]. As kind theory is a relatively new, very rich formal method unfamiliar to most readers, its full form is not used here. Instead, the aspects of kind theory most relevant to this work are explained in terms familiar to most readers, with an emphasis on capturing the important facets of the formalism. The curious reader will find the full details of the original kind theoretic formalization of generic semantic properties in the afore-mentioned dissertation, and a modernized full explanation of the concrete realization of semantic properties for EBON, JML, and Java in a forthcoming technical report and an undergraduate student research thesis [9].

Kind theory lets one describe general purpose reusable assets. Software artifacts and mathematical systems are two kinds of assets that are described, and about which we reason, using kind theory. In its simplest form, kind theory lets one describe *type-like structures* (called *kind*) and explain their interrelationships. The relationships that one describes are *structural*, *subtyping*, *equivalency*, *composition* and *decomposition*, *realization*, and *refinement*.

From a type theoretical point of view, kind theory permits one to describe *multiple type systems* and their interrelationships. The theorems of kind theory support reasoning at the object and the kind level, much like one can reason about types and typed objects in type theory.

A full description of kind theory and its use requires an entire dissertation [8]. For space reasons we only give a flavor of the means by which the semantics of semantic properties is specified here.

$$\frac{\text{(Parent Is-a)}}{\Gamma \vdash K <_p L} \qquad \frac{\text{(Is-a Refl)}}{\Gamma \vdash \diamond} \qquad \frac{\text{(Is-a Trans)}}{\Gamma \vdash K < L \quad \Gamma \vdash L < M} \qquad \frac{\text{(Is-a Asym)}}{\Gamma \vdash K < L \quad \Gamma \vdash \gamma(\bot(K \equiv L)|)}$$
$$\frac{}{\Gamma \vdash K < L} \qquad \frac{}{\Gamma \vdash K < K} \qquad \frac{}{\Gamma \vdash K < M} \qquad \frac{}{\Gamma \vdash \gamma(\bot(L < K)|)}$$

Fig. 2. Example rules written in kind theory

A few examples of kind theory subkinding rules to help the reader get comfortable with reading them are found in Figure 2. The rule *Parent Is-a* states that, if the parent of kind K is the kind L ($K <_p L$) then the kind K *is-a* L ($K < L$). This is akin to subtyping, where L is the immediate supertype of K. *Is-a Refl* states that every kind is a subkind of itself (subkinding is reflexive); *Is-a Trans* that subkinding is transitive. Finally, *Is-a Asym* states that, if $K < L$ and K and L are *not* equivalent ($\gamma(\bot(K \equiv L)|)$) then one can prove that L is not a subkind of K ($\gamma(\bot(L < K)|)$). This last rule hints at the fact that kind theory supports reasoning about proof systems as well as proof artifacts, since proofs and evidence are first-order notions in the theory.

The key foundational axiom of kind theory that supports this refinement-centric work is that properties are preserved under interpretation. Interpretation is simply a

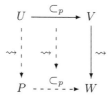

Fig. 3. The Theorem Diagram for (FullInterp Part-of)

(possibly computable) relation between kind, and consequently, between objects that realize those kind. Thus, refinements between BON, JML, and Java in this work are modeled as computational interpretations in kind theory. Such property-preserving relations are described using commutative diagrams, as kind theory is a logic with a categorical feel.

Theorem 1 (FullInterp Part-of)

$$\frac{\Gamma, P \vdash U \subset_p V \quad \Gamma, P \vdash V \rightsquigarrow W}{\Gamma \vdash U \rightsquigarrow P} \qquad \frac{\Gamma, P \vdash U \subset_p V \quad \Gamma, P \vdash V \rightsquigarrow W}{\Gamma \vdash P \subset_p W}$$

Consider the diagram in Figure 3. It captures the essential elements of the proof of the *FullInterp Part-of* theorem, as seen in the two rules in Theorem 1.

Proof. Since V contains U, and $\rightsquigarrow$ fully interprets V to W, then this interpretation also acts upon U. Call the object resulting from the full interpretation P. Since full interpretation is structure-preserving, and $\subset_p$ is a component of that structure, then necessarily $P \subset_p W$. □

What this theorem tells us is that substructures are preserved under full interpretations and, as refinements from BON to JML, and JML to Java, are full interpretations, then substructure relationships in BON are preserved under refinement into JML, etc.

This property is made more clear if we replace this generic commutative diagram with a particular instantiation for our running example. Consider Figure 4, which is an instantiation of this theorem when applied to the single query of the running example.

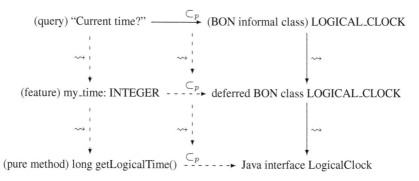

Fig. 4. Full Interpretation of an Informal Query to a Formal (Pure) Feature

Because the high-level design contains this query, (i.e., the BON class chart
LOGICAL_CLOCK contains the query), then according to this theorem, the BON formal
specification of the refinement of the class must also contain this query. *Moreover*, all
properties of the substructure (the query) at the less refined level (the BON informal
level) must be maintained by the more refined level (the BON formal level). In this case
this means that (i) the feature must be of non-VOID type (thus, it is a query), (ii) it
must be pure (i.e., its postcondition must not mention any frame conditions), and (iii)
the documentation of the formal feature must refine the documentation of the informal
query (in this case, they are equivalent, but that's specific to this example).

5   Properties and Their Classification

Thirty-five semantic properties have been identified and defined[1] . All semantic properties are enumerated in Table 1.

Due to space reasons, only a handful of the more interesting properties and their
semantics that we have used in a number of software engineering projects, large and
small, over nearly the last decade are discussed. Also, the following descriptions are
written entirely from the point of view of a *user* of semantic properties (i.e., a software
developer), not a *creator* of new semantic properties (which requires some knowledge
of kind theory).

To derive our core set of semantic properties, the existing realizations that we have
used in two languages for many years were abstracted and unified. First, the set of
predefined Javadoc tags, the standard Eiffel indexing clauses, and the set of basic formal specification constructs were identified and made self-consistent (duplicates were
removed, semantics were weakened across domains for the generalization, etc.). The
resulting set of unique properties are the *core set* of semantic property kinds.

These properties were then classified according to their general use and intent. The
classifications are: *meta-information*, *process*, *contracts*, *concurrency*, *usage*, *versioning*, *inheritance*, *documentation*, *dependencies*, and *miscellaneous*. This classification
is represented using kind theory's inheritance operators, e.g.,:

$$\text{METAINFO} <_p \text{SEMANTICPROPERTYCLASSIFIER} \qquad \text{AUTHOR} <_p \text{METAINFO}$$
$$\text{ENSURES} <_p \text{CONTRACTS} \qquad \text{DEPRECATED} <_p \text{VERSIONING}$$

Many of these semantic properties are used solely for documentation purposes. For
example, the title property documents the title of the project with which a file is
associated; the description property provides a brief summary of the contents of a
file. These kinds of properties are called *informal* semantic properties.

Another set of properties are used for specifying non-programmatic semantics. By
"non-programmatic" we mean that the properties have semantics, but they are not,
or cannot, be expressed in program code. For example, labelling a construct with a

---

[1] The original specification of these properties was defined in the Caltech Infospheres Java Coding Standard (http://www.infospheres.caltech.edu/). That standard has since been refined and
broadened. The most recent version is available via the KindSoftware Research Group's web-
site (http://kind.ucd.ie/)

Table 1. The full set of semantic properties

Meta-information	Contracts	Versioning
author	ensures	deprecated
bon	generates	since
bug	invariant	version
copyright	modifies	
description	requires	**Documentation**
history	**Concurrency**	design
license	concurrency	equivalent
title		example
	Usage	see
Dependencies	exception	
references	param	**Miscellaneous**
use	return	guard
	Process	space-complexity
Inheritance	idea	time-complexity
hides	review	values
overrides	todo	

`copyright` or `license` property specifies some legal semantics. Tagging a method with a `bug` property specifies that the method has some erroneous behavior that is described in detail in an associated bug report. We call these properties *semi-formal* because they have a semantics, but outside of the domain of software (at least for the moment).

Finally, the remaining properties specify structure that is programmatically testable, checkable, or verifiable. Basic examples of such properties are `requires` and `ensures` tags for preconditions and postconditions, `modifies` tags for specifying frame conditions, and the `concurrency` and `generates` tags for expressing concurrency semantics. These properties are called *formal* because they are realized by a formal semantics.

The KindSoftware Research Group coding standard summarizes the current set of semantic properties and is regularly updated to reflect newly identified properties [10]. Each property has a syntax, a correct usage domain, and a natural language summary. As mentioned before, the formalization of semantic properties is found elsewhere [8].

5.1 Context

Each property has a legal scope of use, called its *context*. Contexts are defined in a coarse, language-independent fashion using inclusion operators in kind theory. Contexts are comprised of *files*, *modules*, *features*, and *variables*. Contexts are structured hierarchically; the scope of a property encompasses the context for which it is defined, as well as all sub-contexts.

Files are exactly that: data files in which program code resides. The scope of a file encompasses everything contained in that file.

A *module* is some large-scale program unit. Modules are typically realized by an explicit module- or class-like structure. Examples of modules are classes in object-oriented systems, modules in languages of the Modula and ML families, packages in the Ada lineage, etc. Other words and structures typically bound to modules include units, protocols, interfaces, etc.

Features are the entry point for computation. Features are often named, have parameters, and return values. Functions and procedures in structured languages are features, as are methods in object-oriented languages, and functions in functional systems.

Finally, *variables* are program variables, attributes, constants, enumerations, etc. Because few languages enforce any access principles for variables, their semantics vary considerably.

Each property listed in Table 1 has a legal context [10]. The context *All* means that the property may be used at the file, module, feature, or variable level. Additional contexts can be defined, supporting new programming language constructs that need structured documentation with properties. For example, now that JSR 305 (Annotations for Software Defect Detection) and JSR 308 (Type Annotations) have been finalized the introduction of new contexts may be necessary.

For each concrete language there is a mapping for these contexts/scoping levels. For example, in Java the valid scoping levels are source files, classes/interfaces, methods and variables. Some of the kind theory rules that specify context for a Java method declaration and its documentation are as follows:

$$\text{JavadocMethodDescription} \supset \text{Return} \oplus \text{ParamList} \oplus \text{ExceptionSet}$$
$$\text{JavaMethodSignature} \supset \text{ReturnType} \oplus \text{MethodName} \oplus \text{FormalParameterList} \oplus \text{ThrowsClause}$$
$$\text{JavaMethodDeclaration} \supset \text{JavaMethodSignature} \oplus \ldots$$
$$\text{JavaMethodSignature} \rightsquigarrow \text{JavaMethodDescription}$$

These rules formally define the structure of a Javadoc method description (i.e., the fact that it can contain Javadoc tags like `@return` and `@param`) and the type signature of a Java method. The first line is read, "A Javadoc method description is made up of the composition of a return, param list, and exception set." The third line states that a Java method declaration must contain a method signature, and perhaps more (the elision is not part of kind theory, we are simply ignoring the rest of the formula).

The final line, which is the most interesting one, states that a refinement relationship exists between the Javadoc specification of a method and its declaration. It is read, "One can interpret any Java method signature into a Java method description without any loss of information." This refinement relationship captures two things: (1) a Java method declaration *must* have a Javadoc method description, and, more specifically, (2) how each substructure within a method declaration must be documented in Javadoc. This first properly is generally enforced by several basic tools we use in our software development process (e.g., Javadoc and Eclipse). The second, more specific, property is enforced by our customization of tools like PMD and CheckStyle.

Other structural rules of this form are not enforced by customized versions of third-party tools, but instead by our own, as discussed below.

5.2   Visibility

Visibility is a key notion discussed earlier. In languages that have a notion of *visibility*, a property's visibility is equivalent to the visibility of the context in which it is used, augmented by domain-specific visibility options expressed in kind theory.

Typical basic notions of visibility include *public, private, children* (for systems with inheritance), and *module* (e.g., Java's *package* visibility). More complex notions of visibility are exhibited by C++'s notion of *friend* and Eiffel's class-based feature scoping.

Explicit visibilities for semantic properties are also used to refine the notion of specification visibility for *organizational, social,* and *formal* reasons. For example, a subgroup of a large development team might choose to expose some documentation for, and specification of, their work only to specific other groups for the purposes of testing, or for political or legal reasons.

On the social front, new members of a team might not have yet learned specific tools or formalisms used in semantic properties, so using visibility to hide those properties will help avoid information-overload.

Lastly, a formal specification, especially when viewed in conjunction with standard test strategies (e.g., whitebox, greybox, blackbox, unit testing, scenario-based testing), has distinct levels of visibility. For example, testing the postcondition of a private feature is only reasonable and permissible if the testing agent is responsible for that private feature.

5.3   Inheritance

Semantic properties also have a well-defined notion of *property inheritance*. Once again, in order to avoid new and complicated extra-language semantics on the software engineer, property inheritance semantics match those of the source language in which the properties are used. Our earlier discussion of basic comments for Java methods (a *feature* property context) is an example of such property inheritance.

These kinds of inheritance come in two basic forms: *replacement* and *augmentation*.

The *replacement* form of inheritance means that the parent property is completely replaced by the child property. An example of such semantics is *feature overriding* in Java and the associated documentation semantics thereof.

Augmentation, on the other hand, means that the child's properties are actually a *composition* of all its parents' properties. These kinds of composition come in several forms. The most familiar is the standard substitution principle-based type semantics [11] in many object-oriented systems, and the Hoare logic/Dijkstra calculus-based semantics of contract refinement [12].

These formal notions are expressible using kind theory because it is embedded in a logical framework. For example, automatically reasoning about the legitimacy of specification refinement is supported, much like that seen in Findler and Felleisen work [13].

6   Tool Support

Semantic properties have been used for the past decade in academic and corporate settings. While explicit (and utilized) coding standards, positive feedback via tools and peers, course grades and monetary rewards go a long way toward raising the bar for documentation and specification quality, from our experience these social aspects are simply not enough. Process does help—regular code reviews and pair programming in particular—but tool support is critical to maintaining quality specification coverage, completeness, and consistency.

Templates were the first step taken. Raw documentation and code templates in programming environments, ranging from *vi* to *emacs* to *Eclipse*, are used. But templates only help prime the process, they do not help maintain the content.

Syntax highlighting as well as code and comment completion also helps. Both aid in programmer comprehension and efficiency. Advanced development environments such as Eclipse and Emacs support these features.

Likewise, documentation lint checkers (programs that statically check for the use of improper idioms in a language; e.g., `lint`, `javadoc`, "`gcc -Wall`," or CheckStyle), particularly those embedded in development environments and documentation generators are also useful. Source text highlighting is an extremely weak form of lint-checking. The error reports issued by Javadoc, CheckStyle, and its siblings are a stronger form of lint-checking and are quite useful for documentation coverage analysis, especially when a part of the regular build process. Finally, scripts integrated into a revision control system provide a "quality firewall" to a source code repository in much the same fashion.

But these simple tools are not enough to ensure consistency between artifacts at different refinement levels, nor do they support the automatic updating of artifacts as a system's design, specification, or implementation evolves.

6.1 Checking and Maintaining Consistency

One of the most important parts of tool support for semantic properties is the automation of checking for consistency between abstraction levels. Discrepancies between related artifacts should be detected and presented in a cohesive manner along with other standard errors.

Ongoing research here at UCD focuses on developing the detailed formal theory for automatic consistency checking over multiple refinement levels, with an implementation specifically targeting EBON, JML and Java. We target these languages for a variety of reasons, including local expertise. As seen earlier, the theory itself is applicable to any set of languages for which well-defined refinement relations are defined.

The technique under development supports the definition of all possible relations between two refinement levels, as well as an ordering on these. A consistency check uses automatic deduction of relations (choosing from the set of all possible relations), as well as user-defined relations to determine if artifacts at different refinement levels are consistent.

Part of this work has been the development of the BONc tool[2], a parser, typechecker and documentation generator for BON. It is open source, and available as a command-line tool or as an Eclipse plugin. Our consistency checker is being built on top of BONc and OpenJML, which is, in turn, built atop of the OpenJDK.

To help illustrate the aims of the tool support, consider the following example. A developer is implementing, in Java, a class for which an EBON formal model also exists.

---

[2] Available from http://kind.ucd.ie/products/opensource/BONc/

A sufficiently advanced consistency checker would detect that there is a feature in the class's formal EBON model for which there is no refinement to a Java method. The issue is flagged to the developer inside her development environment in a manner consistent with the presentation of other errors (compilation, etc.). The developer then chooses to automatically fix the issue from a set of suggested fixes—for instance, they might choose to automatically insert a method skeleton with the appropriate signature (calculated from the EBON types and the knowledge of the existing refinement relations).

6.2   Development Environments

As mentioned earlier, a verification-centric development environment, known as the Mobius Program Verification Environment (PVE), has also been built to support design, development, and formal verification using semantic properties.

The PVE is an extension to the powerful Eclipse Platform. It takes advantage of several pre-existing development tools and plugins, including PMD, FindBugs, Check-Style, the JML tool suite, ESC/Java2, and BONc. In the near future our consistency checker will also be integrated.

7   Conclusion

Documentation reuse is most often discussed in the literate programming [14] and hyper-text domains [15]. Little research exists for formalizing the semantics of semi-structured documentation. Some work in formal concept analysis and related formalisms [16,17] has started down this path, but with extremely loose semantics and little-to-no tool support.

Research by Wendorff [18,19] bears resemblance to this work both in its nature (that of concept formation and resolution) and theoretic infrastructure (that of category theory, which relates to kind theory). Development with semantic properties is differentiated by its broader scope, its more expressive formalism, and its realization in tools. Additionally, the user-centric nature of kind theory (not discussed in this article) makes for exposing the formalism to the typical software engineer a straightforward practice.

7.1   Future Work

Our work on the Mobius PVE continues. A graphical modeling environment for EBON is in the works, linking BONc to the Eclipse Graphical Modeling Framework.

Extending JML and other model-based languages like Event-B with semantic properties would follow the same course used for EBON. Because semantic properties are already integrated with Java, and given the existing tool support for JML, inter-domain interpretations will preserve a vast amount of information about JML-specified Java systems in Event-B.

Acknowledgements

This work was initiated under the support of ONR grant JJH1.MURI-1-CORNELL. MURI (via Cornell University) "Digital Libraries: Building Interactive Digital Libraries of Formal Algorithmic Knowledge" and AFOSR grant JCD.61404-1-AFOSR.614040 "High-Confidence Reconfigurable Distributed Control." Recently, the two authors have been supported by several other grants. This work was funded in part by the Information Society Technologies programme of the European Commission, Future and Emerging Technologies under the IST-2005-015905 MOBIUS project. This article reflects only the author's views and the Community is not liable for any use that may be made of the information contained therein. This work is partially supported by Science Foundation Ireland under grant number 03/CE2/I303-1, "LERO: the Irish Software Engineering Research Centre" and by an EMBARK Scholarship from the Irish Research Council in Science, Engineering and Technology.

References

1. Perry, D.E., Wolf, A.L.: Foundations for the study of software architecture. SIGSOFT Softw. Eng. Notes 17(4), 40–52 (1992)
2. Knuth, D.E.: Literate Programming. CSLI Lecture Notes, vol. 27. Center for the Study of Language and Information (1992)
3. Knuth, D.E., Levy, S.: The CWEB System of Structured Documentation, 3rd edn. Addison-Wesley Publishing Company, Reading (2001)
4. Chalin, P., Kiniry, J.R., Leavens, G.T., Poll, E.: Beyond assertions: Advanced specification and verification with JML and ESC/Java2. In: de Boer, F.S., Bonsangue, M.M., Graf, S., de Roever, W.-P. (eds.) FMCO 2005. LNCS, vol. 4111, pp. 342–363. Springer, Heidelberg (2006)
5. Waldén, K., Nerson, J.M.: Seamless Object-Oriented Software Architecture - Analysis and Design of Reliable Systems. Prentice-Hall, Inc., Englewood Cliffs (1995)
6. Kiniry, J.R., Zimmerman, D.M.: Secret ninja formal methods. In: Cuellar, J., Maibaum, T., Sere, K. (eds.) FM 2008. LNCS, vol. 5014, pp. 214–228. Springer, Heidelberg (2008)
7. Janota, M., Kiniry, J.: Reasoning about feature models in higher-order logic. In: Kellenberger, P. (ed.) Proceedings of the 11th International Software Product Line Conference, SPLC 2007. IEEE Computer Society, Los Alamitos (2007)
8. Kiniry, J.R.: Kind Theory. PhD thesis, Department of Computer Science, California Institute of Technology (2002)
9. Kiniry, J., Fairmichael, F., Darulova, E.: Beetlz - a BON software model consistency checker for Eclipse. Technical report, KindSoftware Research Group, University College Dublin (2009)
10. Kiniry, J.R.: The KindSoftware coding standard. Technical report, KindSoftware Research Group, UCD (2005), http://kind.ucd.ie/
11. Liskov, B., Wing, J.M.: Specifications and their use in defining subtypes. In: Proceedings of OOPSLA 1993, pp. 16–28 (1993)
12. Meyer, B.: Applying design by contract. IEEE Computer 25(10), 40–51 (1992)
13. Findler, R., Felleisen, M.: Contract soundness for object-oriented languages. In: Proceedings of Sixteenth International Conference Object-Oriented Programming, Systems, Languages, and Applications (2001)
14. Childs, B., Sametinger, J.: Literate programming and documentation reuse. In: Fourth International Conference on Software Reuse, pp. 205–214. IEEE Computer Society, Los Alamitos (1996)
15. Fischer, G., McCall, R., Morch, A.: JANUS: Integrating hypertext with a knowledge-based design environment. SIGCHI Bulletin, 105–117 (1989)

16. Simos, M., Anthony, J.: Weaving the model web: A multi-modeling approach to concepts and features in domain engineering. In: Devanbu, P., Poulin, J. (eds.) Fifth International Conference on Software Reuse. IEEE Computer Society Press, Los Alamitos (1998)
17. Wille, R.: Concept lattices and conceptual knowledge systems. Computers and Mathematics with Applications 23(6-9), 493–515 (1992)
18. Wendorff, P.: Linking concepts to identifiers in information systems engineering. In: Sarkar, S., Narasimhan, S. (eds.) Proceedings of the Ninth Annual Workshop on Information Technologies and Systems, pp. 51–56 (1999)
19. Wendorff, P.: A formal approach to the assessment and improvement of terminological models used in information systems engineering. Software Engineering Notes 26(5), 83–87 (2001)

Unit Testing of Software Components
with Inter-component Dependencies

George T. Heineman

Worcester Polytechnic Institute
100 Institute Road
Worcester, MA 01609
heineman@cs.wpi.edu

Abstract. Test Driven Development (TDD) is a process for software engineering that advocates constructing test cases before writing actual code; indeed, coding is treated as an exercise in validating the test cases. While such an approach appeals to many software developers, one cannot simply apply TDD to component-based software engineering (CBSE). The primary obstacle is the more complex life cycle for software components that must be packaged, deployed and executed within software containers or deployment environments. In this paper we describe two case studies that show different ways by which TDD can be applied to CBSE. Our focus remains on the dependencies that exist between components and how to manage these dependencies during testing to still enable successful unit testing.

Keywords: Component dependencies, Unit testing.

1 Introduction

Test Driven Development (TDD) is a software development technique that has gained popularity as of late because of the direct benefit of amortizing the testing effort throughout the entire development cycle [2][12]. The primary contribution of this approach is to require automated tests to be written before any code is designed or added to an existing, working system. Using rapid, brief iterations, developers are able to make immediate progress on satisfying specific test cases designed to test external behavior. Then through repeated refactoring effort, the code structure can be improved, and can always be validated against the existing test cases.

The tight iterative development loop consists of several steps:

1. Add a new test case
2. Run all existing tests and validate that the new test fails
3. Write code to ultimately ensure that the test will succeed
4. Run all existing tests and validate that all succeed
5. Refactor code as necessary, and continue with step 1.

The process as described is agnostic with regard to component technology, except for the presumed ability to run a set of tests. One might adopt the strategy that all test

G.A. Lewis, I. Poernomo, and C. Hofmeister (Eds.): CBSE 2009, LNCS 5582, pp. 262–273, 2009.

cases are carried out natively on the code (i.e., as Java classes or C code). However, this point of view will not be satisfactory because the component code is expected to execute as demanded by the underlying component model. In fact, you must test the code in a testing environment that most closely matches the execution environment in which the component is to execute.

The problem identified by this paper is that components invariably have dependencies upon other components. While the ideal case is that each component is wholly independent, it is not always practical or possible. The trouble with software components is that the focus is primarily on the ways in which the components are deployed and composed, rather than on the (often mundane) ways by which the component could be tested. We'll use the following definition in this paper: A **Software Component** is a software element that conforms to a component model and can be independently deployed and composed without modification according to a composition standard [9].

Many of the dependencies that a software component has may never be explicitly declared and may only be discovered at assembly time, or sometimes (even worse) at run-time. The challenge for component testers is to be able to properly assemble the run-time structures necessary for the unit testing required. For this paper, we avoid discussing platform dependencies that a component may have (i.e., it may properly execute using JDK 1.6 but not JDK 1.5) and focus solely on inter-component dependencies.

There are two possible flavors of inter-component dependencies: **concrete** dependencies on other components and **abstract** dependencies on an interface provided by another component. In this paper we present case studies to explore the challenges faced by unit testers having to deal with both of these flavors. A concrete dependency exists when a component makes direct reference to functionality provided by another component outside of any interface construct; we simulate this issue using the C-based product line case study described in Section 2. When an abstract dependency exists, the tester must somehow be able to provide some component that provides the desired interface; we simulate this issue using the CompUnit-based case study described in Section 3. Even though component developers strive to minimize these dependencies, it may not be possible to eliminate them together, which leads to problems during testing.

1.1 Mock Objects

One of the most common approaches to unit testing with dependencies is to introduce mock objects [6] that have clear expectations of the calls they are going to receive. One of the more popular frameworks to support Mock objects is JMock (http://www.jmock.org). The obvious extension is to introduce mock components, yet these components must then also be packaged, deployed, installed and assembled into test applications. Since components must execute within an assembly, you need to prepare a full run-time infrastructure to execute the components. Additionally, whereas it is possible to simply construct mock objects, using standard class constructors, mock components require a larger amount of scaffolding to complete.

1.2 Software Component Life Cycle

Kung-Kiu Lau has described an ideal component life-cycle [14], to identify opportunities for reuse both within component design and component deployment phases. In his view components exist within a component repository during the design phase. Components can be composed with other components to form larger components stored during design or component assemblies during deployment. In the final run-time phase, a run-time infrastructure executes the constructed component assemblies. We consider any testing during this final phase as *integration testing*, so we restrict our attention to the type of testing one might carry out during component design and component development.

The components in the component repository must be independently tested using a unit testing strategy. However, this requirement is challenged by the inter-component dependencies that invariably exist within systems decomposed from components. One must be a bit more careful during design and when developing components, as we discuss in the paper.

1.3 Requirements

Because we had in mind two separate case studies, with different technologies, we defined a set of requirements to guide our effort so we could normalize our results:

- Test cases must be defined separately from the component under test – without such separation, one would be required to repackage and re-deploy software components whenever new test cases are designed.
- A testing framework must be defined separately from the test cases – we must be able to support different testing frameworks, such as JUnit (http://www.junit.org), or home-brewed techniques.
- Testing an individual component must not depend on having all components for the final application – it must be possible to truly test each component in isolation from other components; where necessary, *mock components* are to be written to substitute for an interface dependency.

We believe it is at least plausible that mock components can be written because the communication between components is specified entirely by interfaces. As long as published interfaces have supporting documentation that clearly specifies the behavior being abstracted, one should be able to create mock components.

Our solutions must also reduce as much as possible the manual human element of testing and support the greatest amount of automation. Clearly there is more work to be done to support this principle; in this paper we focus our attention on the "bottom-up" issues faced by component unit testers.

2 Case Study: Product Line Structure

We created a calculator product line composed of features that one might envision having in a hand-held calculator. The Feature Model shown in Fig. 1 captures the various features of this product line using the Czarnecki notation [3].

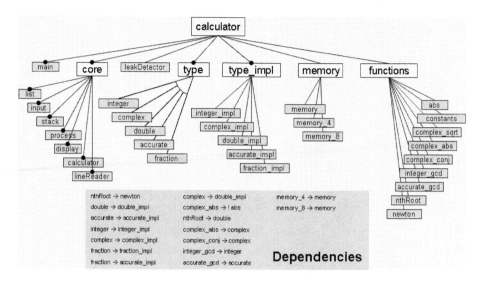

Fig. 1. Calculator Product Line Feature Model

Each gray box represents a feature that is encapsulated as a *feature component* (or component for short). That is, each component has its own source files and can be independently compiled. Features with a black dot at the top are mandatory. The larger white boxes represent feature "families", some of which are also mandatory. For example, the **type** family is mandatory, specifying that one of its child features must be selected. The white "arc" emanating from the **type** node declares that only one of the children is to be included (i.e., XOR functionality) in a product line member. Optional features have no black dot at the top of their box. Dependencies between features are captured declaratively and are provided in the large gray box at the bottom of the figure. For example, the **nthRoot** feature depends upon having **newton**'s method available and that the selected **type** for the calculator is **double**.

The product line was implemented in C. The primary goal of this case study was to demonstrate that one could selectively mix and match desired features in a product line by simply declaring the desired features. Because the C programming language offered no capabilities to support a product line, we engineered a set of constructs and processes to make this happen. This somewhat-academic exercise was intended as a proof of concept, to show that one could devise component models even when the underlying programming language offered no support.

2.1 Integer_gcd Component

It is instructive to show the full details of one of the simpler components. The full case study can be retrieved from the author's web site[1]. Each feature is implemented in its own separate set of C files and is compiled and built by its own Makefile. We intentionally chose to use Makefile specifications rather than design a separate

---

[1] http://web.cs.wpi.edu/~heineman/CBSE2009/CalculatorProductLine.zip

language that captures the same information (such as an XML representation). Indeed, the intent of the Makefile is to produce a single executable `integer_gcd.a` file which can be independently deployed during application assembly. The **integer_gcd** Makefile shown in Fig. 2 defines how to build the component, which simply involves compiling the `integer_gcd.c` source file. However, this Makefile specification also shows how to execute the unit tests for this component (the target "test" in the Makefile).

```
include MakefileCommon
MODULE  = integer_gcd
SRCS    = integer_gcd.c
DEP_MOD = integer_type.c integer_type_impl.c

all: $(MODULE).a

$(MODULE).a: $(SRCS:.c=.o)
        rm -f $(MODULE).a
        ar rv $(MODULE).a $(SRCS:.c=.o)

CORE = input.c process.c calculator.c display.c lineReader.c \
       list.c stack.c

# run tests: Must pre-link in required features (if exist)
test: $(SRCS:.c=.test.o)
        ./ut $(TEST_REMOVE) $(SRCS:.c=.test.c) $(SRCS) $(CORE)
$(DEP_MOD) >> $(PL_TEST)

# invoked by product line architecture
initialization:
        @echo $(LIBS)                    >> $(FINAL_LIBS)
        @echo "$(MODULE)_init(); " >> $(INITIALIZATION)

# clean away the code (including test files)
clean:
        rm -f $(MODULE).a $(SRCS:.c=.o)
        rm -f $(SRCS:.c=.test.gcov) $(SRCS:.c=.test.gcda)
        rm -f $(SRCS:.c=.test.gcno) $(SRCS:.c=.c.gcov)
        rm -f $(DEP_MOD.c=.test.gcov) $(DEP_MOD:.c=.test.gcda)
        rm -f $(DEP_MOD:.c=.gcno) $(DEP_MOD.c=.c.gcov)
```

Fig. 2. Makefile for integer_gcd

A collection of Makefiles are used to build individual features as well as to build an entire product line application member. In this example, the core set of features is defined as the baseline application. That is, no such application member in this product line can be constructed without this base. To describe a potential product line member, then, one need only specify the set of features within the global Makefile. Fig. 3 shows some sample product line specifications.

Description	Definition
Simplest calculator supporting just basic *, – , + and ÷ over doubles	`double_type.c` `double_type_impl.c`
Calculator using complex numbers and supporting small set of complex operators (conjugate, absolute value) as well as a bank of 4 memory registers	`complex_type.c` `complex_type_impl.c` `double_type_impl.c` `complex_sqrt.c` `complex_abs.c` `complex_conj.c    memory.c` `memory_4.c`
Calculator supporting arbitrary-precision accurate integer arithmetic, a bank of memory registers (defaults to 8), some pre-defined constants, and the greatest common divisor function	`memory.c            constants.c` `accurate_type.c` `accurate_type_impl.c` `accurate_gcd.c`

Fig. 3. Sample Product Line Member Applications

We were successful in this effort. We then wondered how we could add unit testing to the underlying development process. Since each component was implemented with its own files, we had to clearly declare its dependencies within its Makefile (note the DEP_MOD variable in Fig. 2). Since the intent is to construct an executable whose purpose is to execute the test cases specified within `integer_gcd.test.c`, we must be able to construct an executable, so all concrete dependencies for the **integer_gcd** component are realized. In this example we use the actual components themselves but this could easily have been rewritten to use mock components.

The result is that each component can be independently built (using make -f component.Makefile) and independently tested (using make -f component.Makefile test). We crafted a unit test utility, **ut,** (referred to in the Makefile) to carry out the unit tests by replicating much of the functionality as specified by JUnit. The `integer_gcd.test.c` source file contains test cases as shown in Fig. 2. While some of the details are unnecessary, one can readily see the use of testXXX() functions to represent test cases and setUp() and tearDown() functions as supported by JUnit. **ut** generates the requisite driver code that launches the four test cases as defined, bracketing these invocations with calls to set up and tear down resources as required.

To complete this case study, the primary Makefile for assembling product line application members was modified to also test the features used within the product line by repeatedly invoking make -f feature.Makefile test on all of the selected features. **ut** uses gprof (the Unix utility for call graph profile data) and gcov (the Unix coverage testing tool) to generate reports showing the code coverage of the test cases, as well as identifying those which failed.

One of the lessons learned from this C-based case study is that the testing of individual features did depend upon having a fully working base. There was no easy way to eliminate the dependency that a feature component has on the base. A corollary of

```c
#include "calculator.h"
#include "process.h"
#include "integer_gcd.h"
#include "integer_type.h"

#include "ut.h"
/* Useful variables for test cases */
static CALCULATOR_PTR calc;
static TYPE_PTR       at;
static TYPE_PTR       bt;
static INTEGER_PTR    ai;
static INTEGER_PTR    bi;
/** Useful test macro */
#define localCheck(expected,tp) {                                      \
  assertTrue ((tp) != NULL);                                           \
  assertEquals ((expected), ((INTEGER_PTR)(tp)->inner)->n);           \
  freeType ((tp));                                                     \
}
/* allocate resources for each test */
void setUp() {
  calc = constructCalc();

  at = newType();
  ai = at->inner;
  bt = newType();
  bi = bt->inner;

  /* initialize module under test */
  integer_gcd_init();
}
/** release resources. */
void tearDown() {
  freeCalc (calc);
  freeType (at);
  freeType (bt);

}
/* this is now a binary operator */
void testisOperator() {
  assertEquals (1, isBinary("gcd"));
}
/* test application */
void testGCD() {
  ai->n = 117;
  bi->n = 13;
  localCheck (13, applyGCD (calc, "gcd", at, bt));
}
void testGCD2() {
  ai->n = 1;
  bi->n = 1;
  localCheck (1, applyGCD (calc, "gcd", at, bt));

}
void testGCD3() {
  ai->n = 14;
  bi->n = 0;
  localCheck (14, applyGCD (calc, "gcd", at, bt));
  localCheck (14, applyGCD (calc, "gcd", bt, at));

}
```

Fig. 4. Sample test cases for **integer_gcd** feature

this lesson was the observation that the base had to be tested as a single unit because of the deep interconnections between the requisite C files that made up the base. See Muccini and van der Hoek [16] for ideas on testing product lines. Nonetheless, each feature can be tested independently by identifying the dependencies of the feature in its Makefile. Another lesson learned was that the unit testing was actually quite effective when using the actual components themselves, rather than stub or mock objects. The reason was the structure of the product line specified a clear tree-like set of dependencies between the feature components, thus it was possible to test small subsets of features first before expanding up to unit test features that depended upon larger collections of features.

3   Case Study: Component-Based Structure

In our second case study, we create a small CAPTCHA (Completely Automated Public Turing test to tell Computers and Humans Apart) utility that involved a client/server system. On the client-side, the user is challenged to identify words in a moving image, and the server processes the messages sent by the user; should the words match, a new user account would be created for the user in a database.

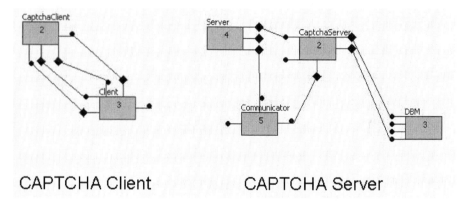

CAPTCHA Client   **CAPTCHA Server**

Fig. 5. CAPTCHA application

To build the application, we used the open source CompUnit component model [8], which has been developed to properly teach issues regarding CBSE at both the undergraduate and graduate level. All components are written in Java and conform to an interaction standard where each component is able to interact with other components only through well-defined interfaces. In short, a component can provide (or otherwise *implement*) an interface and that component can be connected to another component that requires the functionality as defined by that interface. CompUnit components are assembled into applications by connecting components to each other using these defined interfaces. There is a set of tools to help developers package their CompUnit components into stand-alone JAR files that contain the encapsulated implementation; one can also assemble applications using a graphical editor. An application consisting of CompUnit components executes within a run-time environment container called Foundation.

Each component in Fig. 5 is represented by a rectangle. A component may provide a set of services (identified by the "lollipop" handles emanating from the components) and may require services (identified by the lines with diamonds). Components can communicate directly with other components only through such interfaces. The primary modeling novelty of CompUnit is that each component must clearly identify (with meta data) the interfaces which it requires to perform its functionality. CompUnit assumes that each interface, once published, becomes immutable, which ensures the long-term interoperability of components that require and provide the same interface.

Each component is independently built, packaged and installed into a CompUnit environment and then an application is defined by assembling the components together; in Fig. 5, there are two applications. The challenge for the unit tester is to find some way to test the **CaptchaServer** component even though it has three dependent interfaces (one on the **Communicator** and two on the **DBM** component).

We approach this concrete dependency by constructing a mock component to aid the effort. The challenge, naturally, is for the tester to be able to execute the **CaptchaServer** component. Towards this end, we developed a generic **SuiteRunner** component that manages the JUnit test cases to be separately written and packaged with a specific testing component. **SuiteRunner** contains just 126 lines of Java and is used for testing all CompUnit components (not just the ones described in this paper). The final application assembly is shown in Fig. 6.

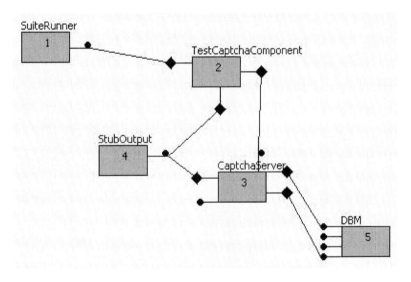

Fig. 6. Assembly to test **CaptchaServer**

SuiteRunner takes over the responsibility of launching the JUnit test cases that are packaged within the **TestCaptchaComponent**. In this way, each component under test can have its own **TestXXX** component that is connected to the common testing infrastructure. Other helper components are written as needed, such as the **StubOutput** component whose sole purpose is to receive responses back from the **CaptchaServer** and enable the **TestCaptchaComponent** to validate the response is as expected.

Each CompUnit component is packaged into a JAR file by a CompUnit utility known as the "Packager" and then installed into a CompUnitEnvironment using the "Installer" utility. Figures 5 and 6 show screenshot captures of the CompUnit utility, "Café" that allows users to graphically construct application assemblies. Each of these CompUnit utilities is actually implemented using CompUnit components.

If one were to truly follow the TDD strategy outlined in the introduction of this paper, then each new test case would require the repackaging and redeployment of a component. While such a process would be developmentally sound, it leads to gross inefficiencies, which is why the case study was carried out entirely within Eclipse (http://www.eclipse.org). For this reason, we briefly explain some details of this process because we believe it shows how to effectively apply TDD to software components.

3.1 Extended Support Provided by Eclipse

Many developers have grown accustomed to the powerful support that Integrated Development Environments (IDEs) such as provided by Eclipse. For example, one can develop web services without ever leaving Eclipse [4]. Clearly such capabilities reduces the effort in developing these services by reducing the overhead of having to package and deploy the requisite code "natively" as required by the various Web-based protocols and Web servers. Much of the development within the CompUnit case study was performed within Eclipse, and we were able to bypass two key phases of the component-based development life-cycle. In particular:

- Installation – once a component was installed into the CompUnit container, there was no need to reinstall it whenever changes were made to the component. This was made possible because the user can set the CLASSPATH within Eclipse to include to the component under development. Thus we only needed to install the component once, and this typically was done when the first few lines of code were written for the component.
- Packaging for deployment – since the component only needed to be installed once, it meant that it only needed to be properly packaged once, just prior to this installation.

Another important productivity enhancer is the ability in Eclipse to allow developers to change code while the system is being debugged [10]. Under most circumstances, Eclipse is able to "rewind" the computation back to the beginning of the method (or earlier depending upon the call stack). As the components are executing, the software engineer can set breakpoints and view the step-by-step execution of the component, rewriting the code as necessary when defects are detected.

These productivity enhancers are not limited to CompUnit; indeed, it must not be the case! Fortunately, the leading IDE vendors for Java (NetBeans and Eclipse) provide various ways to productively test component technologies, such as EJB, servlets, and web services, just to name a few.

4   Related Work

The field of software testing is vast and cannot be captured in a single paper. We focus our attention on the most closely-related efforts for testing software components which has been explored by various researchers within the CBSE symposium series over the years [7][11][17][18][19]. In general, these researchers focused on specific techniques for testing, rather than the complications arising from interdependencies.

Built-in test (BIT) component capability enables the black-box testing of components through fine-grained decorator "wrappers" that enable assertions to be checked as the component executes. Edwards [5] describes a framework that fully automates the process of testing components, including generating the test data and the drivers that execute the components. To incorporate BIT components into a test-driven process, the developer would describe the pre- and post-conditions using the contract-based approach as popularized by Bertrand Meyer [15]. From these contracts, the code to execute the test cases would be generated. Nothing in the wrappers is able to address component dependencies, however.

Throughout the paper we referenced various projects (such as JMock) whose purpose is to enable unit testing of components developed using various technologies. Cactus [1] and JUnitEE [13] also offer similar capability. The unit testing supported by these projects is still complicated by the dependencies that invariably exist between components. The ideas presented in our paper can be used to guide these technologies to handle inter-component dependencies.

5   Conclusion

Unit testing of software components is hard enough without having to deal with the added complications of inter-component dependencies. We constructed two case studies that showed how to address the issue. When component dependencies are concrete, one strategy is to assemble component "sub-assemblies" that enable the construction of an application with the component under test. Should the dependency relationship be cyclic, then the only recourse is to develop mock components using the same component model and define assemblies with the component under test. When abstract dependencies are present, one has greater flexibility in whether to choose actual components or to develop mock components in their place. In both cases, the success of the unit testing is made possible by applying the right tool support and infrastructure to automate the code tests. The full calculator product line can be retrieved from http://web.cs.wpi.edu/~heineman/CBSE2009/CalculatorProduct-Line.zip.

References

1. Apache, Cactus Test Framework (2009), http://jakarta.apache.org/cactus
2. Beck, K.: Test Driven Development: By Example. Addison-Wesley Longman, Amsterdam (2002)

3. Czarnecki, K., Wasowski, A.: Feature Diagrams and Logics: There and Back Again. In: Proceedings of the 11th International Software Product Line Conference (SPLC), pp. 23–34 (2007)
4. Eclipse Foundation, Web Tool Platform (WTP) project (2009), http://www.eclipse.org/webtools
5. Edwards, S.H.: Framework for Practical, Automated Black-Box Testing of Component-Based Software. Software Testing, Verification and Reliability 11(2) (2001)
6. Fowler, M.: Mocks aren't stubs (January 2007), http://martinfowler.com/articles/mocksArentStubs.html
7. Gao, J.: Component Testability and Component Testing Challenges. In: Component-Based Software Engineering Workshop (2000)
8. Heineman, G.: CompUnit Component model (2009), http://sourceforge.net/projects/compunit
9. Heineman, G., Council, W.: Component-Based Software Engineering: Putting the pieces together. Addison-Wesley, Reading (2001)
10. Holzner, S.: Eclipse Cookbook. O'Reilly Media Inc., Sebastopol (2004)
11. Jalote, P., Munshi, R., Probsting, T.: Components Have Test Buddies. In: Component-Based Software Engineering Symposium, pp. 310–319 (June 2006)
12. Janzen, D., Saiedian, H.: Test-driven development concepts, taxonomy, and future direction. IEEE Computer 38(9), 43–50 (2005)
13. JUnitEE (2009), http://www.junitee.org
14. Lau, K.-K., Wang, Z.: Software component models. IEEE Transactions on Software Engineering 33(10), 709–724 (2007)
15. Meyer, B.: Object-Oriented Software Construction, 2nd edn. Prentice Hall, Englewood Cliffs (1997)
16. Muccini, H., van der Hoek, A.: Towards Testing Product Line Architectures. In: International Workshop on Test and Analysis of Component-Based Systems (TACoS), vol. 82(6), pp. 99–109 (2003)
17. Muthu, R.: Testing Software Components Using Boundary Value Analysis. In: Proceedings of the 29th EUROMICRO conference New Waves in System Architecture (2003)
18. Pavlova, I., Akerholm, M., Fredriksson, J.: Application of built-in-testing in component-based embedded systems. In: ROSATEA 2006, pp. 51–52 (2006)
19. Tyler, B., Soundarajan, N.: Testing Framework Components. In: Component-Based Software Engineering Workshop, pp. 138–145 (May 2004)

Author Index